Queer Answers

A Book of Gay Education

Queer Answers
A Book of Gay Education

Written by: D.R. Uribe

DISCLAIMER: This book is offered with the understanding that while the author may have a certain body of knowledge, he is only a reporter of facts and opinion and is not engaged in giving medical, legal, psychological, financial or other professional services or advice. If expert help, advice or counseling is needed, the services of a competent, qualified professional should be obtained. Any application of the contents of this book is at the reader's discretion and sole responsibility. The author and publisher shall have no liability or responsibility for any damage or loss incurred or alleged, directly or indirectly, by any person or entity due to such application.

This book is an expression of the author's point of view. It was created as an educational tool, but it does not hold all information available on any subject. Neither has it been created to be specific to any need or suitable to all situations. While a good faith effort has been made to be factual and to correct errors and/or outdated information, defects may still exist. The reader is encouraged to not rely on this work as his sole source of knowledge.

This book holds non-heteronormative information and sexual content involving sex between men. Those who find that sort of thing to be offensive can either stop reading now or continue reading and thereby expand their understanding of what is all around them.

This book cites hundreds of sources. Citations are offered at the end of the book and the reader is encouraged to use those citations to find and read the source material.

Thoth & Seshat Publishing
Olympia, WA. 98502

Copyright © 2018 by D.R. Uribe
All rights reserved

Thoth & Seshat Publishing
Olympia, WA 98502

thothseshatpublishing@gmail.com

Second edition
ISBN-13: 978-1-7325726-0-7
ISBN-10: 1-7325726-0-7

LCCN: 2018908320

Printed in the United States of America

Contents

Chapter 1 – Basic Questions

1   What is a homosexual?
2   Does having sex with someone of your own sex mean you are a homosexual?
3   What is sexual identity?
4   How many homosexuals are there in the United States?
6   Didn't Alfred Kinsey prove that 10% of men are gay?
6   Why does it matter how many gay people there are?
7   What causes a person to become a homosexual?
10 When in a lifecycle does a person become gay, straight or bisexual?
10 Is being homosexual normal?
12 What is the profile of the average gay man?
14 Is a gay man physiologically different from a straight man?
15 Is gaydar real?
17 Does being a gay man mean you are not a "real man"?
20 What is the "gay lifestyle"?
20 Are homosexuals unhappy and lonely, especially when they are older?
22 Are gay men promiscuous?
26 Are gay men drug abusers?
29 Are gay men alcohol abusers?
30 Are gay people mentally ill?
31 Is there a link between being gay and being a pedophile?
34 Isn't HIV/AIDS a gay disease and aren't all gays at risk of getting it?
36 Is homosexuality immoral?
37 Wouldn't the world be better off without homosexuals?
38 What is the Gay Pride Flag?

Chapter 2 - Gay Historical Context

39 What do we know about gay history and why is it important?

Chapter 3 - LGBT Community Context

65 What is the LGBT community?
65 What is known about the clubber community?
72 What is known about the youth community?
79 What is known about the senior community?
84 What is known about the lesbian community?
90 What is known about the bisexual community?
95 What is known about the transgender community?
103 What is known about the drag community?
105 What is known about the Chub community?
107 What is known about the Bear community?
109 What is known about the BDSM community?
113 What is known about the Leather community?
123 Who else is in the LGBT community?

Chapter 4 - Gays and Religion

126 What is religion and why might gays want to be religious?
127 Is religion antigay?
127 Is homosexuality a sin?
128 How do Christians view homosexuality?
129 Does the Christian and/or Jewish Bible condemn homosexuality?
133 What was Jesus Christ's view about homosexuality?
133 What does the Roman Catholic Church say about homosexuality?
134 What is the Eastern Orthodox Church view about homosexuality?
134 What do Protestants say about homosexuality?
135 What do Baptists say about homosexuality?
135 What do Methodists say about homosexuality?
135 What do Lutherans say about homosexuality?
136 What do Presbyterians say about homosexuality?

136 What do Pentecostals say about homosexuality?
136 What do Episcopalians say about homosexuality?
137 What does the United Church of Christ say about homosexuality?
137 What do Mormons say about homosexuality?
138 What do Jehovah Witnesses say about homosexuality?
138 What do Quakers say about homosexuality?
139 What do Unitarian Universalists say about homosexuality?
139 What do Deists say about homosexuality?
139 What do Muslims say about homosexuality?
140 What was the Prophet Muhammad's view about homosexuality?
142 Does the Qur'an condemn homosexuality?
142 What does the Nation of Islam say about homosexuality?
143 What is the Jewish view about homosexuality?
143 What does Reform Judaism say about homosexuality?
143 What does Reconstructionist Judaism say about homosexuality?
144 What does Conservative Judaism say about homosexuality?
144 What does Orthodox Judaism say about homosexuality?
144 What is the Hindu view about homosexuality?
145 What is the Buddhist view about homosexuality?
146 What does Theravada Buddhism say about homosexuality?
146 What does Vajrayana Buddhism say about homosexuality?
146 What does Mahayana Buddhism say about homosexuality?
146 What does Satanism say about homosexuality?
147 What do Atheists say about homosexuality?

Chapter 5 – Gay Relationship Issues

148 Why are interpersonal relationships important to homosexuals?

148 What is internalized homophobia and how does it influence relationships?
149 How does a person overcome internalized homophobia?
149 What about other people who are homophobic? Aren't they the real problem?
153 What is heterosexism and how does it affect homosexuals?
154 Does heterosexism affect the scientific study of homosexuals?
158 What is HIV stigma and HIV shame?
159 What is gay bashing and what can I do if it happens to me?
163 Is gay relationship domestic violence related to homophobia or heterosexism?
165 Why do men stay in abusive relationships?
165 What can I do if I am the victim in an abusive relationship?
167 Am I abusing my partner and what can I do if I am?
167 Is drug/alcohol use/abuse a factor in domestic violence among gays?
167 How can a person tell if he is in a good long-term relationship?
168 How does a person find a good long-term relationship?
170 Is it possible to have a successful long-term open relationship?
171 Can gays be good parents?
172 How do I go about coming out of the closet?
174 Are gay couple relationships different than straight couple relationships?

Chapter 6 – Gay Health Issues

176 What are the major health issues gay men should be concerned about?
178 What are the basics I should know about HIV and AIDS?
179 What are the symptoms of HIV and AIDS?

- 180 Should I be tested for HIV and, if so, when should I be tested?
- 181 Do teenagers need to be tested for HIV?
- 182 Where can I get tested for HIV?
- 182 What are the advantages/disadvantages in using a HIV diagnosis kit at home?
- 183 Who will know about my status if I test HIV+?
- 184 How does having HIV/AIDS change my insurance coverage?
- 184 Does Medicare and/or Medicaid cover HIV testing?
- 185 Do I qualify for Supplementary Security Income (SSI) if I have HIV or AIDS?
- 186 What is the AIDS Drug Assistance Program?
- 186 What is the Ryan White HIV/AIDS program?
- 186 What does a HIV test cost?
- 187 What do they do when they give you an HIV test and what kind of tests are there?
- 188 Why should I go to counseling if I get a positive HIV test result?
- 189 Can I get HIV from kissing?
- 189 Can I get HIV from fellatio?
- 189 Can I get HIV from being spit on?
- 189 What is the statistical probability of getting HIV?
- 190 Why do men who have sex with men (MSM) have a higher rate of HIV?
- 191 Is there a link between HIV and other STIs??
- 191 What can I do if I think I have just been exposed to HIV?
- 192 What is PrEP?
- 192 If I take a PrEP pill every day am I immune to HIV?
- 193 My partner and I are both HIV+. Is it safe for us to have unprotected sex?
- 193 Is it safe for a HIV negative person to have sex with a HIV positive person?
- 193 What is TasP?
- 194 What are the major sexually transmitted infections (STIs) and sexually transmitted diseases (STDs) found among men in the U.S.?
- 194 How can I tell if someone I want to have sex with has a STI/STD?

- 194 What is chlamydia, how do I know if I have it and what should I do if I get it?
- 195 What is syphilis, how do I know if I have it and what should I do if I get it?
- 196 What is genital herpes, how do I know if I have it and what should I do if I do?
- 197 What is genital human papillomavirus, how do I know if I have it and what should I do if I do?
- 198 What is gonorrhea, how do I know if I have it and what should I do if I do?
- 198 What is hepatitis, how do I know if I have it and what should I do if I do?
- 201 What is trichomoniasis, how do I know if I have it and what should I do if I do?
- 201 What are Fordyce's spots?
- 201 What are pearly penile papules?
- 202 What are lice, how do I know if I have them and what should I do if I do?
- 203 What are scabies, how do I know if I have them and what should I do if I do?
- 203 What STI tests should I have done and how often should I do them?
- 204 What are "safer sex" practices?
- 205 Are some sex acts safer than others?
- 205 How effective are condoms at protecting against HIV and other sexually transmitted infections (STIs)?
- 205 Can I get hemorrhoids from receiving anal sex?
- 205 Does anal sex cause anal cancer?
- 206 Is anal fisting safe?
- 208 Does oral sex cause mouth or throat cancer?
- 208 Is it safe to take part in bondage by being bound?
- 211 Are "water sports" safe?
- 214 Is it physically safe to use sex toys?
- 215 What is electrosex & what are the risks involved in doing it?
- 217 What is "breath play" and what are the risks involved in doing it?
- 219 Are heterosexual men physically healthier than homosexual men?
- 220 Does it matter whether my doctor knows I am gay?

220	How can I find a doctor who is gay friendly and gay knowledgeable?
221	How can I find a HIV knowledgeable doctor?
221	What is substance abuse and substance addiction and what are their health consequences?
222	Why does the LGBT community have a higher rate of drug use?
223	What are the health factors related to using alcohol?
224	What are the risks involved when using cocaine?
225	What are the risks involved in using Ecstasy?
226	What are the risks involved when using poppers?
227	What risks are involved in methamphetamine use?
228	What are the risks involved in using marijuana?
229	What are the risks involved in amphetamine use?
230	What are the risks involved in using Ketamine?
231	What are the risks involved in using GHB?
231	What are the risks involved in using Rohypnol?
232	What are the risks involved in using LSD?
233	Does being a drug user mean I won't be helped by HIV treatment?
233	Is there a link between drug abuse and mental disorders?
233	What is depression, what are its symptoms and what can I do if I do have it?
234	What is anxiety, how do I know if I have it and what can I do if I do?
235	How can I tell if someone is suicidal and what can I do if I think someone is?
237	Are homosexuals less mentally healthy than heterosexuals?
239	Are heterosexual men happier with their bodies than homosexual men are?
239	Do gay men have a higher rate of eating disorders?
240	Does penis size matter?
241	Is there any association between prostate cancer and how often a man ejaculates?
241	Do penis-enlargement products or techniques work?

Chapter 7 – Gay Legal Issues

242 Is being gay illegal anywhere?
242 Do any countries authorize the death penalty for being homosexual?
243 Is anyone trying to criminalize homosexuality in the United States?
243 Why aren't gays treated equally under the U.S. Constitution?
244 Can landlords refuse to rent to LGBT people or evict them based on their sexual orientation or identity? Can sellers refuse to sell property on that basis?
244 Can LGBT people be denied use of public accommodations solely because of their sexual orientation?
245 Are there restrictions on gay men relating to donating blood?
245 What are the rules related to lesbians, gays and bisexuals serving in the military?
246 What is the policy regarding transgender persons serving in the military
247 Have homosexuals who were discharged from the military solely for being gay been treated equally to other soldiers who served honorably prior to discharge?
247 What is the Matthew Sheppard and James Byrd, Jr. Hate Crimes Prevention Act?
248 What is an assault and how is that different from assault and battery?
248 What is the Health Insurance Portability and Accountability Act of 1966?
249 What is the Defense of Marriage Act?
250 What is marriage and why don't some people want gays and lesbians to have it?
250 What rights, benefits, privileges and obligations are associated with marriage?
251 What is the difference between a civil union or domestic partnership and a marriage?
252 Are homosexuals allowed to adopt children?

252	How does being a homosexual impact someone wanting to immigrate to the United States?
253	Does federal law explicitly ban job discrimination?
253	What is the Employment Non-Discrimination Act?
253	Does Title VII of the Civil Rights Act of 1964 protect LGBT people?
255	How do I file a discrimination complaint with the Equal Employment Opportunity Commission?
255	Does the Civil Service Reform Act of 1964 protect LGBT people?
256	Are there any presidential executive orders that protect LGBT people?
256	What protections do the states offer LGBT people?
256	What constitutional right to have counsel during a criminal trial is given under Gideon v. Wainwright?
257	What rights do people in police custody have prior to interrogation under Miranda v. Arizona?
258	What rights to personal safety do LGBT jail inmates have?
258	Can the government criminalize private same-sex sexual intimacy between consenting adults?
259	Can a state pass a law that bans its subdivisions from enacting local measures that would protect homosexuals as a class from discrimination?
259	Does the U.S. Constitution compel states to license marriage between same-sex couples and does it compel states to recognize same-sex marriages legally performed in other states?
259	Can a school be held liable if it acts with deliberate indifference to student on student harassment?
260	Can a school deny a LGBT student the right to express his/her sexual orientation or identity?
260	What constitutional rights do juveniles have during a criminal proceeding in juvenile court under In re Gault?
261	Can private organizations exclude homosexuals based solely on their sexual orientation?
261	What is the Administrative Procedure Act?
262	What is the Affordable Care Act?

263 What is sodomy?

Chapter 8 – Gay Sex Education

265 How do I choose a condom?
266 What is the correct way to use a condom?
268 What should I do if a condom breaks or falls off during sex?
269 How do you choose a personal lube?
270 What is fellatio and how is it done?
277 What is irrumatio and how is it done?
278 What is anilingus and how is it done?
280 What is anal intercourse and how is it done?
286 Why do some tops slap their partner on the butt during sex?
286 What is anal douching and how is it done?
288 What is felching and how is it done?
289 What is "scat play"?
289 What is frottage?
289 What is a "ménage á trois"?
290 What is public sex?
290 What is a "tearoom" and what happens there?
291 What is a JO club and what happens there?
291 What is a sex party and what happens there?
293 Is it alright to talk dirty during sex?
293 How do you clean a sex toy?
294 How do you remove pubic hair/buttock hair?
297 What is a cock ring and how are they used?
298 What is a harness and how are they used?
300 How is a good kiss done?
301 How is a "quickie" sexual encounter done?
302 How is a "one-night stand" done?
303 How does a "fuck buddy" relationship work?
304 How is a coffee date done?
305 How can I make a first date a pleasant experience for both of us?
306 How is the classic pick up done?
307 How do I pick someone up in a bar?
310 How can I find a partner on the internet?
311 What happens in a bathhouse?

313 Does wearing keys or an earring on the right or left side mean anything?
314 What is flagging and how is it done?

315 **Citations**

Chapter 1
Basic Questions

Question: What is a homosexual?

A homosexual is a person who is romantically and/or sexually attracted to his/her own sex on an ongoing and exclusive basis. A heterosexual is a person who is romantically and/or sexually attracted to the opposite sex on the same basis. A bisexual person is persistently attracted to both sexes and an asexual person is attracted to neither sex.

The "and/or" in that definition must be stressed because the romantic attraction a person feels toward another person can be distinctly separate from his/her sexual attraction/behavior and those things may or may not align (American Psych. Assoc., 2008; Savin Williams, 2007; Diamond, 2004; Regan, 2001; Regan, 2000; Sell, 1997). In other words, a romantic attraction can occur without a sexual attraction or behavior and sexual attraction or behavior can occur without a romantic attraction.

It is possible to fantasize about having a homosexual sexual experience without being a homosexual. This is not uncommon among adolescents. However, if the fantasies continue over time or generalize so that several people of his/her own gender are the objects of his/her sexual desire then he/she probably is gay or bisexual.

How a person classifies himself may or may not matter in terms of sexual orientation. A person who is attracted sexually to others of his own sex and acknowledges that attraction is probably gay or bisexual. Similarly, a person who self-classifies as heterosexual but is attracted sexually to his/her own sex is probably also a homosexual or a bisexual person. Those who say a person is not really a homosexual until he/she takes on that identity are confusing a person's sexual identity with their sexual orientation and are ignoring objective reality. A person may believe he is a piece of chocolate cake but that does not mean he is one or that he is delicious.

Homosexuality is often thought of as part of a dichotomy in which one is either heterosexual or homosexual. Factually however, sexuality is more complex than that because each human being exists as a sexual being somewhere on a continuum. On one end of the range is being only attracted to one's own sex (exclusively homosexual) and on the other end is being only attracted to the opposite sex (exclusively heterosexual). Various degrees of bisexuality exist between these two poles. The continuum is bimodal in that a sizeable majority of people are at one end of the spectrum or the other one. Existing at any place within this spectrum is perfectly normal (American Psych. Assoc., 2010; Kinsey, 1948).

A homosexual is more than a sexual being however. He or she is a physical, emotional, social, political, psychological and spiritual being as well. We are part of the communities we live in. We are a valuable element in every socio/economic level, religion, racial/ethnic group and profession. We exist happily as a part of families, friendships and other relationships. Some of us are parents. We take part in every kind of work and leisure activity. Setting aside the cultural bias related to who we are attracted to sexually or romantically and the negative culturally imposed consequences of that attraction, we are pretty much the same as heterosexuals and perfectly normal. We have the same needs and wants, and we have the same kinds of trials and triumphs. In short, a homosexual is a whole human being.

Question: Does having sex with someone of your own sex mean you are a homosexual?

This depends on the age of the people involved and the situation. It is normal for a preteen or teen to experiment sexually with someone of their own gender (Tulloch & Kauffman, 2013; Moore & Rosenthal, 2007; Dreyer, 1982; Kinsey, 1948). This is part of learning about one's sexuality and sexual identity and it is not an unusual or sinful behavior. However, if this experimentation evolves into a sexual attraction to multiple members of his/her same sex and continues over time into the early twenties then the person is probably gay or bisexual. A person's understanding of their sexuality may change over time so in some cases, especially among the young, sexual orientation may be fluid (Reinisch, 1990; Kinsey, 1948).

A person might also have sex with someone of their own gender because of the situation they are in. A person who has sex with a person of his/her own gender because members of the opposite gender are unavailable may not be gay. It depends upon the kind attraction the person has with a same gender partner and what the person would prefer to do if both same-sex and opposite sex partners were available.

This however does not mean that a heterosexual person who has sex with a same-sex person is not involved in homosexual sex or that it is not a homosexual act. All it means is that the person in such a case may not be a homosexual. In most cases, however, those who claim this status are simply trying to get the honey without being bothered by the bees. They want the homosexual contact and emotional intimacy but not the perceived social stigma that goes with it.

Question: What is a sexual identity?
Most people would probably say one's sexual identity is whatever that person says it is. Many researchers study sexual identity on that basis because it is easy to do. All it entails is asking the person how he/she defines himself. Psychologists, sociologists and philosophers know however that the matter is more complicated than that because sexual identity is, like all parts of one's self-identity, multifaceted.

Everyone has an ideal of what his sexual identity should be and we all compare ourselves to our ideal. That ideal is usually something we learn from parents, religious figures or others when we are children. This ideal typically evolves as the person ages and examines the alternatives. When that evolution does not happen, the person keeps the learned ideal.

Many gay men, whether closeted or out, become committed to a heterosexual ideal and they choose to behave based upon an identity that is not biologically natural for them. They know it is not natural because they know who they are attracted to. Psychologists call that "identity foreclosure". This results in internal psychological conflict.

We all have a "real identity" too. This is who a person really is. It is based on a person's values, thoughts, feelings, looks and behavior. A person's belief about his real identity is called his self-image. This belief may or may not match what an objective observer would say the person really is or what his/her ideal is.

Many men who say they are straight meet the objective criteria of being gay or bisexual. Saying you are straight, gay or bi does not make it so because that objective criterion exists. You can accept your real identity or reject it, but it still exists.

Everyone also has a public identity. In fact, we all have many of them because the identity, sexual and otherwise, we show publicly varies based on who we are with and the situation we are in. Some of that is based on deception. It is also not uncommon for someone to have a public identity they are unaware of. This is a result of how people secretly perceive the cues we unconsciously give.

All of this points to why it is important for LGBT people to be out and proud. Coming out to one's self is an acknowledgement of one's true self-identity. Coming out to others is a convergence of that private identity with one's public identity. Doing this with head held high allows a new ideal to bloom. It is only when these three facets (ideal, real and public) align that one's sexual identity is a healthy one.

Question: How many homosexuals are there in the United States?

Nobody really knows what percentage of the United States population is homosexual. It is not possible to accurately pinpoint that since a lot of gays are in the closet and would lie if asked about their sexual orientation. Other people who objectively are gay do not recognize it and thus, if asked, would report their sexual orientation as hetero. There are also people who classify themselves as gay who are not actually homosexual. The definitions used in studies of homosexuality sometimes vary too.

Some researchers use the standard of whether a person has had or has not had homosexual experiences to decide who is a homosexual. Other researchers have measured homosexuality based upon who sees themselves that way. Still others base their definition on who their subjects desire as sexual or romantic partners. All methods have unavoidable flaws thus their results are flawed.

Generally, you get the highest percentage if you measure homosexual attraction and the lowest percentage if you measure open homosexual self-identification. Measuring homosexual behavior gives a result that is somewhere in-between. A 2013 study found that traditional methods used for measuring the size of the gay population substantially underestimate that number (Coffman, Coffman & Ericson, 2013).

There are a lot of figures offered on how many Americans see themselves as gay. A report authored by the Center for Disease Control and Prevention in 2014 states 1.6% of adult Americans see themselves as gay or lesbian and 0.7% see themselves as bisexual. Polls taken between 2008 and 2012 found figures ranging from 3.4% to 4.9%. The National Survey of Sexual Health and Behavior, which is a very large study done in 2010, found 7% of women and 8% of men view themselves as gay.

Looking at all three facets (attraction, behavior and identity) of sexual orientation, we once again find a variation in findings. A 1993 study found that 9% of men and 5% of women have same-sex sexual relationships on an ongoing basis, 4% of men and 2% of women see themselves as homosexual and 5% of men and 3% of women see themselves as bisexual (Janus & Janus, 1993). A 1994 study found that 4.2% of adults see themselves as homosexual, 9.0% have had at least one same-sex sex partner and 15.3% have been attracted to someone of their same sex (Laumann & Gagnon, 1994). A 2011 study said 3.5% of adults report a homosexual or bisexual self-identity, 8.2% report taking part in same-sex sexual behavior and 11% reported same-sex sexual attraction (Gates, 2011).

If we use a 4% figure and 2010 Census data showing the U.S. population at 308,745,538 then reduce that by the number of people under the age of 15 (they either have no sexual orientation or are just beginning to question) it puts the number of gays in the U.S. at 9,879,857. If the 10% estimate is used there are 24,699,643 gays in America. We must remind ourselves however that most of the demographic numbers on sexual orientation are not necessarily exact.

Whether the number of homosexuals there are is 4%, 10% or some other percent the matter of our numbers cannot be fully understood until they are put into context. That context is found when we compare ourselves to other American subgroups. Even 10% may seem small until that comparison is done.

The US Census says the largest subgroup in our country is non-Hispanic Whites. This group is 63.7% of the population. The largest minority group in the United States is the Latino/Hispanic group. That group is 16.3% of the population. African Americans account for 13.6%. Asians are 5% and people age 65 or more are 13.5% of the American population. We see then that whether our number is 4%, 10% or some other amount our number is not as small as it might otherwise seem. We also should remember that homosexuals are members of every other group and that we can influence those groups and interact with hetero and bi allies.

Question: Didn't Alfred Kinsey prove that 10% of American men are gay?

Alfred Kinsey is the father of the field of sexology and the author of the groundbreaking book *Sexual Behavior in the Human Male* which was published in 1948. The widely-held belief that 10% of men are gay comes from Kinsey's statement in that book that 10% of men are predominately or exclusively homosexual for at least three years at some point between the ages of 16 and 55. This, of course, is not the same as saying 10% of men are gay. He wrote that only 4% are exclusively gay for their entire lifetime.

Question: Why does it matter how many gay people there are?

It matters for three reasons. First, the political and social reality we live in is that political and social leaders pay more attention to the rights, needs and desires of larger groups than they do to those of smaller groups. Larger groups are typically able to give more financial and other support to those leaders and the organizations they head. They can offer an elected official more votes and money. It naturally follows therefore that these leaders would tend to respond better to the larger group.

Second, society tends to treat larger minority groups better than it does smaller ones or at least the larger one is better able deal with the society at large. The experience of the African American population in the United States is a case in point. They are about 13% of the total population of our country. They achieved an amazing change in how our society treats them in a relatively brief time not only because they actively demanded change but also because they made it clear that there were 36 million of them that not only were not going to accept discrimination anymore, but they would support only those leaders who supported them. Politicians and judges took notice, laws were changed and, in time, so did American society.

The third reason it matters how many gays there are is that it tells us something about ourselves not only as gay people but also as a species. The number of homosexuals there are in the world tells us something about our diversity and demographics. It also matters to gay people on a personal, self-image level whether we are among of 2.5 % of the world population or part of 10%. We want to know intellectually and emotionally how many people there are in the world like us.

Question: What causes a person to become a homosexual?

Mother Nature does. It used to be thought that homosexuality was a lifestyle choice. That is now known not to be true. We still do not know exactly what causes a person to be homosexual or heterosexual, but it is widely accepted in the scientific community that the cause is largely or wholly biological.

We have known for decades that there is a biological part to sexual orientation because we found differences in the physical structure of human brains based upon sexual orientation (Swaab, 1995; Allen, 1992; LeVay, 1991). We have also found differences in how the human brain works based upon sexual orientation. Sometimes gay and straight male brains use a different process for the same or similar tasks (Hu, 2011; Hu, 2008; Swaab, 2008; Savic, 2008). When that happens the gay male brain and the female hetero brain often use the same or a similar operation. Obviously, the difference in structure and function begins in the womb because that is where brains are made. Development of the human brain continues long after birth but what happens in the womb largely sets the stage for what is possible later.

There are several older studies that support the view that homosexuality is biological. Among these is one published in May 1994 which studied the DNA of gay fraternal and identical twins. The authors of the study assert that genes and brain development in the womb are significant factors in deciding sexual orientation (LeVay & Hamer, 1994).

Other studies support the idea that homosexuality is linked to genes. A well-known 1993 study found a linkage between homosexuality and the maternal genetic line of those studied (Hamer, 1993). Subsequent studies had mixed results in finding that link, but more recent studies have done so (Camperio-Ciani,

2012; Iemmola and Camperio-Ciani, 2009; Camperio-Ciani, 2004). Another found a significant link to homosexuality on two chromosomes (Sanders and Beecham, 2017)).

Another well-known study found stretches on three human DNA chromosomes that strongly suggest a multi-genetic determination of sexual orientation (Mustanski & DuPree, 2005). This supports the idea that it is the interaction of various genes and not a single gene that decides sexual orientation. This cooperation and interplay is common in how DNA decides what characteristics we have. Human height and eye color, for example, are created that way.

It is now thought that a person's DNA makeup and what happens in the womb are the primary determiners in one's sexual orientation. There is still some controversy about whether a child's postnatal environment has an impact on his orientation, but the trend is toward a biological explanation for homosexuality (Balthazart, 2011; Berk, 2010). Even those who still assert that a person's postnatal environment may play a role in sexual orientation agree that that influence would occur in the first few years after birth and that sexual orientation is not a choice.

The evidence shows there is no single specific reason for a person's sexual orientation. Biological factors, including DNA, interact to yield at least a predisposition toward the sexual orientation of the person. Other factors that occur within the womb such as the level and kind of hormones a fetus encounters trigger that predisposition. The bottom line is that straight people are born straight, and gay people are born gay. There is absolutely nothing you can do about it.

It used to be thought that studies done on fraternal and identical twins were a basis for believing a person's environment after birth was a factor in deciding their sexual orientation. A fraternal twin shares the environment within the womb with his twin and an identical twin shares both that environment and his twin's DNA. It was therefore thought that if one twin was straight and the other was gay something other than DNA and the environment within the womb must account for it. That obviously had to occur after birth and therefore had to be environmental in nature.

Now however we know that just because twins share a womb does not mean they have the same experience within it. One twin may receive more testosterone laden blood than the other does thus his brain will be fully masculinized while his brother's will not be. In that case that brother will be gay (Garcia-Falgueras & Swabb, 2010).

Studies in the field of epigenetics seem to confirm this. Epigenetics looks at the mechanisms outside the human genome that switch genes on and off or cause it to function differently. There is not much peer-reviewed research yet about how epigenetics affects homosexuality but what we have leads us to believe that factors both inside and outside of the womb might cause a fetus to become susceptible to the masculinizing effects of testosterone. The behavior of a pregnant women, for example, might be such a factor. Epigenetic markers affecting sexual orientation may or may not be inherited but when they are gay males inherit from their mothers while lesbians inherit from their fathers.

Other studies tell us that the determination of sexual orientation occurs entirely in the womb and that the physical sexual characteristics of a fetus may be at odds with the gender identity in his/her brain because those things are decided at separate times during gestation (Bao and Swabb, 2011; Garcia-Falgueras & Swabb, 2009). In other words, a person might have the physical characteristics of one sex but believe he/she is the other one. A person self-identifying as transsexual might therefore be justified in feeling like he/she is the opposite sex.

Some researchers also assert there is no proof of any kind that social influences play a significant part in the determination of sexual orientation or gender identity. They assert that this is not learned and not a choice. It is purely a function of what happens in the womb (Boa and Swabb, 2011; Garcia-Falgueras & Swabb, 2010).

Despite the dithering of their American colleagues, in 2007 the Royal College of Psychiatrists in Great Britain officially took the position that there is no evidence supporting the idea that the parenting one receives or the childhood one experiences has any role in the formation of that person's sexual orientation. It asserts that sexual orientation is decided by interplay of biological factors. It agrees that the evidence clearly shows that homosexuality is not a choice and that it is perfectly natural.

Question: When, in the lifecycle, does a person become gay, straight or bisexual?

A human fetus builds physiologically along a path of variations as it takes on male or female traits based largely on its genes and the presence or absence of hormones such as testosterone. It is anatomically distinct as a male or female by the end of its 12th week in the womb but the process of differentiation continues. The brain is organized on the same dimorphic (male or female) model during the second half of gestation (Garcia-Falgueras and Swaab, 2010; Swaab, 2007).

A person is physiologically heterosexual, homosexual or bisexual at birth but, while the outcome is unchangeable, identity does not all happen in the womb because the brain continues to develop after birth. A human being's sexual identity is psychologically complete by age 2 although he/she does not understand it then. A child begins to give gender labels to things when he/she is around age 4 but until age 6 or 7 it is common for kids to believe a person's sex can change (Warin, 2000; Kohlberg, 1966). The understanding of the permanent nature of sexuality brings with it another step in the child knowing who he/she is.

As the person ages, he/she continues to develop physically, sexually, psychologically and emotionally, gathers knowledge, becomes increasingly self-aware and interacts with those around him/her. This happens throughout life, but it is especially potent during adolescence. These factors are what really lead a person to who they are. That in turn leads to the question of whether a person is gay simply because he/she was born homosexual or does that happen when that self-identity is accepted, and/or the person behaves romantically and/or sexually as a gay person?

Question: Is being homosexual normal?

It depends upon how "normal" is defined. In the intrapersonal sense, it is simply a person being, believing and acting as he/she typically has. A person who has held a gay personal identity, been romantically attracted to and/or interacted sexually a same-sex partner would probably be right to view homosexuality as normal for him/her. What is "normal" in this sense can change in some cases. An example of this is the moment a person begins to suspect that he/she is gay and begins to grapple with his/her changing self-image and situation.

"Normal" can also be defined interpersonally. This is based on a comparison of individuals using some method or standard which may or may not be valid and this too may change over time. Most Americans, for example, no longer believe homosexuality is abnormal and science has aligned with that view. Among the methods or standards that may be used are mathematics, biological and psychological knowledge and holistic analysis.

Some say that mathematics proves being gay or bi is abnormal because if you plot a distribution chart of sexual orientations heterosexuality is overwhelmingly the mean average and non-heterosexuality is more than one standard deviation from it thus outside of the normal range. That assertion however ignores the fact two standard deviations, not one, would be used on such a chart thus statistically 95% of it would be within the normal range. Certain definitions of homosexuality and bisexuality would in fact put some part of those orientations within that range. Some same-sex behavior and same-sex attraction exist at rates that are well above 5%.

We also must remember that being different is not necessarily a bad thing and being fewer in number does not necessarily have anything to do with "normal". Seckel pears are perfectly normal pears after all even if they are a bit like an apple and exist only as 1% of the market for pears. The key to appreciating them is to accept them as they are and to not expect them to be a Bosc or a Bartlett.

The major problem with using such a chart however is that sexual orientation is not unimodal (one peak). It is bimodal, especially in men (Richards & Hawley, 2011; LeVay, 2011; Rahman & Wilson, 2003; Bailey & Dunne, 2000). A chart of sexual orientations would have a major peak on one end of the continuum (exclusive heterosexuality) and a minor peak on the other end (exclusive homosexuality). In between the peaks is a valley of data that denotes the various manifestations of bisexuality. Hetero men and gay men are in fact two distinctly separate groups and would be better represented on two separate charts. You can compare them, but the comparison would be of the traits of each group rather than the normality of each.

If you define "normal" biologically and/or psychologically then it becomes the state of being free of medical or psychological disorders and within the norms for human intelligence, personality and emotional adjustment. Those norms are based upon what is accepted as biologically/psychologically typical of our species. That basis can be arrived at scientifically or unscientifically.

The scientific approach tells us that a wide spectrum of variation is natural for our species and that homosexuality is a normal part of that variation. It is found in nearly all human cultures (Kirkpatrick, 2000) and has existed in our species since at least the Middle Stone Age (Nash, 2001). Individual-based modeling shows that half of heterosexual men and more than half of heterosexual women may carry a gene that predisposes male human offspring to be gay (Chaladze, 2016). Every major medical, sociological and psychological association in the United States says homosexuality is normal.

The unscientific approach may define homosexuality as abnormal. It however is not a valid method to find normality since it uses political and/or religious dogma or personal bias to color or deny objective science. Homosexuality, in that case, may not be accepted as normal. That, of course, does not mean it is not normal. It simply means that voluntary ignorance and the denial of objective, provable fact is much too common in our species.

If a holistic definition is used, then "normal" is a matter of whether the person is within the range of what the natural processes of gestation and life might lead a human being to be as a complex entity. That process yields so many natural variations that, apart from identical twins, no two human beings have ever been or will ever be genetically identical (National Human Genome Research Institute, 2008). Homosexuality is a natural variation which occurs so often that we can reliably predict a significant part of humanity will have that orientation. It is therefore not only normal but also expected.

Question: What is the profile of the average gay man?
Homosexuals are not studied very much but the information that does exist gives us a partial picture of what is average for gay men. The average gay male in the United States is 34 years old. He is, like the average heterosexual male, around 5' 9" tall but is 50% less likely to ever be obese than other men. He is right handed but has a 39% to 50% better chance (depending upon the study used) of being left handed than a heterosexual male does. He rents his

living space in one of twenty major cities but not in a gay neighborhood. He is not a first-born son. He will enter puberty earlier in his life than the average heterosexual male does.

Both the average homosexual man and the average heterosexual man do not have a college degree, but the gay man is twice as likely to have one. Based upon median income figures he makes slightly less money per year than does a straight man that is similarly qualified. He lives in a single income household. He has more discretionary money than the average hetero man and manages money better. He contributes money to LGBT causes but is not actively involved that community.

The average gay man is happy with his life. He uses drugs and/or alcohol, but he is not a substance abuser or substance dependent. He does not smoke tobacco although a lot of his gay friends do. He is more likely than a hetero man to have an eating disorder and to receive medical and/or mental health treatment for depression. His life expectancy is 74 years, but he has a greater chance of attempting suicide than does the general population. He has a less that 1% chance of getting HIV if he follows safer sex practices and does not share needles with other people. At the same time, his risk of getting HIV is very much higher if he does not follow those practices simply because he is much more likely than a hetero man is to meet a HIV+ sex partner.

The average homosexual man has more sex partners than his heterosexual counterpart, but he will never have children. He does not presently have a romantic relationship going on but has lived with another guy within the past year. He wants a long-term relationship but not necessarily monogamy.

The scent of another gay male sexually stimulates the average gay man. He, like most men, is also very visual in what causes him to be sexually aroused. He prefers masculine looking men as sex partners. He likes porn (straight men do too) and wants it to be graphic (straight men do too) and to feature masculine looking men.

The average gay man masturbates regularly and has had sex with another person by the time he is 17. That person is commonly female. He starts thinking he might be gay when he is a preteen and knows he is by his early twenties. He is "out" to at least one other person but not "out" at work. He fears being discriminated against at work if colleagues find out he's gay.

The average gay man recognizes faces better than heterosexual men. He cannot throw as accurately but has better eye-hand coordination. He sleeps seven hours a night. He washes his hair more often than the average woman does. He is better at detecting others as gay than hetero men are. He is also more verbally fluent and tends to be more empathetic. He does not go to church but is influenced by at least some religious teaching(s). He is politically liberal, or center left and prefers the Democrat party, but he is not politically active.

Question: Is a gay man physiologically different from a straight man?

Human beings are sexually dimorphic in that we are either male or female. A gay man is in nearly all respects physiologically the same as a heterosexual man. More accurately, he falls within the range of what is typical of a male rather than what is typical of a female. Part of that is that he has a male typical size and shape. He has a masculine skeletal structure, musculature and pattern of fat distribution. His hair type and its distribution are typical of his sex. His bodily organs and systems also follow the male pattern. His brain is, like all men, slightly larger than a typical female one and his sex drive is rather robust. He is just as capable of fathering, protecting and raising children as his heterosexual counterpart is.

Testosterone is the primary hormone that brings about masculine physical traits such as those noted above. Studies done in the 1970s gave mixed results on whether there is a difference between straight and gay men in the level of testosterone in the blood. A review of those studies found a failure to show that gay men have lower testosterone levels than other men (Schiavi & White, 1976). In 1984 a meta-analysis of studies found that gay men do not have lower levels (Meyer-Bahlburg, 1984). There have been no peer reviewed studies done since which show that meta-analysis to be wrong.

Some studies report a handful of minor physical differences which may exist between gay and straight men. Among these is that the gay male arm and leg bones may, in some cases, be slightly shorter when compared as a ratio with his overall height. His finger length ratio (index finger to ring finger) is often opposite that of a straight guy. His hands are sometimes slightly smaller, but his penis tends to be bigger.

Differences in gay male brains as compared to hetero male brains have been reported by some studies. The suprachiasmatic nucleus (SCN) of the hypothalamus was reported to be larger in gay men than in heterosexual men and women (Swaab & Hofman, 1990). The third interstitial nucleus of the anterior hypothalamus (INAH3) of gay men was found to be smaller than that found in hetero men but comparable to that of hetero women (LeVay, 1991). The midsagittal plane of the anterior commissure of the gay male brain was reported to be larger than that found in hetero males (Allen and Gorski, 1992). An attempt to replicate that finding failed (Lasco & Jordan, 2002). The symmetry and connectivity of the gay male brain has been reported to be comparable to that found in heterosexual women and dissimilar to that found in heterosexual men (Savic & Lindstrom, 2008).

Other characteristics of the gay male brain are typical of males in general (Safron & Barach, 2007). Gay men do not have a female brain (Swaab, 1995; Swaab, 1990). There is no difference in general cognitive ability/full scale IQ between gays and straights (Rahman and Bhanot, 2012; Tuttle and Pillard, 1991). There is however a study which found that the more intelligent you are, the more likely you are to be gay (Kanazawa, 2012).

Question: Is gaydar real?
"Gaydar" is the ability to recognize intentional or unintentional cues coming from other people that distinguish them as gay. Numerous studies offer evidence supporting the view that gaydar is a real phenomenon. The concept is often criticized as being based on stereotypes. That is obviously true, but it can be more than that.

In one study, for example, viewers of a video of subjects having a conversation could detect who was gay or straight and could do this at a rate higher than mere chance would allow. The detection rate was even better when the subjects were under stress (Silva, 2010). Other studies support the finding that many men can be detected as being gay by elements related to the acoustics of their voice (Valentova, 2013; Pierrehumbert, 2004; Linville, 1998; Gaudio, 1994). Verbal and non-verbal language clues, like the use of certain words, terms and gestures, can also be used by an experienced observer to spot a person who is part of the gay culture.

Another study shows that the way a gay man walks might be a clue that will set off a beep on someone's gaydar. A significant percentage of gay men tend to move their hips slightly more than other men. This was confirmed by objective testing (Johnson and Gill, 2007).

Other characteristics that some studies have found to be common in gay men include a counterclockwise whorl of the hair at the back of the head (Klar, 2004), increased density of the ridges of our fingerprints (Hall, 1994), and slightly longer and thicker penises (Bogaert, 1999). It is also much more common for the index finger of a gay man to be longer than his ring finger than it is for a straight man (Rahman, 2003). Added to that, homosexual men are far more likely to be left handed than straight men are (Lippa, 2003; Lalumière, 2000).

The sense of smell can also be used as a gaydar tool. Each of us, as humans, produces a genetically determined scent which is influenced largely by Major Histocompatibility Complex (MHC) molecules that are associated with the immune system. Our species subconsciously uses this scent as part of how we select or reject potential sexual mates (Payne, 2010).

A piece of this process is that our scent is associated with, among other things, our sexual orientation. Heterosexual men, heterosexual women, homosexual men and homosexual women each produce a scent that is common within their subgroup. People respond to those scents by finding them in varying degrees pleasant or unpleasant based upon the smeller's sexual orientation. Homosexual men prefer the scent of other gay men and heterosexual women over those of heterosexual men and lesbians (Martins, 2005).

Sniffing the air near attractive men is not the best use of these facts however if finding another gay man is the goal. It is more useful to watch people who are not gay men. Straights and lesbians tend to dislike the gay male scent and respond to it negatively (Martins, 2005). The gaydar secret then may be to find a guy that straights and lesbians think smells bad. If, as a gay man, you think the guy smells fine…bingo.

The traits that are useful gaydar tools are not just physical however. Our memory for object location is typically better than that of a heterosexual male (Rahman & Wilson, 2003) and we have better verbal skills and fluency (Rahman & Abrahams, 2003). The most universal characteristic of gay men is, of course, that we are physically attracted to other men thus we look at other men more than heterosexual men do. Gay men have methods of looking at other men that can be distinguished (Nicholas, 2004).

It has been shown that gay men can detect other gay men better than the general population does (Valentova, 2011; Woolery, 2007). It can be done quickly and with relatively little information (Rule, 2008; Ambady, 1999). It is thought that over time gays learn how to detect other gay men because other gay men are more likely to be safe to interact with and because they are a potential partner. The gaydar ability improves over the course of time as one gains experience or is taught by others how to detect other gays.

While this "gaydar" ability points to commonalities that many gays share it certainly is not foolproof. A study done in 2010, for example, showed that even though using masculine and feminine facial stereotypes can be a useful gaydar tool, it must be done right and not overgeneralized if the user wants a better outcome than he would get if he decided based on random chance alone (Freeman, 2010). That, after all, is what gaydar does. It increases the chances of someone recognizing that someone else is gay.

None of the gaydar factors noted above are universal. No study has shown that all gay men can be detected as gay by others without their cooperation in that. This is attested to by the number of gay men that successfully hide in the closet. At the same time, we must acknowledge that successfully being in the closet does not mean other people's gaydar has not worked. It may only mean they have chosen to not act upon what their gaydar has told them.

Question: Does being gay mean you are not a "real man"?

Masculinity is a social construct. As such, it is an idea or perception held by an individual, group or society that is based on their standard of what is ideal or at least proper for a male person. The term "real man" is usually used as an intentionally provocative substitute for the term "masculine man". It carries the heavy message that if you are not a masculine man you are also not a real man.

Masculinity exists primarily as it is compared to the social construct of femininity. The two constructs are commonly viewed as opposite poles on a continuum of gender traits. Femininity then is what an individual, group or society accepts as normal or proper for a female but not normal or proper for a male. A "real man" cannot be effeminate nor have feminine interests.

A large part of our society believes it is not masculine for a man to have sexual or romantic feelings for another man. They view it as grossly unmanly for a man to have sex with another man. Many believe it is not masculine for a man to have any physical or behavioral characteristic or trait that is linked with femininity. They assert that, when sex between men occurs, the insertive person who penetrates his partner is "the man" and the other person who is penetrated is "the women". They also equate masculinity with procreation and being partnered with the woman. This is the heteronormative view. Homophobia is fostered by heteronormative societal forces as a means of support for that norm (Connell, 2005; Morin, 1978).

Homosexual men are not heteronormative. We are naturally attracted to men sexually and/or romantically and most of us have sex with other men. Some of us accept the role of being orally or anally penetrated by our partner's penis and some allow our partner to ejaculate inside us. We have some physical or behavior traits that are more common to females than males. We may or may not share the view that any of this necessarily makes us less masculine.

The problem with the constructs arrives in the fact that masculinity and femininity are flawed concepts. Masculinity and femininity are not opposite poles on a continuum of physical and behavioral traits and interests. Human beings as a species are very widely diverse and each of us holds within us an abundance of characteristics. Traits that are viewed as defining in the stereotypes of masculine and feminine sometimes overlap and blur in the real world. Some of these definitions are utterly untrue.

Even if we could accurately define and agree upon what it is to be masculine or feminine it is likely that virtually nobody could meet the standard completely because each of us would have some characteristics of the other gender stereotype. It is, for example, not uncommon to find heterosexual couples who like variation in who is more dominant during sex and even in which of them is the sexually receptive partner.

Among the factors commonly associated with masculinity are virility and sexual potency. Virility is the ability to procreate and sexual potency is the ability to engage in and complete the act of sexual intercourse. If looked at objectively it is clear that a woman is just as capable of doing these things as a man is. The reason these qualities are viewed as masculine is that historically men have had the exclusive power to define things and men chose to define themselves as the active and powerful source of sexual intercourse and pregnancy. This, of course, is nonsense.

We get the same result if we look at other behavioral traits associated with men such as being brave, strong, logical, confident, courageous, dominant, and a leader. If looked at objectively we find that women can be any of those things and commonly are. Likewise, we find that stereotypical traits for females such a being emotional, dependent, sensual, colorfully dressed, patient, nurturing and gentle can be just as true of a man. Even physical traits can sometimes blur. It is more common, for example, for men than women to be tall but it is not at all abnormal or even uncommon for a woman to be tall and for her to still to be quite stereotypically feminine in her appearance and manner.

We find useful data to support a more critical look at the constructs of masculinity and femininity if we consider the traits of aggression and violent conduct. The stereotype holds these to be masculine traits. If we look at National Crime Victimization Survey done in 2012 we find that males aged 12 and older violently victimized another person at the rate of 25.4% per 1000 while females did so at the rate of 19.8% per 1000 (Truman & Planty, 2012). We can therefore accurately say that men are more likely than women to violently victimize others, but we cannot say that violence is a masculine trait.

It follows then that whether a gay man can be a "real man" depends upon his choices. If he chooses to accept the definitions supporting the heteronormative view of masculinity then "no", a gay man cannot be a "real man". If, on the other hand, he chooses to accept a correct definition of the word "real" he can be. In

English, the word "real" refers to that which is genuine and not false or artificial. If a man understands who he truly is, and he lives as that person, then he truly is a real man.

Question: What is the "gay lifestyle"?
It is a myth. There is no such thing as a gay lifestyle. Similarly, there is no such thing as a straight lifestyle or a bisexual lifestyle.

Some believe the gay lifestyle involves promiscuity, substance abuse and a lot of partying. Others say the gay lifestyle includes a love of opera, ballet, fashion, art, musical theater, and fine cuisine but not sports. Others say if you are male and you adore Cher, Lady Gaga, Beyoncé or Ariana Grande you are not masculine, and you are taking part in the gay lifestyle. Still others say the essence of the gay lifestyle is a life defining hunt for homosexual sex or at least the need for gay companionship.

Human beings exist within a huge matrix of variation. Likes and dislikes vary. Likes and dislikes are sometimes acted upon and sometimes not acted upon. Situations, values and self-identities vary too. All this works to influence what one thinks or does. A lifestyle is unique to an individual and evolves as he responds to his likes, dislikes, values, sense of self and his situation. Sexuality, sexual orientation and how one takes part in gay culture or the gay community are only pieces of what each gay person is, and those pieces do not rule a lifestyle. Sexual orientation does dictate the gender of the people gays are sexually attracted to but that does not define that person's lifestyle. Those who think it does want life to be simple. It's not.

Question: Are homosexuals unhappy and lonely, especially when they are older?
Homosexuals do suffer from some forms of depression at a higher rate than does the general American population. This however is not a product of homosexuality per se but rather is a product of the stress that results from being in a minority group that is discriminated against and sometimes reviled by the heterosexual public at large. Most cases of depression are successfully managed and temporary. Having a supportive network of family and friends is central to that. In the end, the truth is that most gay people are happy and even the ones who are not can be if they get the right kind of help and support.

All people get out of life based upon what they put into it. If a gay person cultivates relationships he will have friends and perhaps a life partner if he wants one. He may even have kids if he wants them. If he does not work at building and keeping relationships, then he may not have those things. This however is also true of a heterosexual person.

It is true that most gays live alone, especially when they get older. It is also true that, on average, a gay person has more friends outside of the workplace than a straight person does (Grant, 2010; Woolf, 2001). These friends are often friends for a lifetime. Because of this gay people are commonly less lonely than heterosexuals as they age, leave the work force and enter retirement.

It is estimated that, depending on demographic factors, 40 to 60% of gay men and 45 to 85 % of lesbians are in a romantic relationship at any given time (American Psych. Assoc., 2008). Most people understand that there is sometimes a difference between a romantic relationship and a committed one. It is widely believed, by both straights and gays, that both kinds of relationships are unstable within the homosexual community.

We should not believe that stereotype. Research shows that from 18% to 28% of gay couples and 8% to 21% of lesbian couples have stayed together ten years or more. A factor in that is that the stability of same-sex relationships may be negatively influenced by the lack of support and recognition that they receive by the society at large (American Psych. Assoc., 2008). This institutionalized reinforcement is not denied to straight people. Since research shows that gay people want basically the same things in a committed relationship that straight people do it is reasonable to think that gay and lesbian relationships will strengthen once that support and recognition arrives.

A 2010 study which analyzed data from the United States Census Bureau found that same-sex couples in the United States number around 581,300 and increased in number by about 3% from 2008 to 2009 (Gates, 2010). If we accept that around 4% of people are openly self-identified as gay, then homosexual couples account for about 15% of the openly gay people in America 24 years of age or older. The number gay couples in America is undoubtedly higher however since not all homosexual couples are out of the closet.

To this we can add that more and more gays are taking on the role of being parents. The Williams Institute tells us that one in three lesbians has given birth and one in six gay men have sired children. Additionally, around 65,500 youths have adoptive gay parents and an estimated 14,100 foster children are in gay homes (Gates & Macomber, 2007). Children, of course, never let you be alone even when you want to be.

Question: Are gay men promiscuous?
Conservative religionists define promiscuity as any sexual act done outside of a valid heterosexual marriage. A more common, albeit secular, definition is that it is having frequent casual sex with multiple partners. That seems straightforward, but it really needs to be put in context if it to be understood since that definition is not universal or based on human biology.

The number of sex partners people have and how often an individual has sex varies based upon age, race, religious affiliation, level of education and other factors such as personal preferences. The numbers also vary from country to country (Wellings and Collumbien, 2006). Men, as a class, are significantly more likely than women to have multiple partners over the course of their lifetime. Over half of American men report that they had five or more partners in that period. American women are far less likely to do so (Chandra & Mosher, 2011; Laumann & Gagnon, 1994). Even so 21.4% of men and 8.3% of women have 15 or more partners in their lifetime (Chandra & Mosher, 2011).

The CDC's National Survey of Family Growth (2010) found the median number of different sex partners for gay men during the preceding year is 2.3. A more recent study found that the median number of partners in the last year for hetero men is 1 while it may be as high as 4 for gay men. The same study found that gay men become sexually active earlier and continue to seek new sexual relationships later in life than straight men (Glick & Morris, 2012).

This gay/straight difference is not because a gay man is more lustful or less moral than straight ones but rather because a heterosexual male's sex partner is a heterosexual female. A gay man has more opportunity to have a variety of sex partners and fewer barriers to prevent him from doing so (Bailey & Gaulin,

1994; Symons, 1979; Kinsey, 1948). If the straight man had the same level of opportunity and risk, he would have a larger number of sex partners too. Even so one large survey found that one third of married hetero men cheat on their wives (Northrup, Schwartz and Witte, 2012) while another study put the figure at around 40% (Reinisch, 1990). Having only one sex partner in the preceding year is strongly correlated to being married to or cohabitating with a woman (Laumann & Gagnon, 1994).

The average male thinks about sex a lot and the male sex drive is stronger than the female one (Baumeister & Catanese, 2001). The part of the brain that deals with sex is 2.5 times larger in a man than it is in a woman. He also has a lot more testosterone and other hormones flowing within his veins that propel his sex drive.

One result of this is that a large majority of men enjoy pornography while only a small minority of women do (Northrup, Schwartz and Witte, 2012; Bailey & Gaulin, 1994). Women do like sex, but they are not as sexually oriented as most men, so they are not as likely to engage in premarital sex (Wellings and Collumbien, 2005) and they typically are not interested in having sex as often as men want it (Northrup, Schwartz and White 2012; Dixit, 2010; Peplau, 2003; Fisher, 1992). At the same time, monogamous, married hetero men, as a global class, have more sex than other men so they are less likely to have to look for it (Wellings and Collumbien, 2006).

Women are also more interested in monogamy than the average man is (Paplau, 2003; Buss, 1993; Midgley, 1981) and they view it differently (Rahman & Wilson, 2003; Buss, 1993; Fisher, 1992). One difference is that she is more likely to view sex in the context of an emotionally intimate relationship than he is (Peplau, 2003). This explains why she views rejection before or after sex more negatively than he does (de Graaf & Sandfort, 2004). It is also why she is far more likely to view a partner having a non-sexual but intimate relationship with someone else as cheating.

She is also more likely to view monogamy as a source of security. One study, in fact, found that within four years of a relationship forming and stabilizing a woman's libido tends to lessen while his stays constant and strong (Klusmann, 2006).

This, not coincidentally at all, is also about the time when she becomes emotionally secure about her relationship.

Men are more permissive than women in their views related to sex (Fisher, 2012; Peplau, 2003; Oliver, 1993). A man, hetero or homo, is much more likely to think of sex as just sex. Gay and straight men have roughly the same higher level of interest in casual sex (Peplau, 2003; Bailey & Gaulin, 1994). Men are also much more likely to accept an offer of sex from someone they do not know well (Guèguen, 2011; Clark, 1989).

It is because of his perception of sex that a man typically does not view his extramarital behavior as necessarily harmful to how he values that primary relationship (Hite, 1982). The straight man however knows his female partner does not agree with that view and that influences his decisions. The gay man is likely to meet much less opposition from his partner to his having other partners than the straight man is. This is because his partner is more likely to share the male view of sex being just sex. This reduced opposition lessens the barrier to having sex with more than one partner. This is perhaps why a non-monogamous committed relationship with one man is the goal gay men most often have (Northrup, Schwartz and Witte, 2012; Hite, 1982).

Men and women are different in what they regret about their history of casual sex. Women are more likely than men to regret having had casual sex with some of their prior sex partners. Men are more likely than women to regret not having more casual sex than they had earlier in their life (Galperin, 2012; Roese & Pennington, 2006). These regrets tend to influence future behavior. The different life situations gay and straight men find themselves in sends them in different directions in terms of what they do about their desire for casual sex.

Simple biology is a very real barrier for heterosexual men. If a male has sex with a woman there is the very real chance of the life altering experience of pregnancy and parenthood. Even if you are careful with contraception heterosexual sex always holds the possibility of pregnancy. Legal and social obligations come with fatherhood. Homosexual men do not have to concern themselves with that risk so it's not a barrier to casual sex.

The social institution of marriage is also a barrier that the heterosexual man faces that most gay men typically do not have. Most straight men are married. Getting a divorce is complicated, stressful and financially draining and it is a failure to succeed in an institution that the culture prizes. Marital unfaithfulness is a major cause of divorce. Once gay marriage becomes an institutionalized norm there is every reason to think that gay couples will experience similar pressure to stay married. The limited evidence we have tells us that gays divorce less often than straights (Badgett and Mallory, 2014).

Society also creates another barrier through giving men much greater latitude in how many sex partners he has than it gives women. Women who have more than one sex partner are often scorned by the community. Common language includes many words like trollop, slut, floozy, tart, and Jezebel for women who violate this standard but few for men who do. He may in fact be called a "stud". Her reality is reflected in her view of what is moral. She naturally expects her mate to be as moral as she is thus society's expectation of her becomes a barrier for him.

Another factor is the natural tendency for people to conform to the standards of the group they associate themselves with. While "slut shaming" is found in the gay culture that community is much more accepting of casual sex than the heterosexual community is. A gay man is more likely to be able to conform to the expectations of his group and not suffer being condemned or ostracized by his peers for having more than one sex partner than the heterosexual man is. The barrier that the heterosexual man faces is, once again, less present for the homosexual man.

The question of whether gay men are promiscuous may be taken to imply that there is something intrinsically wrong with being promiscuous. A survey of human cultures shows this bias is a culturally influenced moral judgment and not one that is based on what is innate and natural for male human beings. There are many human cultures both historically and at present where having more than one sex partner is viewed as normal.

There is, in fact, no evidence that monogamous relationships necessarily offer better cost/benefit outcomes than non-monogamous relationships do (Conley, 2013; Parsons, 2012; Hoff, 2010). In other words, relationship satisfaction is not necessarily a function of monogamy or non-monogamy. There is, of course, a health risk involved in being non-monogamous. Having completely monogamous sex is obviously safer than having sex with two or more people and the more partners you have the more risk you take on. That however may or may not have anything to do with how satisfied a person is with his relationship(s). On that level, there is nothing intrinsically or objectively wrong with being promiscuous.

Promiscuity is viewed as wrong in our society because most Western cultures have accepted the social construct of monogamy as the standard that will be enforced. As noted above, other cultures find having multiple sex partners to be normal and some do not even have the concept of "promiscuity". It can be easily argued that the gay culture is among these.

When gay culture is compared with the culture of straight society, it should be a comparison of traits found on two different charts. We function within most of the norms of the larger society, but we have our own norms too. We do not necessarily define "promiscuity" in the same way the larger culture does, and we are more likely to accept a broader range of what constitutes acceptable sexual behavior. We are also more likely to have members who have had no sexual partners in the past year (England & Brown, 2016; Binson & Michaels, 1995) and members who have had 30 or more (Glick & Morris, 2012). Many of us want a lifetime monogamous partner. Given this diversity, it is incorrect to say that gays, as a global class, are promiscuous. Some of us are and some of us are not.

Question: Are gay men drug abusers?

As a starting place, we must distinguish between drug use and drug abuse. We also must put our community's use or abuse of drugs into the context of what is found in the society generally if we are going to understand how gays fit into the picture. The bottom line is that a large majority of Americans (straight, bi and gay) are not drug abusers or drug dependent (National Institute on Drug Abuse, 2012) but use and abuse are present in all three communities.

Most Americans use drugs. CBS News reports that at least 80% of us use caffeine through our consumption of coffee, tea, sodas and other sources (Neal, 2003). A 2012 poll found that 66% of us drink alcohol (Saad, 2012). The Centers for Disease Control assert that nearly half of all Americans use at least one prescription drug (CDC Press Release, 2004). Nearly 80% of Americans use at least one nonprescription drug to treat their ailments (Consumer

Healthcare Products Assoc., 2012). Homosexuals are part of the American society, so we obviously are part of this drug use pattern.

Drug and/or alcohol use is also often called substance use. It includes everything from occasional use to regular use and everything from beneficial use to maladaptive use such as substance dependence. Substance abuse is associated with the amount used, the frequency of use and/or the kind of substances ingested. It also relates to the problems created by that use.

Illicit drug use is the use of any drug that is illegal under local, state or federal law. It is possible to use an illicit drug in an amount or frequency that is not within the definition of drug abuse. It is not possible to use or have an illegal drug without coming into potential conflict with the law. It is also not possible to use these drugs without becoming at risk of incurring the potential health, psychological and/or social damage that may come with that use. That potential damage is obviously some part of why these drugs are illegal to begin with.

The National Survey on Drug Use and Health (NSDUH) is annually done by the United States Substance Abuse and Mental Health Services Administration. It collects data from state and federal sources and thereby gives us an authoritative picture of the drug and mental health issues facing our country. It and other sources tell us that most Americans are not drug abusers.

The NSDUH for 2011 estimated that 8.7% of all Americans aged 12 or older were illicit drug users. Around 7% of Americans used marijuana. This is around 20 million people. Roughly 1.4 million of us used any form of cocaine. That is around 0.5% of the population at large. Heroin use accounted for 620,000 or 0.2% of us. Around 972,000 (0.3%) of us used hallucinogens. During 2011 roughly 6.1 million Americans (2%) used prescription drugs in a nonmedical way.

Homosexuals are not studied very much and only a small percentage of the research on homosexuals deals with drug use/abuse within that population. Only a fraction of that gives us information that is useful in letting us know the level of drug use within our community or in comparing the rates of drug use/abuse among homosexuals with that of the population at large. There are, however, studies which can be used to meaningfully compare drug use among gays with that of straights.

A 1994 study found that 20% of the gay men studied had used some form of illicit drug during the past month and 32% had done so in the past year (Skinner, 1994). When this study is compared to the data collected in the 1994 National Household Survey on Drug Abuse we find that of the drugs studied in the 1994 research only heroin and crack cocaine were used less by gays than by the Americans generally. Some drugs, such as hallucinogens, were used slightly more by gays while others, such as inhalants, were used a lot more.

Research reported in 2001 found that 52% of the gay men studied had used some type of illicit drug during the preceding six months (Stall, 2001). When the results of this study are compared to the data from the 2001 National Household Survey on Drug Abuse we find that gay men were more likely than the general population to use every category of drug looked at in the 2001 study. Sometimes, as in the case of inhalants, the difference was large while in other cases, such as opiates the difference was small.

A 2004 study directly compared the drug used patterns of homosexuals to heterosexuals of the same gender. It found that homosexuals where at some point in their lives more likely to have used each of the studied drugs and that this difference was significant. The study found however that if only the last month was looked at gays had used only marijuana and hallucinogens more than straights did and the differences were moderate or small (Cochran, 2004).

A research project done in 2011 looked at the role of communities and social networks in the drug use patterns of gays. Part of this research looked at the percentage of the study participants who used meth, ecstasy, cocaine, marijuana and poppers or some combination of those drugs in the last 90 days. When compared to the results of the 2011 National Survey on Drug Use and Health Survey we see that gays in this study used each of the six drugs in a much higher percentage than did the general population.

There are other studies that are also relevant to whether gays are more likely to be drug users or abusers, but space forbids citing all of them. The studies however are consistent. The bottom line is that a higher percentage of gays than straights use illicit drugs. Gays are also more likely than straights to use drugs abusively. At the same time, it must be remembered that the evidence also says that most gays are not drug abusers.

Question: Are gay men alcohol abusers?

The National Center for Health Statistics tells us that 60 percent of American men 18 years of age or older are regular drinkers of alcohol and another 10 percent are infrequent users (Schiller & Lucus, 2012). A 2012 poll supports that figure in that 67 percent of the men polled said that they drink alcohol. When asked how many drinks they had consumed in the preceding seven days the average was 4.2 drinks (Saad, 2012).

It is commonly thought that gay men consume alcohol at higher levels than straight men. It is also commonly thought that gay men, as a group, are significantly more likely to use alcohol abusively or to be alcoholics. This is not just a stereotype that is held by many in the hetero community but is also one that many gays believe. It probably comes from the fact that gay men are more likely than straight men to spend time in venues like bars and clubs that serve alcohol and to use those venues as a hub of social networking (Trocki & Drabble, 2005). Another factor used to support the stereotype is that gays are also more likely to seek professional help for alcohol related issues. The stereotype however is not true.

The National Institute on Alcohol Abuse and Alcoholism (NIAAA) says that overall gay men and heterosexual men have similar patterns of alcohol use and a similar pattern in relation to the rate at which we have problems related to that use. Interestingly, gay men are more likely to be at the poles regarding alcohol use. In other words, gay men are more likely than straight men to either abstain entirely from using alcohol or to drink heavily. Most men, gay or straight, are not alcohol abusers.

There are several peer reviewed studies related to alcohol use/abuse in the homosexual community. A few of these are cited regularly in peer reviewed journal articles and are viewed as authoritative by researchers in the field. Among them are Stall & Wiley, 1988; Cochran & Keenan, 2000 and Stall & Paul et al, 2001. The full citations for these studies can be found in the citation section of this book. These studies are consistent with the view that the alcohol use and abuse patterns of gay and straight men are roughly comparable.

Question: Are gay people mentally ill?
Some people within the gay community do have some form of mental illness. Others have factors in their lives that, while not a form of mental illness, present them with mental health issues. Both things are also true of humans generally.

In no sense is homosexuality itself a mental illness nor are most gays mentally ill. Globally speaking, homosexuals are as mentally healthy as most people in the general population. The American Psychological Association removed homosexuality from its list of mental illnesses in 1973. Every other major medical, psychological and sociological association has followed suit.

Homosexuality is simply one form of healthy social and sexual expression. When mental health issues are a life element for gays it is typically based in the same kinds of biological, environmental and/or psychological factors that bring mental health issues to our species in general. A major difference however is that the mental health issues of gays are often based in the unhealthy way he/she relates to his/her own sexuality or the way others relate to it. LGBTs seeking mental health help often do so because of anxiety or depression issues that occur because of that. This is not unique to homosexuals but rather something that goes hand in hand with any minority group that is viewed disapprovingly or even hostilely by their society.

The assertion that homosexuality is an illness wrongly implies that there might be a cure. There is no cure not only because there is nothing to be cured but also because there is no means to cure homosexuality even if it was an illness. There is evidence however that trying to cure it can result in harm to the homosexual client (American Psychological Association, 2009; Royal College of Psychiatrists, 2007).

Reparative therapy (also called conversion therapy) is sometimes offered by conservative counselors or psychologists, conservative religionists and their allied groups. A few conservative psychiatrists also offer therapy aimed at curing homosexuals. The proof offered in support of reparative therapy is anecdotal and does not stand up to rigorous testing. There is no valid evidence supporting the idea that homosexuality can be cured. This fact has been known for at least two decades and was authoritatively asserted by the United States Surgeon General in 2001 (Satcher, 2001).

In August of 2009 the American Psychological Association adopted the position that it is unethical for a therapist to tell a client or his/her family that homosexuality can be cured or to take part in performing such therapy. This decision followed a statement by the Royal College of Psychiatrists in Great Britain in 2007 that therapy aimed at curing homosexuality is potentially damaging to the client. They conclude that there is no rational reason to treat homosexuals differently from the population at large. In 2012 the World Health Organization (WHO) joined in condemning reparative therapy and called for a worldwide end to the practice (WHO, 2012).

Question: Is there a link between being gay and being a pedophile?

A rabbi, a priest and a deacon walk into a bar. The Jew orders a vodka and tonic with a twist. The Catholic orders a whiskey neat. The Anglican orders a pink poodle. How do you tell if any of them are pedophiles? Answer: There is no way to tell because pedophilia has nothing to do with titles, religion, or beverages. It has nothing to do with sexual orientation either.

To understand why there is no link between homosexuality and pedophilia we need to understand what heterosexuality, homosexuality and pedophilia are. Heterosexuality is the exclusive preference for having opposite sex people as sexual partners. Homosexuality is the exclusive preference for having same-sex people as that kind of partner. The underlying factor for both categories is the sex of their partner.

Pedophilia is the primary or exclusive preference for prepubescent children as sex partners or as the object of a sexual fantasy. A pedophile may prefer a male child victim, a female child victim or he may have no sex preference at all. He always wants the victim to be in a certain age group however. Age, not sex/gender, is his baseline. Pedophiles either have no sexual interest in adults at all or it is secondary.

Most pedophiles are male. Most victims of pedophiles are female. Some pedophiles will switch to a child of the other sex if a child of their preferred sex cannot be found. Some will have consensual sex with an adult, but their primary underlying sexual driver is the youthful age of their preferred partner. Most pedophiles see themselves has heterosexual and may even be married to an opposite sex spouse.

Pedophiles are no more than 3-5% of the population generally (American Psychiatric Association, 2013). They may be male or female although, as noted above, most are male. They may be heterosexual, homosexual or bisexual. He may be a person the victim knows or someone who is a stranger. He may pick his victim with planned intent or through random opportunity (Murray, 2000).

Studies show that 50 to 70% of pedophiles have another paraphilia such as voyeurism, exhibitionism or frotteurism (Cohen and Galynker, 2002; Raymond and Coleman, 1999; Abel and Becker, 1988). Most also have a substance abuse problem (Kraanen and Emmelkamp, 2011). A majority have a diagnosable major psychiatric disorder. Affective disorders, anxiety disorders and personality disorders are a common part of their history (Egan and Kavanaugh, 2005; Cohen and Galynker, 2002; Raymond and Coleman, 1999). None of that is related to any sexual orientation.

Homosexual men who prefer adult men as partners do not respond to sexual stimuli differently than heterosexual men who prefer adult women as partners. Adults of their preferred sex/gender arouse them (Freund, 1989). Children of either sex do not. Sexuality, not age, is their motivator. The development of sexual orientation in humans is an entirely different process than is the development of pedophilia (Freund, 1984). Pedophilia is not associated with an existing homosexual or heterosexual identity (Hall and Hall, 2007).

It is dishonest to assert, as anti-gay people do, that there are more homosexual pedophiles than heterosexual ones. The assertion that, given the low percentage of gays in the general population, gays are overrepresented in the pedophile population is likewise dishonest.

First, we do not know if those assertions are true because, per the U.S. Department of Justice, most pedophilia cases are not reported to law enforcement authorities. We therefore do not know the sexual orientation of those pedophiles. The information we have comes from arrest data and from surveys, studies and the self-reports of offenders to treatment providers. This allows us to have estimates of the incidence of pedophilia but only general sketches of the personal characteristics of pedophiles as a class.

Those estimates do not come from probability samples, so they do not reliably offer a representation of the full picture. They do however tell us that only a very small percentage of pedophiles are gay or lesbian. A well-known study put the percentage at 3.1% or less (Jenny and Roesler, 1994). This fact is so well accepted by authorities that it is rarely studied anymore.

The assertions are also dishonest because a pedophile may have only one victim, or he may have many victims. One pedophile of the latter type can do more harm than ten of the former type. This, in a sense, makes the number of pedophiles there are less relevant because one can devastate a life or a town. Pedophiles are kind of like werewolves and vampires in that way.

Anti-gay forces have, through intent or ignorance, complicated the matter by mixing apples and oranges. They have incorrectly asserted that a homosexual who has violated a same-sex victim has done so because of his/her sexual orientation. This is not true.

Pedophilia is both a sexual interest and a paraphilia, but it is not a sexual orientation (American Psychiatric Assoc., 2013). There is no causal or biological link between pedophilia and any recognized sexual orientation. It has nothing to do with being gay, lesbian or bisexual.

The exact cause of pedophilia is still not known. There is however a growing body of evidence that pedophilia is biological and related to brain structure (Sartorius, 2008; Cantor, 2007; Cohen, 2002) and brain chemistry (Maes, 2001; Maes 2001) that is not found in non-pedophiles. Brain imaging shows that homosexual male pedophiles do not mentally respond in the same way as other homosexual males when seeing the same sexual stimuli (Schiffer, 2008).

The takeaway nutshell is that typical gay men do not hurt anyone unless they don't use enough lube, or someone asks them to make him moan. We would not hurt a kid for anything. Our deal is that we get "that feeling" because the right man was in the right place at the right time. When that time and place comes, a kid would be in the way.

Question: Isn't HIV/AIDS a gay disease and aren't all gays at risk of getting it?
We must distinguish between HIV (Human Immunodeficiency Virus) and AIDS (Acquired Immune Deficiency Syndrome). HIV is not AIDS. It is also not a disease. HIV is a viral infection that compromises the immune system and thereby makes it vulnerable to disease. A HIV+ person may not get AIDS for years even without treatment.

The state of being HIV+ but not AIDS+ can last a normal lifetime if the HIV+ person has a doctor who is knowledgeable in HIV/AIDS and that person follows the treatment plan rigorously. That plan will be aimed at increasing or keeping his/her white blood count and keeping his viral load low. Some HIV+ people have a load level so low that HIV is undetectable. If, on the other hand, the CD4 T-cell (white blood cells) count is below 200 the person is diagnosed as having AIDS.

The myth that HIV and AIDS are gay ailments is believed by some people because the highest rate of HIV and AIDS in the United States is found in the men who have sex with men (MSM) community. The Centers for Disease Control calculate the incidence of a diagnosis of HIV for gays in 2008 at 672 per 100,000 (Purcell, 2012). The same study put the heterosexual rate (men and women) at 21.6 per 100,000 and the rate for hetero men at 10.1 per 100,000. The only risk group the United States in which HIV infection is increasing is gays (Centers for Disease Control and Prevention, 2010). These statistics are sometimes used to support the view that HIV and AIDS are gay disorders.

The fact however is that HIV/AIDS is caused by a virus that any human being can be infected with. Anybody that meets it may get it. It is primarily spread through the exchange of bodily fluids such as blood, semen, pre-seminal fluid (precum) or breast milk. Any behavior that enables that exchange may spread HIV.

The behavior that transmits HIV can be sexual in nature or nonsexual as in the case of sharing contaminated needles. It can be homosexual or heterosexual. Americans tend to think no further than what is happening within our borders but, on a global basis, most cases of HIV are heterosexual or not based on sexuality at all (UNAIDS, 2010). It is rare for a woman to give another woman HIV (CDC, 2014) but the women of the world account for 52% of the HIV cases on Earth. Children account for roughly another 7% and intravenous drug users account for nearly 9% (UNAIDS, 2010). A sizable majority of the latter group is heterosexual.

All human beings share the same HIV risk factors. The prevalence of HIV in the gay community is higher than it is in the hetero community because we come across the risk factors more often and we often do not do what is needed to declaw the risk. Unprotected anal sex is by far the most potent risk factor. That practice is done by both homosexuals and heterosexuals, but we do it a lot more. We also have a greater chance of having sex with a HIV+ partner because the pool of people we get a sex partner out of is a lot smaller and the percentage of our pool that is HIV+ is a lot higher.

If we yield to our parochial instinct and consider just what is in the United States, it at once becomes clear that even here HIV cannot be accurately described as a gay ailment. That point becomes indelibly clear when we consider that, when looking at the subgroups within the United States, we find it is gay women (lesbians) who have the lowest rate of infection (Women's Institute at GMHC, 2009). Since this is the case it is obvious that HIV and AIDS are not gay ailments. If we wish to pursue the line of thought about whose fault American HIV/AIDS is, we must take another look.

African Americans account for 46% of all HIV/AIDS cases and 45% of all new infections. The rate of infection of Blacks is six time that of the general population (National Center for HIV/AIDS, 2010). Since they are only 13% of the general population, HIV/AIDS seems to be an African-American malady. If we add the 17% of HIV cases that are Latino it begins to look like HIV/AIDS is a racial minority problem.

Then again, a sizeable majority of American HIV/AIDS cases are male (Center for Disease Control and Prevention, 2010) so maybe the fault lies in gender. If that is not correct then perhaps the problem is one of age. People age 39 or younger are the clear majority of new HIV diagnoses after all (National Center for HIV/AIDS, 2010; Gayle, 2000).

All of that, of course, is nonsense and only shows us that statistics can be used to serve the needs of any master. The fact is that heterosexuals and even asexuals can get HIV. HIV is a species-wide problem because it can thrive in nearly any human and it travels with any host. As such it must be dealt with globally in a way that is sensitive to the risk factors of our various subgroups. Our method must not discriminate against low status groups such as women, men who have sex with men and intravenous drug users. Such discrimination may make the powerful feel good, but it is lethal for our species.

Question: Is homosexuality immoral?

It depends upon how morality is defined. If we accept the view of the philosopher Thomas Hobbes that morality is whatever a society says it is through its laws and norms then yes, in some places homosexuality is immortal. In others, it's not. As public opinion and the law change so does the status of homosexuality. In the United States, public opinion is shifting rapidly toward the view that homosexuality is moral.

A 2010 poll found that 52% of Americas believed homosexuality is moral. In 2015 the number had risen to 63%. This is a major change in the moral status of homosexuality in the United States since earlier polls showed the majority view was that homosexuality was immoral. If public opinion is the measure of morality then, in the United States generally, homosexuality is moral, but it is not in specific sections of the country or by those who hold certain religious beliefs.

If we accept the view of the philosopher Jean Paul Sartre on what is moral then, once again, maybe homosexuality is moral and maybe it's not. There is, per Sartre, no innate standard of morality and neither law nor other social norms can decide the matter since they are authoritarian, arbitrary and irrational. In his view, each person must decide for himself what is moral. It is a matter of personal choice. In this case homosexuality is only immoral if you personally think it is.

Aristotle said that morality is always found in virtue and virtue is always based on right action, right motives and right manner. He said that the true essence of man is the desire to be happy and that this can only be achieved through reasoning. Reason, he taught, would consistently take you on the moderate and temperate path. For him then, there is nothing about homosexuality per se that is moral or immoral. That is decided in how you practice it.

Many religionists say morality is defined by what is contained in their holy book(s) and by the interpretation of that content. If this is the definition used to judge homosexuality, then it may or may not be immoral. Some religionists interpret their holy book(s) one way, and some interpret it in another. Mainline Islam, Orthodox Judaism and conservative Christianity, for example, view homosexuality as immoral while Progressive Islam, Reform Judaism and liberal Christianity do not.

The standard used by the ancient Greeks to decide what is moral is certainly the most universal one. It is the standard of justice, temperance, fortitude and prudence. These when formed together, but not necessary individually, make a person virtuous and moral. This standard is found in every human culture on earth.

Justice is the ideal of interacting with others fairly, impartially and in a way in which a person gets his due. It is not only something one wishes to receive but also something that one has an obligation to give. Prudence is the exercise of sound judgment using knowledge, insight and reason. Temperance is satisfying one's needs and wants moderately. Fortitude is the ability to be courageous, strong, patient and controlled in the face of adversity or challenge.

None of these are necessarily absent in homosexuality per se therefore there is nothing necessarily immoral about it. All human beings have the natural need to love, to be loved and to fulfill themselves sexually and emotionally. Nature mandates that homosexuals do these things with persons of their own sex. Some might say it would be immoral for us not to do so.

Question: Wouldn't the world be better off without homosexuals?

Would we be better off without Socrates or Aristotle? Are Shakespeare, Noel Coward, Oscar Wilde or Tchaikovsky expendable because they were gay or bisexual? Do we really want to do without Cole Porter or Francis Bacon? It would certainly be a turn for the worse if we had not had Michelangelo or Leonardo da Vinci. Can we imagine a childhood without Han Christian Anderson? Would the grace found in the world be the same without Nureyev?

The world was made happier when Elton John found his way to us and the world changed forever in the hands of Alexander the Great, Julius Caesar, Hadrian, Frederick the Great and James I of England. Do we want to set Lord Byron or Tennessee Williams aside as being expendable? Would not we be less without Arthur Bernstein, Van Cliburn, Andy Warhol and Yves Saint-Laurent? Would the world understand itself quite as well without John Maynard Keynes or Harry Stack Sullivan?

Could we do without the gay fireman that risks his life to save our home or the office workers who do their jobs day after day and thereby make companies and governments function day after day? Perhaps it's the mechanic that repairs your car or the gay plumber that makes you toilet or pipes useful again that you would like to dispose of.

All the people noted above are gay or bisexual. Homosexuals are in all walks of life and contribute in every conceivable way to the welfare of the world. Which of them are we better off without?

Would the world be better off without homosexuals? We must, if we are unbiased, answer "no". It is not just because of the achievements offered by gay people that this is so but also because humanity is improved by its diversity. We are better and stronger as a species because of our differences. We are each better as a person when we understand that.

Question: What is the Gay Pride Flag?
The Gay Pride Flag is also called the "Rainbow Flag". It was created in San Francisco, California by Gilbert Baker in 1978. The flag originally had more colors than the current one does because over the course of time the colors pink and turquoise were eliminated. The current variation of the flag was created in 2008. It includes the colors of red (life), orange (healing), yellow (sunlight), green (nature), royal blue (serenity/harmony) and violet (spirit). The flag should be flown with the red stripe on top. It is recognized world-wide as the symbol of our community, of our struggle and of our pride.

Chapter 2
Gay Historical Context

Question: What do we know about gay history and why is it important?
History is "bunk" or so said Henry Ford (Wheeler, 1916). A more enlightened mind might well see the error in that opinion and prefer the view of Henry St. John Bolingbroke who said, "History is philosophy teaching us by examples" (Bolingbroke, 1735). It offers lessons not only in why and how things can or should be done but also teaches us about ourselves as a species. By showing us the past, history points us into the future with the admonishment that we should pay attention and never surrender.

The timeline offered below is the history of our reality and our truth as homosexuals. It is the basis of our living that reality and truth. These examples are mere tokens of unnumbered others. They, individually and collectively, teach us if we have a mind to take their lessons. They tell us not only of what reality was and is but also what it could be. We should listen.

2400 BCE. The first gay couple to be historically documented was Khnumhotep and Niankhakhum. They were royal servants in the 5th Dynasty of Egypt and are listed in the records of that time as having been royal confidants of the Pharaoh. They were found buried together in a single crypt.

1200 BCE – 323 CE. This is the era, between the end of the Mycenaean civilization in Greece and the death of Alexander the Great, that we now call ancient Greece. In that time and place the homosexual/heterosexual dichotomy did not exist as a concept and same-sex relationships were viewed as ordinary and accepted if they were within certain rules. Slaves, of course, could be used sexually by the master but freemen could also be involved in male with male relationships if the rules were adhered to. Within that boundary, it was a matter of tastes, not one of morality or manliness. The 4th century Theban army, in fact, had an elite force of 300 men (the Sacred Band) that was entirely made up of male lovers.

The activity was viewed as one of status and not one of merely sex. An older man took on the role of mentoring a boy or young man and was expected to be the active person in any sex. The younger male was expected to be the passive one that was anally or orally penetrated by the penis of the older man. When the younger man became old enough to have a beard he became an adult citizen and the relationship was expected to end. It was not illegal for it to not end but it was socially unacceptable for it not to.

722 BCE. The biblical book of Leviticus was written. Two versions of it were penned originally. One was written by a priest from the kingdom of Judah and the other was written by a priest from the northern kingdom of Israel. These were joined together into the form of the book of Leviticus we have now (Friedman, 1997). This book is important to homosexuals because it became a major basis for our persecution throughout much of history.

Religionists try to give Leviticus authority by ascribing its authorship to Moses. Some even say it was dictated to Moses by God. No creditable historian now accepts this ascription as valid (Friedman, 1997; Clines, 1993). Moses is, in fact, viewed by many historians as a mystical figure (Murdock, 2014; Dever, 1993). If he existed, he is dated as living around 1572 BCE.

600 BCE. The first recorded homosexual relationship in the Far East was Pan Zhang and Wang Zhaongxian. They are recorded as falling in love at first sight and living together as a couple for the rest of their lives. They were buried next to one another as well.

509-27 BCE. This is the period of the Roman Republic. During this time, male homosexual relationships were common and acceptable. They were very much like those found in ancient Greece. A man could do what he liked with his slaves, prostitutes or non-citizens but it was restricted by custom (not by law) based on status. Typically, older males took the active role and the younger male took the passive role of being penetrated. When similar age males had a relationship, it was typically within their own socio/economic class.

206 BCE - 220 CE. The Han Dynasty ruled China. Ten of its emperors were recorded to have been homosexual or bisexual. Emperor Ai even tried (unsuccessfully) to make his male lover his heir to the throne.

27 BCE- 476 CE. This is the period of the Roman Empire. Under this scheme the legality or illegality of homosexual relationships was up to which ever emperor was in charge at the time. At the beginning and for quite some time things did not change much in this regard from what existed during the days of the Republic. Over the course of time this began to change.

54 CE. Emperor Nero married two men (Pathagoras and Sporus).

98 CE. Emperor Trajan came into power. He was openly bisexual.

218 CE. Emperor Elagabalus came to power. He married a man named Zoitcus. He was assassinated and replaced by his cousin Severus for that and other offenses.

222 CE. Emperor Severus lowered the status of homosexuals who took the passive role of being penetrated. Under this law these people had greatly reduced status and greatly reduced rights.

346-395 CE. Emperor Theodosius, at the urging of the Catholic Church, instituted Mosaic Law as it applies to homosexuality. Homosexuals were executed.

412 CE. Augustine of Hippo (St. Augustine) upped the ante on homosexuality. He wrote that sodomy was a primary sin and against the will of God. This meant you not only were executed for doing it but also went to hell.

478 CE. The last Roman emperor was deposed by the barbarian chief Odoacer. This was the end of the Roman Empire and the end to the Roman laws against homosexuality. It once again became widespread practice in various parts of Europe.

527 CE. The Justinian Code was put in place throughout the Byzantine Empire. The penalty for homosexuality under this legal code was death.

768-814. Charlemagne was king of the Franks (France). He personally disapproved of homosexuality but did not make it illegal. It was viewed as just another sex act done outside marriage but not one that should be prosecuted.

632 CE. The Prophet Muhammad died. Prior to the rule of Muhammad homosexuality was not an uncommon practice in the Middle East (El-Rouayheb, 2005). Muhammad however disapproved of it and said homosexuals would be judged harshly by Allah (but not by him) and then sent to hell. His successor, Abu Bahr as-Siddiq, began the practice of killing male homosexuals.

794 CE. The form of male homosexuality found in ancient Japan called "nanshoku" or "shudo" was well entrenched at all levels of Japanese society by this time. It took the form of an older man taking the active role and a younger man or boy taking the passive position of being penetrated. The younger man was often an apprentice to the older one.

1050-1080. Pope Gregory VIII affirmed celibacy as a requisite of priesthood and actively enforced it. This was done both because the Church asserted it wanted to follow the example of Christ and the Apostle Paul and because it was much less expensive to have unmarried priests.

1225- 1274. Saint Thomas Aquinas busied himself with thinking and writing. He thinks homosexuality is a personal sin against God and he writes that this makes it among the worst of all possible sins. His writings became one foundation upon which homosexuals were hunted down and persecuted or killed over the next several centuries.

1233. Pope Gregory the IX authorized the papal inquisitions. Church officials and others hunted down both heretics and homosexuals. It was, in fact, thought that being a homosexual was heretical in that it was against the teachings and will of God.

1252. Pope Innocent IV authorized torture to gain confessions from accused heretics and homosexuals. He disallowed priests being involved in the actual torture but did allow priests to authorize it and use the fruits of it in trials.

1256. Pope Alexander IV authorized priests to absolve one another for sins resulting from the torture of accused homosexuals and heretics.

1478. The Spanish Inquisition began. It was initially authorized by Pope Sixtus IV, but he later washed his hands of it because of the brutal course it took and the fact that no appeal to the pope from those convicted was possible. The inquisition's mission was the discovery and elimination of heretics, Jews and homosexuals.

1524. Pope Clement VII authorized Inquisitional tribunals that only dealt with homosexuality.

1533. King Henry VIII of England decreed the first secular law against homosexuality in England. It was known as the Buggery Act. This was more of a political move than anything else however since his targets were primarily Roman Catholic priests. He had declared himself as head of the Church of England and was busy confiscating all the property and wealth of the Roman Catholic Church he could find in England. This law made the matter easier.

1566. The first recorded case of a person being executed in the Americas for homosexuality. Spanish records show that a Frenchman was executed in Florida for this offense.

1637. The word "gay" transformed from meaning simply "carefree and happy" to also possibly meaning the person so described was morally loose. In the 1920s the word again changed when homosexuals began to refer to themselves as "gay". That use broadened into the mainstream of American slang.

1778 (March 15). The first American soldier to be expelled from the military for homosexuality was Lieutenant Frederick Enslin. He was found guilty of sodomy and drummed out of the service publicly with the entire force he had served with as witnesses.

1791. France abolished ecclesiastical courts and established law as a secular function exclusively. The Church could no longer bring homosexuals or anyone else to trial.

1804 (March 21). The Napoleonic Code decriminalized homosexuality. This legal code spread throughout much of Europe and the more liberal view of homosexuality spread with it. This is largely due to the efforts of Jean-Jacques-Reis de Cambacérés who was second counsel in Napoleon's government and a homosexual.

1811. Homosexuality is decriminalized in Amsterdam.

1857. Amboise Tardieu published *Medio-Legal Study of Offenses Against Public Decency*. The book asserted that homosexuals could be recognized not only by behavior but also by physical markings on the penis and anus.

1861. England abolished the death penalty for homosexuality.

1864-1879. Karl Heinrich Ulrichs published the pamphlet series *Paragraph* 175. In it he urged Germany not to adopt anti-gay legislation and asserted homosexuality was natural and therefore not immoral. He became the first person to out himself in 1867 when he began writing in his real name and stated publically that he was a homosexual.

1869. Karl Westphal, MD published an article in which he asserted homosexuality exists prior to birth but is not inherited. He argued that this made the matter one of mental health, not one of law.

1869. Karl-Maria Benkert coined the words "homosexual" and "heterosexual" in his writings. He asserted that homosexuality is innate and unchangeable. He was roundly criticized by most of his contemporaries but has been proven to be correct.

1878. Arrigo Tamassia writes an article in Italy agreeing with Karl Westphal.

1882. Jean Martin Charot writes an article in France agreeing with Karl Westphal.

1886. Richard von Kraft-Ebing publishes *Psychopathia Sexualis*. The book supported Karl Westphal and popularized the term "homosexual".

1886. Toronto, Canada institutes the Morals Division of its police department. David Archibald was the first head of that division. Its purpose was to police the public morals including finding and arresting homosexuals.

1895 (May). Oscar Wilde is prosecuted for "unnatural vices" (homosexuality) in England. He was found guilty and sentenced to two years in prison. His genius as a playwright was never the same again and he died broken and bankrupt in France in 1900.

1896. Havelock Ellis published *Sexual Inversion* in which he challenged the view of the day that homosexuality was unnatural. He argued that it is innate within our biology. He has been proven to be right.

1897 – 1933. Magnus Hirschfeld, MD founded and led the Scientific Humanitarian Committee. The committee was an organization of professionals who worked against anti-sodomy laws in Germany.

1905. Sigmund Freud published *Three Essays on the Theory of Sexuality*. In it he said homosexuality is based on the individual's anxiety at finding out his mother has been castrated. The homosexual, he said, relates emotionally with the mother and takes on the role of a woman with a penis. He then seeks the love of his father and/or of other men. Freud believed bisexuality was universal in humans to one degree or another and that some combination of biology and environment decided how one's sexuality manifests itself. He asserted there was no cure for homosexuality and that it is neither sinful nor shameful.

1914. The word "faggot" was coined in American slang as a pejorative referring to male homosexuals. It was shorted to "fag" in 1921. The term derives from the Yiddish word "feygele" which literally means "little bird" but is now used in Yiddish as a reference to a male homosexual. The term "faggot" has existed in the English language since the 16th century but originally referred to a bundle of sticks. The pejorative "faggot" has spread from American slang into the languages of many countries.

1924. The Society for Human Rights was founded by Henry Gerber. It was formed to support gay rights but disbanded a few months after its start when the police started arresting and harassing members. Its first president was a Black clergyman named John Graves. Henry Gerber was later fired from his job at the Post Office for "conduct unbecoming a federal employee". That conduct was that he was gay.

1932 (June). Henry Gerber published an essay in the journal The Modern Thinker entitled, *In Defense of Homosexuality*. The essay was a rebuttal to another article which had said homosexuals are antisocial, insecure and criminally inclined. Gerber offered evidence for his view that homosexuality was normal and natural and disputed the assertion that it could be cured. He asserted that homosexuality is not just a matter of sexual acts but one of sexual attraction and affection. Interestingly, this is now the view of the American Psychological Association.

1940. Sandor Rado published an article entitled, *A Critical Examination of the Concept of Bisexuality*. The article rejected Freud's theory and argued that bisexuality and homosexuality are pathological (diseases). He said homosexuality is a phobic response to parental bias against expression of sexuality and that this could be cured. The pathology model is still the basis of the idea that homosexuals can be cured.

1948. Alfred Kinsey published *Sexual Behavior in the Human Male*. The book deals with all aspects of male sexuality which of course includes male homosexuality. He asserts in it that 10% of men are exclusively homosexual for at least three years and 37% of men have at least one homosexual experience in their lifetime.

This book created a furor and there were calls for Kinsey to be fired from his job at Indiana University. The president of that university, Herman Wells, defended Kinsey based on academic freedom and refused to fire him. Kinsey is now acknowledged as being the father of sexology.

1950. President Harry Truman signed legislation approving the Uniform Code of Military Justice. One of its measures demanded the removal from the military of any person found to be a homosexual and gives the policies and procedures to do so.

1950 (Nov. 11). The Mattachine Society was founded by Harry Hay, Bob Hull, Chuck Rowland, Rudi Gernreich and Dale Jennings. This organization was among the earliest gay rights groups in American. It faded during the 1970s and 80s as other gay rights groups entered the arena in a more activist and vocal way. It ceased to exist in 1987.

1952 (Feb). Dale Jennings was tried for sodomy. He admitted in court that he was a homosexual but pled innocent to the charge. The jury deadlocked, and he was not retried. The arrest but not the failure to convict was reported by the press.

1953. President Dwight Eisenhower signed executive order 10405 authorizing officials to fire any federal employee who was a homosexual. It also authorized the federal government to aid states and businesses in finding gay persons. This was federal policy until 1993.

1953. ONE becomes the first gay magazine in America. In 1954 the United States Post Office classified the magazine as obscene because it discussed homosexuality and portrayed it in a positive light and refused to deliver it. The publisher, ONE, Inc, sued and won. In 1965 ONE, Inc merged with the Institute for the Study of Human Resources. The magazine is no longer published.

1954. Senator Joseph McCarthy led his Senate investigative committee from solely looking for communists in every corner to also looking for homosexuals in every closet. He asserted that homosexuals were generally communists and therefore enemies of the state. His investigations ended two years later when he was censured by the U.S. Senate for conduct unbecoming a senator. He was not removed from the Senate, but his influence died as he, himself, did in 1957. He never proved a single charge against anyone, communist or homosexual, but his accusations alone were enough to ruin several lives.

1954 (June 7). Alan Turing died as the result of a probable suicide. He was the father of theoretical computer science and artificial intelligence. His work in deciphering codes was instrumental in the Allies winning World War II. He was prosecuted and convicted in 1952 of gross indecency because he was a homosexual. He was chemically castrated. The British government officially apologized on September 10, 2009.

1955. The Daughters of Bilitis is founded by Del Martin and Phyllis Lyon. It was originally intended to be an alternative to the lesbian bar scene for those who wanted to socialize with gay women. It expanded into education, publication, research support and outreach. It folded in 1970.

1957. Evelyn Hooker published *The Adjustment of the Male Overt Homosexual* in which she shows that homosexuals are no worse adjusted psychologically than heterosexuals are. She also showed that when experienced psychology professionals are given the projective tests of homosexuals and heterosexuals, the professionals cannot tell them apart.

1957. Bayard Rustin and Dr. Martin Luther King, Jr. organized the Southern Christian Leadership Conference which became the foundation of the African American quest for equal rights in the 1960s and beyond. In 1960 Rustin was forced to resign from his post as a primary lieutenant of Dr. King by Congressman Adam Clayton Powell, Jr. who objected to Rustin's homosexuality. In 1963 Bayard Rustin was asked to return to the movement and to help Philip Randolph organize the first March on Washington. He did so, and the march is now remembered not only for the huge size of the crowd demanding equal rights but also for Dr. King's "I have a dream" speech.

1957. Frank Kameny was fired from his job at the United States Army Map Service for being a homosexual. He lost at every phase of the appeal process but filed the first appeal related to sexual orientation at the United States Supreme Court. The court declined to hear the case. This is the first civil rights case based on sexual orientation. Kameny was not deterred and went on to become one of the giants in gay rights activism.

1961. José Sarria became the first openly gay person to run for political office in the United States. He ran for the San Francisco Board of Supervisors but lost the election.

1962. Irving Bieber published *Homosexuality: A Psychoanalytic Study*. He supported the idea that homosexuals can be cured with research data showing 27% of those in his study were cured of homosexuality. His work was discredited but is still part of the arsenal used by those who assert homosexuality can be cured.

1967 (Apr. 19). Stephen Donaldson founded the Student Homophile League at Columbia University. It is the first gay student organization in America. Other similar organizations soon followed at other universities. His organization at Columbia University is now called the Columbia Queer Alliance.

1967 (Sept). The Advocate begins publishing. Initially it is in the form of a newsletter called Los Angeles Advocate. It became a national publication in 1969. It was bought by David Goldstein in 1974 and is now the largest gay magazine on earth.

1969 (Apr). The Gay-Straight Alliance (GSA) was founded by high school student Kelli Peterson in Salt Lake City, Utah. She asked for permission to form a gay/straight social club at her high school. The request was denied. At the appeal level the school board was told they had the options under the law to either allow the club or disallow all after school clubs. They chose the latter choice. Initially the state legislature sided with the school board and passed a law which had the effect of banning the GSA. The legislature finally yielded to public pressure and passed legislation authorizing gay clubs to exist in public high schools. The GSA is now in high schools and universities all over America. They offer a safe and supportive environment for gays, lesbians, bisexual and transgender people plus our allies.

1969 (June 28). The Stonewall riots took place. The Stonewall Inn was (and still is) a gay bar in the Greenwich Village area of New York City. On this date the New York Police Department raided the bar for no reason other than to harass and arrest gay men. No law violation had occurred. They were surprised when instead of passively being arrested as they had in the past, these gay men fought back with such force that the police had to withdraw. This single event changed gay history. It was the real beginning of the gay rights movement in the United States. It also influenced the history of gays in other countries in that it was an example that they could and did follow.

1969 (July). The Gay Liberation Front (GLF) was founded by Jim Fouratt and Martha Shelley as a response to the events surrounding Stonewall and the aftermath of that event. The intent was to map out a continuing response to Stonewall, to cease appeasing the heterosexual establishment and to oppose militarism, sexism, racism and capitalism with "in your face" activism. It disbanded in 1972.

1969 (Dec. 21). The Gay Activists Alliance was founded by a group of former members of the Gay Liberation Front who wanted a single issue (gay rights) organization. They were also dissatisfied with the chaotic nature of GLF meetings and the tactics of their former group. This group continues to exist and to actively fight for gay rights.

1970 (June 27). The first Gay Pride March anywhere in the nation took place in New York City. It was organized by Craig Rodwell, Michael Brown and others. There were no floats, music or scantily dressed marchers. The first marchers were cautioned by organizers prior to the march to dress and behave well so that the best possible image would be projected. Initially the marchers were people from various gay action organizations who had agreed to march as a united front. Along the way people spontaneously joined the parade and lent their voice to the chant, "Say it clear, and say it loud. Gay is good, gay is proud". By the time the march ended the marchers numbered in the thousands. The next day parades were also held in Chicago and Los Angeles.

1970 (Dec). Gay activists, led by Franklin Kameny, Barbara Gittings and APA member Dr. Judd Marmor, began to lobby against the American Psychological Association's inclusion of homosexuality in its diagnostic manual. They confronted APA members at the annual meeting of the APA and offered evidence and dialogue. This was repeated every year from 1971 through 1973.

1971. Stephen Donaldson (founder of the first gay student organization) became the first person to challenge a dismissal from the United States military for homosexuality. He lost on every level of appeal and was discharged from the United States Navy in 1972.

1972. Parents, Families and Friends of Lesbians and Gays (PFLAG) was founded in New York City by Jean Manford. She was among the first mothers to march with a son in a gay pride parade. PFLAG is a national organization for homosexual gays and lesbians who are under 21 years old and for their families and other supportive people. It offers support and an accepting environment for such people.

1973. The National Gay and Lesbian Taskforce was founded in New York City by Dr. Howard Brown, Dr. Bruce Voeller, Reverend Robert Carter and Dr. Frank Kameny. This group acts to empower homosexual, bisexual and transgender people by working to stop anti-gay legislation, foster pro-gay legislation, and to organize and train others. This is among the oldest gay rights organizations in America.

1973. The Lambda Legal Defense and Education Fund (Lambda Legal) was founded. The first request for incorporation of this organization was denied by the state of New York because the organization was considered harmful to the interests of public policy. Lambda sued and won. It is now the oldest and largest gay and lesbian legal organization in the country. It works to support and protect the civil rights of gay men, lesbians, bisexuals, transsexuals and persons with AIDS through litigation, education and public policy work.

1973 (Dec). The American Psychological Association officially removed homosexuality as a mental disorder in its listings within its diagnostic manual, the DSM II. The DSM II replaced homosexuality with the diagnosis of "Sexual Orientation Adjustment Disorder". This designation was for those who found their homosexuality to be problematic. The DSM III dropped that diagnosis too because it could not be clinically proved to exist. The current diagnostic manual does not deal with homosexuality per se at all.

1977. Harvey Milk became the first openly gay person ever voted into a government position in the United States when he won election to the San Francisco Board of Supervisors. He was assassinated by Dan White just months later.

1977. Anita Bryant began her anti-gay campaign. In 1977 Dade County, Florida passed an ordinance banning discrimination based on sexual orientation. Bryant organized opposition to this decision and successfully led that opposition to pass a repeal of the ordinance at the polls. She then went on a national anti-gay campaign and was a factor in several states. Gay activists responded all over America with pickets and boycotts of the products Bryant endorsed such as Florida orange juice. The negative publicity her homophobia generated damaged her career as an entertainer and she eventually had to file for bankruptcy. The courts overturned the repeal of the anti-discrimination ordinance in 2008.

1978. Dan White stood trial for the murder of Harvey Milk. He was convicted but then was given the lightest sentence possible.

1978. Human Rights Watch was founded in Helsinki, Finland. It began as chapters in various countries and in 1991 those chapters took the unified name of Human Rights Watch. It is active in defending and protecting human rights internationally and won the Nobel Peace Prize in 1997. Part of its work is in the areas of HIV/AIDS and gay rights.

1980. The national platform of the Democratic Party endorsed the idea of equal rights for gays and lesbians. This was the first time a national political party called for this.

1981 (May). Billie Jean King publically acknowledged that she was a lesbian and thereby became the first major sports figure to do so.

1981(June 5). The United States Centers for Disease Control and Prevention found that five samples taken from individuals in Los Angeles, California held a new, very virulent virus. They initially called it Gay-related Immune Deficiency (GRID) but the name was soon changed to Acquired Immune Deficiency Syndrome (AIDS). The AIDS epidemic had begun.

1983. Representative Gerry Studds of Massachusetts (Democrat) became the first sitting member of congress to acknowledge he was gay. He did so as part of an ethics probe.

1985. The Gay and Lesbian Alliance Against Defamation (GLAAD) was founded in New York City as a response to a story in the New York Post that defamed gay people as a group. It is now one of the primary gay rights groups in the United States and works to give voice to gays in the media and to hold the media accountable.

1986. In the case of Bowers vs. Hardwick the United States Supreme Court ruled it was constitutional for states to criminalize private sexual behavior between consenting adults.

1986 (Oct. 1). The Vatican issued a letter (On the Pastoral Care of Homosexual Persons) penned by Cardinal Joseph Ratzinger (who later became Pope Benedict XVI) which asserted the position of the Roman Catholic Church that homosexuality is an "intrinsic moral evil" and an "objective disorder". The letter instructed all Roman Catholic officials to cease all support of gay organizations. The letter also instructed that violent speech or action against homosexuals is against the teachings of the Church.

1987 (March). The gay activist group AIDS Coalition to Unleash Power (ACT UP) was founded. This organization works internationally through direct action in support of those who have

AIDS and those who deal with AIDS. It functions both through demonstrations and through outreach.

1987. Cleve Jones begins the work of the NAMES Project AIDS Memorial Quilt. The name of every American that dies of AIDS is placed on a patch which is then sewn onto the quilt. The quilt now weighs over 54 tons.

1987 (Oct). The second March on Washington took place. The first March was done in 1963 by the throngs of people led by the Reverend Martin Luther King. This second March was done by hundreds of thousands of people demanding equal rights and equal treatment for gays and lesbians. It included six days of activities including picketing the Supreme Court because of the decision in Bowers vs. Hardwick.

1988. The American Psychological Association publicly announced its opposition to employment discrimination based on sexual orientation.

1989. The Association of Sexual Minorities became the first gay organization in Russia.

1989. Thema became the first gay related newspaper published in Russia.

1990. The American Psychological Association publicly announced its opposition to the exclusion from the military based on sexual orientation.

1990. The Boy Scouts of America expelled Assistant Scout Master James Dale because he was gay. In 2000 the United States Supreme Court ruled the expulsion was legal.

1991. The American Psychological Association publicly announced its opposition to immigration and naturalization decisions based on sexual orientation.

1993. The Congress of the United States overrode President Bill Clinton's objections to Public Law 103-160, Section 654, Title 10 and passed it with a veto proof majority. This law continued the long-standing complete ban on homosexuals serving in the military and authorized the removal any person found to be a homosexual. President Clinton, in response, issued Defense Directive 1304.26. It became known as "Don't Ask, Don't Tell" (DADT) meaning that the military would not specifically ask any service member if he/she was gay but if it found out or the individual told it he/she was gay, that person would be removed from the military.

1993. Allan Berube published *Coming Out in America* which is a history of homosexuality in the military.

1993. Rainbow Law was founded by Elisia and Carrie Ross-Stone. They help gays and lesbians prepare legal documents on the web.

1995. The film *Serving in Silence* starring Glenn Close opened. It is the story of Colonel Margarethe Cammermeyer who was expelled from the United States military for openly being a lesbian.

1996 (March 6). The largest organization of rabbis in the United States announced its support of gay unions.

1996 (May). The United States Supreme Court, in the case of Romer vs. Evans, struck down a provision in the Colorado state constitution that banned jurisdictions within the state from treating homosexuals as a protected class on matters related to civil rights. The Court declared the ban to be a violation of the Equal Protection Clause of the United States Constitution.

1996. Congress passed, and President Bill Clinton signed the Defense of Marriage Act (DOMA) which compelled the federal government to not recognize any marriage other than those between a man and a woman.

1998. The American Psychological Association publicly announced its opposition to any treatment aimed at curing homosexuals.

1998. The National Youth Advocacy Coalition was formed. It was a group that advocated for the rights of LGBT youth and offers education and support to youth and youth related groups. It had the only national 24-hour crisis and suicide helpline specifically for youths in this country. It closed in 2011.

1999. The Black AIDS Institute was founded by Phill Wilson. The mission of this organization is the elimination of the AIDS epidemic in the Black community through education, training and research and through the organization of people and resources.

2000. The American Psychological Association publicly supported same-sex unions.

2001 (April 1). The Netherlands became the first country to legalize gay marriage.

2003. Gene Robinson was made the first openly gay Bishop in a diocese of the Episcopal Church. This created a fire storm and led to a schism within the church.

2003 (June 1). Belgium authorized gay marriage.

2003 (June 26). The United States Supreme Court in Lawrence vs. Texas overruled its earlier decision in Bowers vs. Hardwick. It ruled that states cannot criminalize the private sexual behavior of consenting adults.

2004 (May 17). The Supreme Court of the state of Massachusetts ruled that state laws against same-sex marriage are in violation of the state constitution. The ruling made same-sex marriage legal there. Foes at once began an attempt to rewrite the state constitution to ban same-sex marriage.

2005 (March 22). Pope John Paul II published a book (Memory and Identity) in which he called homosexuality an "ideology of evil".

2005 (July 19). Two teenagers were publicly executed by hanging in Iran for being gay.

2005 (July 20) Canada legalized gay marriage.

2005. Spain legalized gay marriage.

2005. The American Psychological Association publicly supported same-sex marriage.

2006 (Nov. 30). South Africa legalized gay marriage.

2008 (May 15). California Supreme Court declared that state's ban on gay marriages to be unconstitutional. Gay marriages began to be performed in California a month later.

2008 (July 7). The Palmer Center at the University of California released a statement in which 52 retired generals and admirals of the United States military and a former Secretary of the Army supported the removal of all barriers to service in the military based on sexual orientation.

2008 (Sept.8). Rachel Maddow became the first gay or lesbian news anchor on a major television network.

2008 (Oct. 10). A ruling by the Supreme Court of Connecticut made same-sex marriage legal there.

2008 (Nov. 4). Proposition 8 (the California Marriage Protection Act) was passed by California voters. It amended the state constitution and ended gay marriages being performed there.

2009. The True Colors Fund is founded by the singer and entertainer Cyndi Lauper. This is a non-profit charity that promotes gay rights through education, support and outreach.

2009 (Jan. 1). Norway legalized same-sex marriage.

2009 (April 3). The Supreme Court of the State of Iowa ruled there is "no important government interest" in denying gays the right to marry. The ruling made gay marriage legal there.

2009 (May 1). Sweden authorized same-sex marriage.

2009 (Sept. 1). Same-sex marriage became legal in the state of Vermont. Governor Jim Douglas (Republican) had vetoed a bill passed by the legislature that made gay marriage legal there. The legislature overrode his veto.

2010. Iceland, Portugal, Mexico and Argentina legalized same-sex marriage.

2010 (Jan. 1). Same-sex marriage became legal in the state of New Hampshire because of a bill passed by the legislature and signed by Governor John Lynch (Democrat).

2010 (Sept. 4). U.S. District Court Judge Vaughn Walker overturned a 2008 initiative that banned gay marriage in California. Governor Arnold Schwarzenegger and California Attorney General Jerry Brown refused to appeal the decision. An anti-gay coalition of California citizens moved to appeal in the place of California government officials and thus raised the question of whether a non-official has legal standing to appeal.

2010 (Sept 9). U.S. District Court Judge Virginia Phillips declared the "Don't Ask, Don't Tell" policy of the U.S. military to be unconstitutional. The decision was stayed pending appeal.

2010 (Oct. 12). U.S. District Court Judge Virginia Phillips issued a worldwide injunction against the United States military enforcing its "Don't Ask, Don't Tell" policy. The decision was stayed but the court ordered that nobody could be discharged under "Don't Ask, Don't Tell".

2010 (Dec 22). President Barack Obama signed a law ending "Don't Ask, Don't Tell". The bill ending "Don't Ask, Don't Tell" had previously failed in the Senate because of nearly unanimous opposition from Republicans led by Senator John McCain but that opposition was overcome because of the efforts of Senators Joe Lieberman and Susan Collins. The law stated that "Don't Ask, Don't Tell" officially would end when the military and the president certified that end did not hurt the readiness and cohesion of the U.S. armed forces. That happened in September 2011.

2011 (Feb 25). President Barack Obama announced that the United States government would no longer defend the Defense of Marriage Act (DOMA) in court because it is clearly unconstitutional.

2012 (June 15). Denmark approved gay marriage.

2011 (June 24). The legislature of the state of New York passed a bill authorizing same-sex marriage and it is signed by Governor Andrew Cuomo (Democrat).

2011 (July 6). The 9th Circuit of the U.S. Court of Appeals declared "Don't Ask, Don't Tell" to be unconstitutional and ordered its immediate end. The Court later stayed its ruling but ordered that nobody could be discharged under "Don't Ask, Don't Tell".

2011 (Sept. 20). "Don't Ask, Don't Tell" officially ended as a policy of the United States.

2011 (Sept.). Great Britain abolished its law against homosexuals donating blood.

2012 (Jan. 7). The case of Collins v. United States was settled. The federal government agreed to stop the practice of giving gay military personnel just half the pay it gives heterosexuals when they separate from the military service. It also agreed to compensate anyone who received half pay upon discharge on or prior to November 10, 2004.

2012 (Feb. 7). A panel of the United States Ninth Circuit Court of Appeals ruled that the ban on same-sex marriage in California is unconstitutional. Foes of gay marriage appealed the ruling to the U.S. Supreme Court.

2012 (Feb. 13). Washington State governor Christine Gregoire (Democrat) signed a law passed by the legislature the preceding week thus making same-sex marriage legal there. Foes at once began an unsuccessful campaign to overturn the law at the polls.

2012 (Feb. 18). New Jersey governor Chris Christie (Republican) vetoed a bill passed by the legislature which would have made same-sex marriage legal there.

2012 (March 1). Maryland governor Martin O'Malley (Democrat) signed a law passed by the legislature which made gay marriage legal there. Foes at once began a campaign to overturn the law at the polls.

2012 (May 14). The NAACP endorsed same-sex marriage.

2012 (June 22). The National Council of La Raza endorsed same-sex marriage.

2012 (Aug 27). The Republican Party platform supported a Constitutional amendment that defines marriage as between one man and one woman and bans same-sex marriage.

2012 (Sept 4) The Democratic Party platform supported equal treatment under the law for all people and supported same-sex marriage.

2012 (Oct 2). Governor Jerry Brown (Democrat) signed a bill into law that bans conversion therapy (reparative therapy) being offered to minors in the state of California.

2012 (Oct 23). Mexico abolished its law against homosexuals donating blood.

2012 (Nov. 6). Maryland, Maine and Washington State are the first states of the union to approve gay marriage at the ballot box.

2012 (Nov. 6). Tammy Baldwin (Democrat – Wisconsin) became the first openly gay/lesbian voted into the United States Senate.

2012 (Nov. 6). Kyrsten Sinema (Democrat – Arizona) became the first openly bisexual person voted into the United States Congress.

2012 (Dec. 8). Pope Benedict XVI delivered his "Message for the Celebration of the World Day of Peace" in which he followed his customary practice of denouncing gays and gay marriage.

2013 (Jan. 2). Roman Catholic Archbishop Vincent Nichols ordered the halt of the gay friendly religious services that had been done since 2007 in the Soho District of London, England at the Our Lady of the Assumption church.

2013 (March 13). Cardinal Jorge Mario Bergogio of Argentina was chosen pope following the resignation of Benedict XVI. He takes the name Francis. He opposes the oppression of homosexuals but also opposes giving gays and lesbians equal rights. He is staunchly against both same-sex marriage and allowing gays and lesbians to adopt children.

2013 (April 23). France legalized same-sex marriage and the adoption of children by homosexuals. There is fierce and large opposition to this, especially among French Roman Catholics.

2013 (April 29). Jason Collins became the first player in any major American sport to acknowledge he was gay. He thereby made the National Basketball Association the first major sports association to have an openly gay player.

2013 (May 23). The Boy Scouts of America announced that it would no longer ban homosexual boys from its membership but that gay adults still could not be leaders. Fundamentalist Christian organizations denounced this and formed opposition groups saying homosexuals are anti-God.

2013 (June 20). Exodus International announced that it was disbanding. The founder of the organization apologized for the harm his group did. Exodus International was a leading anti-gay organization and a major facilitator of conversion therapy.

2013 (June 26). The United States Supreme Court declared section 3 of the Defense of Marriage Act (DOMA) unconstitutional. This gave homosexual wedded couples the same rights and privileges under federal law as heterosexual couples.

2013 (June 26). The United States Supreme Court declared that the plaintiffs who sought to restore California's ban on same-sex marriage (Proposition 8) had no standing to bring the matter to the court and returned the case to the lower court. Same-sex marriage became legal again the next day when the Ninth Circuit Court of Appeals lifted its earlier order that no same-sex marriages could be done in California until the Supreme Court had ruled.

2013 (June 30). Russian president Vladimir Putin signed a law that forbids the promotion of nontraditional sexual relationships. The law makes it illegal to do anything publically that supports or promotes homosexuality. The law is widely condemned internationally but homosexuals begin to be arrested anyway.

2013 (Aug. 1). Same-sex marriages can be legally performed in Rhode Island.

2013 (Aug. 1). Same-sex marriages can be legally performed in Minnesota.

2013 (Aug. 3) Secretary of State John Kerry announced that henceforth homosexuals married couples will treated equally to heterosexuals when applying for visas to enter the United States.

2013 (Aug. 19). Same-sex marriage became legal in New Zealand.

2013 (Aug 19). Governor Chris Christie (Republican) signed a bill into law that bans conversion therapy being offered to minors in New Jersey.

2013 (Sept. 20). New Jersey Superior Court Judge Mary Jacobson ruled that denying homosexuals the right to marry was unconstitutional and that homosexuals could get married in New Jersey beginning October 21, 2013. New Jersey governor Chris Christie (Republican) appealed the ruling but the New Jersey Supreme Court ruled unanimously against him.

2013 (Sept 29). The 9th Circuit Court of Appeals upheld the legality of California's ban on conversion therapy.

2013 (Oct. 21). Gay and lesbian couples began to get married in New Jersey.

2013 (Nov 7). The United States Senate passed the Employment Non-Discrimination Act (ENDA). The bill, if enacted, would forbid discrimination in the workplace based on sexual orientation or gender identity. John Boehner (Republican) announced that, as Speaker of the House of Representatives, he would not allow ENDA to come to the floor of the Congress for a vote. This killed the bill. It was widely believed that the bill would have passed if it had been given a vote.

2013 (Nov 8) U.S. District Court Judge Freda Wolfson upheld the legality of New Jersey's ban on conversion therapy.

2013 (Nov. 13). Governor Neil Abercrombie (Democrat) signed a bill into law that makes same-sex marriage legal in Hawaii.

2013 (Nov 20). Governor Pat Quinn (Democrat) signed a bill into law that makes same-sex marriage legal in Illinois.

2013 (Dec. 11). India's Supreme Court recriminalized same-sex marriage by striking down a lower court's decision which had legalized same-sex marriage in that country.

2013 (Dec. 19). The Supreme Court of New Mexico ruled that denying homosexuals the right to marry persons of the same sex is a violation of the state's constitution. Same-sex marriage thereby became legal in New Mexico.

2013 (Dec. 20). US District Court Judge Robert Shelby ruled Utah's ban on same-sex marriage to be unconstitutional. He declined to stay his ruling thus same-sex marriage became legal in Utah. Utah appealed the refusal to stay and a stay was granted by the US Supreme Court. Governor Gary Herbert (Republican) then announced that Utah would not recognize any same-sex marriages that had been performed. On 1-10-14 US Attorney General Eric Holder announced that the federal government would recognize those same-sex marriages legally performed in Utah prior to the stay.

2014 (Jan. 13). Nigerian President Goodluck Jonathan signed a bill that criminalizes homosexuality in that country.

2014 (Jan. 14). US District Court Judge Terence Kern ruled than Oklahoma's ban on same-sex marriage was unconstitutional, but he stayed the decision until it could be appealed.

2014 (Jan. 21). The Ninth Circuit Court of Appeals ruled in Glaxosmithkline v. Abbott Laboratories that it was unconstitutional to remove a juror solely because he/she is homosexual. It also ruled that the standard used when dealing with cases of LGBT discrimination is "heighted scrutiny" and not "rational-scrutiny". This will make LGBT cases easier to win in court unless the US Supreme Court overrules this decision.

2014 (Jan.27). The Turkish Republic of Northern Cyprus repealed its law that made homosexual sexual relationships illegal. It was the last European country to have such a law. Most European countries still ban same-sex marriage and adoption by homosexuals.

2014 (Feb. 4). Same-sex marriage became legal in Scotland.

2014 (Feb. 12). U.S. District Court Judge John Heyburn ruled that the state of Kentucky must recognize marriages that are legally performed in other states.

2014 (Feb. 13). U.S. District Court Judge Arenda Wright Allen ruled that Virginia's ban on same-sex marriage is unconstitutional. The ruling was placed on stay pending appeal.

2014 (Feb. 24). Ugandan President Yoweri Museveni signed a bill into law that makes being homosexual in Uganda illegal.

2014 (Feb. 26). U.S. District Judge Orlando Garcia ruled that the Texas ban on same-sex marriage is unconstitutional. The ruling is stayed pending appeal.

2014 (Mar. 14). U.S. District Court Judge Aleta Trauger ruled that Tennessee must recognize the same-sex marriages of three couples who were married in other states.

2014 (Mar. 21). U.S. District Court Judge Bernard Friedman ruled the Michigan ban on same-sex marriage is unconstitutional. The ruling was stayed pending appeal.

2014 (March 21). U.S. District Judge Bernard Friedman ruled Michigan's ban on same-sex marriage is unconstitutional.

2014 (March 29). Same-sex marriage became legal in England and Wales.

2014 (April 14). U.S. District Judge Timothy Black ruled that Ohio must recognize same-sex marriages performed in other states.

2014 (May 9). Pulaski County Circuit Court Judge Chris Piazza ruled the Arkansas ban on same-sex marriage is unconstitutional. The ruling was appealed at once.

2014 (May 10). Michael Sam becomes the first openly homosexual player in the NFL.

2014 (May 13). U.S. District Court Magistrate Candy Dale ruled that Idaho's ban on same-sex marriage is unconstitutional.

2014 (May 19). U.S. District Judge Michael McShane ruled Oregon's ban on same-sex marriage is unconstitutional.

2014 (May 20). U.S. District Court Judge John Jones III ruled Pennsylvania's ban on same-sex marriage is unconstitutional.

2014 (June 6). U.S. District Court Judge Barbara Crabb ruled that Wisconsin's ban on same-sex marriage is unconstitutional.

2014 (June 18). Same-sex marriage became legal in Luxembourg.

2014 (June 25). U.S. District Court Judge Richard Young ruled that Indiana's ban on same-sex marriage is unconstitutional.

2014 (June 25). U.S. Court of Appeals for the Tenth Circuit upheld a lower court's ruling that Utah's ban on same-sex marriage is unconstitutional.

2014 (July 9). U.S. District Court Judge C. Scott Crabtree ruled Colorado's ban on same-sex marriage is unconstitutional.

2014 (July 18). U.S. Court of Appeals for the Tenth Circuit upheld a lower court's ruling that Oklahoma's ban on same-sex marriage is unconstitutional.

2014 (July 21) President Barack Obama signed an executive order that expands employment protections for LGBT people working for the federal government or federal contractors.

2014 (July 28). U.S. Court of Appeals for the Fourth Circuit upheld a lower court's ruling that Virginia's ban on same-sex marriage is unconstitutional.

2014 (Aug. 21). U.S. District Court Judge Robert Hinkle ruled Florida's ban on same-sex marriage is unconstitutional.

2014 (Sept. 4). U.S. Court of Appeals for the Seventh Circuit upheld lower court rulings that same-sex marriage bans in Wisconsin and Indiana are unconstitutional.

2014 (Oct. 6). U.S. Supreme Court refused to take appeals from Indiana, Utah, Oklahoma, Virginia and Wisconsin which sought to overturn lower court rulings which found bans on same-sex marriage to be unconstitutional.

2014 (Oct. 7). U.S. Court of Appeals for the Ninth Circuit upheld lower court rulings that found same-sex bans in Idaho and Nevada to be unconstitutional.

2014 (Oct. 10). It became legal in Virginia for same-sex couples to adopt children.

2014 (Oct. 10). North Carolina legalized same-sex marriage.

2014 (Oct. 12). U.S. District Court Judge Timothy Burgess ruled Alaska's ban on same-sex marriage is unconstitutional.

2104 (Oct. 15). Idaho legalized same-sex marriage.

2014 (Oct. 17). U.S. District Court Judge John Sedwick ruled Arizona's ban on same-sex marriage is unconstitutional.

2014 (Oct. 21). Wyoming legalized same-sex marriage.

2014 (Nov. 4). U.S. District Court Judge Daniel Crabtree ruled Kansas' ban on same-sex marriage is unconstitutional.

2014 (Nov. 6). U.S. Court of Appeals for the Sixth Circuit upheld the bans on same-sex marriage in Tennessee, Kentucky, Michigan and Ohio. This disagreement with other Courts of Appeals set up the likelihood that the U.S. Supreme Court would rule on this.

2014 (Nov. 12). U.S. District Judge Richard Gergel ruled that South Carolina's ban on same-sex marriage is unconstitutional.

2014 (Nov. 19). U.S. District Court Judge Kristine Baker ruled Arkansas' ban on same-sex marriage is unconstitutional.

2014 (Nov. 19). U.S. District Court Judge Carton Reeves ruled Mississippi's ban on same-sex marriage is unconstitutional.

2015 (Jan. 16). U.S. Supreme Court agreed to hear an appeal of the Sixth Circuit's ruling that bans on same-sex marriage in Tennessee, Kentucky, Ohio and Michigan are legal.

2015 (May). The Pew Research Center says that 57% of Americans now approve of same-sex marriage. This is up from 37% in 2006.

2015 (June 9). The U.S. Department of Defense announced that LGBT military personnel will be included in their Military Equal Opportunity policy.

2015 (June 26). The U.S. Supreme Court in Obergefell v. Hodges overruled the Sixth Circuit. It ruled that marriage cannot be denied to Americans purely based on their sexual orientation. Same-sex marriage thereby became legal in all 50 states.

2015 (July 1). The clerk for Rowan County, Kentucky defied a court order that she must follow the Obergefell decision and issue marriage licenses to gay and lesbian couples. She cited her religious objections and her constitutional right to practice her religion. Most of the Republican presidential candidates support her view and again express their opposition to same-sex marriage. She was sent to jail and then released after her deputy clerk begins to issue marriage licenses to same-sex couples.

2015 (July 8). Gallup published a poll showing that 68% of Americans believe that homosexual behavior should be legal. This is up from 37% in 2007.

2015 (July 27). The Boy Scouts of America announced that it would no longer ban openly gay people from employment or positions of leadership.

2016 (June 17). The United States Senate confirms Eric Fanning to be secretary of the Army. He becomes the first openly gay secretary of any U.S. military branch.

2016 (June 24). The Stonewall Inn is named as a national monument. The Stonewall National Monument includes Christopher Park, the Stonewall Inn and the streets and sidewalks around them.

2016 (June 30). The U.S. Department of Defense announces that transgender people will no longer be banned from serving openly in the U.S. military.

2016 (Aug. 5-21). A record number of openly gay, lesbian or bisexual athletes take part in the summer Olympic Games. The number increased from 23 in 2012 to 49.

2016 (Nov. 8). Donald Trump (Republican) won the presidential election and the Republican Party also won majorities in both houses of congress. This begins the most anti-LGBT government in modern American history.

2016 (Nov. 8). Kate Brown was voted into the office of Governor of Oregon. She thereby became the highest-ranking openly bisexual person ever voted into an American political office.

2017 (June 22). The Fifth Circuit Court of Appeals allowed Mississippi's HB 1523 to become law in that state. The law allows discrimination based on sexual orientation because of "religious freedom".

2017 (Aug. 25). President Trump issued a memo to the Department of Defense directing it to stop accepting enlistments into the military from transgender people. The memo obliges the Secretary of Defense to send a plan to the president by 2/23/18 on what to do with those transgender people who are already serving.

2017 (Sept. 7). President Trump nominated Jeff Mateer to serve on the U.S. District Court for the Eastern District of Texas. This nominee is staunchly anti-LGBT, pro-conversion therapy and publicly said transgender children are proof that Satan's plan is working.

2017 (Sept.15). Senate Majority Leader Mitch McConnell (Republican) blocked a bipartisan bill what would have protected currently serving transgender people in the military despite it clearly having enough votes to pass. He did not allow a vote.

2017 (Sept 26). Attorney General Sessions filed a brief with the Second Circuit Court of Appeals in the case of Zarda v. Altitude Express. It argues that Title IV of the Civil Rights Act of 1964 does not give protection from discrimination based on sexual orientation.

2017 (Oct. 4). Attorney General Sessions issued a memo asserting that Title VII of the Civil Rights Act of 1964 does not protect transgender workers from discrimination based on gender identity.

2017 (Oct. 13). President Trump became the only sitting president to ever attend or speak at the anti-LGBT Values Voters Summit.

2018 (Sept. 6) India's Supreme Court rules that country's laws against homosexuality to be unconstitutional.

Chapter 3
LGBT Community Context

Question: What is the LGBT community?
The LGBT community, like all communities, is a collection of diverse individuals and groups which have formed around a common core culture that includes shared values and practices and a shared overarching identity. Within our community are gay males, lesbians, bisexuals, and transgender people of all ages, races, ethnicity, professions, religions and creeds and those others who support LGBT rights and equality. Among the hallmarks of our community is its pride in its diversity, its inherent non-heteronormative identity, its commitment to justice and its active pursuit of liberty.

The LGBT community has several distinct subcultures. A subculture shares the identity, values and practices of its parent culture but also has distinct behaviors, values and attitudes that set it apart from that parent culture. All subcultures of the LGBT community, for example, share a common identity as non-heteronormative and hold values and attitudes that are in line with that identity. At the same time, they are distinctly recognizable. Among these are the clubber community, the youth community, the senior community, the lesbian community, the bisexual community, the transgender community, the drag community, the Chub community, the Bear community, BDSM community and the Leather community.

Question: What is known about the clubber community?
The clubber community is made up of people who either go to school or have jobs during the day and socialize in bars and dance clubs at night. There are various kinds of dance clubs and bars, but the primary types fall into the category of either heterosexual/mixed clubs or those that cater mainly to gay males. There are, of course, bars that cater primarily to lesbians, but they are much less common because lesbians do not go to bars in the numbers that gay men do. It is the gay male places that are dealt with here.

The patrons of gay dance clubs are typically White and under 35 years of age. They are stereotyped as being sexually promiscuous and regular users of drugs and alcohol. It is not at all hard to find members of this community that fit the stereotype. It is also true that many "clubbers" do not.

A study of clubbers in New York found that in the last six months 68.5% had used at least 2 drugs, 43.5% had used 3 or more and 24.9% had used at least 4. Polydrug use was common (Parsons and Halkitis, 2006). Another study found that clubbers had used methamphetamine, cocaine, ecstasy, GHB, and ketamine in the last 12 months and that they had often used more than one drug at a time (Halkitis and Palamar, 2007). A third study found that having sex under the influence of drugs and/or alcohol, having unprotected insertive sex and having sex with partner who has a different HIV status is also common (Flores & Mansergh, 2009).

All the senses are stimulated in a club. There is a lot of socializing, touching, watching and cruising. As the night progresses toward closing time the male scent that gay men tend to love perfumes the air. The whole atmosphere with the thumping music, the lighting effects, the go-go boys and the people dancing close is sensual and sexy. In short, it is a lot of fun.

To understand this community, you must understand the club and bar scenes. The dance club scene is as much about what happens within the club and how to function within it as it is about the people who populate it. The bar scene is less so because there are fewer formal or informal rules and they tend to have a more diverse crowd.

The scene at clubs and bars varies by venue but there are some general things that can be said. It is, for example, common for dance clubs to have an admission charge that is paid at the door. Some clubs have membership cards that allow the user to enter without paying the charge. Those on the owner's "guest list" and, in some cases, those who are friends of the doorkeeper also get in for free. Members and guests typically walk around whatever line there may be at the door or enter through a separate entrance.

The security guy at the door of a club is there primarily to control who gets into the place. He is typically not a guy you want to upset so when he says you cannot go in it is best to leave and find another place to go to. Even if you manage to get past him you are likely to meet the other security guys working in the club as you enter and that is not going to be a good thing. You are likely at that point to find out why they are called bouncers. By that time of course you have committed the crime of trespass because you have entered private property against the wishes of the owner.

The security guy at the door has been given instructions on what qualifies a person to enter the club. His job is on the line, so he is unlikely to bend the rules for you. You are not likely to get in if he sees you are rowdy or already visibly high or drunk. The instruction he gets from the manager may include what "look" the owner wants in the club. That commonly includes a dress code. You can tell what the dress code is simply by looking at the guys who are going in. If you do not look like that you may not get in.

If you love wearing well-worn blue jeans love wearing something else when you go to a gay dance club because in many clubs those blue jeans will get you rejected at the door. Forget about wearing any kind of athletic wear too. Sweaters and jackets are not usually practical because it gets hot in most clubs after the first hour or two. Some clubs (especially larger ones) have "coat check" station at the door for customers to leave coats and things but that is not universal. Some coat check stations are offered free of charge while other clubs involve a small payment.

The safest way to go to a club is to go with one or more people that you already know. You can separate once inside and then check-in with each other periodically throughout the outing. If you find someone at the club that you want to go home with make sure a person you went to the club with knows who you are leaving with. Introducing the guy to your friend is a good safety measure because your friend will know what the guy looks like and the guy will know it.

It is also wise to not wear anything expensive because that reduces your chances of being victimized. Wearing expensive things isn't going to impress anyone for more than a few minutes and it will make you the center of attention of the predators who may be wandering around the club looking for an opportunity. You also may want to leave your wallet at home and just take a credit card, your driver's license or other ID and some cash.

African Americans, Asians and Latinos tend to be disproportionately absent from clubs because most actively avoid them. This is explained by the cultural influences that affect gay African Americans, Asians and Latinos. Those cultures tend to disapprove of homosexuality more than Caucasians do thus gay members of those cultures tend to avoid openly doing things like going to a gay club that would label them as gay (Flores & Mansergh, 2009).

Those racial minorities who go clubbing however usually find they are very welcomed because gay clubbers, like most gays in general, tend to be open and accepting in their views about race. Clubbers are also notorious for liking things that are new or different. Cultural views about homosexuality are changing and with that will come the presence of more and more men of color in clubs.

Once inside a gay dance club you can expect to find lighting effects, loud pulsating music, go-go boys, crowded bathrooms, a lot of young men dancing and guys hooking up for sex. It may also have professional drag queens. The music may be live or, more commonly, offered by a DJ. Most people in a club will be harmless people who are just having a good time, but some may be drug pushers, prostitutes, pickpockets and predators. The best rule of thumb is to stay in control of your senses and listen to them. If something does not feel right it probably is not.

If you are going to a club to socialize or to find someone to take home with you it is best to walk around the club, so you can see who is there and be seen doing it. Moving around lets more people see you and that is the key to advertising the things that make you attractive. It also tells them that you are probably at the club unattached.

It is common however to see men just standing around trying to chat over the loud music or watching other people dancing. Some guys go clubbing night after night and never set foot on the dance floor. Some of these guys are just shy while others are self-conscious about their inability to dance well. Most however can be coaxed to dance if you are confident enough to let them know you really want to dance with them.

Don't waste a dance by just dancing. Talk to the guy...better yet, lean in close and say something nice right in his ear. It's usually fine to touch him on the arm or shoulder when you do that. Touching makes a connection more complete.

It is almost always okay to take off your shirt in a gay dance club if you're hot or just want to dance without a shirt on like many guys do. You can "check" your shirt if the place has a "coat check" service. If not, typically the shirt is tucked into the waistband of your pants at the rear or side but never at the front.

If you have a great ass, you may want to avoid the rear tuck position too since that will hide your asset.

The owners of clubs make their primary living by selling alcohol. Most will have nothing to do with selling drugs because they can lose their liquor and business licenses if they get caught doing that. Bartenders get asked often about whether they sell drugs but if they value their jobs they do not.

Bartenders obviously do sell alcohol however and they are very busy doing it so when you go to the bar to buy a drink know what you want and have your money or credit card ready. In fact, showing a bartender that you have it ready will often get you faster service. Keeping your order simple (A Black Russian, a beer or a glass of wine for example) and giving him a tip will probably get you even better service next time. The bartender (and the club owner) will appreciate it if you do not take up space at the bar after you get your drink.

The smallest tip for a bartender is $1.00 for a beer and $2.00 for a simple mixed drink. A bartender sees a lot of people every shift, so he may not remember you unless you are a heavy tipper. You should also be aware that bartenders work varied shifts so the guy that you have been tipping all night might leave before you do. The guy that takes his place won't know you.

Unprotected sex is strongly related to getting HIV and other STIs, so it is wise to take along your own condoms even though they are available in most clubs. Some clubs have bowls of free ones somewhere on the premises. Other clubs have machines that offer various brands of them for purchase. These condoms are probably fine, but you will know more about the history of the ones you buy yourself.

It is common for guys to feel pressured to not stop to get a condom once they have hooked up with someone and sometimes the machines or bowls are poorly placed. The other clubbers that you might hookup with often won't have a condom with them. The result is that guys that might have used a condom do not have one. The bottom line is that it's up to you to have a condom to protect yourself.

Few club goers will have lube either since many club patrons believe lube is hard to carry in a club situation. If they use lube at all they will use saliva (spit). It is however not hard to carry lube with you to a club. It can be done easily by putting a couple single-use packets in your pocket. Those can be easily bought online. Most guys find that it is simpler to take their hookup home or to go to his place. Having sex at the club will be an entirely different, albeit riskier, experience however.

Spit, by the way, is a poor lube because it is not very slick, and it dries up fast. The danger in that is that a man might over work a condom as he has anal sex because he thinks the spit they have used has lubed their partner when it really has not. The result is that the condom might fail. If a guy's penis is inside you and the condom breaks, the odds are you are not going to know it until he ejaculates inside of you. The Centers for Disease Control and Prevention assert that diseases such as genital warts, hepatitis, mononucleosis, and viral meningitis can be transmitted in saliva.

If you are averse to seeing guys kissing or having sex you probably should not go to a gay club and you certainly should not go into the bathroom at one. There are often signs in the bathrooms saying sex is not allowed but everyone understands the signs are there so the owner can make the health inspector and the police happy. The actual internal policy on this varies by club but commonly owners do not have security patrolling in the bathroom very often and is happy to not know what is going on in there. If you hear nature telling you to use a urinal or toilet it is not a good idea to put off going to the bathroom because you are probably going to have to wait in line to get a urinal or stall.

If the club has go-go boys, they will be dancing either on raised platforms or on the bar. Some clubs allow the dancers to be touched and others do not. That commonly is related to what the local laws are on that subject. If touching is allowed do not touch them in the groin or on the ass because that may not be appreciated. Go-go boys commonly make their money by getting tips from customers. You can either hand it to him or put it in the waistband of whatever he is wearing. Some dancers also hustle on the side.

The main feature that distinguishes a gay dance bar from a gay dance club is the size of the venue. A gay bar may have one or more dance floors, lighting effects and the other things found in a club, but it is always smaller in size. Some gay bars offer live music but generally the music in these establishments is recorded.

Like most bars, a gay bar will usually have a cover charge only when live entertainment or a special event is being offered. It may be collected at the door or after your first drink is served. If you are unsure about whether there is a cover charge or what the "cover" is, you should ask before you order the first drink because the cover charge may be added to that drink.

Not all gay bars are dance bars however. It is not possible to describe a typical gay bar because they vary widely depending upon the type of clientele a place caters to. Some gay bars cater to a mixed crowd of various ages, races and orientation, exclusively to homosexual men and women or exclusively to just lesbians or just gay men. Others may specialize in an older crowd or a younger crowd. There are Leather bars for those who are into the Leather subculture and piano or karaoke bars for those who like to spend the night singing along or listening to others sing. Some bars are only gay bars on some nights of the week and are regular bars the rest of the time.

Most gay bars look like any other bar except that some or all the clientele is gay. These typically have things a pool table, darts, a television and video games. Some of them sell food while others do not. Some have loud music while others have it toned down, so conversation can happen more easily. Most have the lights dimmed but some kick that up a couple notches. Some are places to socialize and some are meat markets that exist primarily as hook up places. If you want to know what is available in a specific geographic area check www.gayellowpages.com to find out.

What is acceptable to wear to a bar depends upon the kind of bar it is. Leather bars, for example, sometimes have dress codes. The owners of regular gay bars are typically unconcerned about what you wear if it's clean, legal and not disruptive.

Some gay bars and clubs have backrooms that are used by the clientele for sex. The room is rarely an official sex room but exists because of the owner's benign neglect about what is going on in the room. Private clubs are an exception to this in some cases because in some legal jurisdictions private clubs have more latitude in what can occur there. It is also not uncommon for sex acts to occur in the alleys that are next to a bar or club. That is a potentially hazardous activity however since alleys are typically dark and secluded.

Straight guys do not typically go into gay bars or clubs so the act of doing so tells those inside and outside the establishment that you are probably gay or bisexual. Most of the clientele in these places do not really care about that since they are already "out". If you are still in the closet however before you go into a gay bar or club you may want to consider what may happen later if someone you know sees you there.

If you are a straight male and you go into a bar that caters to gay men, you should understand that you are in gay man territory and you may get hit on. In this territory, a man hitting on you is a good thing because it means you are attractive. If you cannot accept the compliment you probably do not belong in that bar.

If you go to a bar or club regularly you should expect the other regulars to talk about you. That obviously means they are going to talk to the guys you have picked up there. The result of that is that you will have a reputation among the regulars not only about what you like sexually but also about the kind of person you are. Reputations are often difficult to change so it is wise to carefully build the kind of reputation you want. It is also wise to listen to what is said about other patrons because that can not only tell you who might be a good match for you but also might give you forewarning.

Question: What is known about the youth community?
The youth community is usually defined as including LGBT people from 13-18 years of age. In some cases, however, the definition may include people up to the age of 24 or even 35. This book defines the community as being made up entirely of adolescents (13-18) because that group shares distinct characteristics and issues that draw it together as a whole.

Among the commonalties that make this group a community are that they are no longer completely children but also not yet fully physically or intellectually mature. They also tend to base their world view on the same history. In addition, they commonly share the same slang and music, the same understanding and appreciation of technology and a similar view of the culture around them. Part of that is the unique relationship adolescents have with adults and with authority figures.

In most respects the youths in this community are the same as the youths in the heterosexual community. They have the same drives, needs and desires as every other American in their age group because they are going through the same stage of human development. Where there are differences they are usually differences in degree or specifics rather than kind.

Adolescence is a time of dramatic and stressful change. It is a time when the brain and the body transition from childhood to physical, sexual and intellectual maturity. A primary part of this is the process of going through puberty.

Puberty is sexual maturation of the body. The process of puberty varies not only from person to person but also based on geographic area. This is accounted for by environmental and genetic differences.

In the Western world, the sexual maturation process of puberty in girls lasts from 1.5 to 6 years. It may start as early as age eight and commonly peaks around age 12. It then starts to slow and taper off.

Male puberty, in the West, may begin as early as age 10 and may last from 2 to 5 years. On average, it peaks around age 14 then recedes gradually. This process is the same regardless of sexual orientation. Gays however tend to enter this process earlier than straights (Bogaert & Friesen, 2002).

To understand adolescents, it is necessary to understand what happens to them during puberty. A boy experiences a major growth spurt. In a relatively brief time his body is very visibly changed so that he much bigger and more muscular. His voice deepens, and it is common for his voice to crack when he talks. His genitals also get larger and his scrotal sac becomes bigger, redder and wrinkly. He gets pubic hair and hair on his face and body. He becomes a sexual being and he thinks of himself in that way.

With that come the expectations of the society he exists within, but he understands sexuality and gender incompletely because he has incomplete information. His information comes from things he has heard or overheard, adult role models and information he gets from peers and the media. He begins to have sexual thoughts and concerns, to masturbate and to take part in sexual or romantic relationships. He commonly experiences some confusion and anxiety over all of this. He wants desperately to be accepted by others thus he worries about how his sexuality and his lack of information and experience will affect that.

It is important for boys to understand that puberty affects girls somewhat differently just as it is important for girls to understand what the process is for boys. As noted above, girls typically begin and end the process of sexual maturation earlier than boys do. A girl experiences her body change as it grows bigger but, on average, not as big as the average male. The new hormones that are rushing through her body cause fat to accumulate on her hips and thighs, her voice to deepen (but not typically as deep as an average male), her breast to enlarge and hair to grow around her genitals and in her underarms.

At the end of her puberty process she begins to ovulate and menstruate. She is then also a sexual being who exists within the expectations of her culture and she begins to think of herself in that way. She begins to have sexual thoughts and concerns, to masturbate and to take on sexual/romantic relationships. She typically feels anxious and confused about this and worries about how her sexuality and gender status will affect her ability to be accepted. She usually understands that intercourse may cause her to become pregnant but commonly does not fully understand what a pregnancy would mean in terms of changing her life.

During the time an adolescents body is maturing his/her brain is changing too. Children think differently than mature adults do. They do not have the same level of ability to think abstractly or to reason. They tend to think more concretely. It is during adolescence and early adulthood that the major changes in the way human beings think occurs (Shaw & Kabani, 2008; Piaget, 1972). During adolescence, the brain is neither childlike nor mature.

During adolescence and into the twenties a person's brain is still developing. The parts of the brain responsible for interpreting nonverbal signals like facial expressions and body language, preplanning and choosing priorities is still growing. The brain is also not yet producing chemicals like dopamine at adult levels, so teens are less able to deal with day-to-day stressors. Teens are far more likely than adults are to make errors in judgment as to what is important in the short or long term and to overreact.

As a person progresses through adolescence he becomes more and more aware of abstract possibilities. He also becomes more aware of his existence as an individual separate from his parents and this commonly results in the teen being self-centered. He relates everything to how it affects him alone and he begins to seriously question who he is and how he matches up with his peers. He strives to be like those peers and to be liked by them thus peer pressure becomes a major factor in his life. His physical appearance and his conception of how his peers view him become very important in terms of his self-image and in terms of what his social life is like.

A teen is likely to have an image of his ideal self that is very different from what he really is. He tends to judge himself based on his physical, intellectual, moral and sexual ideals but he does not yet have the experiences or maturity necessary to fairly judge who he is. He tends to goal himself to be like his peers or like some role model that he has chosen based on incomplete and/or inaccurate information. He sometimes needs adult guidance which he generally does not want. All of this is perfectly normal but obviously problematic.

Added to this are the facts that teens are typically financially dependent on their parents and they are forced into a school situation that may be rather unforgiving and unaccepting of differences in appearance or behavior. Adolescents tend to use their parents and family unit as a physical and emotional safety net and their failsafe support unit as they test and use their independence. Their identity as part of that family unit is an important part of their self-image and their self-esteem.

As if the above is not enough, it is during adolescence that a person develops the beginnings of his personal moral code and begins to apply it to those unfortunate enough to fall within his gaze. His newly improved ability to think abstractly finds faults in the adults he once thought of as nearly infallible because he sees other possibilities. He seeks new role models. He begins arguing with his parents about the "fairness" of their principles, rules and decisions. He begins to judge himself as a morally worthy or unworthy human being.

The family unit is just as important to a gay adolescent as it is to a straight one. The problem is that he knows he is gay or at least thinks he is. He is often aware of this possibility prior to puberty and commonly self-identities as gay by age 16 (Ryan & Futterman, 1998). He is also aware that his sexual orientation makes him different and he fears it makes him unacceptable to his parents, his family unit generally and to his peers. This fear is obviously part of why many gay teens stay in the closet. That decision is stressful because he is constantly worried about his secret being discovered.

About 46% of gay teens say their family is the source of a lot of negative messages about LGBTs and 33% say their family has rejected them because of their sexual orientation or gender identity (HRC, 2012). Another study found that when a teen "came out" to his/her parents they were kicked out of the family home 43% of the time (Durso & Gates, 2012)). Others are physically or emotionally abused (Thompson & Sayfer, 2001).

The result is LGBT adolescents are found among the homeless in greatly disproportionate numbers. An often cited 2012 study by the Williams Institute found that 40% of the homeless in America are LGBT youths. To fully understand this, it must be remembered that gays are just 4-10% of our population. Sadly, a 1998 study by the U.S. Department of Human Services also found the figure of 40% (Robertson & Toro, 1998).

The importance of an accepting, nurturing home for adolescents cannot be overstated. LGBT youth that experience family rejection are over 8 times more likely to try suicide, nearly 6 times more likely to suffer from severe depression, 3.5 times more likely to use illicit drugs and engage in unprotected sex and 7 times more likely to be a crime victim (Ryan & Huebner, 2009). Adolescent homelessness is directly related to their dropping out of high school (Yumiko and Cooper, 2015), and to using "subsistence prostitution" (selling sex to obtain the essentials of life) and other forms of delinquency (Ferguson and Bender, 2011) as a means of survival.

If being "out" at home may be problematic doing so at school is often more so. In a 2003 survey done by the Gay, Lesbian, Bisexual and Transgender Education Network 84% of LGBT youth reported being verbally harassed and 39% reported being physically assaulted at school. In another study, LGBT teens were found to be three times more likely to be involved in a physical fight that needed medical attention and 4 times more likely to be threatened by a person with a weapon in school (Massachusetts, 2008). Childhood abuse and/or victimization is directly linked to an elevated risk of developing an eating disorder later in life (Feldman and Meyer, 2007).

Gay teens are normal teens, so they internalize this rejection and it affects their self-image. They are different however in that they typically feel alone and unsupported. They commonly do not have friends to act as buffers against the problems they are having at home or school like other kids do. Many of these kids isolate themselves from others as a means of defense. This, of course, compounds the problem because it reduces the chance of finding the support and acceptance that all humans need.

Many gay teens may also believe, based on what they have been taught as children, that they are grossly immoral because they are gay, that God disapproves of them and that they are doomed to hell. If they have been raised to value religion and its norms this is extremely stressful. Members of their faith, including clergy, may deliver homophobic messages that the youth internalizes. This too affects the teen's self-image.

All teens have a natural desire to be independent and are often embarrassed when talking about things related to their sexuality, their fears and being the target of peer harassment. This commonly prevents them from seeking help from adults. The problem is compounded for gay teens because many do not know an adult who can act as a gay role model or even one that they view as supportive of them as a LGBT person (Sessions-Stepp, 2001). The result is that their grades suffer and they many skip or drop out of school because they feel unsafe and/or unwanted there. One study found a rate of skipping school of 22% (Garofalo & Wolf et al, 1998), and another found a dropout rate of 28% among LGBT teens. Their dropout rate is more than 3 times the national average (Chase, 2001).

The three top causes of death among American youth 15 to 24 years of age are accidents, homicide and suicide. As noted above, LGBT teens are 8 times more likely to try suicide. Per the 2010 Time Almanac over two-thirds of the deaths by accident in the 15-24 age group occur in automobiles. Gay teens are far more likely than heterosexual teens to engage is risky behavior such as not using a bicycle helmet, driving drunk, riding with a person who is drunk or not wearing seatbelts (CDC, 2016). Experts assert that many of these accidents are really suicides (Wright, 2010).

It is important to note that homosexuality per se is never the cause of suicide in adolescents or anyone else. The risk factors for suicide are depression, hopelessness, drug and/or alcohol abuse, a suicide attempt by a peer or relative and experiencing victimization (Russell & Joyner, 2001). Among gays the self-identification as gay at an early age and internal conflict about that, family dysfunction and non-disclosure about being gay are added elements (Remafedi & French, 1998) that increase the risk. The bottom line is that gays do not think about or commit suicide because they are gay. They do so because of their inability to find another means of coping with the negative way others treat them.

As one looks at these risk factors through the context of adolescence it is easy to see why gay teens are at increased risk of suicide. They are sexually aroused by others of their same gender and there is not anything they can do about it. They are very aware that this makes them different from most of those around them and they do not fit in. They are also aware that much of society, at least some of their peers and possibly their family disapprove of them and pressure them to change but they do not think they can change. They know first-hand that even a few intolerant people can make their life hell. They view the world as a hostile place, they do not know how to cope with it and they cannot find help. At some point, it becomes an overwhelming burden.

Most gay teens find a way to cope and pass into adulthood successfully (Saewyc, 2011). If you are a LGBT adolescent who is having trouble coping you need to know that it gets better after high school. This is not to say that after high school there won't be problems but there will be a lot fewer of them. There may be some homophobes from time to time but in most cases the bullies will be gone. You will become more independent once you go to college or join the adult work force. You may have friends who accept you just as you are. Even if you do not, you can have that if you are willing to change your environment so that you set aside people and things that are toxic and gather in people and things that are supportive. Lots of people are waiting to like you.

Don't let the jerks that harass you chase you out of school because if you do not have a high school diploma you are setting yourself on a path that will in most cases mean you will earn less than others in your age group. That lets the bullies win. The jerks lose when you are happy and successful. You really can be happy and gay. Lots of gay people are doing it right now as you read this. You can too.

Seek out supportive adults that you know or that people you know vouch for because they will offer you acceptance and respect. You can also learn from them and find connections through them. These adults can also give you a voice if you find the system only listens to adults. It may be hard for you, as a teen, to accept but mature adults do, on average, have better cognitive and reasoning skills than you may have. They also usually have more experience. If you do not know any adults like this contact a local chapter of Parents and Friends of Lesbians and Gays (PFLAG). All the adults there will be supportive because they have kids who are gay, and they will know what resources are available for you because they have already found them for their kids.

Embrace who you are because you are a worthy, normal person. You are not alone or powerless so find others like you in your community or online. Join the Gay/Straight Alliance group in your school if there is one. If there is not one, start one. You can find out how to do that at the Gay/Straight Alliance website which is: https://www. gsanetwork.org.

If you are a Christian, you can find others like you who know that God loves you at www.rainbowchristians.com which is a dating and social networking website. If you plan to go to college look for ones that have an active and open LGBT community. If you are an LGBT youth or the parent of a LGBT person you can find support at the Federation of Parents and Friends of Lesbians and Gays (PFLAG) through www.pflag.org. ***If you are a youth who is in crisis or thinking about committing suicide call the National Suicide Prevention Lifeline (1-800-273-8255) or the Trevor Lifeline (1-866-488-7386).*** The call is free and open 24/7.

Question: What is known about the Senior Community?
The Senior Community is made up of those gays that are 65 years of age or older. They are people of every race, socioeconomic status and religious belief who are bound into a community because of their age. It is because of their age that they share much of the same history, similar issues and many of the same problems and pleasures. They also, of course, share the common trait of being in the last stage of life.

Old age is both a subjective experience and an objective one. Whether a senior is truly old or not depends upon the definition that is used. If the definition used centers on the number of years a person has lived, or the number actuarial charts say are left, then being 65 or more years of age is old. On the other hand, if the definition used is related to ability and/or attitude whether a person is old or not depends on the state of being of the individual person. There are some things that are common to the people in this community however.

All people who are 65 years of age or older share the experience of living through the cold war and the "red scare" of former Senator Joseph McCarthy. They all remember living under the threat of nuclear holocaust, the Viet Nam War, the peace movement of the 1960s and the rise of the drug culture. They all recall the civil rights movement headed by Martin Luther King, the women's liberation movement, and the presidency and assassination of John Kennedy. These experiences and others may be central and formative to whom these people are.

Gay seniors who were open about their sexuality also share the experience of being actively discriminated against not only by ordinary members of their society but also by the police and the government. They know the experience of living through or hearing about police raids of gay bars and of job loss and/or social isolation for being gay. Even those who stayed closeted share the knowledge of what living in fear is like. They all know what it feels like to be classed as mentally ill by mental health "experts" because they were born gay.

The Stonewall riots and beginnings of the gay liberation movement are also memories they share. The history of AIDS/HIV affects all seniors too because most either know someone who died of AIDS or they know someone who knows someone who did. These things are also part of what shaped those in this community.

Seniors additionally share, in various measures, the physical, emotional and psychological impact of getting old. Vision tends to stabilize after 60 years of age, but many seniors find they have problems with decreased depth perception and with the ability to see in the dark. They also commonly find their hearing is not what it once was, and food seems to be less flavorful. After 55 years of age the heart's rhythm slows slightly. High blood pressure becomes more common too. Teeth and gum problems may increase. The body is not able to recover from stress as readily and it loses muscle mass. The reflexes also slow.

A person's physical appearance also changes during old age. The skin becomes paler and less elastic. Wrinkles, blotches, skin folds and maybe even a "turkey neck" appear. Varicose veins are more abundant and prominent. Hair becomes thinner and it whitens.

Most seniors are emotionally and psychologically healthy. Seniors, as a group, are happier and more content than younger people (Scheibe, 2012; Yang, 2008). They tend to deal with problems better too (Grossman, 2010). Staying active and involved helps support that.

Depression is a widespread problem among seniors however. Most seniors do not seek treatment for it beyond their primary care physician (Olfson & Pincus, 1996). Primary care physicians miss symptoms of depression about half of the time (Sandovsky, 1998).

Around 80% of depression cases can be treated with medication. The other 20% need the intervention of a mental health professional (National Institute of Mental Health, 1999). Treatment is essential because depression is a major risk factor in suicide. Seniors are disproportionately present in suicide statistics. They account for 16.37% of completed suicides but only 13.75% of our population (American Assn of Suicidology, 2012). Statistics separating LGBTs out of this whole are not kept.

Among the greatest fears of seniors is that they will get Alzheimer's disease or some other form of dementia. It is commonly believed that memory loss is always just part of getting older and that memory impairment is always permanent. It is true that minor memory loss, such as momentarily forgetting a word or name, is an ordinary part of advanced age (National Institute on Aging, 2009) but only around 5% of Americans between 65 and 74 years of age have Alzheimer's disease.

Seniors need to have the truth about memory loss. Alzheimer's disease is not a normal part of aging, not all memory loss is due to normal aging and some causes of memory loss are reversible (Mayo Clinic, 2009). It is also true that the effects of Alzheimer's disease can be slowed if it is detected early on (Mayo Clinic, 2009). It is therefore critical that seniors consult with a doctor about any symptoms or concerns they have related to their lapses in memory function.

Seniors are also sometimes concerned that as they age their intellectual functioning may be dulled. This does happen in many cases, but it does not always have to. Research shows that mental acuity in old age is directly related to what the person does throughout his/her lifetime. If the person keeps a good diet, stays mentally and physically active, interacts with others socially and can relax regularly throughout their life the outcome is often better mental acuity in old age (Middleton & Barnes, 2010). Often seniors can compensate for any reduction in cognitive ability by using their elevated level of experience and ability (Nunes and Kramer, 2009; Morrow, 1997).

LGBT elders are a normal part of the senior population of the country so naturally they experience most of the things heterosexual seniors do. There are some differences however. Many gay elders have spent their entire lives either living in the closet in fear of being discovered or they have been "out" and actively discriminated against. They therefore tend to not use the resources available to them because they simply do not trust government or other officials (Grant, 2010).

Gay seniors often find that they are dismissed or discriminated against because they are homosexual. Senior services are almost universally set up to serve heterosexual people. Service providers either do not know about the special needs of gay seniors or they do not fill those needs through neglect or intent (Grant, 2010). Many heterosexual seniors continue with their lifelong belief that gay people are abnormal and immoral and they openly shun or abuse the gay seniors in their midst.

The American public at large does not value its elders. Being old is viewed negatively. An LGBT senior must deal not only with that stigma but also the stigma that comes with being LGBT. Even parts of the gay community tend to discriminate against him/her. He/she, for example, is often viewed as sexless, useless and ugly. The pejorative term "troll" is sometimes directed at him by young gay men who should know better. They, after all, know what it feels like to be called names by bigots.

The stereotype is that LGBTs are isolated and lonely when they get old. It is true that these seniors are very vulnerable to that and live alone more often than straight seniors do (SageUSA & MAP, 2017) but that does not mean LGBT seniors are necessarily lonely. Half of them are partnered or married (Fredricksen-Goldsen, 2017) and gays tend to form new relationships more often than heterosexuals do so they commonly have better skills related to meeting new people. They also tend to have a wider circle of friends outside of the workplace and many of those friends become like family. That family relationship continues into old age (Woolf, 2001). Gay seniors tend to have a smaller social network than younger gays, but they interact within it more often (Cromwell & Laumann, 2008).

Gay seniors are much less likely to have children when compared to heterosexual seniors. This has two effects. First, the lack of children denies the childless gay senior a source of support that a gay or straight parent may have. It also means that the gay senior who has no children will never experience the depression that often comes with the "Empty Nest Syndrome" as children leave the home in young adulthood. This syndrome happens because parents tend to focus their lives on their family and work while childless gays tend to focus their lives more broadly (Woolf, 1998).

It is also commonly thought that gay seniors live in poverty. Seniors in general are overrepresented among the impoverished and gay seniors are disproportionately present among impoverished seniors (DeNavas-Walt, 2010). This is largely explained by the greater likelihood of gay seniors living in a one income household and of not having a high school diploma. Gays in all age brackets who do not have more than a high school education tend to earn less than similarly qualified heterosexuals. On the other hand, gay seniors who have a college degree and a committed partner do better financially after retirement than heterosexual couples (Albelda, & Badgett, 2009).

If you are a gay senior there are organizations that have services for you. You can find services for seniors in the yellow pages of your phone book or online but most of those will be tailored for heterosexuals. They do deal with issues generic to an older clientele however so some of them might still be a useful choice.

Services or organizations specifically tailored to older gays are few. Some websites that are designed specifically to help gays and lesbians find information and aid do not have a listing for seniors. The result of that of course is that it is often difficult for LGBT seniors to find resources.

The primary organization for older LGBT people is Service & Advocacy for GLBT Elders (SAGE). It offers direct services, referral and education to gay seniors and to those who work with them. They have independent chapters in localities around the country. If you need to contact SAGE quickly their hotline number is (888) 234-SAGE. The central office is in New York at (212) 741-2247 or find them on the internet at www.sageusa.org. You should note that sometimes SAGE is called "Senior Action in a Gay Environment" but do not be confused. It is the same organization and has the same phone number and web address.

The Senior Pride Network also functions solely to service senior LGBT people. It runs primarily in Canada but has international affiliations. Information can be obtained at www.seniorpridenetwork.com and their email address is www.spntoronto.com.

If you are looking for a hookup or a relationship with an older man, there are websites that will offer access to that. Among them is www. GrayGay.com. It offers news and information.

As a word of warning it should be noted that, while most of the people on sites like these are probably harmless, some of them may be predators. Be cautious. Don't give your social security number, your financial information or other personal information to people you meet online. It is also unwise to respond to pleas for financial or personal aid. These pleas are almost always scams.

If you are a senior citizen who is thinking about suicide call the National Suicide Prevention Helpline at 1-800-273-8255. The call is free. It is available twenty-four hours a day and seven days a week. It is safe to tell them you are gay.

Question: What is known about the lesbian community?
Lesbians, of course, have always existed. There is not a lot of history written about them because, frankly, men historically have authored most history books and until relatively recently what women did with other women was not viewed as worthy of entry into the books men wrote. Among the earliest writing about lesbian love were done by the 6th century BCE lesbian poet Sappho. Most of her writing has been lost.

The term "lesbian" refers to the Greek island of Lesbos where Sappho lived. Originally the term "lesbian" meant anything that came from Lesbos but that changed in the last part of the 19th century when it came to mean a sexual relationship between two women. The term came into prominent use thanks to the writing of the British physician Havelock Ellis who, among other writings, authored the seven-volume work entitled *Studies in the Psychology of Sex*.

In his writings, Ellis asserted that lesbianism, like all homosexuality, was an inversion from the norm in which the person takes traits of the opposite gender. He said that lesbianism, in most cases, was a passing phase that changed eventually but that some women stayed "inverts" for their entire lives. He viewed homosexuality as an abnormality and a form of mental illness. His view was widely accepted and was, unfortunately, rather long lasting. The American Psychological Association, for example, viewed homosexuality as a mental disorder until 1973.

Historically gay women have always been and continue to be a minority within a minority. Homosexuals are a minority within the American population generally and there are fewer lesbians within the LGBT community than there are gay men. We do not know precisely how many fewer because that cannot be accurately measured. We do know that studies consistently show the size of the lesbian population to be smaller than the gay male population.

One well-respected study found that if we define homosexuality as romantic or sexual attraction to one's own sex 7.7% of Americans are gay men and 7.5% are lesbians. If we measure homosexuality in terms of open self-identification as homosexual 2.8% of men and 1.4% of women are gay. If having sex exclusively with members of one's own sex is the measure then 3% of men and 1.6% of women are homosexual (Laumann & Gagnon, 1994). Other studies give other figures, but most conclude that there are more gay men than lesbians. This may seem to be unimportant but that is not the case.

Researchers tend to use open self-identification or sexual behavior as their measuring stick. Because of this most of the research done related to homosexuals is about gay males. This is at least partly because it easier to find a statistically significant sample of gay men. It may also be partly due to researchers wanting their work to be applicable or beneficial to a larger population. Another factor may be that society in nearly every culture has historically viewed sexuality through a male favored lens.

We therefore do not have as much information about lesbians as we do about men in general or gay men as a subgroup of them. One study that reviewed the sexuality related research done from 1975 through 2001 found that homosexuals were studied less than 1% of the time and lesbians were studied in less than half of that (Lee & Crawford, 2007). There are some things that we do know however.

There are no distinct categories of sexual orientation in terms of the masculinization or feminization of the brain. We cannot point to certain areas of the brain that are masculinized in all lesbians and feminized in all homosexual men. What exists is a spectrum of individualized variations (Muscarella and Elias, 2004).

In most respects lesbians are, as a group, like other women. It has been shown, for example, that there is no difference in the hormone types or levels found in heterosexual and homosexual women (Banks & Gartrell, 1995; Dancey, 1990). Similarly, there is no significant difference in femininity as measured by psychological tests although lesbians do tend to score higher in some measures of psychological masculinity such as assertiveness and autonomy (Finlay & Scheltema, 1991). There are also no differences in lateralization of language or visual tasks in the brain, in personality traits, depression scores or the level of satisfaction they have with their bodies (Sanders, 1997). The lesbian body is, with few exceptions, the same as that of heterosexual women.

Lesbians, as a group, do tend to have some characteristics that are more like heterosexual men than like heterosexual women or gay men. Lesbians and hetero men, for example, have a similar finger length ratio when the index finger and the ring finger are measured (McFadden and Schubel, 2002). As another example, the lesbian startle response is comparable to the heterosexual male response and dissimilar to the heterosexual female or gay male one due to a masculinization of the limbic area of the brain (Rahman and Kumari, 2003). Moreover, homosexual women respond to certain smells in a way that is typical of straight men but not straight women (Savic and Berglund, 2006). Lesbians, as a group, also tend to be more like straight men than heterosexual women or gay men in verbal fluency (Rahman and Abrahams, 2003).

The differences in some characteristics between lesbians and others are sometimes only partial. A team from the University of Texas, for example, found that the responses of lesbians to auditory stimuli was neither typical of men (gay men and straight men are the same in this) nor of straight women. Heterosexual women generally have a stronger auditory response than gay or straight men do. The lesbian response however was in-between the male one and the heterosexual female one (McFadden and Pasanen, 1998).

It has long been known that homosexual men, on average, earn less than similarly qualified heterosexual men. Lesbians do not, on average, suffer that same bias however. Depending upon which study is looked at there is either very little difference between what a lesbian makes, and a similarly qualified heterosexual woman makes (Ahmed & Hammarstedt, 2010) or lesbians earn more (Berg & Lien, 2002; Romero & Baumle, 2007; Carpenter, 2008). At the same time lesbians are more likely than heterosexual women to live in poverty (Albelda & Badgett, 2009). This is at least partly due to higher levels of unemployment among lesbians and her not having the higher level of household income that comes from being coupled with a man.

It is also known that homosexuals smoke at a significantly higher rate than does the American population generally. American smokers as a group are 20.6% of the public at large. Men smoke more than women do. Lesbians smoke 1.2 to 2.0 times the rate of heterosexual women. This may be largely due to the stress lesbians feel related to the stigma of being gay and the highly addictive nature of nicotine (American Lung Association, 2010).

Lesbians, as a group, are more likely than other women to be overweight or obese (Conron and Mimiaga, 2010; Boehmer, 2007). It is not known why this is the case, but the evidence suggests that many lesbians simply reject the cultural norms about body weight and physical appearance. This together with their increased rate of smoking and alcohol consumption puts lesbians at greater risk than other women of breast, ovarian and colon cancer (Mayo Clinic, 2009).

Lesbians are also different in some ways from heterosexuals and gay males in how they manage their relationships. Cohabitating lesbians report higher rates of intimacy and equality than either married heterosexual couples or cohabiting gay couples. It is speculated that this may be the product of the fact that it is two women involved in the lesbian relationship and women tend to value intimacy (not to be confused with sex) and equality in a relationship more than men do (Kurdek, 1998).

Many lesbians are labelled as either butch or femme. Any person (male or female) who is characterized as "butch" is being defined as a person with at least some stereotypically masculine attributes. A butch lesbian then is a homosexual woman who has some stereotypically masculine attributes or interests. A "femme" on the other hand is a lesbian who is much like a heterosexual woman except in her sexual orientation.

It must be understood that while the butch and femme designations are generally accepted by the public at large and even by many gays they do not characterize all lesbians since there is a wide diversity of traits within the lesbian community. Many lesbians reject these labels entirely. At the same time, self-identified butch and femme lesbians have been studied and there are differences between them.

One study, for example, found that butch lesbians tend have a higher waist-to-hip ratio like men do while femmes commonly have a more female typical ratio. Both femmes and butches reported gender non-conformity as children in that they did not like or do some female typical things, but they did like male typical things. This however was found to be more pronounced in butch lesbians (Singh and Vidaurri, 1999).

Butch lesbians tend to have more female sex partners than femmes do, but femmes are likely to have more male ones. There are more women who are perceived as butch than there are women who classify themselves that way. Butches tend to be more comfortable with self-identifying openly as lesbian than femmes are and more likely to be involved in the gay community. Femmes are more likely to say they are bisexual (Rosario and Scrimshaw, 2009).

Butch lesbians, as a group, tend to be less likely to want to give birth than femmes. Femmes, on the other hand, tend to want that more than straight women do. Butch lesbians tend to be more likely than femmes to take the dominant role in sex. They also tend to have a history of more sexual relationships than either femmes or straight women (Singh and Vidaurri, 1999).

A study concerning preferred partner characteristics found that heterosexual women preferred a partner who was older, taller, heavier, more muscularly developed and more sexually dominant. Homosexual women preferred a partner who was older, taller and more muscular than them but also lighter. Femmes commonly preferred a partner that was taller than the partner selected by butches (Muscarella and Elias, 2004).

Many people define lesbians by their romantic attraction to other women and/or by their preference for same-sex sex partners. This may seem natural and logical since that is a primary difference between them and other women. In defining lesbians that way however the observer misses most of what lesbians are. They are much more than their sexual preference. All lesbians are normal, whole people who have the same physical, psychological and emotional needs as everyone else. They fulfill those needs in the same way too.

One of those needs is that of having intimate relationships and intimate sexual contact with another person. They do the things that others do in that regard. They love, communicate, share, kiss, caress, nibble, hug, rub and have mouth to genital, hand to genital, and genital to genital contact with one another. Many lesbians, like women in general, love to touch and snuggle. Obviously, they are not able to have penis to vagina contact but sometimes an artificial penis is used. All of this is within what is normal for human beings.

The sexual part of a lesbian relationship is just that...part of it. There is much more to it just as there is in a heterosexual or gay male relationship. This is especially true if the people involved are friends or committed partners.

As with most humans, a sizeable majority of the relationships lesbians have with other people are not sexual at all. They are work related or social. From that perspective, it becomes less logical to define lesbians or anyone else by just the sexual part of how they interact or feel about other people. Our species would take a large stride forward if we would all stop doing that.

Question: What is known about the bisexual community?

Bisexuality is the sexual and/or romantic attraction to and/or the sexual interaction with both sexes. Very little research is done on bisexuals. When it is done, they are usually lumped in with homosexuals. One analysis of the literature from 1990 through 2004 found that of the 2,859 articles published in which the word "bisexual" was found in the abstract, in the title or as a key word only about one-third (1,002) did not attach bisexuals to homosexuals. The term "bisexual" was very commonly used as a catch word to count non-heterosexuals. Only 8.4 % (240) of the articles referred to bisexuality as a self-identity (Pitts, 2005). Male and female bisexuals are commonly lumped together too even though they have many distinctly different traits.

There are those in both the straight and gay communities who believe bisexuality does not actually exist. They believe people who say they are bisexual are simply homosexuals who have not admitted to themselves that they are gay or who know they are but do not want to be labelled as homosexual. This belief may be true in some cases but overall is not based on fact.

There are studies that have failed to find a bisexual pattern of genital arousal in men. Other studies have found that pattern however (Rosenthal, 2012; Cerny, 2011). There are also studies that have found a bisexual pattern in some men using data related to pupil dilation responses to sexual stimuli (Rieger, 2012; Hess, 1965). The weight of the evidence clearly shows that bisexuality does exist. That should however not be taken to mean that everyone who claims to be bisexual is so.

One of the difficulties in measuring bisexuality is that it rarely manifests itself as an equal attraction to both sexes. That happens only 0.6% of the time. Bisexuals typically prefer one sex or the other to some degree but are attracted to both. Their sexuality is unique from homosexuality, heterosexuality and asexuality.

It has been shown that physical attraction and romantic attraction are neurobiologically independent phenomena. MRI imaging shows the regions of the brain dealing with romantic activity and those dealing with sexual arousal are separate and do not overlap (Diamond, 2004). Many people, in fact, experience falling in love with someone before they become sexually attracted to them. Indeed, some people have ongoing romantic relationships without being sexually aroused by the other person.

Sexual orientation is therefore not exclusively measured by the presence or absence of a genital response to stimuli. Some find that they are attracted to one gender differently than they are to the other one. A person, for example, might be more physically attracted to one gender while being more romantically attracted to the other one (Rust, 2002).

It used to be thought that lots of people were to some degree bisexual. Alfred Kinsey's groundbreaking research told us that 15-25 % of women (Kinsey, 1953) and 33-46% of men (Kinsey, 1948) are bisexual. This is not widely accepted as true anymore but there is no agreement on how to measure it. If, for example, behavior is the measurement used the researcher must decide how much bisexual behavior over what timespan counts. Is it one contact in the last month, two or more in the last year or some other measure? Does the fact that 62% to 79% of self-identified homosexual men and 74% to 81% of lesbians have had sex with a person of the opposite sex (Reinisch, 1990) make them bisexual? Problems also arise when self-reported attraction or self-identity is measured. Thus, we do not know how many bisexuals there are, but we have some indications.

It is now believed that the frequency of bisexuality is much less than what was given to us by Alfred Kinsey. A well-respected study measuring sexual orientation based on attraction, behavior and self-identity found 0.8% of men and 0.5% of women say they are bisexual. The same study reported that in terms of sexual/romantic attraction 2.6% of men and 2.7% of women are bisexual but mostly attracted to the opposite sex, 0.6% of men and 0.8% of women are attracted to both sexes equally, and 0.7% of men and 0.6% of women are bisexual but attracted to mostly their same sex. Finally, in terms of behavior, the study offered that 0.7% of men and 0.3% of women had had sex with both men and women in the last year and 4% of men and 3.7% of women had done so since age 18 (Laumann & Gagnon, 1994).

Other studies have given other results. The Janus Report, for example, found that 5% of men and 3% of women self-identified as bisexual (Janus and Janus, 1993). The 2002 National Survey on Family Growth reported that 13% of women and 6% of men said they felt some attraction to both sexes but only 2% label themselves that way. A 2015 survey found that 4% of people say they are bisexual but at the same time 16% describe their sexuality as being to some degree bisexual (Moore, 2015). Most studies have found there are more gay men and women than there are bisexual men and women.

The attraction to both sexes does not necessarily yield behavior that matches that attraction. Bisexuals do not necessarily have sex with both genders. Many prefer one gender while being attracted to the other. They behave and/or label themselves in line with their primary attraction or with the one that yields the least negative fallout. There are undoubtedly a lot of closeted bisexuals who say they are straight and behave as heterosexuals since they can easily pass as that. Doing so lets them avoid the prejudice, discrimination and scorn that sometimes come with being non-heterosexual. Many homosexuals, of course, do likewise.

It seems counterintuitive but there are also bisexuals who label themselves as gay. One might think that self-identifying as bisexual would mean you are part of both the straight and gay communities and accepted by both while labelling oneself as gay would get you some level of stigma that you would not get as a bisexual. This however is not necessarily the case because human society tends to think in terms of two sexual orientations.

Human society tends to categorize people as either heterosexual or homosexual. If you are bisexual, you are both and neither of those. Instead of being accepted by both communities some bisexuals find they are subjected to prejudice from both. Some bisexuals who are primarily attracted to their same sex simply find it simpler and less stressful to label as gay.

Bisexual men may that find their sexual orientation affects their heath and the medical treatment they receive. He, for example, may be at more risk of having the higher HIV, anal wart and mood disorder rates of a homosexual man and the higher obesity, genital wart and psychosis rate of a heterosexual man. Studies show that bisexual men, as a group, have a higher rate of heart disease, asthma and depression than either homosexual or heterosexual men. It is therefore important for the bisexual man to find a doctor he can talk to openly about his sexuality, concerns and symptoms.

One of the myths that have caused a stigma to attach to bisexuality is that bisexuals are the reason the heterosexual community was infected with HIV/AIDS. The reasoning behind the myth is that HIV/AIDS is mistakenly viewed by some as a gay disease that was transferred to heterosexuals by bisexuals. The myth is sometimes even fostered by researchers who wittingly or unwittingly associate bisexuals with the spread of the infection (Pitts, 2005). That idea, of course, is nonsense both because it ignores how viruses spread from animals to humans and it is ignorant of the history of HIV.

The parent virus of HIV has existed within African primates for at least 14 million years (Gifford and Katzourakis, 2008). The virus moved from chimpanzees and gorillas to humans in the form of Simian immunodeficiency virus (SIV) around 1876 (Sousa and Müller, 2010). It is theorized that that occurred via a bite or a blood spatter. The oldest form of Human immunodeficiency virus (HIV) is dated as being from the late 19th or early 20th centuries (Worobey and Gemmel, 2008).

There are two major theories about how HIV spread among humans. One of them faults the use of unclean needles during the various mass inoculations that occurred in Africa during the late 19th and early 20th century. The other theory faults the widespread prostitution and drug use that came with the rapid growth and urbanization caused by the colonization of Africa.

Whichever theory is right the odds are heavily in favor of HIV being a virus that initially infected heterosexuals then spread to homosexuals and bisexuals. This is the case simply because of the demographics of our species and of HIV. Ninety to ninety-five of humanity is heterosexual. On a world-wide basis, most cases of HIV/AIDs are heterosexual or not sexually transmitted (UNAID, 2010). A large majority of prostitutes and drug users are hetero. Most people who give inoculations are too. Dirty needles are a known source of HIV.

Another stigmatizing myth is that bisexuals are, by nature, promiscuous. The fact that bisexuals are attracted to both genders is taken to mean that they, as a group, not only have sex with both genders but that they do so often. There is no evidence to support this. In fact, human beings, as a species, are not promiscuous (Fisher, 1992). This naturally includes bisexuals.

It is sometimes said that bisexuality is a phase that people go through on their way to homosexuality or, in a minority of cases, heterosexuality. This is true in some cases. Bisexuality may or may not be a phase in how a person understands their sexuality. This naturally follows from the fact that sexual orientation is fluid in some people but not in others. At the same time, it must be added that bisexuality is not a phase for most people (Dickson and van Roode, 2013; Savin-Williams, 2012; Ott and Corliss, 2011).

Many people believe that bisexuality is not a sexual orientation that is distinct from homosexuality and heterosexuality. They think of it as some ratio of heterosexuality to homosexuality. In other words, bisexuals are thought of as being this much heterosexual and that much homosexual. Bisexuals, if asked, will be quick to say that this is not what they are.

Nature does not make a bisexual the way a bartender makes a martini. They are not three parts of this and one part of that with a garnish tossed in. You cannot make one the same way every time. Each human being, whether bi, gay or straight, is a complex and widely diverse mixture of characteristics. Many of their traits are impactful in how he/she responds to his/her sexuality and gender identity and to that of others.

Bisexuals as a group have some distinctly different social characteristics from homosexuals. They are far less likely to be "out" about their sexual orientation or to say their sexual orientation makes a difference in their life (Pew, 2013). A large majority of them are in a heterosexual committed relationship and have at least one child (Herek & Norton, 2010). They are much more likely to link with the Republican Party and much less likely to identify with the LGBT community (Herek & Norton, 2010).

Sexual orientation is a matter of biology, of attractions, behaviors and identities and of emotion, psychology and physicality. Pieces of that may change over the course of time and they do not necessarily align (Saewyc, 2011). Bisexuals are a distinct community because of the central thread within that mix that they share with other bisexuals but not with other sexual orientations. Their way of responding to males and females is that thread.

Understanding bisexuality entails the abandonment the notion that sexuality is straight, gay or some combination of straight and gay. You must accept that there are four archetypes of human sexual orientation: heterosexual, homosexual, bisexual and asexual. As with all archetypes they are distinct, and they act as ground for the wide spectrum of sexuality that branch out from them. Specifics within these branches may overlap but the root of a person's sexual orientation is always one of these archetypes.

The problem that bisexuals have is that all human beings fall within one the archetypes, but sexual orientation is also bimodal (two peaks). Most human beings are either heterosexual or homosexual, so a graph of human sexuality would have a major peak at one end of the spectrum (heterosexuality) and a minor peak (homosexuality) at the other one.

What most people see when they look at a bisexual appears very much like it is this much hetero and that much gay. This is because they do not experience bisexuality the way bisexuals do, and the straight/gay model is what is normative for them. When most people see a couple kissing, for example, almost none of them think one or both of those in the kissing couple might be bisexual. We assume homosexuality or heterosexuality.

That will not change until bisexuals come out of the closet, so they can be seen, and they can educate. It also will not change unless bisexuals and their allies actively push for change. Bisexuals have natural allies in the LGT community. Everyone in our LGBT community understands what it is to not be understood or accepted. Bisexuals need to find those allies and enlist them to join the push. At the same time, they must understand that our community may hesitate to help them if they deny being part of it which, sadly, many bisexuals do.

Question: What is known about the transgender community?

The transgender community is made up of people who define themselves as being outside of society's traditional definition of two genders. Each of the groups within the transgender community is distinct in some way. It includes transvestites, bi-gender and androgynous people, genderqueers, and transsexuals. This community is therefore based on gender identity and not sexual orientation.

Some also include those people who are intersexed as part of the transgender community, but they are properly part of it only if they classify themselves as being outside the traditional model of the male or female genders. Not all intersexed people do. Some see themselves and behave as male or as female despite not having some of the biological characteristics of that sex. Gender identity is an entirely personal matter, so this is entirely proper.

To understand the transgender community, you must grasp the difference between sex and gender and between sexual orientation and gender identity. A person's sex is totally about the status of being biologically male, female or intersexed. A person's gender, on the other hand, relates to the cultural norms and expectations society places on male and female people because of the sex they are. Sexual orientation relates to whether a person is sexually and/or romantically attracted to others of his/her own sex, the opposite sex, both or neither. Gender identity is about how a person defines himself and how he feels and behaves in terms of society's norms for masculinity or femininity.

Some people do not believe transgender people properly belong under the umbrella which covers LGB people. They assert that the LGB community is based on the sexual orientation of its members and that sexual orientation is not the defining feature of most transgendered people. They accept that some transgender people are part of the LGB community but insist that this inclusion is because those people are gay, lesbian or bisexual and not because of the nature of their gender identity.

Others assert the LGBT community is at its core about civil rights and supporting diversity in sexual identity. They insist that transgender people are defined by their sexual identity just as LGB people are and as such are rightfully a part of our community. They also point out most gays and bisexuals do not conform to the heterosexual standard of what men and women should be and that, like transgendered people, our sexual identity is often viewed as abnormal. They add that the transgender community and the LGB community share issues, values and goals and we are share the fight against discrimination by those who support conformity to a heterosexual standard of sexuality.

A transvestite is a person who dresses in the clothes of the opposite sex and who may also take on the manner of that sex. This person may wear only one item, a few items or a whole wardrobe of opposite gender apparel. The person may be bisexual, homosexual or heterosexual. Most, but not all, transvestites are male. If asked to classify themselves in terms of gender their response would say that their gender identity matches their biological sex identity. They have no interest at all in changing sexes through sexual reassignment surgery. They do however have an interest in feeling feminine and they accept that what they do to obtain that puts them outside the larger society's definitions related to their gender.

Transvestites cross dress because of the emotional gratification obtained by doing so. They may or may not also obtain sexual stimulation by doing this but that is not an essential feature of transvestitism. It is not therefore a characteristic of transvestitism per se. In heterosexual men (but not homosexuals) this feature may take the form of transvestic fetishism. Transvestitism per se is not a mental disorder.

A bi-gender identity and an androgynous identity are opposite sides of a coin. A bi-gender person presents a masculine gender identity in some situations and a feminine one in other situations. This is not the same as being bisexual because bisexuality is about sexual orientation while bi-gender is about gender identity. A bi-gender person could be heterosexual, homosexual, bisexual or asexual.

In some ancient cultures androgyny was viewed at the ideal because it combines male and female into a unified whole. An androgynous person does not link with either gender and does not present himself that way. A neutral observer would find neither the appearance nor the behavior of a clearly delineated masculine or feminine identity. The androgynous person presents this identity across all situations. He/she may be bisexual, homosexual or heterosexual.

Genderqueer is an umbrella identity. Genderqueer people might see himself as being neither masculine nor feminine or both masculine and feminine. They might also completely dismiss the whole matter of gender as being irrelevant or assert that genderqueer is a third gender which is neither masculine nor feminine.

If the intersexed are classed as transgender they are the largest group within it. It is generally accepted that a person can be intersexed in five ways: 1) number and type of chromosomes, 2) gonad type (ovaries or testicles), 3) type of sex hormones produced, 4) internal anatomy, and 5) external anatomy. There are multiple variations within the intersex schema. Around 1% of live births are intersex in some way.

In some cases, intersex characteristics are clear at birth while in other cases they become so later in life. Sometimes they won't become noticeable at all unless they become so because of a medical examination such as a chromosome test or a fertility test. Some intersexed people are involuntarily given "normalizing" surgery as infants or children, some undergo it voluntarily as adults and some choose to not take that course.

The reader should understand that, like all LGBT people, the intersexed person's sexuality is not average in some way, but they became who they are through a natural, normal process. At the same time, it may be useful to remember that person cannot be reduced to one or two of the facets of what they are nor is it possible to predict what he/she will become on that basis.

For more information go to the website of the Intersex Society of America at: www.isna.org/faq/what_is_intersex. A booklet aimed at the parents of intersexed children can be found at: dsdguidlines.org/htdocs/parents/index.html. The animated video found at intersexday.org/en/aotearoa-youth-video-2017 is highly recommended.

A transsexual is a person who feels that his/her biologically assigned birth sex does not match his/her gender identity. Such a person connects strongly with the opposite sex and believes that he/she should have been born as a person of that sex. Some transsexuals see themselves as transsexual but make no overt action to behave like the opposite sex. This leads to the charge by some that these people are not actually transsexual. Others present themselves as a person of the opposite sex and see themselves that way but take no action to change their birth sex. They keep the sexual characteristics they were born with and simply live as a person of the opposite sex. Still others have or want to have sex reassignment surgery (SRS).

Like all transgender people a transsexual could be heterosexual, homosexual, bisexual or asexual. This is not as straight forward as it sounds however because of the conflict the transsexual has between his/her birth sex and his/her gender identity. A transsexual person who is sexually or romantically attracted to their persons of their own sex is homosexual in terms of sexual identity but may not be homosexual in terms of gender identity since their identity aligns with the other sex. Some transsexuals classify their sexual orientation based on their birth sex, but others define it based on their gender identity. Researchers typically do the former when studying transsexuals. It is polite to use the gender pronouns that are in line with the transsexual person's preference.

Some people believe that transsexuality is the same thing as a gender identity disorder. This is not true. Gender identity disorder is a psychological diagnosis that was replaced in 2013 by the psychological diagnosis of gender dysphoria. This diagnosis (like gender identity disorder) is not limited to transsexuals. It entails two things: 1) the person is in some way transgender and 2) the person is experiencing significant personal or interpersonal problems because his/her gender identity. Being transgender per se therefore is not a mental health issue. It becomes one only when it becomes the root of mental health issues.

Most transgender people do not experience such an impairment of functioning and thus do not have the disorder. Their level of self-esteem and psychological adjustment does not differ from that of the public at large. A study done in 2009 supports this view (Bockting and Benner, 2009).

Transsexuals are the most studied group within the transgender community although they are not studied a lot. One area of study is the prevalence of transsexualism and the male to female ratio of them. An often cited 1990 study in the Netherlands found 1 in 11,900 people to be male to female (MTF) transsexuals and 1 in 30,400 to be female to male (FTM) transsexuals (Bakker and van Kestern, 2007). Another study asserts the number of transsexuals who have had or will have sex reassignment surgery in their lifetime is 1 in 2500 MTF and 1 in 4,200 FTM. The same study concluded that if undiagnosed transsexuals are considered the incidence of transsexualism increased to 1 in 750 MTF and 1 in 1400 FTM (Horton, 2008).

A third study found the incidence of transsexualism to be between 1 in 1000 and 1 in 2000. The study also shows that more recent data suggests the incidence might be 1 in 500 or more (Olyslager and Conway, 2007). If 1 in 500 is correct then 0.2% of all people are transsexual. If the Netherlands study is correct then 0.008% of all people are MTF transsexuals and 0.003% of all people are FTM transsexuals.

The fact that transsexualism is rare does not mean it is abnormal. It just means that it is not average. The evidence is that transsexualism has at least some roots in biology. It certainly is not a choice.

There is a growing body of evidence that sexual orientation and gender identity are decided in the womb. A fetus is male, female or intersexed by the end of the 12th week of gestation. The brain locks in the fetus' gender identity during the second half of a typical 40-week pregnancy (Garcia-Falgueras and Swabb, 2010; Swabb 2007). A child's sexual orientation and identity continues to develop after birth, but the outcome is largely settled at birth.

Children develop a conscious sense of gender identity by age 2. In other words, they think of people as being as a boy or a girl at that age (Stipek and Gralinski, 1990). They view themselves as a boy or a girl by age 4 and they behave based on that identity. This is before they are intellectually capable of understanding sexuality or gender identity thus they are not able to make conscious choices related to that. They behave in the way that feels natural to them although they do not yet understand that their sex cannot change (Warin, 2000; Kohlberg, 1966). That happens around age 7 and in most cases gender identity tends to be very stable afterwards.

Transsexuals are not an exception to this. They however experience a misalignment of their biological sex and their gender identity. They have the body of one sex but link psychologically with the opposite sex or with both sexes. The anxiety this causes often resolves itself once the person produces the hormones that develop him/her sexually and their brain matures. Less than a quarter of people who enter preadolescence experiencing gender dysphoria (anxiety or anguish) continue to experience it after they have become fully mature people (Steensma and Biemond, 2011).

There is evidence from family studies that transsexualism has a biological part. Siblings of a transsexual person have a significantly higher probability of also being transsexual than does the population generally. Brothers are more likely than sisters to also be transsexuals (Gomez-Gil, 2010). This, of course, may be to some degree the result of environment but it falls in line with the fact that most transsexuals are biologically male at birth.

There are also grounds to believe that the brains of MTF and FTM transsexuals are different from each other and, in some ways, also different from the brains from non-transsexuals of the same sex. The first study showing a female brain structure in MTF transsexuals was reported in 1995. It found that a part of the brain (the bed nucleus of the stria terminalis) was the same size in MTF transsexuals as it is in non-transsexual women and smaller than it is in other men (Zhou, 1995).

In 2000 another very well-known study found that gay and straight men have nearly twice the number of neurons in a certain region of the brain as women. It also found that MTF transsexuals are comparable to women and FTM transsexuals are comparable to men in this regard (Kruijver, 2000). The authors of the study plainly state that this points to a neurological basis for transsexualism.

More recent research offers further evidence of a biological influence in transsexualism. MRI imaging of the brain was used in one of these studies. It showed the brains of homosexual MTF and FTM transsexuals differ from brains of cisgender heterosexual males and females which may imply brain intersexuality (Guillamon, 2016).

Other studies have also used brain imaging. One done in 2011 showed that some white matter structures within the transsexual brain are closer to what is typical for the person's gender identity sex than they are for his/her biological sex (Rametti and Carrillo, 2011). Another study found that white matter within the untreated transsexual brain is typical of neither male nor female but rather is in-between the two (Rametti and Carrillo, 2011).

A study of dichotic listening and handedness shown that the brain of MTF transsexuals is organized in a similar fashion to non-transsexual women and that the brains of MTF transsexuals and FTM transsexuals are not the same (Govier, 2010). A 2009 study revealed that gray matter in a region of the MTF brain resembles that found in a female brain. The authors said that this supports the idea that brain anatomy is a factor in gender identity (Luders and Sanchez, 2009). There are other peer reviewed articles related to this view, but space prohibits listing them.

Research shows that genes are a factor in transsexualism. One study found a genetic difference between FTM transsexuals and non-transsexual women on the CYP17 gene but did not find the same sort of difference in transsexual and non-transsexual men (Bentz, 2008). Researchers at the University of Vienna have found a variant of a gene that boosts testosterone levels in FTM transsexuals and in some non-transsexual women. The variation is much more common in transsexuals however (Geddes, 2008). Another study found three genes that may have at least a partial effect on whether a person is an MTF transsexual (Henningsson, 2005).

It is commonly thought that being transsexual means a person is transitioning from being one gender into being the other one and that part of that is undergoing sex change surgery. This is often untrue since transitioning may involve surgery but it not uncommon for it not to. In this case the person takes on the life he/she feels he/she was born to lead and that, of course, means acting in accord with the gender role found within that life and not the one associated with the sex he/she was born with. Some transgender people use the pronouns commonly associated with his/her transgender identity while others prefer to use his/her name or a sex neutral term.

Transgender people tend to have some health issues that should be discussed with a doctor. These include substance abuse, hormone use, smoking, heart disease and receiving healthcare that is sensitive to the person's transgender situation. Transfolk, as a group, also tend to not practice safer sex techniques so they tend to have high rates of STIs.

The major health issue for this community however is certainly HIV. The Centers for Disease Control and Prevention (CDC) say that this group is among those at highest risk of getting HIV. A 2012 study shows that transgender women are nearly 49 times more likely to be infected with HIV than are other women (Baral, 2012).

Like most minorities, transgendered people often face discrimination and prejudice. Transgender people are more likely than others to perceive their family as unsupportive. They are more likely than their siblings to be highly educated but, because of discrimination, less likely to financially gain from that education. They are also more likely to be harassed (Factor, 2007). A study on gender violence reported that 59.5% of transgendered people experience some form of violence or harassment during their lifetime and 47% experience some form of assault (Lombardi, 2001). Thirty-three states have no law against firing someone purely for being transsexual.

Many LGB people are among those who discriminate against transgender people. This is particularly unsettling since, having been on the receiving end of discrimination, LGBs should know better. It is especially hard to understand once you know that transfolk got their gender identity the exact same way gays, lesbians and bisexuals got their sexual orientation: biology.

Those needing further information about transgender issues should go to the True Child website (www.truechild.org), the National Center for Transgender Equality website (www.nctequality.org) and/or the Human Rights Campaign website (www.hcr.org).

Question: What is known about the drag community?
The drag community is made up entirely of cross dressers. To be "in drag" is to be in the clothing of the opposite gender but it is also more than that. Being in drag is also about presenting a persona. A persona, of course, is an image or role a person presents to other people. If a person in the drag community is male, he is called a drag queen. If the person is female she is called a drag king. There are far more drag queens than drag kings.

The fact that a person is in drag does not in itself make that person part of the drag community. A person, for example, might go to a costume party in drag but would not be part of the drag community. Similarly, a person that dresses in drag purely to obtain sexual gratification is not part of that community.

It is sometimes thought that a drag queen is the same thing as a transvestite. This is usually not true. While both drag queens and transvestites may be asexual, homosexual, bisexual or heterosexual most drag queens are gay and most transvestites are straight. Unlike some transvestites, drag queens do not try to pass as a member of the opposite gender. Most transvestites cross dress privately or even secretly while the drag queens are very public. The primary difference however is the motivation behind their cross dressing.

A transvestite wears female attire primarily because of the emotional and possibly sexual gratification he gets by doing so. He views himself as outside of the cultural norms of masculinity or femininity regardless of what he is wearing because of that need. Even if he is not wearing any feminine attire at all the need is still there. This is who and what he is twenty-four hours a day, seven days a week.

A drag queen, on the other hand, cross-dresses to obtain monetary gain, situational power and/or the attention of others (Berkowitz, 2010; Hopkins, 2004). He may refer to himself or other people who are in drag as "she" but that designation is not about gender identity. It is about being "in character" and possibly about sexual orientation. At the end day, a drag queen takes off his opposite gender clothing and the opposite sex persona that goes with it. While many in the drag community find emotional gratification or affirmation though their opposite sex persona they never believe that persona is truly who they are. They are entertainers.

There are two kinds of drag queens: performance artists and non-performance artists. The latter never go on stage and do not get paid for being in drag. They simply choose to go out sometimes dressed in drag and that act is a kind of performance. They are sometimes seen in gay bars or even in the audience at drag shows. For some this is the first step toward becoming a drag performance artist. Others simply enjoy doing it for some period of their life and it does not progress beyond that.

The former type of drag queen dresses in drag as part of a performance done to entertain or they do so in a socio/political context such as a gay pride rally or parade. They typically earn money for their performance by getting tips from the audience although sometimes they also get part of whatever cover charge there is at the bar or club they are performing in. Tips are either handed to the artist or tucked into his clothing when he comes near. Any tips that fall to the floor are gathered after the show by someone associated with the performer but rarely by the performer himself. Most never make much money as a drag performer but they find other benefits in performing.

Drag queens present either an exaggerated female persona or they impersonate some renowned female star or other female person of note. Like all entertainers, they spend a lot of time perfecting their act which includes selecting music and perfecting their choreography, costumes, makeup and hair. Some of them have solo acts while others perform as a troupe. Members of these troupes commonly form tight bonds with one another. It is possible that a transvestite could perform as a drag queen but that is far more the exception rather than the rule.

The content of the acts varies from performer to performer but generally they revolve around humor, singing and/or lip-syncing to music while staging a well-rehearsed choreography. Many drag queens use interaction with people in the audience as a theatrical devise. It is also not uncommon to see a drag queen acting as a host or emcee for other performers or at a gay community event. Some become well known and their celebrity helps attract people to these events.

Audiences at drag performances are often some mixture of straight and gay patrons. This underscores the fact that drag acts are about entertainment and having fun and not about gender identity. It is in these venues that many straight people first feel they have anything in common with gay people. A drag queen may be the first person they have ever heard talking about the gay world and good-naturedly poking fun at it. Many straights do not realize it but when they leave after the show they feel somehow less threatened by gay people. It is hard to be threatened by someone who laughs at the same things you do.

Drag kings are roughly the female equivalent of a drag queen except that the performer is a female who is performing as a male persona. This typically involves not only the use of male clothing but also the use of male mannerisms, the binding of the performer's breasts to make them flatter, the addition of simulated male genitals and the use of make-up or hair attached to the face with theatrical gum to give the appearance of male facial hair. The performances are usually done in a lesbian oriented venue such as a lesbian bar. The actors typically are part of a troupe although some solo artists do exist. The acts are similar in content and form to that of the drag queen although, of course, from another perspective.

Question: What is known about the Chub community?
The defining characteristics of a Chub are that he is gay or bisexual and that he is overweight or obese. The former trait makes him, like other LGBs, at odds with much of the heterosexual majority. The latter compounds that by placing him outside of what the modern Western world views as beautiful. It is arguable that the standard of "thin" being an essential element of beauty is more entrenched in parts of homosexual male

community than it is in other parts of our society, but it is a pervasive standard in that larger society as well.

The Chub community began in the late 1960s and early 1970s as response to the liberation and sense of gay pride/power fostered by events such as the Stonewall riots and the socio/political activity that followed. It was also a response to the exclusion many Chubs felt at the hands of others in the gay community. For many in the gay community, just as in the larger society, beauty equates with worth.

All humans have the innate needs for acceptance, the feeling of self-worth and the feeling that we are valued by others. Our species tends to fill those needs in a variety of ways. One of these is simply associating with others who are like they are. Chubs are, of course, no exception.

Chubs found that when they were in a group of Chubs their weight was not an issue. Who they were as people and what their individual likes/dislikes were became the primary factors. They found in these groups not only camaraderie but also people who view them as physically attractive. Among these admirers are men who are not obese themselves but are attracted to those who are. These people are called "Chub Chasers".

The process of Chubs forming together into groups started in a few locations and has spread from coast to coast and even internationally. Chubs have certain local bars that they tend to frequent and social organizations such as Girth and Mirth that center less on the bar scene and more on gatherings like picnics, going to parties, having dinner together, going on cruises or even simple things like going to a movie together. Most chapters of Girth and Mirth are members of the umbrella group called the Affiliated Big Men's Clubs. Most charge a fee for membership. Chubs tend to be welcoming and accepting so anyone can attend a Chub function if they appreciate Chub culture.

Chub organizations also have regional and national events. The national event in the United States is called "Convergence". It is basically a circuit party in that it is held in a different city each year normally around Labor Day. Part of that is a competition among regional contestants for the national title of Mr. Chub International or Mr. Chaser International. There are also excursions of local points of interest, group activities and private parties. Things are normally toned down in public but that is not necessarily so at the private affairs. Naturally people who find each other attractive may pair off privately which, of course, is what gay men sometimes do.

All subgroups of the LGBT community have issues that relate particularly to them. Chubs are not the exception. They, as noted previously, often face disapproval and discrimination because of their size. Part of that may be that people point to the health issues that are common among people who are significantly overweight. These include coronary artery disease, osteoarthritis, type 2 diabetes, sleep apnea and hypertension.

Chubs are very aware of their size and that there may be medical issues related to that. They would be appreciative if you did not find the need to point it out to them. Physical characteristics define no one and personal worth has nothing to do with one's girth. All human beings are multi-dimensional and complex. It is an error to judge someone based solely on their appearance.

Question: What is known about the Bear community?

The Bear Community grew out of the Chub and Leather communities in the late 1980s (Wright, 2013; Hennen, 2008). It was a natural evolution in that both Chubs and Bears are typically large men. There are be some differences however. These differences separate the two communities in some ways and give each its own identity. The same is true for Bears and Leathermen.

The stereotypical Bear is a heavyset man who is hairy. He has some degree of facial hair and a hairy body. Some Bears wear leather, but most prefer working class kinds of clothing like denim jeans and cotton (commonly flannel) shirts. They tend to have a stereotypically masculine appearance both in what they wear and in their attitude. They celebrate being men. They celebrate being large.

While a Bear is usually heavyset they can also be lean or at least in decent shape physically. He might even be muscular. This does not mean that a Bear cannot be a Chub because there is some overlap in many cases. It simply means Bears tend to embrace the Bear identity and not the Chub one and they tend to conform to what that identity entails.

A Bear is, and overtly means to be, the incarnation of working class maleness. He typically does not worry about having a lean, chiseled body. He does not worry about looking young. He does not give a damn about what is in the pages of GQ. He does not care about the vintage of what he drinks but wants his beer cold and if it comes in a bottle rather than from a tap he does not need a glass.

There are several types of Bears. Cubs are younger Bears. Otters are furry men with a thinner frame. Muscle Bears are Bears with a muscular build. Polar Bears are men with gray or silver hair. A Ginger Bear is a man with red hair. A wolf is muscle Bear with a dominant disposition. A daddy Bear is an older man who has or wants to have a relationship with a cub. Some daddy Bears are dominant, and some are not. A dolphin is a Bear that has no fur. They are becoming easier to find but are still not what Bears usually look like. There are several other kinds of Bears too. What they all share however are certain values and an attitude.

Bears tend to travel in packs. They are typically friendly and accepting unless you mess with them. If you mess with one of them you should prepare to defend yourself against the entire pack because they will be giving you their attention. Some of them will not mind hurting you at that point.

While Bears present themselves as stereotypical working-class men they may really come from any walk of life and social class. Many are very well educated. Many are very computer and technology literate. What they share is a view of what it means to be masculine and a rejection of the gay male stereotype of being effeminate or trendy. They can join nearly seamlessly with heterosexual working-class males and can be nearly invisible among them.

The Bear community is primarily White. It has been reported that around 96% of Bears are Caucasian (Hennen, 2001). Several reasons for this have been suggested but note should be taken that other subgroups within the gay community are primarily White too. The clubber community is an example of that.

Studies of that phenomenon show that the reason for this is not usually racial discrimination but rather the product of how various races treat open homosexuals (Flores, 2009). Racial minority groups tend to be less accepting of that than Whites. Gay men of color, as a group, are more often faced with the choice of being known as an open member of the gay community or as a respected member of their family and racial group. Generally, it is simply harder for many men of color to associate with a group that is known to be gay. This however is changing.

Bears tend to congregate in their own bars and social organizations. Sometimes they can also be found sharing space with Chubs or Leathermen. They are probably the most commercialized subculture in gay America because you can buy just about anything with a paw print (the symbol of Bears) on it. They also often have their own local or regional events such as camping weekends and their own regional, national and international events such as the International Bear Rendezvous. These tend to be more raucous when they move out of the public view but are always fun if you enjoy the company of large, masculine men.

Bear functions tend to be social functions. Anyone that wants to come to one of these events is welcome so long as they appreciate and respect the Bear culture. Social functions may have a sexual element but that usually revolves around two guys hooking up after socializing or a spontaneous party rather than anything that is organized. In other words, these functions offer an environment that sex may evolve from. There is never any guarantee that if you go you will have sex...or that you won't.

Question: What is known about the BDSM community?
The BDSM community is known to its members as the "Scene" (spelled with a capital "S"). Calling it the "BDSM community" is technically not quite correct since many of its members are participants in some sort of fetish and/or kink but are not involved in BDSM (bondage, discipline, dominance/submission, sadism/masochism). The Scene may or may not involve sexual behavior and the sexual orientation of the participants may or may not matter in terms of what occurs in a scene.

To understand BDSM/Kink/Fetish relationships you must understand that a "scene" (spelled with a small "s") is a setting and a moment in time in which BDSM and/or kink activity takes place between a top and a bottom. One of the differences between the sadomasochist (S/M), the Dominant/submissive (D/s), the bondage and the kink communities is how the term "scene" is defined and what happens during one. The same act may have different motivations and effects depending upon whether it is done within an S/M, a D/s, a bondage or a kink relationship.

Understanding this world also entails knowing the difference between a Dom and a top and between a sub and a bottom. A Dom is a person who guides, controls or possibly owns a sub. A top is a person who is the active/penetrating partner in sex with a bottom or who is the active person in an S/M scene. A sub is a person who is guided, controlled or possibly owned by a Dom. A bottom is a person who is the receptive/penetrated partner in sex or who is the recipient of whatever happens in an S/M scene.

A Dom is typically also a top, but tops are sometimes not Doms. Likewise, a sub is usually also a bottom, but bottoms are commonly not subs. Tops and bottoms may trade roles back and forth (this is called a switch) but Doms and subs typically do not. A sub may become a Dom, or a Dom may (rarely) become a sub but there is never a switch.

SM relationships involve a scene in which one person (a top) is the active inflictor of pain and/or humiliation on another person (a bottom). They both derive pleasure from their roles in this. There is dominance and submission only in the sense that one person is the active inflictor of pain or humiliation during a scene and the other is the recipient but there is no servitude. There may be bondage in the sense that the bottom may be restrained to advance some other activity. There is fetish kink involved only to the extent that the participants agree to make it part of the scene, but it may not exist at all. The scene lasts for minutes or hours but after the scene is over the top and the bottom drop their role personas and have some other kind of relationship.

A bondage relationship is based on the pleasure one person gets from immobilizing another person through some sort of bondage technique and the pleasure the other person gets from being immobilized in that manner. Dominance and submission are involved only in the sense that the immobilized person is helpless and at the mercy of the person who bound them or, for that matter, anybody else that comes into the room. S/M or kink may or may not be involved but it is always secondary to the pleasure that comes from binding or being bound. Again, the scene only lasts for minutes or hours. Once it is over the people involved assume a different relationship.

A kink relationship primarily involves some activity that revolves around a sexual fetish. A sexual fetish is defined by the sexual or erotic stimulation a person gets from a physical object or a specific activity or situation. This includes a great many activities such as fisting, water sports, erotic piercing, wearing uniforms and role playing erotic situations. S/M, D/s and bondage may or may not be involved but it is secondary to or an enhancement of the fetish activity. A role play, for example, may be about a prisoner who is bound and dominated. This relationship lasts for minutes or hours and then the participants take on a different relationship.

D/s relationships are centered in a voluntary transfer of power and control. The submissive (sub) person relinquishes some or all the power and control he/she has over his existence. The Dominant (Dom) person accepts that power and control and takes on the responsibility of seeing to the subs welfare to the extent that the sub has agreed to it. This relationship is nearly always based upon a negotiated agreement (usually written) between the parties. A Dom or a sub can try to negotiate a change in the agreement unless the sub is a slave. A slave has no rights beyond the few that the contract calls for. The parties may live in this relationship on a 24/7 basis or it may be part time. The sub may or may not wear a collar.

There are several kinds of collars. The specifics related to collar types are beyond the scope of this book but there are two broad categories of collars: 1) BDSM related "play" collars which are functionally used as equipment in a BDSM scene and 2) status collars. There are no status collars in the pure S/M, B&D and kink worlds although they might exist if such a world is mixed with D/s elements. A status collar not only distinguishes the wearer as a D/s submissive (sub) but may also pinpoint the type of relationship he is in. Some of these collar types are recognized pretty much universally within D/s but others are not.

Each kind of status collar relates to a distinct situation and dynamic between people in the D/s world. A sub who has no current relationship with a Dominant (Dom) may still wear a collar. In other words, a sub can buy a collar and wear it to signify his/her status as a sub but that is not the tradition or general rule. This is because custom says that Doms are the true owners of collars. A collar is almost always owned by a Dom. The sub who wears a self-purchased collar is stopping Doms who may be interested in him/her from acting on that interest because it says the wearer is taken and therefore not available.

A sub typically gets to wear a collar only after accepting it from a Dom. Once the collar is accepted the Dom, in most cases, holds the exclusive rights to both the collar and the sub. If a Dom/sub relationship ends custom requires that a collar be returned to the Dom that owns it. The Dom is not supposed to use that collar again to collar someone else or to give it away.

People within the BDSM world are normal human beings so they tend to interact with others who have similar interests and identities. They typically have "play" partners and they often belong to a BDSM related club. Clubs commonly have gatherings such as "munches" or play parties. A munch is a public, nonsexual social gathering of like-minded people. A play party is a private gathering during which BDSM, kink and/or fetish activity will take place. Joining one of these groups removes some degree of privacy but it also eases learning about the BDSM world and finding others with similar interests. They can also offer a safer "play" environment.

There are websites that cater to the interests of BDSM, kink, fetish or D/s people. Some sites are better than others. Even the good ones have problematic users. FetLife.com seems to be one of the more highly rated ones. This is not a dating site but rather one that lets you find out what is happening near you and meet real people. Most dating websites allow a user to make a BDSM related profile.

The BDSM world is very diverse and tolerant. There are rules however that tend to be staunchly adhered to. Among them are:
1. Play must be between consenting adults and those involved must be capable of freely and knowingly consenting.
2. Play must be done safely, and the bottom must have a "safe word" that will instantly stop a scene.
3. It is impolite touch anyone or their things without permission.
4. Pseudonyms are often used in this world. Use whatever name or pronoun a person prefers when addressing them or talking about them. Don't use their real name at BDSM gatherings without their permission and do not use their pseudonym in public.
5. Don't take pictures without the permission of those involved.
6. Don't take on a scene or a D/s role without negotiating it first.

There is some debate about whether the BDSM community is part of the LGBT community. Most of its members are heterosexual after all and being LGBT may not be a factor in the activity of a participant. It is clear however that most of these people are part of our community because even if they are not LGBT they are LGBT allies.

It is also clear that mere membership within the BDSM community does not single out a person as mentally unhealthy (Wismeijer and van Assen, 2013; Richters and de Visser, 2008; Connoly, 2006). The Diagnostic and Statistical Manual of Mental Disorders, ed. 5 (DSM-5) of the American Psychiatric Association agrees that BDSM activity is not a psychological problem unless it causes a person significant distress or impairs his/her functioning.

Question: What is known about the Leather community?

The gay Leather community began at the end of World War II as an outgrowth of biker clubs in Los Angeles and San Francisco and rather rapidly spread across the United States and Europe. The movement was propelled by a lot of gay men who did not like being associated with the stereotype of gay men being effeminate and wanted to present a much more masculine image. They also did not like much of mainstream culture's idea of "go along to get along" and, like the bikers they emulated, preferred the image of an outsider. It was natural therefore that Leathermen took on the masculine look of bikers, policemen and military men and that BDSM and various form of sexual kink was embraced.

Originally the Leather community was entirely male. It also was based upon strict adherence to a set of protocols and a well-defined formal power structure. New members had to be sponsored by an established member and had to start as a pledge or trainee. They worked their way up in the hierarchy whether they wanted to or not. There was no switching of roles between a Dominate/top and a submissive/bottom. Trainees were always bottoms and subservient to a Dom/top. Eventually the pledge would become a "senior" and would then be assigned to a master who he served. Over time he was expected to also become a Dom/Master and a Top.

Few Leathermen now use all this system which is called "Old Guard". "New Guard" rules for the most part replaced the "Old Guard" during the 1990s. Many clubs and individual Leathermen still use parts of the Old Guard way however. This results in a situation in which customs and definitions vary from place to place depending upon what mixture of Old Guard and New Guard exists locally.

Generally, a person now can join a club without being sponsored and can become an officer in the club relatively quickly. A member can take on the role of a top or of a bottom or even switch back and forth. A sub can continue as a sub if that is what he wants, and a Dom does not necessarily have to ever be a sub. Ageism has never been an issue in this community.

Many in the New Guard welcome women into their community. Many women have responded to that by embracing the Leather and BDSM cultures. Some of them have joined clubs or formed their own Leather clubs. They are sometimes even found in bars that were once entirely a male domain. This typically does not extend into gay Leather bars and clubs however. The presence of Leatherwomen is mostly seen in lesbian or heterosexual leather clubs and bars and in establishments that cater to a mixed crowd.

The Leather community is not just gay anymore. Most of the members of this community are heterosexual or bisexual. The gay Leather community is one of the subcultures within the larger Leather, BDSM and gay communities. Domination/submission (D/s), bondage and discipline (B&D), Sadism/Masochism (S/M), fetishism and/or other forms of kink are still practiced by many members but not by all.

In some ways, the Leather community has more rules than other communities but in other ways it is a lot freer. There are, for example, expectations about how to behave while watching or taking part in a scene but at the same time there is little or nothing within the realm of sexuality between consenting adults that is taboo. The central rules are that everyone should be treated with respect and that activities must be safe, sane and consensual. That means participants must be adults that have the physical and mental capacity to consent, know the risks involved and freely do consent to taking part in the activity.

Relationships within the gay Leather world is an area that may confound a person that is new to this reality because it has a wider range than is typically found in the other LGBT communities. This community has the casual sex, roommate, lover, "fuck buddy", boyfriend and spouse relationships found elsewhere in the gay male universe although the Leatherman's version of them might be a little different because his values and tastes may be different. It also has relationships that are foreign to and largely misunderstood by the vanilla world.

The relationship types that the Leather world is known for are probably the ones based on the power or authority transfer found in Dominance and submission (D/s). There are three major kinds of D/s relationships in the gay male Leather world: Master/slave, Sir/boy and Daddy/boy. Each is distinct from the others.

The M/s relationship is usually based upon a mutually agreed upon written contract which spells out the duties and rights of each party. It may call for the relationship to be part-time or 24/7. Part-time ones vary in how much control and submission is involved when the two are apart. Each Master/slave relationship is different from all other ones because of the differences in what each contract calls for and what each Master and slave brings into the relationship.

Theoretically, a Master is in complete control of every aspect of the slave's life. The slave has only the freedoms his Master and his contract give him, so he can better see to the needs/desires of the Master or function publically in society. He has no vocalized opinion on anything unless his Master asks for it and no property. That includes the slave's body which is owned, controlled and used by the Master within the limits of the contract. He typically does have the right to bring disagreements about the contract to a third party when he feels the Master is violating it.

A slave usually keeps legal authority over his finances but actual day-to-day authority over the use of those assets is often overseen or managed by the Master. Slaves commonly have a job but may not have control of the money he earns from it. A slave is theoretically a slave for life. Slaves can be sold, passed to another owner or inherited. A true slave will cooperate in that. It is common however for slaves to transition out of slavery if they become unhappy with it.

A more common sort of D/s relationship is the Sir/boy or the Daddy/boy relationship. The term "boy" as used here does not connote anything to do with age but rather refers to an adult man who is deferential and even submissive to his Dom. The level of deference or submission depends upon whether the relationship is Sir/boy or Daddy/boy. A boy will call any Dom "sir" even if he's not in a relationship with him.

A boy serves his Sir by seeing to the Dom's needs and comfort. He is probably sexually intimate with his Dom. He also probably wears a collar that signifies he is taken (not available) and he probably is learning the rules of the culture and techniques of BDSM and/or kink by being on the receiving end of it. He may or may not be owned but a Sir is always stricter with his boy than a Daddy is. This relationship is usually based upon a mutually agreed upon contract.

A Daddy/boy relationship is centered on the Dom teaching and offering experiences and balance. The boy is learning and working to find his place in the Leather world and to perhaps also find his place in the world at large. Boys are expected serve the Dom, to do what they are told as a means of learning and to appropriately ask questions for the same reason. He is not property thus not owned like a slave is and the relationship is not completely centered on his service to the Dom. It is a tradeoff. Each person gives and gets based upon what is negotiated by the parties involved.

As noted above, D/s relationships are usually governed by rules the people involved negotiate and agree upon. There is often one set of rules (protocols) that are used in private and another set that are used in public. It is also guided by the rules of their club. The boy is nearly always expected to either be in school or have a job.

A D/s relationship may last months or years but, like all relationships, it may end. The negotiated, written agreement between a Dom and a boy nearly always has a specified time limit although it is renewable. Doms understand that their boy may want to become a Dom too and they celebrate that transition. At the same time, they understand that some people will not find happiness in that. No real Leatherman thinks less of a person because he is a sub.

It surprises people sometimes when they learn that the Leathermen they may view as sexually and socially intemperate are rather conservative where respect, honor and loyalty are concerned. Not abiding by their written agreement, quickly throwing off a committed relationship or, worse, going from relationship to relationship runs against that ideal. In this ideal Leathermen are as traditional and staid as a Southern Baptist preacher.

It is reasonable perhaps to think that all people in the Leather community wear leather, but this is not true. For most people wearing leather is a means of self-expression and being in a Leather oriented group is a matter of socializing and sharing values. Some in the Leather community never wear leather at all but socialize and connect with the community none the less. Other people within this community choose to wear fetish gear, uniforms, western (cowboy) gear or clothing reminiscent of motor cycle gangs.

Men new to the Leather world can get gear on their own but sometimes items will be awarded to a man by a Dom or a club. When purchased by the individual himself, it should be bought with the help of someone who is familiar with the Leather world and with the quality, fit and function of what is worn in that world.

The new man can buy Levi 501 blue jeans (some clubs accept black) and plain white or black t-shirts. Footwear should be heavy black boots (usually military style) or plain masculine looking cowboy boots. Most Leathermen have at least one leather vest. He also has some black belts. Most of these are plain except for possibly the buckle. The leather of a Leatherman is always well cared for. A man who is a sub or planning to be one should buy nothing without the permission and guidance of his Dom.

It is not at all unusual to see Leathermen wearing a harness on his torso. The purpose of any harness worn by a Dom or top is to display masculinity and to make the man look good. A bottom or sub wants that too, but he commonly wears one that has functional, well-secured straps that can be used by a top to hold onto during sex. Doms won't allow their harness to enable someone else to control or use their body. That is why you won't see them wearing a harness style that has a strap going between the legs or that has rings, grommets or snaps that allow things to be attached.

As noted above, many gay Leathermen (and Leatherwomen) have their own clubs and social organizations. Some meet in public bars while others have private or semiprivate clubs. Typically, a Leather club or bar will have the Leather culture's flag (black and blue stripes with a white stripe in the middle and a heart in the upper left corner) on a wall. The Leather culture also has magazines and websites that are specifically directed at its members and at those who are interested in it. The Leather community has its own national/international events as well. Among these are the Folsom Street Fair in San Francisco and the International Mr. Leather contest that is held annually in Chicago.

It is common for local clubs to have their own events too. That might be a "run", a "munch", a play party, a black party, a ceremony, a contest or other gathering. A run is a Leather community event that is traveled to and often involves various clubs meeting somewhere. A munch is a public or private social that usually involves food and drink but usually does not involve sex or kink. A play party is a private gathering that revolves around sex and/or BDSM/fetish activity. A black party is a Leather themed party that is open to anyone who wants to come. It usually involves BDSM and fetish activity, people having sex and the consumption of drugs and alcohol. Those who do not want to do that are still welcome to come if they are open to that kind of experience.

Gay Leather bars are a lot like other gay bars. There is usually rock or country music playing, a television set, a dart board and a pool table. Some serve simple kinds of food, but alcohol is the main thing consumed. The bar usually has a happy hour, and most have discount nights where beer is a bit cheaper than it normally is. Some have a patio which is where most guys go to socialize when they want a smoke. Most Leather bars do not have a cover charge unless something special is scheduled and that seems to happen at least a couple times a month. Like all bars, a Leather bar is a place where you can have a drink, a conversation and relax.

Gay bars commonly have difficulty staying in business both because the local authorities are hostile to them and because they do not have enough patrons to make the place work financially. This is even more the case for many Leather gay bars. In response to that bar owners commonly have Leather nights or Leather events on the calendar on a part-time basis. The rest of the time the bar is a regular gay bar or a regular bar. In other cases, a Leather bar may become formally or informally a club that members support with patronage and dues. It is not unusual for gay Leathermen and gay Bears to share a bar. There is, in fact, a branch of the gay Leathermen called "Leather Bears".

There are, of course, differences between a Leather bar and other bars. The first one is that they have a dress code. Some enforce the code all the time while others do so on certain nights. When the code is not in force you can wear pretty much anything you want to so long as it is clean and not disruptive. When the code is in force patrons must dress to match those requirements. That typically means patrons must wear leather outfits or leather and blue jeans but that is often expanded by the house to include uniforms, fetish wear or even just underwear or a jockstrap.

Most gay Leather bars have the lights dimmed. They often have dark corners and darker out of sight places where patrons can go to entertain themselves with a willing someone. Some also have a backroom that is used for events like demonstrations of various kinds of kink, bondage or instructional lessons in that. This room might also be used by a top to conduct an S/M "scene" which can be watched by the others in the bar.

Should you happen to accept an opportunity to watch one of these scenes there are rules that should be followed. These may vary from place to place but there are general ones that are widely accepted.

It is customary practice to not go to watch a scene unless you have been invited. You can ask for an invitation but in Leather culture "no" always means "no" and that decision must be respected. You should stay quiet while watching the scene. You should not smoke, talk or do anything else that might disrupt the scene. You can briefly respond to something the top or dungeon master says directly to you but not to anything the bottom says. The dungeon master's word is law. You should never at any time be between the top and the bottom or position yourself so that you interfere with what is happening in the scene. That certainly means that you can never be in the top's playing space unless he invites you. You can leave anytime you like but you are expected to slip out quietly. You may find the scene to be sexually stimulating but it is unacceptable to do anything sexual while watching the scene.

If you are not part of the Leather culture and you want to go to a Leather bar it is probably best, at least for the first few times, to go with a Leatherman that you know or a friend of yours knows. It probably would work out fine if you went alone because the Leather culture values the ideals of everyone deserving respect, sex being done only when it is consensual and not intentionally scaring vanillas. The atmosphere of the bar will change when you walk in however because you are an unknown, uninvited outsider coming into Leatherman territory. If you go with a Leatherman, then you become an invited guest and your host can run interference for you if that is necessary.

You should expect some or all the guys in the bar to check you out. These guys are just as gay as you are, so you should not be surprised if one or two of them cruise you. It is normal if you feel intimidated and a bit lost because you do not know what you should or should not do and you may have heard the stereotype that Leathermen are potentially aggressive. You should therefore ask for and follow your friend's advice about what is or is not okay. There are also some general rules that you should know before you go into a Leather club or bar.

1. If you are not part of the Leather culture you should not wear leather into this place because it may be taken as disrespectful. Instead wear something that looks conservative and masculine. Wearing a leather jacket is alright if it is brown or black, masculine looking and not designer made.
2. Experienced Leathermen will take what you wear as a message. Ill-fitting leather, wearing the wrong kind of leather and leather worn incorrectly will be taken as the mark of a wannabe. Poorly cared for clothing signifies the wearer lacks discipline and self-respect. Wearing bright colors or designer clothing may be taken as being effeminate. Flashy shoes are completely out of place here and show you are clueless. The content and location of visible tattoos and piercings will be noticed. Things worn on the right side (e.g. keys or an earring) may be taken to mean the person is a bottom while things worn on the left side may signify a top.

3. Don't wear cologne or scented personal care products.
4. Stay in control of yourself. Don't get drunk. Domestic beer is usually a good choice. Drink it out of the bottle unless it was on tap.
5. Don't touch anyone or their things unless you have permission.
6. Don't do anything like lighting someone's cigarette or going to the bar to get a round of drinks because that will be taken as service. That's a sub's job.
7. Be honest about your lack of experience in the Leather world and about your interest in it. You will easily find Leathermen who will appreciate your interest and honesty and who will be willing to help. Don't go home with any of them however until you know them better.
8. Don't ask anyone personal questions like what they do for a living, where they work, where they live and so on. Understand that Leathermen often use a different name and persona when they are in the Leather world than they do at other times. That name and persona is all you need to know.
9. Treat everyone with respect.
10. Don't be rude or pushy because that won't end well for you.
11. If someone hits on you politely say "no" even if you are interested. You can come back after you have thought about the offer and had the chance to privately ask your friend about it. When a Leatherman takes you home it may involve things beyond anything you are used to.
12. If you do something wrong you are expected to sincerely apologize by saying (without excuses) what you did wrong, that you are sorry for doing it and that you will not do it again. You can also politely explain misunderstandings.

The definition of acceptable behavior in a gay Leather bar/club and in the Leather culture generally is based on good manners, club rules and what a person's status is. Subs must be respectful to Doms. Doms are expected to behave as Doms when dealing with subs and to give other Doms respect.

Subs can usually freely interact with other subs, but collared subs do not usually interact with Dom's without permission. To interact with a collared sub or a slave you should first get the permission of his Dom. If someone standing next to you is giving you his attention but saying nothing, he is probably an uncollared sub who identifies you as a Dom and is waiting for you to start talking. A slave probably won't talk to anyone without his Dom's okay.

Cruel Doms are often tolerated by their peers but never held in esteem. The same goes for submissives who are not deferential Doms or who bring shame to their Dom or to the club. Having respect in this world has nothing to do with being a Dom or a sub. It is about a person's behavior and attitude.

The word that gives the sub/bottom true power is "no" because in the BDSM and Leather worlds "no" is expected to be honored. An experienced bottom will always tell his top what his limits are, and those limits will almost always be respected. A bottom always has the right to stop BDSM scenes whenever he feels he must do so. A sub always has the right to refuse to accept a collar from a Dom.

A good Dom does not often hear his sub say "no" because as a Dom he honors the contract he and his sub agreed to and he communicates with his sub a lot. He listens to the input of others. A Dom always considers the welfare and desires of his sub. At the same time a good Dom makes sure that the sub always knows who is in charge and who is making the decisions. He will use the tool of punishment if that is needed.

The behavior of a sub always reflects on his Dom. The Dom is always personally responsible for that behavior and for the good or ill that behavior causes. Poor behavior on the part of a sub should be reported to his Dom but only that Dom can correct it or punish the sub unless that Dom gives his permission for it to be otherwise. If the Dom does not correct his sub other Doms will probably give him feedback suggesting that it should be done.

Old Guard rules allowed a top to do pretty much what he wanted to do to a bottom once he got him home. Under New Guard protocol the top and the bottom negotiate about what will happen in a general way. They outline what they like to do and do not like to do and have at least a broad agreement about what will and will not happen during a scene. They also reveal any health or personal issues that may affect the scene. The top's job is to make sure the bottom is safe and that the only things that happen to him are things he has consented to.

It is wise for a bottom to make sure the top he has hooked up with is a man of his word and that someone knows where he is when he is with a top. This is important because he may be at the mercy of the top if he is put in restraints or the top ignores their agreement. There are tops who believe their experience allows them to take a bottom passed the edge of the bottom's stated limits. This is a form of edge play. There is some debate within the Leather community about whether doing that is ethical.

It is very important to remember that a Leatherman is part of the Leather culture because he accepts that identity but that is not all of what he is. His identity has many sides in the same way that every other human being does. In most ways, he is probably not very different from those around him. He has the same basic kind of needs and wants that other humans do. He simply chooses to fulfill some of them in a way that is different from most other people. Those differences do not make him weird or dangerous. Most Leathermen have no desire to hurt anyone unless they want him to. Acknowledging his differences and acting on them does make him honest however.

Question: Who else is in the LGBT community?
The gay community is not just a bunch of gay subcultures that have been brought together because of common values and issues since you don't have to be gay to be part of this community. Its foundation is the principle that basic civil rights and liberty are fundamental to all people regardless of sexual orientation or gender identity. All you must do is believe that basic principal and act on it. You can do that as an individual or as part of a group.

There are a lot of organizations that are part of the gay community because they share that belief. Among these are:
- Accord Alliance (Intersex advocacy & support)
- ACT UP (HIV/AIDs Advocacy)
- Affirmation: LGBT Mormons, Families & Friends
- American Veterans for Equal Rights
- Athlete Ally (Education & advocacy in sports)
- BiNet USA (Bisexual advocacy & support)
- Campus Pride (College student support)
- Children of Lesbians and Gays Everywhere (COLAGE)
- Equality Federation (Social justice)
- GLBTQ Legal Advocates & Defenders (GLAD)
- Gay and Lesbian Medical Association (GLMA)
- Gay & Lesbian Victory Fund (Political candidate support)

- GLAAD (Advocacy & support)
- GSA Network (Racial & social justice)
- Human Rights Campaign (HRC) (Social justice)
- Immigration Equality
- interact (Intersex youth advocacy)
- Keshet (Jewish social justice)
- Lambda Legal (Civil rights & law)
- Matthew Shepard Foundation (Advocacy & support)
- National Black Justice Coalition (NBJC) (Civil rights)
- National Center for Lesbian Rights (NCLR)
- National Center for Transgender Equality
- National LGBT Chamber of Commerce
- National LGBTQ Task Force (Advocacy & support)
- Out & Equal (Workplace equality)
- OutServe (U.S. military support)
- Parents and Friends of Lesbians and Gays (PFLAG)
- Point Foundation (College financial aid)
- Pride Foundation (Advocacy & college financial aid)
- Services & Advocacy for GLBT Elders (SAGE)
- Transgender Law Center
- The Williams Project (Education & advocacy)

Many corporations are also part of the gay community because they support equality. The Human Rights Campaign Foundation (HCR) publishes a report card each year on corporate America in terms of whether they treat their gay, lesbian, bisexual and transgender employees equally with other employees. Many corporations, such as Boeing, Alaska Airlines, Levi Strauss, U.S. Bancorp, and Microsoft do so in a way that earned a rating of 100% in 2017. Other major corporations such as Farmers Insurance, Dick's Sporting Goods, Bed, Bath & Beyond and Las Vegas Sands Corp earned a score of less than 50 out of 100. Several corporations such as Tractor Supply Company, News Corp and DISH Network got a score of zero.

Some corporations support the gay community economically by contributing to organizations that act to support gay equality. As an example, Lambda Legal (a network of lawyers who work both inside and outside of the courtroom in support of equal rights for gays) is supported by several corporations. Among these are American Airlines, MasterCard, GILEAD, Pillsbury, and AARP.

Americans tend to give religious institutions low marks in how they deal with LBGT people and issues, so it may come as a surprise to some that many churches are also part of the gay community. Religion is sometimes thought of negatively in our community because we only hear about the fundamentalists of all religions who regularly and loudly condemn gays and others who are not like them. They however are not the voice of religion. Religion has several voices. Some of them are gay friendly and some are not. Our community should embrace gay affirming and/or accepting religious people and organizations. These people and organizations can, perhaps better than others, make the point that fundamentalists are not the face of religion.

Chapter 4
Gays and Religion

Question: What is religion and why might gays want to be religious?
Religion in its broadest sense is any system of fervently held beliefs or principles related to mankind's relationship with the force(s) governing the universe. In the narrower more sectarian sense it is a system of beliefs and practices related to the serving and worship of a god, gods or some other spiritual essence. Religion is universal in humankind in that it is found in every culture on earth.

Some say the need to worship or acknowledge a higher power is innate in the human species. Others say that religion is universal because it is highly functional in terms of fulfilling the social, psychological and political needs of those within our species. While the former view can be debated at length, the latter is clearly true. We see this as we look at the hierarchy of human needs as offered by the psychologist Abraham Maslow.

Among the needs all human beings share is the need to feel secure, the need to belong to a group, the need to be accepted by others and the need to self-actualize so that one's full potential is realized (Maslow, 1954). Religion offers an avenue to these. It is thus of value to straights and gays alike.

Belief in a higher power may offer the individual the anxiety and stress reducing sense that even if things are beyond what he can manage, they are not beyond what their deity can manage or at least that there is some reason for what is happening. Religion allows an individual to see himself as a member of a group, to interact socially within the group and to then take on the norms of that group as his own. Through the religious group and its norms, he has the chance to gain the esteem of others. It also allows the individual the possibility that he might grow as a person so that his evolving belief system might become the basis for solving problems that are outside of him in a way that is independent of his culture.

Homosexuals are normal human beings so naturally we have the same needs as our heterosexual brothers and sisters do. We have the potential to fill those needs in the same way others do also. This naturally may include taking on religious beliefs and associating with others with who have similar beliefs.

A survey done in 2009 showed that 72% of all Americans and 60% of gays hold religious faith as important in their lives. At the same time gays are only half as likely to go to church as straight people are (Barna, 2009). Many of we LGBTs feel judged or simply do not feel welcome in a church, so we do not go. The operative questions then become: 1) Where can the gay person go to fulfill his/her natural needs through affiliation with a religion and 2) What is the status of a homosexual within the context of religion. Helping the reader answer those questions is the purpose of this chapter.

Question: Is religion antigay?
As will be shown below, some religions are antigay, and others are gay friendly.

Question: Is homosexuality a sin?
In the religious sense sin is the violation of divine law. For sin to exist its necessary parts must exist. Those parts are: 1) The actual existence of a deity or deities, 2) The actual existence of an expression of a deity's will and 3) a violation of that will.

If the second part exists the third can be taken as a given since human history clearly shows that, regardless of who issues it, if a rule exists someone will break it. If the first part exists, the second part is possible but not proven since logic shows both that a deity could have rules with or without them being known and that a deity could exist but not have rules. The second and third parts are meaningless however until we prove the first part: the actual existence of a deity or deities.

Human beings have two general ways of proving things. The first is an "a posteriori" proof which is dependent upon experience and empirical evidence. The other is an "a priori" proof which is based purely on reasoning and independent of experience and observation. Multiple philosophers have shown that mankind's experience and powers of perception are so flawed that they cannot be relied upon in the pursuit of truth. A few a priori arguments alleging proof of the existence or non-existence of a deity(s) have been offered but none has been accepted universally as true. This is the nub of why religion is based on belief instead of objective fact. We cannot objectively prove or disprove the existence of a deity.

Religionists of all types will assert that they have a factual, uncorrupted expression of their deity's existence and will and that it can be found in the holy texts of their religion. They will also insist that their holy texts say what will happen because of following or not following that law. All of that is problematic because none of it can be proven without first accepting the tenants of their faith.

What can be proven is that through some process that may or may not involve a deity a very diverse range of life exists on our planet. Each of these life forms has a range of characteristics that is natural and normal for it. Human beings are one of those life forms, so we naturally have a range of characteristics that are normal for us. Among those characteristics are a variety of sexual orientations that are not unique to our species.

This variation in orientation has existed for around 200,000 years. It is not the root of any kind of harm to anything on the planet. It can be objectively shown that it is in fact a positive adaptation that enhances the chance of survival of any species that has it. The biological factors that produce it have not been extinguished through natural selection or any other natural process. If a deity exists and it has a will then variation among and within all species is clearly part of it. No sexual orientation is a sin.

Question: How do Christians view homosexuality?
Around 73% of Americans label themselves as being Christian. That includes the forty-two percent of LGBT Americans who do so (Pew, 2013). There are many denominations or sects of this religion each of which assert some views that are distinctly different from the other branches of the faith. There are some core beliefs however that all or at least most Christians hold as true.

The primary prerequisite of the Christian faith is the belief in the person, the spirit and the message of Jesus Christ. All mainstream Christian religions believe in the death, resurrection and ascension of Christ and in Christ's second coming which will bring forth the Day of Judgment and the salvation of those who have been faithful. Most Christian faiths also believe that Christ is part of the Trinity of God the Father, His Son and the Holy

Spirit which is within the being of God. A large majority of Christians accept the Bible as a holy book although not all accept it as the literal, unerring word of God.

Christianity however has not come together as one on the matter of homosexuality. Various views on the subject can be found within it. Central to this disagreement is whether the Bible is to be taken literally as the unerring word of God or as a spiritually pure but physically imperfect holy book. Parallel to that is the disagreement about how the Bible is to be interpreted and what exactly the Bible's teachings are. When looked at in context then homosexuality becomes one of many areas of disagreement all of which flow back to the same central issues.

You cannot therefore say that Christianity per se has any view about homosexuality. You can only say that this branch has this view and that branch has that view. Each branch, of course, thinks it is right but none has the right to speak for the others. None can say it speaks for Christianity. It can only say it speaks for a specific branch.

Question: Does the Christian and/or the Hebrew Bible condemn homosexuality?

There are various versions of the Christian and Hebrew Bibles. All versions have verses that at least some factions say condemn homosexuality. In the Old Testament, they are Genesis 19, Leviticus 18:22, and Leviticus 20:13. In the New Testament they are Romans 1:26-27, I Corinthians 6:9-10, I Timothy 1:9-10 and Jude 1:7.

Genesis 19 is the story of the destruction of the cities of Sodom and Gomorrah which has historically been used to persecute gays. There is no archeological proof that those places ever existed (Greenberg, 2000; Mulder, 1992; Miller and Hayes, 1986). The Bible says in Genesis 19:24, Deut. 29:23, Hosea 11:8, and Jude 1:7 that there were two other cities (Admah and Zeboim) that were destroyed with Sodom and Gomorrah. Those cities have not been found either. That of course is not the same as showing these cities did not exist. Either way the story is in the Bible. Some sources say the story is a myth (Carden, 2004; Greenberg, 2000).

Fundamentalists sometimes point to the ruins of the ancient cities of Bab edh-Dhra and Nameira as being the ruins of Sodom and Gomorrah, but this has never been accepted as creditable by most nonsectarian archeologists. Various other locations for Sodom and Gomorrah have been offered but none has been proven. That of course does not stop religionists from claiming the cities have been found and that their ruins support the Genesis account. The available evidence does not support these claims.

Even if we accept the existence of Sodom and Gomorrah as real cities which were destroyed by God it does not mean homosexuality was the reason for that destruction. The Bible, in fact, makes clear in Isaiah 1, Ezekiel 16:49-50, Jeremiah 23:14 and Amos 4:11 that those cities were destroyed because of pride, greed, sloth, not giving hospitality to travelers, the failure to help the needy and the poor and for, in so doing, turning away from God. Christ himself refers in Matthew 10 to the inhospitable nature of Sodom and Gomorrah. If this view is accepted, then Genesis 19 does not condemn homosexuality.

It is noteworthy that God decides to destroy these cities in Genesis 18 but the alleged attempt to sexually assault Lot's male guests does not happen until the next chapter. Obviously, these cities were guilty in God's eyes of something before that happened. We see in the verses noted above that Sodom and Gomorrah were known for being inhospitable to travelers and that was viewed at the time as a great sin. It is also noteworthy that the cities of Admah and Zeboim were destroyed with Sodom and Gomorrah despite having nothing whatever to do with the attempted sexual assault on Lot's guests.

Some historians place the date of the destruction of Sodom and Gomorrah in the early second millennium (2300-2000 BC). Biblical chronologies place Abraham (who pleaded with God to spare the cities) at circa 2166-1991 BC or circa 1952 BC (Rose, 2005). Nonsectarian authorities however say the facts offered in the Bible place him in the Iron Age (1200-550 BC) (Van Seters, 1976; Thompson, 1974) and many say his existence is fiction (Moore & Kelle, 2011; Finkelstein & Silberman, 2001; Graves & Patai, 1964). The story of Sodom and Gomorrah therefore cannot be literally true. In this case the story is in the Bible but the facts that refute it are in it too.

Leviticus gives the Law of Moses concerning male homosexual sexual behavior. Leviticus 18:22 (King James Version) says, "Thou shalt not lie with mankind, as with womankind: it is abomination". Leviticus 20:13 says a violation of that law must result in death. Even if you accept these verses as rational there are two problems that persist.

First is that the Law of Moses applies to Jews but not to Christians. The religious law for Christians was formulated around 50 A.D. at the Council of Jerusalem. That law is called the Apostolic Decree and is found in Acts 15:5-29. It bans eating anything previously sacrificed to an idol, eating any animal that was strangled, eating blood and all acts of porneia.

"Porneia" is one of the Greek words used in the Bible to refer to forbidden sexual behavior(s). It has several definitions and how it is defined decides what it condemns. When conservatives read Acts 15 they find a ban of all sexual behavior outside of a valid heterosexual marriage. When progressives read it, they find a ban against harlotry, adultery and incest but nothing about homosexuality. Acts 15 therefore may or may not condemn homosexuality.

Secondly, many Bible scholars say the word "abomination" as we understand it now does not exist in the original Bible text because the word "toevah" was mistranslated. They assert the Bible does not say that same-sex sexual behavior per se is a "sin" but rather that it is an unclean temple practice that is not allowed by God (Robinson, 2009; Helminiak, 2000; Kellogg, 1900).

This is better understood when one knows that at that time some non-Jewish religions such as Ashtoreth worship had male and female temple prostitutes. The ancient Hebrews reviled these prostitutes (see Deut. 23:18-19) and viewed them as unclean. Had the authors of Leviticus meant to condemn all same-sex sexual behavior they would have used the word "zimah", which means "sin" and not the word "toevah" which means "unclean" (Helminiak, 2000). If this view is accepted, then homosexuality per se is not condemned in Leviticus.

Only ten nations on earth follow the practice of killing gays. That practice comes from their use of Muslim Sharia law. The penalty is therefore not based on the Christian or Hebrew Bible. No Christian or Jewish majority country supports killing homosexuals.

Paul wrote the condemnation of homosexual behavior found in Romans and 1st Corinthians. He influenced (posthumously) the ones found in 1st Timothy and Jude. He is the only major figure in the New Testament that mentions it in any context. He spoke/wrote about sex repeatedly. He did so because he believed celibacy was the best choice for those that wanted to go to heaven. He said the end of days would happen in his lifetime and only those who were pure could enter God's kingdom. He saw heterosexual sex outside of marriage and homosexual sex as disqualifying.

There are many instances in which Paul contradicted Christ or taught ideas that neither Christ nor the Apostles ever mention. As a result, what he taught is called "Pauline Christianity". He, for example, created the idea of original sin (Romans 5: 12-21 & 1st Corinthians 15:22) which was not actually religious doctrine anywhere until the 2nd century A.D. when Irenaeus, the Bishop of Lyons, made it so. The idea of original sin is therefore in the Bible but it's not a teaching of Christ or any of his twelve disciples.

The same is true of homosexuality. Paul wrote at least 13 of the 27 books in the New Testament. His very negative view of homosexual behavior is therefore in the Bible. In Romans 1:26-27 he casts homosexuals in with murderers, haters of God, backbiters, boasters, liars, fornicators and those who disobeyed their parents. He branded these people as apostates which simply means they had left the faith. He preached that God allows apostates to choose wicked behaviors and that in so choosing they were doomed to hell.

It is worth noting that Paul is seen by Jews as either an apostate and a charlatan or as a bridge between Judaism and Christianity. Muslims view him as a deceiver. Thomas Jefferson wrote that Paul was the first corrupter of Christ's teachings (Jefferson, 1820). Nothing written by Paul is in the Jefferson Bible because of that.

The bottom line is that fundamentalist Christians have generalized the few verses in the Bible that may be interpreted as banning homosexual behavior so that they become an overarching principle. They contend that all male homosexuality is banned. In fact, only penetrative anal sex is forbidden even under the most conservative construction of what the Bible says. A great many homosexuals never do that.

Question: What was Jesus Christ's view about homosexuality?

Some religionists say we know he was opposed to it because he spoke against adultery, sexual immorality and fornication and because he was a practicing Jew. We do not really know his view however because he is not recorded as having ever mentioned it. When Christ spoke about sexual matters it was nearly always within the context of marriage. He was a staunch supporter of that institution and of marital fidelity. The closest he ever came to mentioning homosexuals is in Matthew 19:11-12 which is also a statement about marriage. He says there that some men are born with no interest in women and he spoke positively about that. He is also recorded to have supported ideas that were contrary to traditional Jewish practices so the fact that he was a Jew holds no weight in this debate.

Question: What does the Roman Catholic Church say about homosexuality?

The Roman Catholic Church is the largest unified branch of Christianity in America. Roman Catholicism does not view homosexuality per se as sinful but rather sees homosexual desire, which is a hallmark of being gay, as being a disorder. It views homosexual acts, whether done by gays, bisexuals or heteros, as against nature and therefore sinful. It welcomes openly gay members, but gays cannot receive the sacrament of Holy Communion until after they have properly repented. It denies homosexuals most of the other sacraments on the same basis. It does not ordain openly gay men into the clergy and does not support gay marriage. Around 14% of LGBT Americans and 22% of all Americans are Roman Catholic (Pew, 2013).

Roman Catholics divide sin along the lines of mortal sin and venial sin. A mortal sin instantly separates the sinner from the grace of God and, unless repented correctly, condemns the sinner to hell. For an act to be a mortal sin it must be a grave matter and done deliberately and knowingly by the sinner. Homosexual acts are mortal sins but can be forgiven through the Sacrament of Reconciliation. Part of that is the repentance of the sinner and the commitment to not sin again. In other words, the homosexual would have to become celibate.

The Church calls upon all homosexuals to stay celibate and chaste. It is opposed to any effort to make homosexual activity legitimate while at the same time calls for the decriminalization of homosexuality around the world. It counsels people to treat homosexuals with compassion and stands against violence in any form being done to those who are LGBT. The bottom line message of the Roman Catholic Church however is that if you are actively gay you are acting against nature, are morally depraved and will, unless you get properly forgiven, go to hell.

Question: What is the Eastern Orthodox Church view about homosexuality?
The Roman Catholic Church and the Eastern Orthodox Church were once part of a single church, but they split into separate churches in the eleventh century AD. The Eastern Orthodox Church is primarily represented in the United States by the Orthodox Church in America. It views homosexuality as contrary to scripture and as a sin. It asserts that, like all human beings, homosexuals should be treated with compassion and justice. It does not allow openly gay people to take the Holy Sacraments until after they have properly repented through the Sacrament of Confession. It does not ordain openly gay people into the clergy nor does it support gay marriage or unions. It calls upon homosexuals to struggle against the sin of homosexuality and to stay celibate and chaste.

Question: What do Protestants say about homosexuality?
If Roman Catholicism is the largest unified branch of Christianity in the United States Protestantism is easily the largest non-unified one. Nearly half of Americans view themselves as of a Protestant faith but only a quarter of LGBT people do. Protestantism has abundant limbs however each of which embodies a distinct form of Christianity. Among the many issues in dispute among them is how to respond to homosexuality. Protestantism per se therefore does not have a view on homosexuality.

Question: What do Baptists say about homosexuality?
The Baptist church is the largest Protestant denomination in this country. There are however several variations within the Baptist church. The largest body is the Southern Baptist Convention. The American Baptist Churches USA is the third largest group within the Baptist faith. Both groups hold homosexuality as sinful. The former group takes the matter further through their position that homosexuality is an abomination in the eyes of God.

Other Baptist churches such as the National Baptist Convention, USA, Inc. (the second largest body of Baptists) and the Cooperative Baptist Fellowship hold no official view of homosexuality at all and leave the matter up to individual congregations. Still other Baptist churches such as the Alliance of Baptists and the Association of Welcoming and Affirming Baptists not only welcome gays and allow full participation in their church but also support gay rights.

Question: What do Methodists say about homosexuality?
Methodists are the second largest denomination of Protestants in the country. The United Methodist Church is the largest body of Methodists. Generally, Methodists hold homosexual behavior but not homosexuality itself to be sinful. It takes the position that all people have "sacred worth", are due basic civil rights and that everyone is welcome to attend their worship services. Methodists do not support gay marriage but do accept the ordination of openly gay clergy so long as they are celibate. The Reconciling Ministries is a Methodist branch that is completely gay friendly.

Question: What do Lutherans say about homosexuality?
Lutherans are the third largest Protestant denomination is the United States. The main body of the Lutheran church is the Evangelical Lutheran Church in America. This church allows but does not compel congregations to accept openly gay non-celibate clerics and allows pastors to perform same-sex unions. It welcomes homosexuals as fully participating members and does not view homosexuality as a sin. Smaller branches of the Lutheran church such as the Lutheran Church-Missouri Synod, the Wisconsin Evangelical Lutheran Synod and the Evangelical

Lutheran Synod (ELS) completely disapprove of homosexuality based on their belief that it is unnatural, against scripture and therefore sinful. They do not allow openly gay people to serve as pastors and do not support same-sex unions.

Questions: What do Presbyterians say about homosexuality?
The largest body of Presbyterians in this country is the Presbyterian Church (USA). This Protestant church welcomes openly gay worshipers and has removed all barriers to the ordination of openly gay non-celibate clergy. It does not view homosexuality as a sin. It allows pastors to officiate at same-sex marriages. Other branches of the Presbyterian Church such as the Presbyterian Church in America, the Associate Reformed Presbyterian Church and the Orthodox Presbyterian Church view homosexuality as unnatural and sinful and do not ordain openly gay people into the clergy. There are also branches of the church such as the Covenant Network of Presbyterians and the "More Light" Presbyterians who are completely gay friendly.

Question: What do Pentecostals say about homosexuality?
The Pentecostal Church is another Protestant faith. It has a lot of branches within it, but the primary body is found in the Assemblies of God. It, like most Pentecostal churches, views homosexuality as a sin and forbids gay marriage and openly gay people from serving as clergy. Some denominations of Pentecostals also forbid gay people to be part of their congregation. At the same time, some Pentecostal denominations, like the Covenant Network, the Global Alliance of Affirming Apostolic Pentecostals and the Fellowship of Reconciling Pentecostals, welcome gays as fully participating members of their church.

Question: What do Episcopalians say about homosexuality?
The Episcopal Church of the United States of America (ECUSA) is the primary body of the Anglican Communion in this country. It does not view homosexuality as a sin. It welcomes openly gay members and accepts openly gay non-celibate people as clergy. It

also allows clergy to perform same-sex marriages and openly opposes any effort to limit marriage to heterosexual couples. The Anglican Communion itself and smaller bodies within the Anglican Communion in the United States, such as the Anglican Mission of the Americas and the Convocation of Anglicans in North America oppose all of that and view homosexuality as against scripture and sinful.

Question: What does the United Church of Christ say about homosexuality?

The United Church of Christ is a completely gay friendly Protestant church in most instances, but it allows individual churches within its body to make decisions related to issues like homosexuality. Those that are gay friendly take on the designation of Open and Affirming. A large majority of local churches within this denomination welcome gay members as fully participating members and accept openly gay people as ordained clergy. Most also support same-sex unions and gay marriage.

Question: What do Mormons say about homosexuality?

There is some dispute over whether the members of the Church of Jesus Christ of Latter Day Saints (Mormons) are Christians. They assert that since they worship Jesus Christ, view him as the Savior and endeavor to follow his teachings they are indeed Christians. Others assert a contrary view citing several factors which they hold as disqualifying including using the Book of Mormon as a holy book, the rejection of the concept of the Trinity and the refusal to accept the spiritual authority of other Christian churches to act in Christ's name.

The Mormon Church views homosexual behavior as a sin but not homosexuality itself. It accepts that homosexuality is not a choice but allows homosexuals to be members only if they are celibate and chaste. Mormons do not have the concept of a clergy, so ordination of homosexuals is not an issue. They actively oppose gay marriage and support the concept that marriage must be between one man and one woman. Mormons also believe that all sex done outside that union is sinful. Persons in a same-sex marriage or involved in same-sex sexual behaviors are viewed as having left the faith and their children will not be allowed to fully take part in the church until they are at least 18 years of age.

Mormons hold the view that homosexuals must be dealt with compassionately.

Question: What do Jehovah Witnesses say about homosexuality

Jehovah Witnesses count themselves as Christian because they believe in and worship Jesus Christ as the Son of God. Others do not view it as Christian however because it does not accept the doctrines of the Trinity or the immortality of the soul and it has its own version of the Bible. It also does not accept the concepts of heaven and hell.

This church views homosexuality as a sin. Gay members are expected to stay celibate and chaste. Even homosexual thoughts and desires are forbidden. Sex is allowed only within a marriage which is defined as being only between one man and one woman. Masturbation is also forbidden. Those members who violate the churches rules are subject to "disfellowship" which means complete ostracism. The primary exception related to homosexuality is that family members can interact with a homosexual member when within the home, but they cannot talk about matters related to the church. This church requires that homosexuals be treated compassionately and forbids hateful speech or actions directed against homosexuals.

Question: What do Quakers say about homosexuality?

Most members of the Religious Society of Friends (Quakers) view themselves as Christian. They view Christ as being a great teacher but not holy. They have no sacraments or creed. They have no clerics, priests or similar positions so the ordination of homosexuals is not an issue.

Some Quaker organizations in the United States support gay rights and are gay friendly and some are not. Among the gay friendly Quaker organizations in this country are the Friends General Conference, the North Pacific Yearly Meeting and the Pacific Yearly Meeting. The latter two of these are meetings of local Quaker organizations that come together to discuss policy. Among the organizations condemning homosexuality are the Friends United Meeting and the Evangelical Friends International.

Question: What do Unitarian Universalists say about homosexuality?
Unitarian Universalists may or may not be Christian. This body has no creed or dogma. It allows members to decide individually what their personal religious truth is. Since this association has roots in Christianity it is common for members to subscribe to some parts of that tradition. At the same time, other traditions are present as well.

In line with its tradition of freedom of thought and speech Unitarian Universalism is completely gay friendly. It allows gay members to be clergy or lay leaders and supports gay marriage. It opposes all forms of discrimination directed against homosexuals.

Question: What do Deists say about homosexuality?
There is some dispute about whether Deism is a Christian religion. The only things all Deists have in common with Christians are the belief in the existence of God, the belief that God is the only God and the belief that God is the Creator of our universe. Deists do not share Christian belief that God is an active force now but rather hold that God created everything He needed to create at the beginning, so He does not have to intercede or amend now. They also believe that God's will can be discovered through reason, so we have no need of prophets or revelation.

Deism has no creed or dogma beyond that said above. It leaves the individual believer to discover his/her own truth. Many Deists choose to believe in the person, message and spirit of Jesus Christ. These believers generally accept Christ as a great teacher and do not deal with the matter of whether he was holy or not since that cannot be objectively proven. There are few Deist congregations in the United States so those Deists wishing to fulfill themselves through such a group commonly find that by joining a Unitarian Universalist congregation. Deism is gay friendly.

Question: What do Muslims say about homosexuality?
Islam is both a religion and a system of laws. There are two major divisions within Islam. A large majority of Muslims are Sunni and most of the rest is Shiite. The mainstream of both branches condemns homosexual behavior as being against the will of Allah

(God). Such behavior is also a violation of Islamic religious law (Sharia).

Within Sunni and Shiite Islam are various schools of jurisprudence that interpret Sharia. Each of these schools teaches its own doctrine about what Sharia calls for and that includes how the law should deal with alleged homosexuals and how convicted homosexuals should be punished. Some say the death penalty is called for and ten Muslim countries follow this path. Some say the judge should decide punishment. Some say no penalty is called for because the Qur'an never mentions homosexuals being punished until Allah does it on Judgment Day.

Mainline Islam does not allow any form of homosexual relationship, especially between men, so gay unions of any kind are impossible. An openly gay person also cannot have any official position, such as imam, within this faith. Islam asserts actively gay people are condemned to hell unless they repent and cease all homosexual activity.

Not all Muslims follow Sharia however. Many believers follow their own interpretation of the Qur'an and their own conscience using modern knowledge and reason. Some states in the Muslim world separate church and state and follow secular law. In a few of those, such as Turkey and Jordon, homosexuality is legal. No Muslim country allows same-sex marriage.

The primary progressive Islamic organization in America is Muslims for Progressive Values. There are few LGBT friendly mosques in the U.S.A., but LGBT Muslims compensate for this by gathering in homes or in other borrowed or rented spaces. The good news is that acceptance of our community is rapidly growing in the Muslim community. A recent publication, in fact, asserts that a small majority of American Muslims now say homosexuality should be accepted by society (Pew, 2017).

Question: What was the Prophet Muhammad's view about homosexuality?

Abü al-Qāsim Muhammad ibn 'Abd Allāh was born in the city of Mecca in 570 A.D. He married his first wife, Khaddijah, in 595 A.D. when he was 25 years old. He stayed monogamous and faithful until she died.

Tradition says Muhammad began to have revelations from Allah given to him through the angel Gabriel in 610 AD. These revelations are the basis of the Qur'an (Islam's holy book). He was not particularly popular in his birth city of Mecca because of his religious views so he was glad to accept an invitation from the city of Medina to move there and become their leader. He moved there in 622 AD. Using Medina as a base he then went on to unify nearly all the Arabian Peninsula through either negotiated treaties or war. He died in 632 AD. A record of his sayings and actions (the hadith) along with the Qur'an form the primary basis of Islamic law and the Muslim religion. There is disagreement among Islamic factions as to which parts of the hadith are authentic and to be followed by the faithful.

What we know about Muhammad's view of homosexuality comes primarily from the Qur'an and the hadith. Various parts of the hadith conflict on that point. Most sources tell us that he did not approve of homosexuality per se but felt that nothing should be done to a homosexual so long as they stayed celibate. He felt that if punishment was correct for homosexuality it was a job for Allah and not for mankind.

Muhammad's view toward homosexuals who actively engage in homosexual sex is less clear. Some scholars cite evidence that he did nothing. Some say he believed banishment was the correct response. Other scholars cite evidence that he believed that behavior merited death. Islam is still not united on this point.

It is clear however that Muhammad believed that if a homosexual stopped having gay sex and genuinely repented nothing should happen to him so long as he had stopped before he was caught. Once caught however the person was doomed on the Day of Judgment to go to hell.

It has been asserted by a small number of people that Muhammad was himself gay. They cite passages from the Qur'an and the hadith to support that view. Those passages do exist, but they must be squeezed quite significantly for them to yield that juice. The fair interpretation of what we know is that Muhammad was very much in love with his first wife and he had four daughters and two sons with her. He also had a son with his wife Maria al-Qibtiyya (a Christian who converted to Islam before her marriage). It is also clear that he felt his wife Aisha was very attractive and he loved her.

Question: Does the Qur'an condemn homosexuality?
No, the Qur'an does not condemn homosexuality. It does however condemn homosexual lust and/or homosexual behavior. Most mainstream authorities say the Qur'an specifically does this in seven places: suras (chapters) 7:80-84, 11:77-83, 21:74, 22:43, 26:165-175, 27:56-59 and 29:27-33. These refer to the story of the destruction by God of the cities of Sodom and Gomorrah.

The suras (chapters) noted above either do not mention a punishment that is to be meted out or suggest that if the behavior does not stop banishment will occur. The Qur'an says God will punish homosexual behavior after the sinners die but does not make homosexuality per se a crime punishable by man. A few passages in the hadith do however. Sadly, much of Islam does not follow the Qur'an in this regard.

Several Muslim nations arrest and imprison people just for being homosexual because of what they interpret to be in the hadith. All countries having the death penalty for homosexual behavior are Muslim majority nations. Twenty of the fifty-seven Muslim majority nations on earth have no laws banning homosexuality or homosexual behavior.

A minority of scholars disagree with the notion that the Qur'an bans homosexual behavior. They cite scientific evidence that homosexuality is natural and normal for some people and that that sexual orientation is not chosen. They further say that Allah, who is always just and fair, would not punish anyone for something He created as an unchosen way of existence. They point out that the Qur'an clearly says that God does not punish people for things that are not their fault. They also point out that the Qur'an is completely silent about homosexual love that is not acted upon sexually. Romantic love between people of the same sex is, of course, sometimes what homosexuality is.

Question: What does the Nation of Islam say about homosexuality?
The Nation of Islam (Black Muslims) views itself as a branch of Islam. It exists primarily in the United States. They assert their belief in the Five Pillars of Islam and their use of a version of the Qur'an as its holy book as the proof of their status as a Muslim organization. Others disagree because the Nation of Islam teaches that its founder, Wallace Fard Muhammad, was the incarnation

of God, that Elijah Muhammad (a primary figure in their movement) was the last prophet of God and they do not accept that the Qur'an was revealed to Muhammad by Allah. All of this is blasphemy to a mainline Muslim.

The Nation of Islam is very much anti-homosexual. It views homosexuality as a primary evil and asserts the death penalty is fitting for those who are gay. Obviously therefore being openly gay within this organization is out of the question. The same holds true for being White and/or Jewish. Both are primary evils also.

Question: What is the Jewish view about homosexuality?
Judaism per se has no view about homosexuality. Its various denominations have doctrine and dogma about it, but none can say it speaks for all Jews. Most Jewish faiths are tolerant of homosexuality and, within limits, are also tolerant of homosexual behavior.

Question: What does Reform Judaism say about homosexuality?
Reform Judaism is a progressive branch and the largest body within the Jewish faith in the United States. It believes that the Tanakh (Hebrew Bible) is spiritually pure but also that it includes some errs which must be interpreted using modern history and knowledge. It therefore does not accept the view that homosexuality is a sin. It accepts gays as fully participating members and allows sexually active gays to become rabbis or cantors. The faith also allows, but does not compel, rabbis to officiate at same-sex marriages.

Question: What does Reconstructionist Judaism say about homosexuality?
Reconstructionist Judaism is another progressive branch of Judaism. It does not view homosexuality as abnormal or sinful. It has basically the same beliefs about homosexuality as Reform Judaism. It however encourages, rather than merely allowing, rabbis to officiate at same-sex unions.

Question: What does Conservative Judaism say about homosexuality?

Conservative Judaism authorizes individual rabbinical schools to choose whether they will or will not ordain openly homosexual people as rabbis. It allows individual rabbis to decide whether they will officiate at a same-sex marriage. It also allows each congregation to choose whether it will accept gay members, cantors and/or rabbis. It expressly does not allow members to engage in anal sex and holds this practice as a violation of Biblical law. It however does not assume that this practice will be part of a gay relationship.

Question: What does Orthodox Judaism say about homosexuality?

Only a few years ago, there was a nearly unanimous voice within Orthodox Judaism that homosexuality is an abomination in the eyes of God and that there is nothing about it that is natural, normal or acceptable. All forms of homosexual behavior were universally condemned. A homosexual could not become an Orthodox rabbi. The fact that homosexuals were demanding equality was viewed as the arrogance of sinners. That view is no longer unanimous.

There is now a divide within the Orthodox community. Some continue to hold the belief that homosexuality itself is unnatural and sinful. Some hold that homosexuality per se is natural but homosexuals should stay celibate. Others hold that homosexuality is natural (not sinful) and that homosexual sex is acceptable unless anal penetration is involved. Still others accept homosexuality and homosexual sex as natural and normal.

There are now Orthodox rabbis who are either gay or gay friendly. Some Orthodox rabbis openly question whether those rabbis are truly Orthodox. Generally, gays and lesbians are welcome at Orthodox synagogues and events. Orthodox Judaism teaches that homosexuals should be dealt with compassionately. Orthodox Judaism does not support same-sex marriages.

Question: What is the Hindu view about homosexuality?

Hinduism is made up of four major divisions: Shaivism, Shaktism, Vaishavism and Smartism and all these are present in the United States. Hinduism has a long tradition of being tolerant of homosexuality which includes the concept of the "third gender". A third gender person is in some ways male and in some ways female and may include gay men, lesbians and transsexuals. Its holy books do not mention homosexuality at all and the religion does not say marriage must be heterosexual.

All sides of the issue of homosexuality tend to view it in terms of whether it is a path that can lead to a good karma. One's karma, of course, controls whether an individual is reborn after death or becomes part of the universal truth of Brahman. Conservatives tend to think homosexuality is unnatural and based on lust and thus generates a poor karma. They tend to be intolerant of gays. Liberals believe homosexuality can be a very natural form of intimacy and love and thus is a positive factor in karma. They tend to be open and accepting.

Hindu priests are supposed to be celibate so homosexuality within the priesthood is rarely talked about. Priests are allowed, but not compelled, to perform same-sex unions. Even with this background an openly gay person may or may not be welcomed at a Hindu temple. Some are welcoming, and some are not. Hinduism is primarily practiced in India.

Question: What is the Buddhist view about homosexuality?
Buddhism's three major branches are Theravada, Mahayana and Vajrayana (Tibetan). There are a lot of limbs growing from these branches including Zen Buddhism. All Buddhist monks are supposed to be celibate and chaste so homosexuality in the clergy is rarely an issue. All branches of Buddhism say that homosexuals should be treated with the compassion that is due all human beings and deplore the violence and hate that is sometimes directed at gays.

The Buddhist view of homosexuality is divided generally into the liberal, conservative and moderate camps. Each camp uses the teachings of the Buddha to find a view about homosexuality, yet they get different results. We can therefore say that there is no Buddhist view about homosexuality. There is only what this camp or that camp says is right. No camp speaks for all Buddhists.

Question: What does Theravada Buddhism say about homosexuality?
Theravada Buddhism asserts that sexual orientation is like race and gender in that a person is born with it. It judges heterosexual and homosexual relationships on the same scale based upon what goes into and comes out of the relationship. A relationship is wrong only if it is the result of sexual misconduct such as forced sex or abusive interactions. It is right if it brings the people within it happiness and fulfillment. This view supports gay marriage.

Question: What does Vajrayana Buddhism say about homosexuality?
The conservative Buddhist view is espoused by Vajrayana (Tibetan) Buddhism. It supports only penis/vaginal sex and says that all other sex (including masturbation) is wrong because it uses organs (hands, mouths and anuses) for sex that were not intended for that purpose. It views this as sexual misconduct and says the Buddha specifically said sexual misconduct was wrong. This branch of Buddhism does not support gay unions or relationships.

Question: What does Mahayana Buddhism say about homosexuality?
Mahayana Buddhism asserts that homosexuality is not objectively right or wrong. It says that so long as nobody is harmed, and the relationship stays part of the private lives of the individuals involved, society should tolerate it. Marriage, per this branch of Buddhism, is a social construct so a society will define it based upon whatever values it has but those can change. As a rule, so long as homosexuals are not harming anyone and not breaking laws, they should be allowed to marry if they believe that is right for them.

Question: What does Satanism say about homosexuality?
Satanism supports all sexual orientations and the behaviors that rise naturally from them. It stands for the free expression of human sexuality between consenting adults. It also supports same-sex marriage and the agenda of equal rights for LGBT

people. It welcomes homosexuals as equal and fully participating members.

Question: What do Atheists say about homosexuality?
Atheists do not have a unified dogma about homosexuality because they coalesce as a group based upon their shared disbelief in a deity and not because of a shared sociopolitical view. It would be fair to speculate however that most atheists are pro-gay because most of the arguments against homosexuality are based in religion and upon the assertion that some deity abhors homosexuality. A 2013 poll showed that 15% of gays are atheist and an another 7% are agnostic (Pew, 2013).

Chapter 5
Gay Relationship Issues

Question: Why are interpersonal relationships important to homosexuals?
Homosexuals are normal human beings. Human beings need other human beings. This is true across all demographics including sexual orientation. One's mental health, physical health and self-image are largely the result of their interactions with other people. People who do not have contact with other humans do not thrive and sometimes die. We are social animals naturally but a large majority of our interactions with others are not sexual. They relate to survival, safety, social belonging (family/friends) and self-esteem (Maslow, 1954). Gays are not an exception.

Question: What is internalized homophobia and how does it influence relationships?
People are born heterosexual, homosexual, bisexual or asexual. They have an intact sexual identity by around age 2 but do not begin to understand it until around age 7. That early identity is only part of a person's self-concept however. A self-concept is how a person thinks about himself. It is based in one's childhood experiences and the intentional or unintentional feedback he gets from others about their perceptions of him (Rogers, 1959).

A person who suffers from internalized homophobia is a LGBT person who has had the misfortune of having grown up in an anti-LGBT environment but has not yet effectively dealt with it. He knows his "real-self" is LGBT but the ideal he holds for himself (his ideal-self) is not. The result is internalized homophobia.

Internalized homophobia is self-loathing. It may or may not be related to whether the person is out or not since it is possible to be openly gay and still not at peace with it. It is not necessarily related to how connected the person is to the gay community either since it is possible for a gay person to be actively involved with that community and still detest his own sexual orientation (Frost, 2009).

Internalized homophobia is related to both depression and to relationship problems. These relationship difficulties may be general or more narrowly focused on the person's partner or others who try to get close. It is typically the stress and depression generated by the self-loathing that is at the root of the relationship problems (Frost, 2009).

Many gay or bisexual people experience internalized homophobia. It is sometimes a phase people go through as they move to a psychologically healthy balance of their real self and their ideal self (Cass, 1979). They start with the learned belief that being gay is bad but over time they grow through that by testing the validity of that learned standard. They are also able to make use of the support they find in the gay community and, hopefully, within their family and friendships. Other people, however, get stuck in their self-loathing.

Question: How does a person overcome internalized homophobia?

The process of moving through internalized homophobia is not hard to understand but it can be hard to do. Human beings tend to be emotionally attached to their core beliefs and to think and behave as they have in the past. Overcoming that emotional attachment entails the person challenging what he believes and setting aside the fact that he learned those things from people he cares for and trusts. He must objectively examine the underpinnings of his own homophobia.

He must also find his positive attributes and interlace those with the fact that he is gay. This is how he begins to change his mindset that being LGBT is a negative into one that accepts that it is simply part of being the person he is. Sexual orientation and gender identity have little to do with personal worth. That is achieved by leading a life of positive meaning and purpose.

It is very helpful to have friends who are gay or gay friendly as one goes through this process both because gay/gay friendly friends can act as a support group and sounding boards. It is also often easier to see the positives that exist in gay friends than it is to see those that exist in one's self. Perhaps the hardest thing in this process is to leave relationships that support homophobia. It is difficult to heal if you continue to drink the poison.

Question: What about other people who are homophobic? Aren't they the real problem?

Homophobia is the irrational hatred or fear of (Webster's New World Coll. Dict., 2006; Weinberg, 1972) and/or the feelings of anger/disgust at (Herek, 2004) homosexuals or homosexuality. It is an umbrella term that includes not only prejudice against gay men but also against lesbians (lesbophobia), bisexuals (biphobia), transgender people (transphobia) and others within the LGBT community. At the root of homophobia is a negative emotional response to that which is different. This, of course, is also the root cause of racism, anti-Semitism, sexism and other forms of irrational prejudice.

It will hardly come as a surprise to most LGBT people but there is a lot of anti-gay bias around. Polls show that half of Americans hold antigay views on at least one LGBT core issue. A large minority believe denying LGBT people one or more of their civil rights and constitutional protections is the right and moral thing to do. Many also believe it is right to deny LGBT people the necessities of life such as housing and employment. Some hold that LGBT people should be imprisoned or even killed. The 2010 Republican Party platform in Montana and Texas, for example, called for homosexuality to be criminalized.

Most homophobes are content to keep their homophobia private or at least to go no further than active or passive discrimination. Some however take their bigotry to the point of verbal or physical bashing. That group is busy. A survey done in 2009 showed that 20% of gays have experienced a crime against their person or property as the result of their sexual orientation and about half have experienced harassment or verbal intimidation (Herek, 2009). A 2012 study shows the numbers are much worse in rural areas of the country (Gay, Lesbian & Straight Education Network, 2012).

The Southern Poverty Law Center said in 2010 that LGBT people are far more likely than any other minority group to be the victim of a violent hate crime. A hate crime is any criminal act that is motivated by prejudice or bias against the victim's race, religion, sexual orientation, gender identity, class, ethnicity, national origin, color, age or disability. A violent hate crime is a hate crime wherein the offender uses force or the threat of force upon a victim. Examples of hate crimes include assault (causing a reasonable fear of physical injury), physical battery, property damage, bullying, harassment, verbal abuse and sending hate mail if bias is the motivation.

Federal Bureau of Investigation and Department of Justice statistics show that hate crimes in general are grossly underreported and that hate crimes based on sexual orientation are more so. The Department of Justice, for example, reports that from 2007 to 2011 there were 259,700 nonfatal hate crimes committed in the United States (Bureau of Justice Statistics, 2013). The hate crimes reported to the FBI during that same time interval totaled 40,893 (Federal Bureau of Investigation, 2011).

The disparity comes from the fact that most law enforcement jurisdictions are not obliged to report hate crimes to the FBI. Some states do not report hate crimes at all because they have no laws that make anything a hate crime. Other states have laws against some types of hate crimes but do not include crimes motivated by the victim's sexual orientation among them. Another factor is that reporting a crime as a hate crime is left entirely to the discretion of local authorities. In that case an assault against a homosexual, for example, might be reported as an assault but not an assault involving a hate crime.

Race is the single most common motivation for hate crimes. Around 33% of reported hate crimes (violent and nonviolent) are motivated by race and nearly 72% those are against Blacks. Sexual orientation is the motivation for hate crime 21% of the time. Male homosexuals are the target nearly 57% of the time in those cases (FBI, 2011).

FBI statistics also show that in 2011 59.0% of hate crime offenders were White and 20.9% were Black (FBI, 2011). To put this into context it must be remembered that per the 2010 census 72% of Americans are White and 13% are Black. This is noted here as relevant because crime tends to be intra-racial rather than interracial. African Americans, as a group, tend to be less tolerant of homosexuals than Caucasians and this is more pronounced in Black men than in Black women (Lemelle and Battle, 2004; Herek, 1995). These facts help explain why so many African American gay men are closeted or on the down low.

American homophobes are overwhelmingly male and conservative politically and/or religiously which of course means they overwhelmingly tend to be Republicans. They tend to be from the South or Midwest. They also tend to have little or no contact with LGBT people, so they are not able to test their biases against reality (Herek, 2000).

This problem is compounded by the fact that homophobes, as a group, tend to have less ability to reason abstractly when compared to more tolerant people (Keiller, 2010). They also tend to be less well-educated as adults and less intelligent as children than non-prejudiced people (Hodson and Busseri, 2012). Interestingly, homophobia seems to cut around 2.5 years off a homophobe's life (Hatzenbuehler and Bellatorre, 2013). The reader is hereby absolved for any uncharitable thoughts concerning the justice of that.

Studies show that, as might be expected, homophobes are made and not born. Homophobic boys and girls have gotten their prejudiced views by the time they are 12 or 13 years old (Poteat and Anderson, 2012; Baker and Fishbein, 1998). Generally, both boys and girls may become less bigoted as they move through adolescence. That varies based upon the environment they are in, but girls tend to do better at dealing with that. Boys tend not to change their views toward homosexual men significantly but do moderate concerning lesbians. Racial minority teens tend to decrease their level of homophobia less than Caucasian teens (Poteat and Anderson, 2012).

Studies also show that homophobes are prejudiced against more than one class of people. Again, this is not surprising. Predictably, people who are prejudiced against homosexuals are prejudiced against transgender people too (Nagosi and Adams, 2008). They also tend to accept the rape myth which, of course, is the belief that the victims of rape are blamable for the rape (Aosved and Long, 2006) and to be sexist and racist (Kimmel, 1994).

Many people believe that homophobic attitudes and behaviors may be based in the homophobe's own repressed homosexuality. In other words, it is a defense mechanism called a "reaction formation" in which the person must go to extremes to defend his ego against unwanted thoughts and feelings. In this case his repressed feelings of self-loathing are unleashed on someone he sees as showing the homosexuality that he hates in himself. There is a sound basis to believe this but the motivation behind homophobia is not the same for all homophobes.

Multiple authorities support the idea that homophobes may think and behave as homophobes as they try to deal with their own inner conflict concerning their sexuality and/or because they want to be seen by others as masculine by being anti-gay (Weinstein, 2012; Parrot, 2009; Franklin, 2000; Herek, 2000; Theodore, 2000; Adams, 1996). Other homophobes may think and behave that way to support and enforce the heteronormative stereotype of masculinity which is the standard that is part of their belief system (Parrott, 2009; Herek, 2000).

Another theory about homophobia is that it is based in biology. There is a growing body of work that points to brain structure and genetic predispositions being a factor in a person's political and social belief system (Kanai and Feilden, 2011; Settle and Dawes, 2010; Oxley and Smith, 2008; Amodio and Jost, 2007; Alford, and Funk, 2005). This points to the possibility that conservative and liberals respond to the world differently because they cognitively perceive it differently for both environmental and biological reasons.

The theory is that the conservative's biology leads him to prefer tradition, order and hierarchy and to view what is new or different as a potential threat. The liberal on the other hand naturally likes progress and egalitarianism and views what is new and different as a potential positive. We liberals are more adaptive (Shook and Fazio, 2009; Amodio and Jost, 2007). One theorist posits that liberals simply have more of the kind of intelligence that allows our species to embrace what is new and different (Kenazawa, 2012).

This model makes it easy to understand the conservative's response to homosexuality. From their perspective, LGBTs pose a threat to their values and standard of order. Their biology and experience predispose them to resist that threat, to resist change and to avoid ideas and people that conflict with their views. That may result in homophobic actions based on anger and fear. Anger and fear, even if grounded on biology, do not excuse the behavior of homophobes either legally or morally however. They are still responsible for what they do.

Question: What is heterosexism and how does it affect homosexuals?

Heterosexism is the attitude that heterosexuality is what is normal for humans and that it should be favored over homosexuality, bisexuality and asexuality. Some heterosexists are homophobes while others are not since heterosexists are not necessarily motivated by hate, anger or fear. They do consciously or unconsciously support some form of discrimination against gays and bisexuals however. They tend to discriminate against bisexuals more (Herek, 2002).

Heterosexism is widespread in the United States. As noted previously many religions are heterosexist and some are blatantly homophobic. Many universities are too because they do not have policies in place that ban discrimination against LGBT people or protect those who have a non-heterosexual identity. Some colleges refuse in enroll LGBT people and use heterosexuality as a basis upon which to make employment decisions. Polls suggest that nearly half of the people in the United States are heterosexist as well because they support the view that heterosexuality should be legally favored over homosexuality and bisexuality. This however is rapidly changing.

It is no surprise then that most state governments are also heterosexist. Some do not allow gay couples to adopt children. Several states have made it clear that they disagree with the Supreme Court's decision which legalizes gay marriage and they still want to ban it. Twenty states have no laws that make crimes based on sexual orientation or gender identity hate crimes. Twenty-nine states have no laws barring discrimination based on sexual orientation. Around 10% of gays have experienced overt discrimination in employment and/or housing because of their sexual orientation (Herek, 2009). If we assume that 4% of Americans are gay that is 1,244,000 citizens who have been denied housing or employment solely because they are gay.

Question: Does heterosexism affect the scientific study of homosexuals?

Heterosexism unfortunately exists in the scientific fields that study or report on sexual minorities. It is very easy to find reports wherein gays, lesbians, bisexuals, and/or transfolk are described as doing less well than heterosexuals in this or that. It is also easy to find reports that some sexual minority is at more risk than heterosexuals of having this or that negative happen.

What is rarely found is a study or report that says some sexual minority did better at this or that than heterosexuals did. What is not found are reports that say some sexual minority is less at risk than a heterosexual is of having some negative health, psychological or interpersonal issue happening. When LGBT people are found to be less at risk or have better results, we are almost universally folded back into a larger category and not shown to have a positive factor. When gay men, for example, do better than hetero men we are folded into the larger category of "men".

The authors of these reports may mean well. Issues cannot be discussed if they are not found and reported on and the authors often want our betterment. What they do not grasp however is what it is like to see study after study and report after report say that you are less.

It is not uncommon to see researchers make sweeping, broad statements through overgeneralization from the limited data they have. It is very easy, for example, to find reports saying that LGBTs have a "higher psychiatric morbidity" (negative psychiatric outcome) or a "higher incidence of mental health disorders" or "poorer mental health outcomes". The fact that LGBTs use outpatient mental health resources at higher levels is even used sometimes to support that narrative. That narrative unfortunately functions to stigmatize and denigrate the LGBT community by making it look as if we LGBTs are less well than heterosexuals.

The truth however is that the diagnostic manual of the American Psychiatric Association includes twenty overarching mental health categories and each of those has multiple distinct diagnostic sub-types. It is well-known that homosexuals, as a group, have a higher incidence of some of those sub-types because of the stressors that society directs our way. This is not however the case in other diagnostic areas.

The broad claim that we gays and bisexuals have a higher rate of mental health/physical health morbidity or that we have poorer mental/physical health outcomes is not correct since that implies that we do less well in terms of mental and/or physical health generally. That is not true. In the large majority of mental and/or physical health categories we, as a group, are either not different from or we fare better than heterosexuals as a group (Hellman and Sudderth, 2002; DeAngeles, 2002; Gay and Lesbian Med. Assoc., 2010; Cochran, 2001; Muehrer, 1995).

The narrative that LGBTs are less well also does not acknowledge that the size difference between the rate of illness of groups is sometimes small. It likewise does not speak to the fact that some mental/physical health issues are more serious than others and that some tend to be transitory rather than on-going.

If a study is going to claim, for example, that homosexuals have a higher rate of depression or cancer it needs to say which specific kinds of depression or cancer the study looked at and what the specific difference between groups was. It also needs to clearly say how large or small the population having the issue is. It is, as a case in point, easy to find reports that gay men have an elevated risk of an eating disorder, but it is harder to find out that the population of men (hetero and homo) with eating disorders is 2.0% or less of men in general.

The problem of inaccurate reporting is compounded when researchers load the dice. This happens in a variety of ways. Studies on health, for example, sometimes ignore the historically much higher rate of illness caused by HIV/AIDS and lump HIV/AIDS positive and negative people into the same group when comparing homosexuals to heterosexuals. That skews the result and gives a false impression of the overall well-being of homosexuals as a class. If HIV+ men are removed from the data, we find that gay men are not less healthy than hetero men.

It is also common to see homosexuals and bisexuals lumped into one study group when, in fact, they are distinctly separate. The use of sample populations that are not culturally or demographically representative of homosexuals as a group is also a common bias. All of this is based on the conscious or unconscious heterosexist view that all homosexuals are the same.

More disturbing is when researchers do not report all the data as in the case of a 2001 study in which the author wrote that he was not including some data because it showed a low prevalence of the studied disorders. In another equally disturbing case a researcher who was studying the reactivity of men to sexual stimuli wrote that he had removed part of the men from the study because they were not sufficiently reactive. One might hope that at some point someone will explain to these researchers that a "low prevalence" and low reactivity is a meaningful result and that the support of the heterosexual norms of society is not a legitimate goal of research.

Another rather transparent example of heterosexism is found in a 2001 study that allegedly compared the incidence of certain mental illnesses in homosexuals and heterosexuals. The study defined homosexuality as any same-sex sexual contact done in the last year. No sexologist who knows the field would accept that definition.

Whether homosexuality is defined based on sexual attraction, romantic/emotional attraction, sexual behavior or some combination of those things it must be an enduring phenomenon that lasts over a significant timespan. In this researcher's mind if a straight person, even once, has any form of homosexual sex for whatever reason he/she is instantly transformed into a homosexual, but he did not assert the reverse to be true. In other words, this researcher did not define heterosexuality in a way that if a homosexual has heterosexual sex for some reason he/she is heterosexual. This inconsistent rationale can only exist where heterosexism is accepted. Sadly, this researcher's definition is found in a lot of studies including U.S. government studies.

In one instance while writing this book it was found that a researcher reported that the data supported her hypothesis that homosexuals had a higher incidence of mental health morbidity in some of the studied areas, but it did not support the hypothesis of a higher level in all of them. She then wrote that despite that she was sure later data would. Let's be clear. The data was not supportive, but she was sure gays where worse. More than that, she was willing to use her status as the author of a peer reviewed article to assert something that the data refuted.

It should also be pointed out that supporting a narrative that LGBTs have a higher rate of mental health problems by using the level of at which LGBT people use mental health resources is unprofessional and dishonest. Using mental health services is not a mental health negative and that use does not by itself support the notion that LGBT people have a higher level of mental health problems. It may simply show that heterosexuals do not use mental health services. It may also show that homosexual men are less attached to the macho ego structure that prevents straight men from getting help (Sánchez and Bocklandt, 2013). The assumption that it means LGBT have a higher morbidity rate is heterosexist since it assumes that what hetero men do in terms of seeking help is normal.

Undoubtedly the most disturbing thing about the heterosexism that is found in scientific studies is that the statements/findings that come from those venues are sometimes blindly accepted and repeated. Each of the studies noted above appeared in well-respected journals and have been cited as authoritative in other peer reviewed articles. More than one of them has been cited hundreds of times. This has happened because editors and researchers accept the work of others too uncritically and because they lack cultural competence when dealing with the LGBT community. They accept ignorant assertions because they lack the competence to know better.

The article that used a faulty definition of homosexual, for example, should have been rejected because of a design flaw. Its definition of homosexuality doomed the study to not measure what it was intended to measure. The entire study was based on the variable of sexual orientation and it defined that variable incorrectly. That error created the possibility that study participants were misclassified and that their results were made part of the results of the wrong study group. This error makes the study worthless. Instead of being rejected this study has been cited as authoritative over three-hundred times. This occurred because some very smart and very skilled people lacked the cultural competence to detect the incorrect definition. On the other hand, the matter is not altogether disagreeable because it gave this writer an excuse to have a second splash of Scotch.

Those who do studies or write reports about the LGBT community should read the guide offered by the American Psychological Association entitled *Avoiding Heterosexist Bias in Psychological Research* (Herek and Kimmel, 1991). It is always wise if one does not know the trail to follow those who do.

Question: What is HIV stigma and HIV shame?

A stigma is literal or figurative mark placed upon something or someone that acts to tarnish the reputation and detract from the accepted value of anything that is so marked. Placing a second-place ribbon on something at the county fair, for example, marks it as not as good and not as valuable as the thing that got the first-place ribbon. Shame is the hurtful human feeling that one's reputation and worth have been reduced in the eyes of other people and that one is not measuring up to the accepted standard. It can also be what others expect you to feel if you are so marked.

HIV stigma is a figurative mark some people place upon anyone who has HIV. It is the basis that they use to justify discrimination directed at those so marked. HIV shame is the hurtful feeling of disgrace that HIV+ people may feel or are sometimes expected to feel because of their diagnosis. It is based upon the incorrect belief that HIV+ people are less reputable or worthy after their diagnosis than they were before their diagnosis.

It would be a lie to say that a HIV+ person is not different after their diagnosis than they were before it. They know afterwards that they have a serious medical condition and that many people will respond to it with dread, social distancing and unjust behavior. It would also be a lie to say that HIV+ people merit that response. HIV stigma and HIV shame are purely the products of fear and ignorance.

If there is any group of people anywhere on Earth that should understand the consequences of being unjustly stigmatized because of fear and ignorance it is we LGBTs. We have a long history of living with that burden. Many legions from our community have been persecuted, imprisoned and murdered because of it. We have no excuse for putting that sort of burden on others. We, likewise, have no excuse for standing quietly on the sidelines as the yoke of HIV stigma is placed on someone who needs the justice and comfort that we can give him.

Our history gives or should give the members of our community an understanding of HIV. That condition has stalked us like it stalked no other, but we have fought it and brought it to the place and time where it will be defeated. That defeat will not be complete until our community uniformly and assertively stands for the principle that HIV+ people are not less or less valued after their diagnosis than they were before it. That defeat will also not be complete until the ignorance and fear that clothe HIV is stripped away and the truth is laid bare. It is simply not dangerous or disgraceful to be around HIV+ people and no stigma or shame is due.

Question: What is gay bashing and what can I do if it happens to me?

Gay bashing is verbal and/or physical abuse directed at a LGBT person because of their LGBT identity or their perceived identity. It can occur in person, by electronic messaging or through things like rumors, graffiti or hazing. It is most prevalent in middle school or high school but can happen to a person of any age. It may or may not involve a hate crime.

It is very common for victims of bashing to feel fear, rejection, anxiety, anger, depression and/or helplessness. It is also common for bashing to have a negative impact on the victim's self-esteem and his relationships and attitudes. Victims are always chosen because they seem different, isolated and/or vulnerable.

Dealing with bashing has two parts. First, the greatest harm bashing can do occurs when the victim internalizes the negatives being directed at him/her and makes them part of his own pattern of thinking and feeling. The lasting damage of bashing occurs when the victim begins to think he deserves being bashed or that maybe the abuser is right. Let's be clear. No characteristic a victim has or is perceived to have justifies bashing being directed at him/her. Dealing with bashing calls for the victim to keep in touch with his personal worth and with the real reason the bashing occurred. That reason is the personal character negatives of the abuser.

The second part in dealing with bashing is action. A bully picks a victim because he believes he can get what he wants through abusing that person and he can get away with it. He must be shown that he is wrong and that his behavior is going to cost him. That will occur when the victim shows, using his personal power, that he is not going to quietly accept the role of victim. This starts when the victim begins to document the situation. That includes listing the names of perpetrators and witnesses, dates, places and a description of what happened. A victim's response should usually be nonviolent.

A violent or threatening response to a basher is rarely a useful tool in the long run because our society typically reacts negatively to such responses. It also lets the abuser paint himself as a victim and gives him the opportunity to claim self-defense when he responds back. It is usually more productive for a victim to consider who might help him deal nonviolently with the problem. The exception of course is when immediate self-defense is necessary. In that case, it is useful to know local laws related to that.

It is not unusual for others to watch or know about the bashing but to do nothing because they support the basher or at least they do not like gays. They might also not want to be involved in someone else's problem or not want to risk becoming a victim too. This is part of why documenting is important. People tend to respond better to official interventions than to private ones and officials can do a better job if they have useful information.

Victims sometimes help the abuser by not using the resources available to them. This happens for one or more of six reasons: 1) They are intimidated, 2) They think doing anything about the bullying will cause more trouble, 3) They think they deserve what is happening, 4) They do not think anything will work and nobody will help, 5) The abuser is anonymous, 6) They do not know about the resources available to them. These rationales must be defeated.

Often a victim cannot think of think of anyone who would help, or he tries to get someone to help but gets none. He needs to "brain storm". Brain storming is thinking of every possible person or group that can help. It includes getting input from others about that. He needs to use the best ideas. It is critical that he not keep the problem a secret. There are lots of help possibilities. Among them are:

Friends and/or family. Talking to friends helps relieve the pressure a victim may feel and gives a sense of support. If there are not any friends, then join a support group. If immediate family members won't help, branch out. Talk to aunts, uncles, cousins and/or grandparents. Pick anyone who might be supportive. They might not only help but they might also pressure immediate family members to do so.

School or community officials. These people are important because they have local power that they can bring to the problem at once. Consider which of them has the power to help but is not a homophobe and then ask for it. Document who you talk to, what was said and what happened later. If they won't help, document that. If the situation is happening at school and a school official refuses to help a victim may wish to talk to a lawyer about bringing a lawsuit for negligent supervision. Do not worry about making the problem bigger because the abuser wants the situation to be small and unnoticed by those with power.

School or local groups that are LGBT oriented or friendly. Groups are often more effective at dealing with problems than individuals are because they offer a lot of support and more people equates to more resources and more ability to bring pressure to those with the power to act. Groups are good if you need to find an anonymous abuser because increases the odds that someone will know him or know of him.

One such group is Parents, Family & Friends of Lesbians and Gays (PFLAG). It is a gay friendly support group that has local chapters across the nation. Another group is the Gay-Straight Alliance. It is a support group related to the welfare and safety of LGBT high school and college students.

U.S. Department of Education/Office of Civil Rights (OCR). A victim of a bashing at a school may be able to file a complaint with the OCR under Title IX. File a complaint at: www2.ed.gov/ocr.

Law enforcement agencies/courts. Research the local, state and federal laws related to bashing and use them as a tool. The law and those who enforce it can not only be used to directly intervene in bullying but can also be used indirectly as well. A basher may back off when he becomes aware that the victim knows the law and he is not afraid to use it. All victims of bashing should become familiar with both the criminal laws related to assault, battery and hate crimes and with civil laws that may be the basis of a lawsuit such as the intentional infliction of mental distress. You can get enough information about this using a computer search engine to know when you should call a cop or a lawyer.

Local newspapers. A victim always has the choice of making his abuse issue public. He can talk to a reporter or write a letter to the editor. Neither a bully nor an official who has refused to help will like the public knowing about the situation. It may be wise to discuss the matter with a lawyer before publicly naming or characterizing anyone, but the general issue can be brought to light. The ensuing investigation will name people.

State and national LGBT or LGBT friendly groups. Every state has at least one such group. Among them are: The Gay, Lesbian & Straight Educators Network (GLSEN), the LGBT National Help Center (Hotline: 1-888-843-4564), Gay & Lesbian Association of Retiring Persons (GLARP), Gay, Lesbian Alliance Against Defamation (GLAAD) and Pride at Work.

Groups that support and promote civil rights. Among these are: The National Association for the Advancement of

Colored People (NAACP) (www. naacp.org /pages/find-your-local-unit), UnidosUS (formerly called the National Council of La Raza) (www.undosus.org), the American Civil Liberties Union (www.aclu.org/affiliates) and Lambda Legal Defense and Education Fund (www.lambdalegal.org/about-us/contact-us). Few school or government officials will ignore a letter or call from any of these organizations.

Business officials. Most social media businesses such as Facebook or Twitter have a means of addressing their site being used abusively by bullies. Some businesses take that abuse more seriously than others, but an abuse victim should try to use that process and document it. A victim can also talk to local gay friendly business owners about any anti-gay situation or abuse happening locally. These owners have more clout with local officials than most victims do.

There are other things victims can to do to help themselves if physically attacked:

1. Seek medical attention even if the injury does not seem serious. Some injuries such as concussions do not always have obvious symptoms. The police need to know not only that you were injured but also how serious the injury is. A defendant's lawyer may use a victim's failure to seek medical help as part of his defense. Seeking aid also creates a medical record.
2. Report the attack to the police at once. A defense lawyer may use the victim's failure to quickly report the attack as a tool to help his client escape justice.
3. Document who you talk to (including badge numbers) and what happens.
4. Get a business card from anyone you talk to if they have them.
5. Check to see that an official police report is filed. If a report is not filed a victim has the right to file a complaint. That complaint becomes part of the official record.

Question: Is gay relationship domestic violence related to of homophobia or heterosexism?

The Department of Justice defines domestic violence as "a pattern of abusive behavior in any relationship that is used by one partner to gain or maintain power and control over another intimate partner". The abuse may be physical, verbal, emotional, economic or psychological. The goal of an abuser is control of the victim and through that control to achieve a sense of authority and power. The abuser most often employs the emotions of fear and/or dependency on the part of the victim to gain that power. Those emotions are often sustained both by an ongoing pattern of abuse and by the abuser isolating the victim, so the victim has no support network he/she can use to deal with the problem.

Both homophobia and heterosexism can be part of the domestic violence picture in a gay relationship. Psychologists generally assert that abusers tend to have low self-esteem. A gay man may find his homosexuality repugnant and will compensate for that through the sense of power and worth he gets by dominating someone else. He may also find the homosexuality of his partner a reflection of what he dislikes about himself. He may respond to that by physical and/or verbal abuse of the other person.

The victim of domestic abuse also sometimes has self-esteem issues. He may feel that he is not really a worthy person and he deserves the abuse he is getting. This, of course, compounds the problem because it feeds into the mindset of the abuser and makes his control stronger. It also significantly reduces the likelihood that the victim will look for help. The fact is however that domestic abuse is never the victim's fault and he does not deserve it.

Heterosexism is also often part of the reason domestic abuse situations continue. Homosexuals grow up learning heterosexual norms and ideals. One of those ideals is that a long-term monogamous relationship is what should be strived for and that in achieving that sort of relationship both parties in it must preserve it through better or worse. Many gay men want a long-term relationship but, of course, there are a lot fewer possible mates in society for him than the heterosexual man has available to him. Some gay men respond to that by accepting abusive behavior as part of the relationship. This may especially be the case if a victim has been isolated and has come to believe that the abuse is normal for domestic couples.

Many homosexuals also find heterosexism is a barrier when they do seek help. This is especially true for homosexual men because lesbians can hide their sexual orientation when they seek help simply by saying their abuser is male. This fits the heterosexist model which assumes a male perpetrator and a female victim. They will then receive services.

Many people who work in the law enforcement and the social work fields are simply not trained to deal with male on male domestic violence. Some discount the merit of abuse complaints they receive from gays because of their attitudes about homosexuality. They may also have the attitude that men are supposed to be able to take care of themselves in an abusive situation. Homosexual men who are abused may share that belief and may be embarrassed to ask for help as well. Consequently, help may not be offered or looked for. When it is offered, it is often inadequate because the system is commonly designed and funded to help female abuse victims but not male ones. There are, for example, few shelters in the United States for male victims of abuse (Freiss, 1997).

Question: Why do men stay in abusive relationships?

The question of why people stay in abusive relationships is often asked. This is especially true in the case of male on male abuse because it is assumed that men are not subject to feelings of dependency or intimidation. The fact however is that men stay in these relationships for the same reasons women do. These are: financial dependence, inexperience in domestic relationships, love, hope that the abuser will change, loneliness, commitment to the relationship, emotional dependence, fear, guilt, low self-esteem, physical attraction/dependence and/or feeling that there is no practical alternative to the relationship (Cruz, 2003).

Question: What can I do if I am the victim in an abusive relationship?

If you are in an abusive relationship it is critical that you know what to do in advance of the next incident. It is also important that you seek professional help through local domestic violence services. Here are some other recommendations.
1. Know what domestic abuse is. Disagreements and arguments are a normal part of domestic relationships. They become abusive when the language used is demeaning, intimidating or threatening or when one partner physically assaults or tries to psychologically or physically control the other.

2. If an abusive situation starts, try to go to a room that you have previously found to have no weapons in it and has more than one way out. If it escalates into physical abuse such as hitting or throwing things, or you feel you are in danger leave the house or apartment at once.
3. Take off items like necklaces, scarfs or neckties that can be used for choking.
4. Teach children in the home how to get help and where they can go that is safe. This will increase their sense of empowerment and reduce the sense of victimization that seeing the abuse may bring. Talk to them so that they know why the abuse is happening and that it is not their fault. Let them ask questions.
5. Have a phone accessible as much as possible. Call 911 as soon as possible after the incident to report what happened and then call a friend who will help you. Get the badge number and name of the police officer that responds and ask for the case number.
6. If the police do not make out an incident report you can file a complaint with the police department. This will put the matter on someone's desk for resolution and it will be an official record of the incident.
7. If you are physically assaulted and you cannot get away make yourself as small a target as possible by rolling into a ball in a corner and protect your head with your arms.
8. Let friends and neighbors know about your situation. Talking to them about your situation might be embarrassing but they cannot do anything to help you if they do not know about it.
9. Create a plan to leave the relationship and follow the plan.
10. Know in advance who to call and where to go. Do not tell the abuser or his friends what the plan is.
11. Create an emergency kit holding money, medication, clothing and copies of critical paperwork such as identification and court orders. Store the kit at a friend's house.
12. Get medical help if you are injured and, if possible, take pictures of the injury(s).
13. Make use of local domestic violence services.
14. **Call the U.S. Domestic Violence hotline (1-800-799-7233) or the LGBT National Help Center hotline (1-888-843-4564).**

Question: Am I abusing my partner and what can I do if I am?
If you intimidate, threaten, demean, try to control or physically assault your partner you are abusing him. It may be that you don't think you can stop doing it because you get so angry or jealous that you do things you regret later, and you may really care about your partner and fear that you are losing him. Those feelings are real, but they don't excuse being abusive. You can and must stop the abusive behavior now.

The first step in doing that is taking responsibility for what you are doing. Throw out all the things you tell yourself to justify what you are doing because your partner does not deserve what is happening and what you are doing is not his fault even if he is doing something you hate. He does not control your behavior, you do. If you are using drugs and/or alcohol you should stop. You should then seek out the help of a professional therapist that specializes in domestic abuse issues. Your sessions with the therapist should be individual ones and not part of couple's therapy. Couples therapy may or may not come later.

Question: Is drug/alcohol use/abuse a factor in domestic violence among gays?
Drugs and alcohol are disinhibitors. They act on the mind so that the user will do and say things that he otherwise would not do or say. Drugs and alcohol are also widely used and abused within the gay community. Some of them, like Chrystal Meth, are very addictive and may cause the user to become violent, paranoid or confused. This may result in an ongoing cycle of use that fuels an ongoing cycle of abusive behavior directed at a partner. Substance abuse and depression are the factors that are strongly related to domestic abuse among gay men (Houston, 2007).

Question: How can a person tell if he is in a good long-term relationship?
These are the factors that are common to most good relationships:
1. Effective communication. There is a lot of it and both parties feel open to it. Both parties actively and non-judgmentally listen as well as talk and both are comfortable talking to the

other one. They also ask questions to clarify what has been said.
2. Honesty and trust. Both parties are honest with and trust their partner. Each feels worthy of the trust of the other and believes the other is honest with them. Each feels comfortable in putting his welfare in his partner's hands. Neither partner will ever intentionally embarrass the other in public.
3. Openness. There are not a lot of secrets in the relationship because both men believe they can share with the other person without fearing that person will betray a confidence. Both partners are willing to admit when they are wrong, and they express their opinions without fear that their partner will respond negatively to that. The partners may disagree, but they are open to hearing an opinion they do not share and do not respond with personal put downs, anger or sarcasm.
4. Fairness and equality. Neither of the partners is "the boss" and the partners openly try to fill the needs of the other. Decisions are made jointly and when disagreements happen the partners are willing compromise without having hard feelings about it.
5. Individuality. Each person is free to be an individual, to express that individuality and to have his own identity. The partners are comfortable in both doing some things without the other person and with the other person doing some things without them.
6. Support. Each of the partners believes he can rely on the other for support and help in troubled times. He also believes he can rely on his partner to share the joy in good times.
7. There are many more positive verbal and nonverbal messages going between the partners than negative ones.
8. Each of the partners really likes and respects the other person and likes to be with him. The relationship is not viewed as a burden by either partner and they are not staying together because that is what others expect of them.

Question: How does a person find a good long-term relationship?
The first step is being willing to having one. Not everyone wants to be involved in that kind of relationship and that is a valid choice although one wonders if it is ever wise to say "never". Hearts are

funny things and sometimes things happen without intent when fate intervenes.

Long-term relationships are always intentional acts. Sometimes a person goes out looking for that kind of relationship. Sometimes a person starts a relationship with no intention of continuing it, but it continues anyway. Either way the relationship evolves into something that lasts. That evolution can only occur if the parties involved allow it to. It is based on the attitude and the intentional act of valuing one's partner so much that the inevitable rough spots do not end the relationship.

A guy who wants a long-term relationship also must understand the kinds of relationships gay men have and kind of relationships he himself typically has. People typically gravitate to certain types of people and certain kinds of relationships. A guy who historically has gravitated toward backroom sex, one-night stands or serial relationships will need to assess his desires and situation honestly because behavior patterns can be hard to overcome. Similarly, a guy who gets dumped repeatedly or never tries to connect needs to assess himself and his situation honestly.

It is often thought that love is a key to a long-term relationship. That is true, but love tends to morph as the relationship continues over the course of time. This obviously is because people change. It is also true that sometimes even people who love each other simply cannot live together. The secret behind successful long-term relationships therefore is that the couple is compatible at the beginning of the relationship and they work to stay that way.

There are many people who have successful relationships with a long-term partner who do not share that partner's religious, political or social views but the odds are against that happening. Relationships involving people with dissimilar sexual/intimacy wants and needs typically do not last either. Disagreements about pets, kids and money are often hard to reconcile too. The baseline factor is that the couple let their differences become wedges instead of using them as building blocks. The cardinal rule related to compatibility is that each partner feels valued, respected and trusted by the other one.

If you want a long-term relationship you can use websites such as onegoodlove.com or match.com to find people that the website judges to be compatible with you. Websites like these that are goaled toward long-term relationships typically collect, analyze and compare data their clients give them to find matches. You can also go places where you are likely to find people who like at least some of the same things you like. Either way once you find a compatible person you are going to have to get your hands dirty getting to know that person and letting that person know you. You are also going to have to be willing to spend some time on it.

There are three things you should not do. First, do not act on the basis that there is only one person out there who is meant for you and that kismet will put you together. There are lots of people out there that you can have a happy long-term relationship with, but fate is rarely a good matchmaker.

Second, do not settle for just any relationship just because you want a long-term partner. If you want a relationship that lasts you must keep looking for it until your gut, your head and your heart agree that you found "him" then you are going to have to earn what you want.

Third, do not walk away from a relationship because things have gotten tough. Every long-term relationship occasionally meets a briar patch or two. That is not to say that walking away is never the best choice, but long-term relationships are not made that way.

Question: Is it possible to have a successful long-term open relationship?

Around half of gay couples have a relationship that lets each of them to have sex with men other than their life partner (Northrup, Schwartz and Witte, 2012). These open relationships are based on the same general factors as other successful long-term relationships but there are a few differences. The most important of these is that the partners should agree at the beginning of the relationship that it is an open relationship and set up rules to govern what is acceptable and not acceptable. It is imperative that the process of rule creation be frank and honest, that the partners are willing to compromise, that the rules are fair to both parties and that they can be changed if both parties agree.

Honesty and trust are key ingredients in any long-term relationship, but it is especially important in one that is not sexually exclusive. Each person must fulfill his part of the agreement he makes with his partner and thereby be worthy of being trusted. Each of them must also trust that his partner is fulfilling his responsibilities under the agreement. This environment is supported by honest communication, mutual support and the love that is shared between them.

One of the factors that must be dealt with when making rules governing an open relationship is what sexual practices are allowed or not allowed. Nonexclusive sex increases the odds of catching a STI or HIV so an agreement about when safer sex techniques must be used should be part of that discussion. Each of the partners should also talk about sexual things they will want to do with those outside the relationship and things they do not want their partner to do. The conversation should also deal with whether they tell each other about the sexual liaisons they have or keep it private. If the partners agree to not talk about the sex they have with other people, they should also agree that it can be talked about if a sexual encounter goes bad or if they need help/support for some reason.

Question: Can gays be good parents?

Absolutely, yes! The US National Longitudinal Lesbian Family Study shows that gays can be as good as or better at parenting than heterosexuals are. It followed the male and female children of lesbian mothers from birth to age 17. The research showed these seventeen-year-old children rated higher in total competence and in academic and social skills while rating lower in rule breaking and aggression than were the children of heterosexuals. The study only dealt with lesbian mothers and did not deal with the children of male homosexuals, but the authors of the study explicitly say study shows that same sex parents can raise psychological healthy children (Gartrell, 2010).

The definitive statement on the arguments surrounding gay parenting was offered by the American Sociological Association (ASA) in an Amicus Curiae brief to the United States Supreme Court in the case of Hollingsworth v. Perry (2013). In this brief, the ASA noted the weight of the evidence that has been collected over decades shows same-sex people in a stable relationship are just as capable of raising well-adjusted children as opposite-sex couples are. It also refuted the arguments presented by those opposed to same-sex couples parenting children and said flatly that there is no creditable evidence supporting that opposition. The ASA asserted that the primary factors in raising well-adjusted children are giving the child parents that are in a stable two parent relationship, giving a stable parent–child relationship and the greater socioeconomic resources two parents can provide.

A gay man can father his own child and usually can adopt or have a foster child. The fact that you have a child does not mean you are a good parent however. Good parenting has been studied a lot and certain factors are clear. Among these are:

1. Being a good role model. A good parent not only gives standards verbally but also shows the child what to do through his own behavior.
2. Giving lots of love, not lots of things.
3. Being involved in the child's life while allowing him to be appropriately independent.
4. Allowing the child to grow by adjusting to the child's changing needs.
5. Setting up and enforcing rules and values while not micromanaging the child's life.
6. Being willing and able to explain rules and values to the child so he/she knows why the expectations exist.
7. Being consistent and fair.
8. Showing the child respect and expecting it in return.

Question: How do I go about coming out of the closet?
The act of acknowledging one's LGBT identity is known as "coming out". Nobody can really tell another person how they should come out because everyone's situation is different. Each person is dealing with different people and different dynamics. There are some general guidelines that might be considered however.

The first step in coming out is coming out to yourself. The second step is being okay with who you are. You must accept that: 1) you are LGBT, 2) your sexual orientation/gender identity is not likely to change, 3) being LGBT is natural and normal and 4) you can have a happy life. If you do not reveal who you really are, nobody can have a relationship with that person.

It is always wise to think before you act. The first person you pick to come out to should be the one you are surest of. It should be a person you believe will support you and continue to care about you after you have spilled the beans. It is not a good sign if this person thinks of Donald Trump as a personal role model. It is not a good sign if this person can quote Romans 1:18-32 verbatim or thinks the story of Sodom and Gomorrah is true. You should also pick someone else if this person ever orders a decaf cappuccino. He who does not understand the need for caffeine in cappuccino understands nothing.

Openly tell your first pick that he/she is the first person you have told because you trust him/her most and ask him/her to allow you to be the one to tell others. If the person asks why you have not mentioned it before be genuine with him/her. A common approach for that is to simply tell him/her that you only recently came to terms with it yourself. It is okay to ask him/her what he/she thinks about what you have told him/her and to have a conversation about it. It is also okay to put that off until later if that seems right to you.

If it is wise to think before you act, then it is also wise to prepare before you act. There are three general types of responses you might get when you come out to someone. Being prepared to respond to each of them will somewhat ease the anxiety you feel before you tell them you are gay, and it will also allow you to have your facts and thoughts collected. The three kinds of responses are: 1) genuine support, 2) acceptance (I'm not rejecting you, but I wish you were not LGBT) and 3) rejection. Rejection often morphs into acceptance eventually, but it rarely becomes support.

It is wise to prepare yourself for the possibility that someone you thought would be supportive and caring does not do that and may even be hurtful. There really is no way to not feel the pain involved in that. It is the innate human response people naturally feel when experiencing rejection and loss.

It is important that you not let that setback end your coming out process. The reasons you decided to come out in the first place are still valid and other people will be supportive. Those supportive people will be more important than ever at this point because the person who rejected you is probably going to be busy outing you every chance he/she gets.

There are lots of gays who are out to some people and not to others. Coming out is not about becoming a martyr. A lot of us, for example, are out to some friends and family members but not out to others because of the perceived risks involved. It is common to be out to people you are close to but not out at work. At the same time, it is also common to be out to everyone. Only you can decide what you want to do. That decision should be thought out and feel right to you before you do it.

There are choices in how to tell other people you are gay. You can throw caution to the wind and take the attitude that people will either accept you or not, but you are not going to hide who you are from anyone. This might be the basis of coming out through one mass email or on Facebook. This naturally ends the selective, support driven approach suggested above and tells your close friends and family that they are all equal in your eyes. That can cause some hurt feelings. People who feel close to you may feel less close if you do this. Perhaps it might be better to come out to everyone after you have personally told those you care most about.

If you choose the more personal approach you can come out by slipping it into a conversation. You can also be bold and do it by forthrightly telling the person you have something important to tell him/her, then just doing it. Each method of coming out has consequences. Sometimes those are good and sometimes they're not. Never tell someone you are gay unless you are reasonably sure it is physically safe to do so.

Your sexual orientation is not a negative and should never be used as one. It is unwise to tell someone you are gay because you are angry, or you want to hurt them. If you do that they will always associate your sexual orientation with that even if they may eventually forgive you.

The gay community is a valuable resource for those who are in the coming out process. It is wise to connect with others in it before you come out because other gays have been through the process and they will be supportive. You can do that through a gay resource center or by just talking to gay friends. Most gays are verbally fluent, so the conversation might also be delightful.

Question: Are gay couple relationships different than straight couple relationships?

Yes, in some ways they are and no, in some ways they are not. It has been known for some time that heterosexual couples and gay or lesbian couples are similar in many ways. A 1983 study, for example, found that straight couples and gay couples are similar in problem solving, values and the ability to negotiate to solve relationship problems. The study also noted some dissimilarity.

An example is that one partner making more money than the other one affects the balance of power in straight and gay relationships but does not typically affect lesbian ones (Blumstein and Schwartz, 1983).

A 1994 study found the conflict resolution styles of gay and straight couples to be similar. Interestingly, they found that much of the difference existing between homosexual couples and heterosexual couples is the result of gender and not of sexual orientation. In other words, it is because the couple consists of two men or a man and a woman. The study also found that gay men make more effort to resolve conflicts than heterosexual men do and that they are more adaptive/flexible, and less role bound (Metz and Rosser, 1994). Gay couples also tend to be better at communicating with one another than straight couples are (Northrup, Schwartz and Witte, 2012).

In 2004 another study of relationships found that in 50% of the qualities measured by the study there was no significant difference between heterosexual couples, lesbian couples and gay couples. Where differences were found gays and lesbians were better functioning than straights 78% of the time. The only major area where gays and lesbians were less well-functioning was in the support their relationship got from family. Aside from that gays and lesbians are better able to adjust to relationship stress, better able to constructively settle disputes, more positive in relationship style, more equal in how they shared power, more positive in their communication style and less prone to use a command/withdraw relationship style (Kurdek, 2004).

More recently another study showed that there are differences between gay, lesbian and straight couples in their primary relationships, but these differences are sometimes small. Gays and lesbians receive somewhat more support for their relationship from friends but a small amount less from family. They also were slightly more equal in status within their relationship and they distributed the household labor more equally. They also have fewer institutionalized barriers to ending their relationship thus are more likely to separate (Kurdek, 2006)

Chapter 6
Gay Health Issues

Question: What are the major health issues gay men should be concerned about?

The National Institute of Health recommends gay men to talk to their doctor about:

1. ***HIV/AIDS*** – Men who have sex with men (MSM) have much higher rates of HIV/AIDS than any other group. A gay man should talk with his doctor about any risk factors he has for getting HIV such as intravenous drug use or unprotected sex and about being tested for AIDS/HIV. He should also tell the doctor about symptoms such as flu-like symptoms, fatigue, rashes, weight loss or enlarged lymph nodes since these may signal newly acquired HIV. HIV+ men should be under the care of a physician because there are treatments available that can be used to manage the condition very effectively. All gay men should have a discussion with their doctor about the use of PrEP.
2. ***Substance Use*** – Gay men use some drugs more than does the general American population. This use can have negative health consequences. The doctor should be made aware of any drugs you use both because of their direct effect on your health and because of possible interactions with other substances being used.
3. ***Depression/Anxiety*** – Gay men suffer from some forms of anxiety and depression at higher rates than do straight men and the American population generally. These feelings can have serious health consequences, including drug addiction and death. If he is worried or depressed, he should discuss it with his doctor.
4. ***Hepatitis Immunization*** – Men who have sex with men have higher rates of hepatitis than does the general American population. Hepatitis can cause damage to the liver and can lead to cancer of the liver and death. All MSM should be talk to their doctor about being immunized against hepatitis A and B.
5. ***STIs and STDs*** – All people who have sex are at risk of catching a sexually transmitted infection (STI) and of it becoming a sexually transmitted disease (STD). Some of these

can be cured while others can, at best, only be managed. A gay man who thinks he may have an STI should see his doctor at once because waiting can have grave consequences. The risk of catching a STI is reduced by practicing safer sex methods so having a discussion with a medical professional about how to do these methods is important.

6. ***Prostate, Testicular, and Colon Cancer*** – These cancers are, of course, found in men of all sexual orientations and we are not an exception. A gay man would be wise to have a discussion with his doctor about being tested for them and what the symptoms are. The sooner treatment begins for any form of cancer the better. The Centers on Disease Control and Prevention state that cancer is a leading cause of death in all men including those who are gay.

7. ***Skin Cancer*** – Skin cancer is a very common form of cancer in humans generally, but gay and bisexual men are twice as likely to get it as heterosexual men are.

8. ***Alcohol Use*** – Everyone should make their doctor aware of their alcohol use since even low levels of use can have physical consequences including liver and/or kidney disease. Those gay men who abuse alcohol should seek help through an alcohol treatment professional who is sensitive to the needs of gay men. A doctor who is sensitive to these needs can be a valuable resource in finding such a professional.

9. ***Tobacco Use*** – Gay men use tobacco at much higher rates than straight men do. Tobacco use has been strongly linked to heart disease, high blood pressure, lung cancer and several other diseases. A gay man who smokes should talk to his doctor about methods of stopping the use of tobacco.

10. ***Fitness*** – Gay men tend to be more critical of their body image that straight men are. They are therefore more likely to have an eating disorder such as bulimia or anorexia. A poor self-image also can lead to using substances like steroids which can cause serious long-term health consequences. Other gay men such as Chubs and Bears embrace their body image which tends to be overweight or obese. This can lead to health consequences such as diabetes, high blood pressure and heart disease. Per the Centers for Disease Control and Prevention, heart disease is the number one killer of men, including gays, in the United States.

11. ***Anal Papilloma*** – Many gay men have anal and/or genital warts. These warts are caused by the human papilloma virus. It is very contagious and can lead to anal cancer. Gay and bisexual men, as a group, have a higher risk of anal cancer than hetero men do. Men who have sex with men should talk to their doctor about routine screening using an anal Pap smear, so they can detect such a cancer early and about treating the existing warts.

Question: What are the basics I should know about HIV and AIDS?

Being infected with HIV is extremely serious. HIV is a virus that is very efficient in reproducing itself in the human body. It does that by invading and taking over immune system cells. If left untreated the virus rapidly replicates itself inside those cells and the cell is eventually killed. As the virus replicates more and more immune system cells are attacked, taken over and killed. This weakens the body's immune system and over time the immune system can no longer effectively fight disease. It is commonly one of these diseases that becomes the official cause of death.

HIV exists primarily in two forms: HIV-1 which is the form typically found in the North America and HIV-2 which is found primarily in Africa. HIV-1 and HIV-2 each has multiple strains (sub-types) so the HIV a person has may not be the same as that of another person. It is possible to have more than one strain at the same time.

HIV is becoming more and more a chronic condition rather than one that usually leads to AIDS and death. HIV can be well-controlled and when it is controlled a patient can reasonably expect to live a normal or near normal human life span (Rodger & Lodwick, 2013). It is becoming more common for HIV+ people to have an undetectable viral load. At the same time, HIV+ people can easily sabotage their own treatment. An example of this is that smoking tobacco while HIV+ can lead to a significantly reduced life span (Helleberg & Afzal, 2013; De & Farley, 2013).

The key to living with HIV is to have a doctor that is knowledgeable in the diagnosis and treatment of HIV/AIDS, strictly following the treatment plan and openly communicating with the doctor. Part of that communication is talking about the emotional aspects of living with HIV and the problems the patient is having with following the treatment plan.

The goal in treating HIV is keeping the viral load (level of HIV in the blood) low and the level of CD4 cells (cells that activate the immune system) high. This is done using highly active antiretroviral therapy (HAART) which is a cocktail of drugs prescribed by a doctor for each patient. HAART is sometimes also called combination antiretroviral therapy (cART). Many of these drugs are available in a generic form and may be covered by insurance and/or Medicare. Some HIV patients are now being treated using a combination of drugs that are given in one pill, once a day. HIV treatment medications may have side effects that should be discussed with the prescribing doctor.

If HIV is left unmanaged or HIV treatment does not work the immune system may become so weak that a diagnosis of Acquired Immune Deficiency Syndrome (AIDS) will be given. The person will become chronically sick because his body can no longer fight off disease. A person with untreated AIDS may live one to three years unless he develops an AIDS related disease.

AIDS however can often be managed through the rigorous use of a treatment plan. This may even move the viral load and CD4 cell levels back to HIV levels. The diagnosis of AIDS won't change however. The AIDS patient must work diligently to avoid getting any other disease or infection. AIDS is the sixth leading cause of death in the U.S. in the 25-44 age group.

Question: What are the symptoms of HIV and AIDS?

Per the US Department of Health and Human Services website (AIDS.gov) many people with HIV have no symptoms initially. Others develop flu-like symptoms within two weeks to three months after getting the human immunodeficiency virus (HIV). During this time, they may have a fever, a sore throat, feel fatigued, have chills and/or night sweats and may also experience unexplained weight loss, rashes, ulcers in the mouth and/or enlarged lymph nodes in the neck, groin or armpits. Patients commonly describe this as the "worst flu ever". These symptoms may pass within a week or two and the person may feel fine again. This phase of the condition is called acute retroviral syndrome (ARS) or primary HIV infection.

During this phase, the person has a high load of the virus in his blood and is very infectious. It is also during this phase that the person's body begins to create antibodies to fight the HIV invasion. This is called "seroconversion". This term simply means that the person's blood has converted (changed) from having no antibodies in it related to fighting HIV to having those antibodies. These antibodies are what most HIV tests look for.

Once the person passes through the early stage of HIV infection he moves into the chronic phase (also called the latency phase) of the condition. During this phase the HIV virus is still present in the blood and it can be transmitted to other people but is less active. Some people have reoccurring symptoms during this phase, but many have no symptoms at all. This stage can last ten years or longer even without HIV treatment.

The fact that a person is HIV+ does not mean he has AIDS. AIDS is the final stage of HIV infection. It most commonly occurs in HIV+ people who have not gotten HIV treatment.

The website MedicineNet.com says that a diagnosis of AIDS requires that a person have confirmed HIV+ test results and have some other AIDS defining medical condition, a level of CD4 cells in the blood measuring less than 200 cells per milliliter or a laboratory result showing fewer than 14% of lymphocytes in the blood are CD4 cells. AIDS patients often have fatigue, diarrhea, nausea, vomiting, fever, chills, night sweats, and wasting syndrome. They often also catch other infections. The proper and correct diagnosis and treatment of HIV/AIDS demands the services of a doctor who is knowledgeable in the area.

Question: Should I be tested for HIV and, if so, when should I be tested?

The Centers for Disease Control and Prevention recommend that all men who have sex with men be tested for HIV at least once even if they do not think the risk factors for HIV apply to them. It further recommends that you should have yourself tested at least once a year if you inject drugs or steroids, have sex for pay, have sex with a HIV+ person, have more than one sex partner since your last HIV test or have sex with someone who has had other partners. Getting tested is also wise if you are sexually active with a partner who has an unknown HIV status and you have symptoms like those associated with HIV.

The US Department of Health and Human Services website (AIDS.com) says that many medical authorities believe persons who are involved in high-risk behavior (i.e. injection drug use and/or unprotected sex with others who engage in high-risk behavior) should be tested every 3-6 months. The website also suggests that sexually active people make having an HIV test part of routine medical exams. If you want to be tested because you are concerned about a possible exposure to HIV you should have an honest discussion about it with your doctor at once after the possible exposure.

When to get tested also is related to the type of HIV test you are going to take. The most commonly used tests done in this country measure HIV antibodies and it takes two weeks to three months for those antibodies to develop (depending upon the person). If you take the test too early your test may not be correct. The testing site may ask you to undergo another HIV test a few months after the first one if they believe the first test was done too early or was for some other reason faulty. If your test is positive you may be scheduled to take another HIV test of a different type to confirm the result.

The other kinds of HIV tests either look in the blood for the virus itself or for the genetic material of the virus. These tests can be done within 1-3 weeks of being infected. These tests are not as commonly given as the antigen kind of tests. You are probably not going to have a choice about what kind of test you are going to get since most testing sites only give the antigen kind of test during original testing because of costs. A discussion with the testing site about the kind of test(s) they offer and what your window period is for having the test done could be useful.

Question: Do teenagers need to be tested for HIV?
The Centers for Disease Control and Prevention (CDC) recommend that all people who are sexually active or inject drugs get tested for HIV. Since teenagers are often sexually active and/or use needles to inject drugs this recommendation includes them. Unfortunately, teens, as a group, are the least likely to get tested. This is because they do not know where to get a test, they do not want to be seen at a HIV testing site or they do not think they have much chance of getting HIV (Phillips & Ybarra, 2015).

The CDC says that one in four people with HIV are in the 13-24 age category and most do not know they have the infection.

Question: Where can I get tested for HIV?
There are several places you can get tested for HIV. These include doctor's offices, clinics, local health departments, and Planned Parenthood clinics. Gay resource centers either offer this service or can direct you to a place to have the test done. You can find a testing site by logging on to AIDS.com then entering your ZIP code in the proper space. Another way is to call the CDC information line at 1-800-232-4636. The CDC representative will tell you where to go for a test locally.

Some places do anonymous testing which matches a code number to your test sample rather than your name while other places do confidential testing which matches your sample with your name but holds that information as private. Testing sites typically will not give testing results over the phone. You can also buy kits that allow you to test yourself at home.

Question: What are the advantages/disadvantages in using a HIV diagnosis kit at home?
The privacy and convenience offered by HIV tests done in the home are the obvious advantages of them. Some of these kits are not reliable however. Only one (Oraquick) is approved by the Federal Drug Administration (FDA). It is simple to take and is usually reliable if you follow the instructions exactly. Any mistake you make you make in doing a home test may affect the result of the test, so you may incorrectly test as HIV positive or negative. A professional who does these tests routinely in a clinic is unlikely to make such an error and are more likely to catch false positives and false negatives. The clinic also will be able to retest using another kind of blood sample test if needed, quickly deal with some treatment issues, check for other health issues and will be able to offer the needed counseling prior to the test and afterwards. Some home testing kits offer a phone number for counseling services but that may not be adequate if you test positive.

Question: Who will know about my status if I test HIV+?
Most testing sites offer confidential but not anonymous testing. If you want anonymous testing, you can get information about that by calling your local health department or by calling the Centers for Disease Control and Prevention (CDC) at 1-800-232-4636. You can also just call around to the various testing sites in your area to find a location offering it. Anonymous testing sites give a number to the person being tested and that number is then used to match the person with his test. In this case, only you and the people you tell will know you are HIV+.

A site offering confidential testing will take identifying and other relevant information from you. That information will be used to match you with your test, to create a record and to do counseling. Obviously then a few people at the site will know if you test HIV+. That information is protected by privacy laws so, with a few exceptions, it cannot be shared with others.

A doctor who refers you for HIV testing or takes a testing sample will be notified of the test results and can have access to your record. Certain medical staff will also have access to your record if they are related in some way to your case. Others who may see your record include people you authorize, the police if for some reason a bullet wound is involved in your case and certain government agencies that are bound by law to check and/or report HIV cases. Correctional facility inmates may have special rules that apply to the disclosure of their HIV+ status.

Federal law compels HIV testing sites to report positive HIV testing results to the state health department. This is so the health department can see whether HIV+ people are getting treatment and so it can check the incidence of HIV in their state. Federal law also compels state health departments to report HIV+ test results to the CDC but that report is only that a positive test has occurred and does not name the HIV+ person.

Some states have partner-notification laws which require that a newly identified HIV+ person's sex partners and/or needle sharing partners be notified of the HIV+ person's status. If this obligation is a concern a person can call the local health department or ask testing site staff about whether his state has such a law. In any case, newly diagnosed HIV+ persons nearly always go through a period of trying to decide who, if anyone, to tell about their status. This can be a challenging process and is one of several reasons one may wish to accept counseling. The newly diagnosed HIV+ person may wish to consider the morality of telling or not telling prior sex partners or needle sharers that he has been diagnosed with HIV.

Question: How does having HIV/AIDS affect my insurance coverage?
Per the US Department of Health and Human Services website (AIDS.com) under the Affordable Care Act (Obamacare) no insurer can deny coverage to HIV+ children and insurers must cover HIV testing as part of offered coverage packages. The website for the Centers on Disease Control and Prevention (cdc.gov/hiv/topics/ testing/resources/qa/print/ qa/_general-public.htm) says that insurers should not drop a policy holder because he becomes HIV+. The website for the US Department of Health and Human Services (AIDS.com) says that under the Health Insurance Portability and Accountability Act of 1996 (HIPPAA) an insurer cannot drop a member of a group insurance policy, such as those offered by employers or professional organizations, because a family member becomes HIV+. Under Obamacare insurers are not allowed to deny insurance coverage to anyone because of a preexisting condition, to deny coverage to HIV+ people or to impose lifetime caps on insurance benefits. It is unknown at present what, if any, affect the Republican plan to "repeal and replace" Obamacare will have.

Question: Does Medicare and/or Medicaid cover HIV testing and/or treatment?
The website Medicare.gov says that Medicare coverage or noncoverage depends upon whether a service or treatment is considered medically necessary and what Medicare plan you are in. Generally, it covers hospital care, skilled nursing care, hospice care, doctor visits and doctor ordered lab tests. Lots of HIV+ people are covered by Medicare.

Patients may, in some instances, find they are compelled to pay some percentage of the cost related to service. A patient, for example, may have to pay 20% of the cost of a doctor visit or a copay for medications under Medicare Part D. A list of what Medicare covers can be found at http://www.medicare.gov/Pub/pdf/10116.pdf. A person with Medicare questions related to their situation should call Medicare at 1-800-633-4227, refer to the website Medicare.gov or discuss it with a qualified medical professional.

Medicaid is a federal and state partnership program directed at aiding qualifying low-income, elderly and disabled people. Both levels of government give dollars to support the program. The federal government has instituted some requirements all states must follow but the states run the programs and, within certain limitations, may expand what is offered beyond the federal requirements. The federal government has mandatory services that must be offered. These include, among others, inpatient and outpatient hospital services, lab services, doctor related services and certain long-term care services. Some states have opted to expand Medicaid programs so that more HIV/AIDS patients will qualify for services while others have not.

Medicaid is the single largest source of aid going to HIV patients. It offers a range of critical health care services for qualified individuals but what specifically is covered may vary from by state. It typically pays part or all the cost of HIV medications. Some states charge a fee or copay for some services. Some people qualify for both Medicaid and Medicare and some of these may qualify to have their Medicare premiums paid for by Medicaid.

Persons with questions about how Medicaid fits their situation should visit the website Medicaid.gov and name their state of residence in the right box. This will give the viewer a summary of what is offered in their state and a list of other resources. A person may also wish to discuss medically related Medicaid questions with their healthcare professional. The reader is cautioned to keep current on the requirements and benefits offered by Medicaid because it is subject to change.

Question: Do I qualify for Supplemental Security Income (SSI) if I have HIV or AIDS?

The Supplemental Security Income (SSI) program is run by the federal Social Security Administration. It offers cash payments to qualified low-income people who are blind, disabled and/or over 65 years old. There are a lot of people who have HIV or AIDS that get these payments but having one of those ailments is not a guarantee that you will qualify. To know if you qualify you must fill out an application and go through the screening process. For more information see: www.ssa.gov/pubs/EN-05-11000.pdf.

Question: What is the AIDS Drug Assistance Program?
The AIDS Drug Assistance Program (ADAP) is a state run federal program that offers HIV medication to qualified low income people who have HIV or AIDS and have no insurance or are underinsured. It may also pay for health insurance coverage for qualified people. General information about ADAP can be found at: http://www.kff.org/hivaids/fact-sheet/aids-drug-assistance-programs/. For specific information about what is available to you contact the program in your state.

Question: What is the Ryan White HIV/AIDS program?
The Ryan White program is administered by the US Health Resources and Services Administration (HRSA). This program does a variety of things which, among others, include helping qualified people who have HIV/AIDS, and do not have insurance coverage or the financial ability to afford treatment and lack resources through other programs. The program primarily serves large metropolitan areas because that creates service availability to the most people. Among the services offered are: outpatient and ambulatory medical care, AIDS drug support, AIDS pharmaceutical aid, oral health aid, early intervention services, health insurance cost sharing, medical nutrition therapy, hospice services, home and community-based health services, outpatient substance abuse care and medical case management services. Persons interested in obtaining more information about this program can go to the HRSA website (hrsa.gov).

Question: What does a HIV test cost?
It varies depending on where it is done, and the type of test given. Some clinics offer them for free, some have a sliding scale based on income level and others have set fees. A home test can be bought at most pharmacies (prices vary) and online at Amazon for around $40.00. Obamacare compels insurers to offer HIV testing at no added cost. It is unknown as this is being written whether the Republican effort to "repeal and replace" Obamacare will change this.

If you are paying for the test yourself, you may want to either call around to find a place you can afford to go to or check with a local LGBT resource center. A resource center may be able to guide you to a place where you can get the test for free or for a small payment. The bottom line however is that a person may have to choose between the welfare of their health and the welfare of their wallet.

Question: What do they do when they give you an HIV test and what kind of tests are there?

Per the website AIDS.com the most common category of HIV tests are antibody tests. They look for antibodies that fight the HIV virus. Within this category are a few kinds of tests such as the enzyme immunoassay (EIA) and the enzyme-linked immunosorbent assay (ELISA) tests which use a sample of blood, oral fluid (not saliva) or urine.

The oral fluid is taken by putting a device between the cheek and gum for a short amount of time. The test using blood requires that a sample be drawn from a vein. The test using urine involves the person being tested to urinate in a cup. The results from these are available anywhere from 20 minutes to a couple of weeks depending upon the kind of test.

Tests using urine are somewhat less exact than blood or oral fluid tests and an oral fluid test may be slightly less exact than blood-based tests. Antibody tests are labelled by medical professionals as generation 2, 3 or 4 based upon which specific antibody or factor is being tested for. Some antibody tests do not detect HIV-2 (which primarily occurs in Africa) and/or some uncommon strains of HIV-1. A person wanting to take an HIV test may wish to discuss with the testing site the accuracy and sensitivity of the test he is being given.

Another type of antibody test is the Rapid HIV test. This test requires that either a sample of oral fluid (not saliva) be taken or that a small blood sample be taken by pricking a finger with a small needle. This test will, in 10-20 minutes, yield either a result of HIV negative or HIV preliminary positive. The latter result will cause the person to be tested again with another kind of test. He will also receive counseling about what "preliminary positive" means (antibody tests sometimes give a result of positive when the person is truly HIV negative) and what precautions he should take until the results of his second test come back. He will then probably be scheduled for a time to receive the results of the second test. This is usually done in person with a counselor or medical professional.

Another category of antibody HIV test is called the Western blot. It requires a blood sample to be taken from a vein. This test works by detecting how antibodies react to certain proteins in the blood sample. The Western blot is primarily used as a follow up test after an original HIV+ result is found using another test.

The indirect fluorescent antibody (IFA) test is yet another category of antibody test. It is also used primarily to confirm or reject an earlier HIV+ test. It is however not widely used because of cost factors and the availability of the Western blot.

The final kind of HIV test discussed here is the nucleic acid amplification test (HIV NAAT). It is more commonly called a viral load test, a PCR test or an RNA test. This test looks directly at genetic material in a person's RNA. This test is primarily used once a HIV patient is in treatment to check the amount of HIV virus (the viral load) the patient has in his blood or to confirm or reject an earlier HIV+ test. The time frame for doing this test will be decided by the patient's doctor.

Question: Why should I go to counseling if I get a positive HIV result?

Receiving a positive HIV test result can be a major blow emotionally. Human beings are genetically programmed to need other human beings. We are social beings. A newly diagnosed HIV+ person naturally fears not only the health consequences of his diagnosis but also the social consequences. He fears that his HIV status will result in social rejection. This fear is completely natural and normal.

A counselor who is familiar with HIV/AIDS can help you deal with the stress and anxiety that often goes with a HIV+ diagnosis. He/she can also give you helpful information and may be able to both aid you in finding a support group and in working through who, if anyone, you should tell and how to tell them about your diagnosis. If you follow the suggestions of your counselor and your doctor you probably will be guided to effective treatment that will help you manage the condition.

The importance of a support group cannot be overstated. If you are HIV+ you need one. Others in the group will need your support too. The give and take of support within a group can be emotionally healing.

Question: Can I get HIV from kissing?
The Centers for Disease Control and Prevention say there is no risk of getting HIV from closed mouth kissing. There is a small risk of getting HIV from "deep, open-mouth kissing if there are sores or bleeding gums and blood is exchanged". The CDC recommends that HIV+ people refrain from this deep, open-mouthed kind of kissing.

Question: Can I get HIV from fellatio?
The Centers for Disease Control and Prevention say it is possible to get HIV through participating in fellatio. There have been a few documented cases of this occurring, but it is not common. The Stop AIDS Project reminds us that HIV enters the body through mucous membranes such as the lining to the mouth. It recommends that those giving a blow job keep the lining of their mouth healthy and abrasion free by not brushing their teeth, flossing or doing anything else that might damage the lining of the mouth for at least 45 minutes prior to oral sex. It is also wise to either spit out or swallow semen at once since the longer you have it in the mouth the more likely it is to infect you with HIV or another STD. Better yet, use a condom.

Question: Can I get HIV from being spit on?
The Centers for Disease Control and Prevention say that, while HIV has been detected in spit in very low amounts, there are no known cases wherein being spit on was the means of transmitting the virus.

Question: What is statistical probability of someone getting HIV?
The Centers for Disease Control and Prevention (CDC) say the per-act probability of getting HIV from an infected source depends upon what the act causing exposure to HIV was. It lists these probabilities: blood transfusion: 9,250 per 10,000 exposures to HIV; needle-sharing during injection drug use: 63

per 10,000 exposures to HIV; receptive anal intercourse: 138 per 10,000 exposures; insertive anal intercourse: 11 per 10,000 exposures; receptive penile-vaginal intercourse: 8 per 10,000 exposures; insertive penile-vaginal intercourse: 4 per 10,000 exposures. Both receptive and insertive oral intercourse has a low probability per 10,000 exposures. The risk is increased if another STI, acute and late-stage HIV, or a high viral load is involved. Use of a condom decreases the risk by as much as 80% and using PrEP can reduce the risk by as much as 96%. Using both together reduces the risk by as much as 99.2% (CDC, 2014).

Surveys show that some people view HIV as just another STI and believe that the chances of getting HIV are so low that it is safe to not use condoms or take other safer sex measures to reduce the risk. This is a very stupid gamble especially given how simple the protective measures are and what the consequence of losing the bet is. Practically nobody who has HIV thought they were going to get the infection either.

Question: Why do men who have sex with men (MSM) have a higher rate of HIV?

The truth is that MSM do the things that spread HIV more often than other people do and we are much more likely to have a sex partner who is HIV+. The things that increase the risk of HIV transmission are:

1. ***Unprotected anal sex.*** Semen and seminal-fluid (pre-cum) are very efficient mechanisms for transferring HIV from person to person. The anus (male or female) and intestines (male or female) are very efficient at moving the virus into the bloodstream. Penis to anus sex is 18 times more efficient at transmitting HIV than is penis to vagina sex (Beyrer and Baral, 2012). MSM have unprotected anal sex much more often than other people do.
2. ***Choosing sex partners from a pool that has a high prevalence of HIV.*** In 2011, MSM accounted for 62% of all new HIV diagnoses and 50% of all of those living with HIV. MSM are less than 10% of the American population. We are simply more likely to have a HIV+ sex partner.
3. ***Trading sex roles.*** It is common for MSM to be versatile in their sex roles. They are the anally penetrated person sometimes and the penetrator at other times. This puts both

partners at risk. In heterosexual sex, the norm is for only one person to take the role of being penetrated and that reduces their overall risk exposure.
4. ***Accepting semen being ejaculated into the mouth or anus.*** MSM commonly have bareback (unprotected) sex and bottoms often will allow a top to ejaculate inside them rather than asking him to pull out before he ejaculates.
5. ***Underestimating the risk***. It is very common for MSM to not practice safer sex because they view the risk of getting HIV as very small.
6. ***Low rates of HIV testing***. Around 33% of MSM have not been tested for HIV in the last 12 months. Those who are unaware of their HIV status are more than twice as likely to have unprotected sex and to do that with a person who does not have the same HIV status they do. One in six people who are HIV+ do not know it. This obviously means that they have done nothing to reduce their HIV viral load.
7. ***Substance use.*** MSM, as a group, use some drugs at higher levels than does the general American society. Drug use has been linked to an elevated risk of getting HIV.
8. ***Homelessness and/or isolation***. Gay and bisexual men and boys are much more likely than other men to be homeless and/or isolated. Both situations are closely linked to drug use. Homelessness is also closely linked to subsistence prostitution which is yet another risk factor for getting HIV.

Question: Is there a link between HIV and other STIs?
Yes. The Centers for Disease Control and Prevention assert that having another STI increases the chances both of getting HIV and of transmitting it to another person. It is not necessary for the STI to cause a sore or other break in the skin for HIV transmission to occur but break in the skin will make it easier for HIV to enter the body. STIs also trigger an immune response that increases the likelihood of transmission. A HIV+ person with a STI is 3-5 times more likely to pass on HIV than is a HIV+ person without a STI.

Question: What can I do if I think I have just been exposed to HIV?
The US Department of Health and Human Services website (AIDS.com) states that a person in this situation should see his

doctor as soon as possible after the potential exposure. The doctor will decide what the right course of treatment is and may be able to begin post-exposure prophylaxis (PEP). PEP is a 28-day course of taking certain prescribed antiretroviral medications that may reduce the patient's chance of getting HIV. PEP must begin within 72 hours of HIV exposure. Please note that PEP and PrEP are not the same even though they sound similar. The existence and use of PEP is one reason a gay man needs a doctor who knows about gay issues.

Question: What is PrEP?
PrEP is a short way of saying "pre-exposure prophylaxis". It is an FDA approved pill (Truvada) that is prescribed by a doctor. It has been shown to be very effective in reducing the chance of getting HIV if it is taken daily. The testing done so far shows that PrEP is safe, but it does have possible side effects. It is covered by most insurance plans.

The Centers for Disease Control and Prevention (CDC) say that PrEP is intended for those who are at elevated risk of getting HIV. This includes HIV negative gay men who are not celibate and not in a fully monogamous relationship with another HIV negative man, those who are in a sexual relationship with a HIV+ partner, those who take part in unprotected anal sex and those who have been diagnosed with an STI in the last six months. PrEP should be taken as part of a risk reduction plan that includes the use of condoms, monthly HIV testing, managing other STIs and reducing risky behavior. The CDC says this regimen will reduce the risk of getting HIV by 99.2%. It should be noted that while PrEP is effective in protecting against HIV it does nothing to protect against other STIs. If you want to use PrEP, you need to discuss it with your doctor.

Question: If I take a PrEP pill every day am I immune from HIV?
No. The CDC says PrEP is up to 96% effective in preventing HIV negative people from becoming HIV positive, but it does not make a person bullet proof. There are confirmed cases of men getting HIV while on PrEP. It is intended to be used as part of a risk reduction plan and not as a whole plan. You should also use

condoms, be tested for HIV regularly, work to prevent other STIs and reduce risky behavior.

Question: My partner and I are both HIV+. Is it safe for us to have unprotected sex?

There are various strains of HIV and it is possible for a HIV+ person to get another strain. This can complicate the treatment of HIV. Before two HIV+ people have unprotected sex, they should discuss it with a qualified medical professional.

Question: Is it safe for a HIV negative person to have sex with a HIV positive person?

Per the Dept. of Health and Human Services (AIDS.gov) a HIV negative person cannot be completely safe from getting HIV if he has sex with a HIV positive person. The risk involved can however be minimized if a condom is correctly used and the HIV+ partner takes his medication and follows his treatment plan so that his viral load is as low as possible. It is possible for an HIV+ person to have an undetectable HIV viral load and that greatly reduces the risk of transmission. The couple can also reduce their risk by always following other safer sex practices. They should talk with their doctor about this topic and about the HIV negative person taking PrEP.

Question: What is TasP?

TasP is an acronym for "treatment as prevention". It is a preventative strategy that may be used by two people who are in a fully committed, discordant relationship. That means one person is HIV+, the other is HIV- and they are completely monogamous. The concept behind TasP is that if the HIV+ partner is taking part fully in antiretroviral therapy (ART) and thereby gets his viral load to a non-detectable or a nearly non-detectable level he will be protecting his partner from getting HIV. The HTPN 052 trial study showed that this makes the HIV+ person 96% less likely to infect his partner than he would be if he was not involved in ART. This is not a substitute for using condoms. This treatment approach is something that a couple should talk to their doctor about before beginning it. There are no national guidelines in place as of the date this book was published so being under the care of a HIV knowledgeable doctor is important for TasP couples.

Question: What are the major STIs/STDs found among men in the U.S.?

Per the Centers for Disease Control and Prevention the major sexually transmitted afflictions found among men in the U.S. are: chlamydia, syphilis, genital herpes, hepatitis, genital human papillomavirus (HPV), gonorrhea, HIV/AIDS, lice and scabies.

Question: How can I tell if someone I want to have sex with has a STI/STD?

It is common for STIs and STDs to not have observable symptoms. In that case the only way to know a sex partner has one is if he has been tested and he tells you. If he knows he is infected and he is having sex with you anyway he is unlikely to volunteer that information. You therefore need ask about it and hope for honesty. You should ask every new sex partner when he was last tested for STIs and HIV and be willing to share your information about that with him.

Sometimes however a STI/STD will have symptoms you can see. The symptom will be a rash, sores, redness or a discharge of pus, blood or other fluid. You can also see lice, lice eggs and the signs of scabies if you know what to look for. A condom will not prevent lice or scabies from moving to you, but condoms are very effective at protecting against STIs. It should be remembered that you cannot check for any of that if the lights are off or low.

Question: What is chlamydia, how do I know if I have it and what should I do if I get it?

Per the Centers for Disease Control and Prevention (CDC) chlamydia is a sexually transmitted disease that is caused by bacteria. It is transmitted by oral, anal or vaginal sex. It can also be transmitted by a mother to a child still in her womb. Women, hetero men and bisexual men have a higher risk than gay men do but this disease is common in our community. Most men who have chlamydia do not know it because it often has no symptoms. If symptoms appear it is during the first few weeks after infection, then they disappear. In men, the symptoms are a discharge from the penis, a burning sensation when urinating or a burning/itch at the opening of the penis. In some cases, the testicles hurt.

If you think you might have chlamydia, see a doctor. Chlamydia is often diagnosed using a urine sample while in other cases a sample must be taken from the penis using a swab. Undiagnosed chlamydia can be very serious for women. In men, the result of undiagnosed chlamydia ranges from no long-term consequence to pain in the testicles or sterility. The disease is normally cured with antibiotics. The CDC recommends yearly testing for this disease.

Question: What is syphilis, how do I know if I have it and what should I do if I get it?

Syphilis is a sexually transmitted disease that is caused by bacteria. Per the Centers for Disease Control and Prevention in 2016 fifty-eight percent of all cases of this disease occurred in the gay community. The disease is spread from person to person through direct contact with a syphilis sore which usually is found on the genitals or anus. The sore is sometimes inside the anus. It is commonly spread through oral, anal or vaginal sex. It is also sometimes passed by a mother to an unborn child in the womb. It is not passed through contact with things like toilet seats, hot tubs, clothing or eating utensils.

The CDC reports that many people who have syphilis have no symptoms for months or years. Many others develop one or more firm, round, small and painless sores during the primary (initial) phase of the disease which can last up to 90 days. This sore develops at the place the infection entered the body. It will go away without treatment, but the disease lingers on past this stage if treatment is not given.

During the next (secondary) phase of the disease the infected person may develop a skin rash on various parts of the body, lesions in mucous membranes, a fever, swollen lymph glands, a sore throat, patchy hair loss, weight loss, muscle aches and fatigue. These symptoms will commonly pass without treatment. The infected person however still has the disease and will move on to the next phase of the disease.

The third phase of syphilis is called the latent phase. It is also often called the hidden phase because there may be no symptoms. This phase may last for years.

The final stage of syphilis is called the late stage. It is during this stage that damage to the brain, bones and internal organs occurs. The infected person may gradually become blind, paralyzed or uncoordinated and may develop dementia. This phase is often fatal.

Per the CDC syphilis is diagnosed either by examining a sample from a syphilis sore under a dark-field microscope or by a blood test. Obviously, that involves the service of a qualified medical professional. There are no over-the-counter treatments for syphilis, but a doctor can prescribe medication that will usually be effective during the earlier phases of the disease. The damage the disease does prior to treatment is permanent however. The infected person can spread the disease to another person during all phases of the disease.

Question: What is genital herpes, how do I know if I have it and what should I do if I do?
The CDC reports that genital herpes is a sexually transmitted disease that is caused by a virus. There are two types of the virus: type 1 which is known as HSV-1 and type 2 which is known as HSV-2. HSV-1 can cause genital herpes but more often causes blisters in the mouth and on the lips, which are sometimes called "fever blisters" or "cold sores". HSV-2 is the usual source of genital herpes and can only be transmitted through sexual contact with an infected person. Both forms of the disease are very contagious. The virus is released from sores the virus causes but these sores are not necessary for transmission.

It is common for people with genital herpes to have no symptoms. In some cases, one or more sores may present themselves, the infected person may have a fever and possibly swollen glands. These symptoms pass. It is common for the person to have multiple outbreaks of the disease within a year.

In most men, genital herpes presents no serious health threat. Gay men should take note that herpes may make them more at risk of getting or transmitting HIV. People with a disease called atopic eczema may develop a very serious condition called eczema herpeticum if they become infected with the herpes virus. The virus also sometimes may infect the eyes which can cause vision problems. In other cases, the virus may cause a very serious brain condition called herpes encephalitis. The disease often causes suffers emotional discomfort which is typically based in the fear of a negative reaction to their disease by others.

Even though genital herpes is not typically a serious health threat and it cannot yet be cured it should be managed by a qualified health care professional. Such a professional can diagnose and treat any complications the disease may cause, and he/she can offer medications that may make the patient less contagious and the outbreaks of symptoms shorter and less painful. The professional can also make sure through lab tests that what you have is herpes and not something else.

Question: What is genital human papillomavirus, how do I know if I have it and what should I do if I do have it?
The Centers for Disease Control and Prevention (CDC) say the genital human papillomavirus (HPV) is a virus that causes genital warts. The virus may not only infect the penis and anus but also the mouth and throat. The virus can be passed through both oral and anal sex through skin-to-skin contact.

Many men who have the virus never develop symptoms. Some develop warts. Some develop penile cancer, anal cancer or head/neck cancer. Men who have sex with men are 17 times more likely to get anal cancer than are heterosexual men, but the disease is not common.

The CDC recommends that men be on the lookout for growths on the penis, testicles, groin, thighs or anus since these genital warts may signal the presence of HPV. The signs of anal cancer include anal bleeding, pain and itching, a change in bowel habits or the shape of feces and swollen lymph nodes in the groin. The signs of penile cancer include changes in the tissue of the penis including skin color and thickness, build-up of penal tissue and sores/growths on the penis. Signs of head/neck cancer include (among others): sore throat, lasting ear pain, constant coughing, a problem with swallowing or breathing, unexplained weight loss and/or a lump in the throat. If you have any of these symptoms see a doctor.

Per the CDC there is currently no test for HPV in men and no approved laboratory test for penile cancer. Doctors can however perform an anal pap test to screen for anal cancer in men. They can obviously also see genital or anal warts and any abnormalities that may exist on the penis or around the anus. There is a vaccine called Gardasil™ that treats four of the 40 or so types of HPV. It works only if you do not already have the virus at the time you are vaccinated.

Question: What is gonorrhea, how do I know if I have it and what should I do if I do?

The Centers for Disease Control and Prevention (CDC) inform us that gonorrhea is a sexually transmitted disease caused by bacteria. In men, it multiplies quickly in the penis, anus, mouth, throat, and eyes. It is spread by contact with an infected person's mouth, anus, penis or vagina. Newborn babies sometimes get the disease during the birthing process if the mother is infected.

Many men who are infected with gonorrhea have no symptoms. Others develop symptoms sometime within fourteen days after being infected. Symptoms of gonorrhea in the penis include a burning sensation while urinating, a discharge (white, yellow or green) from the penis and sometimes painful testicles that may or may not become swollen. Symptoms of anal gonorrhea may include anal itching or soreness, anal bleeding, anal discharge or painful bowel movements. Gonorrhea of the throat may cause a sore throat but commonly causes no symptoms at all.

If you think you might have gonorrhea you should be checked by a qualified medical professional. Gonorrhea can be detected using a sample swabbed from the urethra (opening of the penis) or through a urine test. The disease can be treated with antibiotics although there are some strains of the disease that are growing resistant to them. Gonorrhea makes getting and transmitting HIV easier. Untreated gonorrhea can cause damage to the testicles and can spread to the blood or the joints. This may be fatal.

Question: What is hepatitis, how do I know if I have it and what should I do if I do?

The Centers for Disease Control and Prevention (CDC) state that hepatitis is an inflammation of the liver that is usually caused by a virus. There are five forms of this virus: Hepatitis A (HAV), Hepatitis B (HBV), Hepatitis C (HCV), Hepatitis D (HDV) and Hepatitis E (HEV). Only HAV, HBV and HCV are commonly found in America.

Hepatitis A is normally acquired through the ingestion of fecal matter. This does not entail more than in microscopic amount since you can get thousands of virus particles on the head of a pin. The trace of fecal matter can be on objects and in drinks or food which is why restaurants demand that employees wash their hands after using the bathroom. It can also be acquired by sexual activity such as rimming or sharing sex toys and by using illicit drugs. The virus can live on objects for months.

Hepatitis A sometimes presents no symptoms but when symptoms do occur they include: fever, fatigue, nausea, vomiting, abdominal pain, loss of appetite, dark urine, clay-colored feces, joint pain and jaundice. The symptoms typically last less than two months but can last six months. The disease is never chronic but can be lethal.

Most people only get this disease once because the human immune system normally creates antibodies for HAV that last a lifetime. An immune globulin that gives short term protection is available for those who believe they have been exposed to HAV. Hepatitis A can usually be prevented entirely by vaccination for people who are 12 years of age or older. The CDC recommends that all men who have sex with men get vaccinated for this disease.

The Centers for Disease Control and Prevention (CDC) assert that hepatitis B (HBV) is usually acquired from an exchange of blood, semen, saliva or other bodily fluids. The CDC lists the following as common means of transmission: sex with an infected partner, sharing needles or drug preparation equipment, birth from an infected mother, contact with blood or open sores of an infected person, needle sticks or sharp instrument exposure and sharing items such as razors or toothbrushes. The CDC explicitly says that HBV cannot be transmitted through food or water, breastfeeding, hugging, kissing, hand holding, coughing or sneezing. The hepatitis B virus can live outside the body for at least seven days.

A person with HBV may have no symptoms. When symptoms exist, they are typically the same as those for HAV and usually last for several months. The disease can be short-term or chronic. Untreated chronic HBV can lead to cirrhosis of the liver or liver cancer which means it can be fatal. It is therefore critical that people with symptoms of the disease see a doctor to find out if they have the disease and, if so, what course it is taking.

There is a vaccine available that will immunize people against HBV. The CDC website lists those it recommends this vaccine for. Among these are men who have sex with men, people with sex partners who have HBV, people who have or may have another STD and those people who are HIV+. The list also includes all people who want protection from the disease. The vaccine is administered in two or three doses over time. The CDC recommends that HIV+ individuals be tested for HBV prior to taking the vaccine. The CDC also says that persons who have already had HBV receive no benefit from the vaccine but can still take it.

The Centers for Disease Control and Prevention state that hepatitis C (HCV) is the most common chronic blood borne disease in the United States. It is most commonly transmitted via shared needles including those used for drug injection and those used for unlicensed tattooing or body piercing. It is not typically transmitted sexually but the CDC states that having another STD, being HIV+ and having sex with multiple partners appears to increase the risk of getting HCV. It is also sometimes (but not commonly) transmitted through sharing personal items such as razors and toothbrushes. The CDC asserts that HCV is not spread by breastfeeding, hugging, kissing, holding hands, coughing or sneezing.

People infected with HCV may have no symptoms but when symptoms appear they are often those of HAV and HBV. The disease may be acute or chronic but if left untreated the disease commonly becomes chronic. Chronic hepatitis C can lead to cirrhosis of the liver or liver cancer. It is therefore obviously critical that those persons who think they may have HCV see a doctor.

In people without symptoms chronic HCV is usually detected because of a routine test of liver function done in a doctor's office. Many people with chronic HCV will have a normal liver function test result however because their liver function may be going up and down. There are blood tests available for hepatitis C, but they are not routinely given. The CDC recommends that those who have engaged in risky behaviors or are HIV+ be tested for this disease.

There is no vaccine for HCV, but it may be cured using medication which must obtained through a doctor. Other treatments for the disease are available which must also be administered and managed by a doctor.

Question: What is trichomoniasis, how do I know if I have it and what should I do if I do?

The Centers for Disease Control and Prevention state that trichomoniasis is a STI that is caused by a vaginal parasite. It can be transmitted between women and between a woman and a man but not usually between two men. That being the case, it is a disease that may infect a bisexual man but usually not men who are exclusively homosexual. Trichomoniasis may increase the chance that a HIV+ woman can spread HIV to a sex partner.

Most men who have this disease do not have any symptoms. Those that have symptoms experience short term irritation in their penis, burning after urinating and/or a discharge from the penis. It is diagnosed using a laboratory test but is harder to diagnose in men than in women. If a sex partner tells you he/she is infected with this disease it is wise to consult with a doctor. Trichomoniasis can be cured with prescription medication.

Question: What are Fordyce's spots?

Fordyce spots are small white, yellow-white, red or skin colored raised spots or bumps that occur on the face or genitals of many people. They are perfectly normal, not harmful and not an indicator of a STI/STD or cancer. They are not contagious. More information and pictures can be found at: http://www.genitalwartsreport.com/fordyce-spots-genital-warts or http://www.soc.ucsb.edu/sexinfo/article/fordyce-spots.

Question: What are pearly penile papules?

Pearly penile papules (PPP) are growths that appear on the ridge of the penis of many men. The formal term for them is hirsuties coronae glandis. They are typically pearly white or skin colored and they tend to appear in one or two rows. They are often confused HPV warts, but they are not an indicator of a disease nor are they contagious.

If you have any growths on your body that you are concerned about you should consider asking a medical professional about them. You can get more information about and pictures of pearly penile papules at: http://www. youngmenshealthsite .org/pearly_penile_ papules.html or at http://www.soc.ucsb .edu /sexinfo/ article/ pearly-penile/ papules.

Question: What are lice, how do I know if I have them and what should I do if I do?

The Centers for Disease Control and Prevention tell us that lice are parasitic insects. That means they are insects that feed on the blood of their host. There are three kinds of lice that live on human beings. They are head lice, body lice and pubic lice.

Head lice, as their name implies, live on the head and neck of the host. Body lice live on the clothing or bedding of the host and only go to the human body to feed. Pubic lice (also called crabs) typically live in the pubic area of the host but also may live in eyebrows, chest hair, armpits, beard or mustache.

Lice cannot hop or fly so they spread solely via contact with a person who already has them. In the case of pubic lice that contact is typically sexual in nature. Body lice often spread due to crowded or unclean living conditions or through sharing clothing/bedding. Head lice or pubic lice infestation may however have nothing to do with such crowded or unclean conditions. You cannot get human lice from any breed of a dog or cat.

Lice bites typically cause itching and may become inflamed. In some cases, the bites can cause enlarged lymph nodes. These symptoms and visual inspection are typically how lice are discovered.

The CDC notes that there are approved over-the-counter lotions and shampoos that will kill lice if they are used exactly per instructions. There are also prescription shampoos available such as Lindane that should only be used while under the care of a doctor because of possible side effects. There are products that are not approved by the Food and Drug Administration. These should not be used.

The CDC states that in addition to killing the lice on his body with an approved product an infected person should manually remove all visible nits (eggs) from his hair with his finger nails or with a fine-toothed comb. He should put on clean clothing and launder (using hot water and a hot dryer cycle) all bedding or clothing that may be infested. Any items that cannot be laundered can be dry cleaned or placed in a sealed plastic bag for two weeks. All people who may have become infected should be notified and the infected person should stop sexual activity until he is sure the lice and nits are gone. The treatment may need to be repeated in ten days or so if live lice are found again.

Question: What is scabies, how do I know if I have them and what should I do if I do?

The Centers for Disease Control and Prevention report that scabies is a skin condition caused by the human itch mite. The mite is microscopic in size, so it cannot be seen by the human eye. Scabies occurs when the mite burrows into the skin where it then lives and lays its eggs. The CDC states that the most common symptoms of scabies are a pimple-like rash and a severe itching in the infected area.

The human itch mite (scabies) is spread via skin to skin contact. This contact may or may not be sexual in nature. Therefore, those who have had sexual contact or other close personal contact with an infected person should be checked for scabies.

Scabies is diagnosed by the symptoms and by visually looking for burrows. The diagnosis is often confirmed by a doctor examining the mite, an egg or the mite's fecal matter under a microscope. There are products available that will kill the scabies mite and its eggs, but they are only available with a doctor's prescription. All bedding, clothing and towels that have been used by an infected person must be laundered (hot water and a hot dryer setting), dry cleaned or sealed in a plastic bag for at least three days.

Question: What STI tests should I have done and how often should I do them?

The Centers for Disease Control and Prevention (CDC) state that all people who are sexually active or are planning to become sexually active should have a talk with their doctor about their sexually transmitted infection (STI) risk factors, how to reduce those factors and which STI tests are recommended based upon those factors. Everyone ages 13 to 64 should be tested for HIV at least once. Anyone who shares IV drug equipment or engages in unsafe sex (e.g. unprotected sex with a new partner, multiple sex partners, sex with a sex worker, anonymous sex) should be tested for HIV at least once a year. Anyone having sex with someone who has a chronic infection such as HIV or hepatitis B or C should be tested at least every six months.

The CDC offers special guidelines for men who have sex with men (MSM). We should get tested for chlamydia (urethra & rectum), gonorrhea (urethra, rectum & pharynx), syphilis and HIV at least annually. The CDC recommends that all MSM be tested for the hepatitis B surface antigen (HBsAg). MSM should also be tested at least once for hepatitis C if they were born between 1945-1965 or if they have other risk factors. Each of us should talk to our doctor about what testing is needed and how often it should be done.

Question: What are "safer sex" practices?
There is no such thing as completely safe sex because it is possible that you can do everything right to avoid it and still get a STI. There are practices however that will lower the chances of getting one. The National Institutes of Health suggests the following:
1. Always use a condom for oral, anal or vaginal sex.
2. Use lubricants. A lubricant will reduce the chance of the condom breaking during use.
3. Use only water-based or silicone lubes because oil-based and petroleum-based lubricants can weaken a condom.
4. Have the condom in place during the entire time sexual activity is occurring.
5. Know your partner. Get to know your partner before having sex with him. This includes discussing the sexual health of each of you and about any involvement in IV drug use. Intravenous drug use increases the chance of getting a STI.
6. Do not be coerced or pressured into having sex or into not using a condom.
7. Stay sober. The use of alcohol and drugs negatively affects judgment, communication and the ability to correctly use a condom.

Question: Are some sex acts safer than others?
Yes. Planned Parenthood states that masturbation, mutual masturbation, cybersex, phone sex and verbally sharing fantasies

have virtually no risk in terms of getting a STI. Kissing, fondling, oral sex with a condom and using sex toys that have not been shared have a minimal risk of infection. Oral sex without a condom is safer than vaginal or anal intercourse. Unprotected anal intercourse is the riskiest activity of all. It is 18 times more efficient at passing HIV than penis to vagina sex is (Beyrer and Baral, 2012). It can be made at least 80% safer by properly using a condom that is in good condition (WHO, 2009).

Question: How effective are condoms at protecting against HIV and other sexually transmitted infections (STIs)?

The World Health Organization states that condoms are at least 80% effective in preventing the transmission of HIV and other STIs when properly used (WHO, 2009).

Question: Can I get hemorrhoids from receiving anal sex?

A hemorrhoid is an enlarged, twisted vein in the anus or rectum that can become painful and/or bleed. Per the Mayo Clinic, being the receiving person in anal sex is one of several potential causes of hemorrhoids. This however does not mean that if you have anal sex you will get hemorrhoids. It simply means you are at risk of doing so. The same is true for anal fissures which are tears or sores in the lining of the anus.

Question: Does anal sex cause anal cancer?

Per the American Cancer Society nobody knows what causes anal cancer. We do however know some factors that increase the risk of someone getting this disease. They are: 1) being over 50 years of age, 2) being infected with the human papilloma virus (HPV), 3) having anal sex, 4) smoking, 5) having a weakened immune system, 6) having chronic anal inflammation such as found with anal fissures, and 7) pelvic radiation such as found with radiation treatment for prostate or bladder cancer. Anal cancer is not common, but it is much more common in men who have sex with men than in other people.

Question: Is anal fisting safe?
Anal fisting is also known as handballing. Its formal name is brachioproctic intercourse. It is the act of putting the entire hand and possibly the forearm into the buttock of another person. This is not a widespread practice both because fisting is viewed by many as dirty and because people are averse to the risk of damaging their rectum and anal sphincters. The practice of fisting is not a gay activity per se because people from all sexual orientations do it.

Many of those who take part in fisting report that when it is done correctly it is a safe activity that brings with it a deep connection between the parties involved. These people will very sincerely assert that the negatives associated with fisting are based on myths and are not supported by the facts. There are serious dangers associated with fisting however that may involve the need for emergency room treatment, surgery or death (de Bakker, 2012; nam aidsmap, 2009; Cohen, 2004).

A person who is considering either being fisted or being the one doing the fisting should thoroughly understand what he is thinking about getting involved in. He should know both what usually happens and what can go wrong. Not only can one or both parties involved be injured but legal consequences might also arise.

The injured party may decide to sue because of a physical injury or a perceived emotional one. The authorities in some jurisdictions might also pursue criminal charges if fisting violates existing definitions of assault. Courts do not necessarily have to accept the defense that the behavior was consensual or that the injured party accepted the risks involved.

The tissue inside the rectum and the lower colon can be easily damaged or torn and tissue of the colon has no pain receptors, so a problem may go unnoticed for some time. The lower colon makes a sharp turn about eight inches up from the inside of the anus. The fist and forearm of most people is longer than that so fisting may straighten out that natural bend. That can move the colon away from its natural course or tear the tissue which in turn can cause internal bleeding or peritonitis (a serious inflammation of the abdominal cavity and its lining).

A lot can go wrong while a person is being fisted. A sharp fingernail, an aggressive movement or just ignorance on the part of the insertive person can have very serious consequences for the person being fisted. An unexpected movement on the part of the person being fisted can cause the inserter to do something he did not intend to do which also can have grave consequences.

The use of drugs and/or alcohol has no place at all in the practice of fisting because they reduce the receiving person's ability to feel pain or other warning signs and they cloud judgment. Pain is the body's way of saying something is wrong. Desensitizing products like benzocaine should not be used. Drugs should not be placed in the rectum because they will be taken into the body very quickly and very potently through the anal and intestinal tissues. Again, those interested in being part of a fisting situation should thoroughly research it prior to going ahead. It should not be an impulsive decision.

There is no way to predict how the anal sphincters will respond to a hand and wrist passing through them. Anal sphincters are very elastic, so it is possible that no long-term damage to them will be done by fisting. At the same time, they are human tissue, so they can tear or lose elasticity. This could result in either a very unpleasant surgery or anal incontinence wherein fecal matter leaks from the anus (Stark, 2011; Critchlow, 1985; Navin, 1981). In some instances, this entails the use of an adult diaper. If you agree to be fisted, you are accepting the potential long-term consequences.

It is generally agreed that the person being fisted has a low probability of getting HIV from this activity since no fluid is being exchanged from the person doing the fisting. The exception of course would be if the person doing the fisting is bleeding or had semen on his hand before he inserted it into the anus. The person who is doing the fisting on the other hand is at more risk because he has a good chance of encountering blood if the person being fisted bleeds at all internally which is not an uncommon occurrence. If the insertive person has any breaks in his skin like a cut, sore or other wound he could become infected if the other person is HIV+ which is one reason he should wear gloves.

There are studies showing that fisting is directly linked to the acquisition of hepatitis C in men who are HIV + (Tohme, 2010; Turner, 2006). Since getting any kind of infection is a serious matter for HIV+ people it would be wise for these people to avoid this activity.

Question: Does oral sex cause mouth or throat cancer?
Not under usual circumstances. The Centers for Disease Control and Prevention (CDC) say that most cancers of the mouth and throat are caused by tobacco and alcohol use. There is however a link between throat cancer and unprotected oral sex with a partner who is infected with genital human papillomavirus (HPV). About 25% of mouth cancers and 35% of throat cancers are linked to HPV. The CDC supports the view that using a condom during oral sex is an effective mechanism in reducing the chances of being infected with HPV. Having oral sex with a non-infected partner on a monogamous basis is a safer sex method of having oral sex.

Question: Is it safe to take part in bondage by being bound?
Bondage is the act of physically restraining someone or being physically restrained. It may be done as part of a sexual encounter or it may be separate from anything sexual. It is always an expression of dominance and submission however so there is both a physical and psychological aspect to it. People who are new to gay sex should get comfortable with participating in that before taking part in bondage.

Whether bondage is safe depends upon who is doing the restraining, who is being restrained and what is being done. If the person doing the restraining (a top) and the person being restrained (a bottom) are mentally and physically healthy, know what they are doing and follow certain safety rules bondage is a relatively safe activity. If the restrainer happens to be a sadist, mentally unstable or has a medical condition that could make him unable to respond to the needs of the bottom very bad things could happen. If the top does not know what he is doing damage can happen unintentionally. In any of these cases the submissive would be restrained and therefore helpless to prevent harm from coming to him.

Very bad things can also happen if the bottom has a mental health or physical condition that might be triggered or aggravated by what may happen during a bondage scene. Bottoms that are new to bondage are at increased risk because they are more apt to experience anxiety during a scene. These bottoms should avoid advanced bondage activities such as the use of sensory deprivation until they become more comfortable in a bondage situation. Both parties involved in a bondage scene should thoroughly know or know about the other person before taking part in bondage with them.

Bondage should always be consensual. The bottom must always hold the power to stop the bondage scene if things get too intense or any pain involved becomes too much. The top and the bottom should agree on a "safe word" which when said by the bottom will stop the scene. They should also agree on a "safe action" which will stop the scene in those cases where the bottom cannot talk such as when he has a ball gag or a bit gag on. Both the safe word and the safe action should be easily remembered things that are not common but will be easily recognized by the top.

A top should assure that he can release the bottom quickly if that becomes necessary. This means keeping cutting tools and keys readily at hand in an area where they cannot be misplaced or lost. The cutting tools should not include any kind of sharp, pointed objects like knives or regular scissors since these can easily damage the bottom. Blunt tipped medical shears are a preferred choice. A working telephone, a fire extinguisher and a first aid kit should also be in the room.

The bottom should not be restrained very tightly because that can damage muscles and tendons and restrict the circulation of blood. He also should not be restrained with his hands behind his back and then placed on his back with his weight on his hands. This also can damage muscles and tendons and can easily cause cramping. This is especially true if handcuffs are used. The bottom should not be kept in any position very long.

It is not uncommon for a bottom to be restrained with his hands secured above him. This should only be done for short periods of time because it can interfere with the bottom's breathing and blood circulation. He should also not be restrained so that his full weight is supported by any of his joints because this can cause dislocation and tear tissue. Suspension is an advanced bondage practice which demands advanced skills. The top should never leave a restrained bottom alone and this is especially true in the above situations.

The top should constantly pay attention to the bottom's breathing and physical state. He should periodically ask the bottom if he is alright and check to see if his limbs are numb, cold or discolored. Blue or purple skin, numbness or coldness means the bottom is having a blood circulation problem. Again, a person who is in bondage should never be left unattended.

Care should be taken when placing a bottom face down, in a kneeling position or in a situation that puts weight on him. These positions can interfere with breathing and cause unconsciousness or death due to positional asphyxia, so they should be used for only short periods of time.

It is advisable for tops to avoid taking part in bondage with a bottom who is drunk or high. These bottoms are typically not good partners anyway, but they present increased risks in a bondage scene. They commonly do not feel pain as well as a sober person so are more likely to be seriously injured. Their breathing can be interrupted more easily too. They also not uncommonly vomit or pass out. If the bottom happens to vomit while he has a gag in, is positioned face down or face up or has a hood on he is in real danger of inhaling his own vomit. That can rapidly evolve into a medical emergency.

It is also advisable for a bottom to avoid taking part in bondage with a top who is drunk or high. Drugs and alcohol impair judgment. Since a restrained bottom will be helpless against the actions of the top the bottom will rightly want the top to be in full command of his mental faculties. A restrained bottom will also find himself in a serious situation if the top passes out or has an incapacitating medical problem.

Tops should take care when doing anything that will obstruct the mouth and nose whether the bottom is drunk/high or not. Gags, muzzles and hoods may create anxiety in a person new to them. They will make it difficult for even a sober person to evacuate vomit from the mouth and throat and can cause a bottom to inhale his own vomit. Hoods, gags and muzzles can also make it more difficult to breathe so they should be selected and used with that in mind. It is the tops responsibility to ensure the safety of the bottom, so he must stay aware of the bottoms breathing.

Question: Are "water sports" safe?
Any sexually related activity involving urine falls under the category of "water sports". This activity can involve the drinking of urine, being urinated on by another person or urinating on another person. The latter two of these activities are commonly referred to as a "golden shower".

Water sports are also known as urolagnia. They are classified as paraphilias which means they are viewed as abnormal sexual behavior by our society. That is not necessarily a reason to not take part in water sports because lots of things, including homosexuality, that were once viewed as abnormal are not classed as such now. Participants should understand that there are risks however.

There is a lot of information in the popular press and on the internet about the safety of water sports. Much, perhaps most, of that is mere opinion offered by people who are simply repeating information they have gotten from hearsay, media reports, the internet or some other source of mixed reliability. That information may be true, untrue or partially true and false.

There is little authoritative information about the safety of water sports per se. Urolagnia is practiced by a small minority of people thus it is not authoritatively written about or studied very much. One can however find information relevant to the safety of the practice by broadening the search into the areas of disease transmission, microbiology and urology.

Many people who take part in water sports assert the activity is harmless because the urine in a human bladder and the urethra (tube that carries urine from the bladder to urethra's outer tip where it is excreted) is usually sterile. They can easily find authoritative sources to support this assertion so their belief that water sports are safe seems, at first blush, completely reasonable and correct. Other factors however must be considered.

It is commonly accepted by authorities that urine may not be sterile in the bladder if the person in question has an infection anywhere in the urinary tract (Porter, 2007; American Association for Clinical Chemistry, 2013). The urinary tract, of course, consists of the kidneys, ureters, bladder, and urethra. Authorities also accept that most of these infections are the result of microorganisms that enter through the outer tip of the urethra and then work their way up into the higher regions of the urinary system. If there are organisms present in the urinary tract or on the outer penis/vagina skin those organisms can be transmitted to another person in urine.

The premise that urine is normally sterile while in the human bladder may not be true. One study found that both pathogenic and non-pathogenic bacteria that are not found by standard methods of analysis can exist in urine samples and can be detected using another method of analysis. The result of this is that earlier work which has been used to show that urine in the bladder is sterile may only show that the standard method of analyzing urine is flawed in that it can miss bacteria that are there (Wolfe & Toh, 2012).

Any microorganisms that are present in the urinary tract and/or on the outer skin of the penis or vagina may or may not be harmful to humans depending upon what they are. Many forms of bacteria, for example, are not harmful while viruses are usually pathogens. The most common contaminate found in the urinary tract is Escherichia Coli (E. coli) bacteria (Porter, 2007). That bacterium has earned a rather nasty reputation. Some forms of it deserve that reputation while other forms of it do not.

There are a variety of pathogens that can be transmitted in urine. The viruses causing the STIs chlamydia and gonorrhea (Healthcommunities.com, 2011; Gaul, 2010) are among these. They can be transmitted to tissues of the throat through urine if it is contaminated and is swallowed. Cytomegalovirus (herpes) and Hepatitis B can also be acquired from urine (Gaul, 2010). Typhoid, staphylococcal organisms, and the Epstein-Barr virus are on the list as well (Utah Dept. of Health, 2005). Epstein-Barr causes a variety of diseases but the most widely known one is infectious mononucleosis. There are no known cases of HIV being transmitted through urine but people who are HIV+ should avoid water sports because of the possibility of getting an infection.

A man who takes part in water sports with a woman is at greater potential risk than he is if does so with another man. Women are 50 times more likely to have a urinary tract infection (UTI) than is a man who is under the age of 50 (Porter, 2007) thus she is more likely to spread an infectious organism through her urine. About 12% of young healthy men get a UTI at least once (Urinary Care Foundation, 2013). Older men have a higher average rate of urinary tract infections than younger men because they are more prone to have medical conditions like prostatitis (Porter, 2007). Conditions like kidney stones, diabetes or an enlarged prostate increase the chances of having a UTI even in young men.

People who receive golden showers and have a completely intact skin covering are at much less risk of getting any urine transmitted disease than those who do not because the skin acts as a barrier. Microorganisms such as hepatitis and herpes will however pass through breaks in the skin such as cuts, scrapes or sores. The longer pathogens such as these stay on the skin, the more likely they are to enter the body. Taking a shower at once after receiving a golden shower is therefore wise.

The United States Army field manual recommends against drinking urine as a means of survival. Urine is a waste product of the body. Drinking urine will therefore increase the amount of wastes in the kidneys. The wastes include, among other things, concentrations of salt, minerals and some level of whatever drugs or supplements the person has taken. The only way the body can remove the added wastes in the kidneys is to urinate more which of course also removes water from the body. This dehydrates the body.

A person drinking urine may react negatively to any drugs that exist in it if he is allergic to it or he is taking medications or other drugs himself. Drinking urine can cause kidney failure in some circumstances such as when sizeable amounts are consumed, it is done repeatedly or where the drinker has a preexisting kidney condition. Drinking alcohol before or after consuming urine is ill-advised because alcohol also dehydrates the body.

People who choose to take part in water sports should avoid getting urine in their eyes. It is not only painful to have urine in the eyes, but it also puts the person at risk of damaging their eyes or even of becoming blind. This may occur if any microorganisms that exist in the urine meets the tissues of the eyes. There are documented cases, for example, of people getting gonorrhea of the eyes through the introduction of urine into the eyes (O'hElineachain, 2008). The chlamydia trachomatis bacterium is often found in contaminated urine and that is a cause of eye disease among humans (Resnikoff, 2004).

Given all the above, whether water sports are safe depends on the health of the urinating person, the health of the person being urinated on or in, the type of microorganism, if any, being transmitted and the level of the load of any organism that is being transmitted. A high load level of a pathogen obviously makes it more likely to have ill effects. Some microorganisms are more dangerous than others. Some do not harm humans at all. Healthy people typically are less likely to spread a pathogen and more likely to fight off disease than unhealthy people. In the end, those who engage in water sports have the responsibility of doing so safely and they assume the risks.

Question: Is it physically safe to use sex toys?
Sex toys are very commonly used by both heterosexual and heterosexual people. It is reported that 78.5% of gay and bisexual men use or have used at least one kind of them (Rosenberger and Schick, 2012). Whether they are safe to use depends upon what is used and how it is used. A properly selected, stored, cleaned and used vanilla (non-kink) sex toy normally presents little physical risk but things can go wrong. If you use a sex toy the risk and responsibility is yours.

Multiple sources offer these guidelines:
1. Do not share any toy that will ever be inside your body.
2. Do not count on your ability to clean your toys as a means of preventing the transmission of disease.
3. Do not orally use any toy that has ever been used anally.
4. Keep your toys clean and stored in a cool, dry place that is away from pets and dirt and protect them from damage.
5. Do not put any toy inside your body that does not come with a reliable means of getting it out. Items placed in the rectum, for example, can be sucked up into the body and not come out without medical intervention in an emergency room.
6. Do not put toys in your body unless it has a wide base that prevents the toy from going entirely inside you. This is especially true for oral toys that go into the mouth or throat and could potentially block the airway.
7. Do not use any toy until after you have inspected it to assure that it is in good repair, it is not discolored (a sign of age and wear), it does not have any sharp edges or seams and it is not

torn, cracked or chipped. This is especially important if the toy is going inside you, it is electrical, or it is made of glass.
8. Always use lots of lube on toys that are going inside your rectum but never use silicone lube on a silicone toy.
9. Always use fresh batteries. Old ones can leak toxic chemicals.
10. Assure that toys you place in or on a body fit properly. Toys that are the wrong size can cause medical problems. A too small cock ring, for example, can cause blood flow to the penis and testicles to be severely restricted and will be hard or impossible to remove without the help of a medical professional.

Question: What is electrosex and what are the risks involved in doing it?

Electrosex is any sexual activity (heterosexual or homosexual) involving the use of electricity as a means of sexual stimulation. It is also called erotic electrostimulation (e-stim). It is a form of kink thus is beyond what is typically viewed as conventional sexual activity. It is also a form of "edge play" which means it sits on the very thin edge between things going well and things going very badly. Any mistake made while involved in electrosex could have very serious consequences. Moving into the realm of electrosex is a serious decision that should be based on thorough research and thought.

Electrosex involves the use of a power control box, wires, a correct kind of lube and at least one of the several kinds of connections offered in the marketplace that interplay with the body. These can be expensive. The boxes generally fall into the categories of TENS (transcutaneous electro-neural stimulation) units and EMS (electro-muscle stimulation) units.

When buying a control box, you should research it well, not buy one on the cheap and not make one yourself. The same goes for the accessories. The buyer should be aware that manufacturers commonly make their accessories so that they will only fit the boxes they make. Adapters are often available however to overcome that problem.

The buyer will also need to decide if he wants a box that has a variety of selectable settings that are preset or if he wants the freedom and the responsibility of having a box that allows custom settings. Any control box bought should have a cutoff switch that will instantly stop the flow of electricity.

TENS units were originally designed as a medical tool used only by medical professionals. Some are capable of being plugged into to a household wall socket, but most have at least the possibility of being run independently using batteries. They typically are more powerful than EMS units and should be used only by well-experienced people who know what they are doing. It is particularly dangerous to use a box that plugs into a wall socket since that can greatly increase the amount of electricity flowing through it.

EMS control box units tend to be lower power ones. They can still cause serious harm or death but are usually safer than many TENS units. They typically run only on batteries thus they cannot put more electricity into the body than the battery(s) provides.

Practitioners of electrosex report that they often achieve deeper and more frequent orgasms than they do with conventional sex. That, obviously, is one of the lures that cause people to take part in the activity. Still, there are health risks (potentially serious) involved that demand safety measures being followed. Among these safety measures are:

1. Do not use e-stem devises without having proper training or supervision.
2. Do not use e-stem devises if the top and/or bottom have any sign of illness such as a fever or nausea.
3. Do not use e-stem devises if the top and/or bottom have an internal or external injury or an inflamed or swollen area of the body.
4. Do not use e-stem devises if the top and/or bottom is pregnant.
5. Electrosex is not for anyone with a preexisting health issues such as a heart condition, a condition causing seizures, a nerve condition, use of an insulin pump, history of stroke or who has an electrical or metal devise in his body.
6. The electrodes that connect to the body should not be placed anywhere above the navel because doing so may cause a heart attack, a seizure, brain damage or a stroke.
7. The electrodes should likewise not be connected near the heart, brain, or spine and should not be placed on the nipples or in the mouth.

8. The electrodes should also not be attached to piercings because the metal will concentrate the electrical charge to that area which may lead to burning or other tissue damage or worse.
9. The electrodes should be placed on one side of the body only.
10. If used on a bottom during bondage, he must be able to move freely within his bindings because the electricity will cause him to move quickly and involuntarily thus immobility may easily cause harm.
11. The user must always remember to appropriately apply electrosex lube at the electrode attachment sites on the body. The exception to this is if the contact electrode has a special kind of pad that does not need lube. Silicone lube should not be used because it does not conduct electricity well.
12. Do not hook up more than one person to a devise at the same time.
13. Be aware that electricity will pass from one person to another person easily even if you do not intend for it to happen. Be careful about what/whom you are touching.
14. Sweat and any other form of water that is not pure will conduct electricity so keep the situation as dry as possible and stay well away from sources of water.
15. Be aware that electrostatic devises like an ultraviolet wand work by ionizing the air. That ionization creates a lot of heat and can cause tissue damage.

It is easy to find electrosex accessories that are designed to insert into the vagina or anus or that attach to the penis or testicles. Using these has been done without apparent harm but electrosex can cause burning or other tissue damage if not done correctly. Damage to these areas is very serious. There are no studies on the long-term consequences of electrosex. Know what the risks are before you take them because those risks and the consequences for taking them will be yours.

Question: What is "breath play" and what are the risks involved?

It is any behavior that heightens the intensity of an orgasm or produces a sense of euphoria by reducing or ending oxygen delivery to the brain which is why it is called erotic asphyxiation or erotic strangulation. This is typically done either by some form of strangulation wherein blood flow in the neck is restricted or by covering the face/head with plastic. **THIS IS EXTREMELY DANGEROUS!**

The problem with breath play is that uses pressure on the neck (strangulation) and oxygen deprivation (suffocation) to achieve its goal. Among the critical features within the neck are the tongue, the larynx (vocal cords), the vagus nerves and the carotid arteries. Strangulation can cause the tongue to swell and/or damage the larynx which may impair or stop the victim's ability to talk or breathe and possibly make it impossible to for the victim to communicate that he is having a medical problem. He may also suffocate to death.

Impairment of the ability to speak may be permanent. Swelling of the tongue or larynx may cause the victim to be unable to swallow and he will therefore aspirate things into the lungs. This may be lethal.

The vagus nerves send signals from the brain to regulate (among other things) the beating of the heart and the ability to breathe. The carotid arteries send oxygen rich blood to the brain and the brain is a shameless pig where oxygen is concerned. Damaging either the vagus nerves or the carotid arteries can easily be fatal therefore putting any undue pressure on the neck is rather stupid especially if all you get for taking the risk is a seconds-long rush.

The brain uses most of the oxygen a human body produces, and it does not respond well to not having it on an ongoing basis. It begins to chemically and functionally change very quickly when oxygen is not available in a large enough supply. A person will lapse into unconsciousness within mere minutes and the brain begins to die. Brain damage or death will follow.

Intentionally reducing or ending the delivery of oxygen to the brain is stunningly stupid given what the brain may do in response. Doing so by enclosing the face or head in plastic is stupidity at several levels higher however because there is a good chance that doing so will result in unconsciousness. If that happens the person is very likely to suffer serious brain damage or death. Participation in helping somebody else with breath play risks being charged with an assault or homicide. The costs involved in breath play may be huge, but the benefits are almost nonexistent.

Question: Are heterosexual men physically healthier than homosexual men?

No. Homosexual men, as a group, do have certain health conditions at a rate that is higher than that of heterosexual men. Among these are HIV, asthma, hepatitis A & B, human papillomavirus (HPV), anal cancer, syphilis, chlamydia of the rectum and gonorrhea of the throat. This is because our community is involved in risk factors like unprotected oral and anal sex, smoking, social stress and drug use at a higher rate and not because of anything that is intrinsic to being gay. We have other health conditions such as diabetes and heart disease at about the same rate as straight men.

Some people point to the fact that homosexual men, as a group, have a higher incidence of cancers such as Kaposi's sarcoma and non-Hodgkin's lymphoma to support the idea that men who have sex with men (MSM) have higher cancer rates than heterosexual men. The fact is that most of the studies done on cancer in the homosexual community have been about HIV related cancers such as Kaposi's sarcoma and non-Hodgkin's lymphoma. There are not very many studies about how cancer affects the part of our community that is HIV negative however.

There is no doubt that men who have sex with men, as a group, do have a higher incidence of anal cancer. There is also no doubt that our community has a higher incidence of the HIV/AIDS related cancers. However, when HIV/AIDS related cancers and anal cancer are excluded from the picture we find that the evidence shows the cancer rates of gay men and their straight peers are not significantly different (Boehmer and Miao, 2014; Boehmer and Miao, 2011; Frisch and Smith, 2002; Koblin and Hessol, 1996).

At the same time let's give credit where credit is due. Gay men, as a group, tend to be leaner and less likely to be overweight or obese than straight men (Conron & Mimiaga, 2010). We are more likely to be tested for prostate and colorectal cancers (Heslin and Gore, 2008). We are more likely to undergo a colonoscopy or sigmoidoscopy to screen for cancer after the age of 50 and to be tested for HIV (Conron and Mimiaga, 2010). We are more informed about HPV and more willing to be vaccinated for it (Gilbert and Brewer, 2011). We have a lower rate of prostate cancer and a higher cancer survivor rate (Boehmer and Miao, 2011). We are also much more likely to see a doctor about health concerns than hetero men are (Bakker & Sandfort, 2006). These are positive health factors.

Question: Does it matter whether my doctor knows I am gay?

Yes. Many gays intentionally do not tell their doctor about their sexual orientation because they fear the consequences of doing so. Those fears might be reality-based because a doctor may respond negatively to hearing that a patient is gay. Gays, however, have special needs and risk factors related to their health that the doctor needs to be aware of if he/she is going to properly do his/her job. Doctors typically do not ask patients about their sexual orientation, so it is up to the patient to bring up the subject. The bottom line is that all patients need a doctor they can be honest with and who they can have a positive relationship with. If you are gay and your doctor is not gay friendly you have the wrong doctor.

Question: How can I find a doctor that is gay friendly and knowledgeable?

Go to the website of the Gay and Lesbian Medical Association which is: http://www.glma.org. Click "Find a Provider" on the menu then fill in the requested information. Gay friendly medical practitioners will then be listed on the screen if any are known to be available in the location you select.

You can also find a physician by asking for information at a local LGBT resource center if your community has one or you can check at www.gayellowpages.com for what is available in your area. You can also ask a counselor at a site that gives HIV tests. People who hold these jobs deal with a lot of gay people, so they hear about which doctor is gay friendly and which is not. Another way is to ask around among your gay friends and associates to find out who they go to. Still another way is to telephone doctor's offices and simply ask some questions. You may have to settle for a doctor that is gay friendly but who does not know much about the special needs of gay patients. This is especially true outside larger cities. This way is not ideal, but that doctor will at least work with you to find answers if you need them.

Question: How can I find a HIV knowledgeable doctor?
Go to the website www.HealthGrades.com. You will find there a method of filling in information and then it's a matter of doing a simple mouse click in the proper box. You will then get both a list of HIV knowledgeable doctors in your area and patient satisfaction scores related to each doctor. You can also go to the website of the HIV Medical Association (www.HIVMA.org) to find out what qualifies a doctor to be an HIV specialist or you can inquire at a local LGBT center.

Question: What is substance abuse and substance addiction and what are their health consequences?
The American Psychological Association says substance abuse is a pattern of drug and/or alcohol use that interferes with a person fulfilling his obligations, puts him or others in physical danger, creates legal problems for him, or creates repeated interpersonal problems. Substance dependence (addiction) is a pattern of substance use that leads to three or more of the following in a twelve month period: an increased tolerance for the substance, withdrawal symptoms if the substance is not used, an increasing dosage or use, a desire or an unsuccessful effort to control or stop usage, the use of a lot of time and/or effort in obtaining the substance, other activities or interests are given up or made secondary because of substance use, the substance use is continued despite the problems it is causing. The American Psychiatric Assn now uses the term "substance-related and addictive disorders" when dealing with substance issues.

The National Institute on Drug Abuse states that drug addiction is a brain disease in that it causes an alteration of genes and of brain circuitry. It is these changes in the brain that lead to the addict craving his drug. Drug or alcohol addiction can lead to cardiovascular disease, stroke, cancer, HIV/AIDS, hepatitis, lung disease and mental disorders. Alcohol abuse can also cause weight gain, high blood pressure, a depressed immune system, liver disease, heart failure, respiratory failure, vitamin deficiency, sexual impotence, central nervous system damage and memory loss. Drug abuse (depending on the drug used) can cause nausea, seizures, coma, heart and/or respiratory failure, psychosis, depression, paranoia, lung damage, liver damage, a weakened immune system, a rapid heartbeat, cognitive and memory problems, ruptured blood vessels, skin disorders and even death. Mixing drugs and alcohol is especially dangerous.

Substance use is directly linked to taking part in risky sex and to exposure to HIV (Klein, 2009; Mansergh and Shouse, 2006). This includes practices such as anal sex, not using a condom and semen being ejaculated into the receptive person's body. Unprotected sex is associated with acquiring HPV, anal cancer, and other sexually transmitted diseases.

Question: Why does the LGBT community have a higher rate of drug use?

The Centers for Disease Control and Prevention state that LGBT people are less likely than heterosexual people to abstain from using drugs and more likely to be drug abusers. There is however nothing about homosexuality, bisexuality or transsexuality per se that makes us more likely to abuse drugs. The primary thing that is different is the way the heterosexual society we live in treats us and the discrimination and violence we experience. Drug use is often a means to temporarily escape the feelings of depression or anxiety that often goes with not being accepted by the larger society. This view is supported by several studies (Wong & Weiss, 2010; Meyer, 2003).

Another reason for our higher level of drug use is that our community tends to accept drug use more readily than much of the mainstream heterosexual community does. This weakened preventative barrier may be compounded by forces in our lives that enable drug use. Our higher rate of drug use in some ways feeds and sustains itself.

Studies show that higher levels of drug abuse among LGBT people tends to start in adolescence and it continues into young adulthood. It is higher among bisexuals than among homosexuals (Marshal & Friedman, 2009; Corliss & Rosario, 2010). It is in adolescence that one's sexual orientation begins to appear, and the LGBT person learns that he/she is different. Feelings of not fitting in, fear of rejection and actual rejection happen. Anxiety about being "outed", rejected, bullied and even being a victim of violence are common among LGBT teens. This may be worse for uncloseted bisexuals since they are often not accepted by either the straight or the gay community.

Question: What are the health factors related to using alcohol?

The National Institute on Alcohol and Alcoholism (NIAAA) is an agency within the National Institutes of Health and one of the country's leading authorities on alcohol and alcoholism. It defines moderate drinking for men as 4 or fewer standard-sized drinks per day or 14 or fewer drinks in a week. This may cause some confusion because the US Department of Agriculture and the US Department of Health and Human Services, through their widely-published pie chart of dietary guidelines and other material, defines moderate drinking for men as 2 or fewer drinks per day. The confusion lifts however if we look at the Report of the Dietary Guidelines Committee on the Dietary Guidelines for Americans, 2010 which is used to create, among other things, the previously mentioned pie chart. It tells us that the weight of peer reviewed research defines "moderate drinking" for men as an average over time of 1-2 drinks per day and no more than 4 drinks in a single day.

The NIAAA tells us that 71.8% of American men consume alcohol at some level. Heavy drinking is defined as any level of drinking that is higher than the definition of moderate drinking. Binge drinking is consuming five or more standard-sized drinks in two hours or less or any amount of alcohol that will result in a blood alcohol level of 0.8 g/dl or higher. A standard-sized drink is 12 ounces of beer, 5 ounces of wine or 1.5 ounces of distilled spirits. All of this is agreed upon by experts in the field.

It is also agreed that light or moderate drinking can have beneficial results on the human body for most people. It may reduce the risk of cardiovascular disease, dying of a heart attack, having a stroke, having gallstones or having diabetes. These possible benefits are not absolute however and do not apply to everyone. No authority supports the notion that anyone should start drinking to obtain health benefits. Overall, a person is better off not to drink alcohol.

Heavy drinking and binge drinking often result in negative health consequences for the drinker. It can physically change the biology of the brain so that mental functioning is impaired. That can affect the ability to reason, change the drinker's mood and behavior patterns and negatively affect his coordination. Heavy drinking also often causes problems related to the heart, liver, pancreas and immune system. It is one cause of various kinds of cancer. Added to this may be the social and legal problems that can come with being an alcohol abuser.

Certain people should not drink at all. This includes those with a history of stroke, liver disease, disease of the pancreas, breast cancer or conditions related to the heart. People with a history of alcoholism or alcohol abuse should abstain also. Alcohol should not be used by those who may be involved in an activity that may endanger themselves or others because alcohol impairs judgment, perception and reaction time. This obviously includes driving a vehicle or operating machinery. It is unwise to use alcohol if you are taking are medications that may interact with alcohol because the result may be serious. This is especially true if you are HIV+.

Alcohol should not be used in an enema because it can damage the lining of the rectum and intestine and it will be absorbed into the body quicker and more potently than if it was consumed orally. This, of course, increases the risk of alcohol poisoning. The user should also note that alcohol can make an erection difficult or impossible to achieve.

Question: What are the risks involved when using cocaine?

Cocaine is a powerful stimulant. It moves very rapidly to stimulate the pleasure centers of the brain. It initially increases the user's sex drive, sense of euphoria, alertness and energy. In addition, it negatively affects the user's ability to organize thoughts, to concentrate and to sustain fine motor control. The user may think that impact is positive but, over time, it won't be so and those functions will be impaired.

Cocaine increases the body's heart rate, blood pressure and rate of breathing. This may negatively and seriously affect a person with a preexisting medical condition and more than doubles the user's chances of having a heart attack. Snorting cocaine will damage the lining of the nose over time. Smoking it may damage the throat or lungs. Most cocaine users experience a very unpleasant "crash" as the effects of the drug wears off. This can include a bout of depression so those with an ongoing history of depression should understand that the drug will compound their problem. Cocaine is highly addictive.

Question: What are the risks involved when using Ecstasy?

Ecstasy is a synthetic "designer" drug which means that it is manufactured from chemicals by someone. The formula of ecstasy is customarily some mixture of amphetamine or methamphetamine and a hallucinogen like mescaline, but that formula is sometimes altered by manufactures to increase profits or because a typical ingredient is not available. This of course means that the user has no way to judge the strength or purity of the drug and no way to tell what, if any, ingredients have been used as an altering agent. Ecstasy is commonly known as MDMA, Molly, "E", "X", or "XTC".

Ecstasy increases the level of a neurotransmitter found in the brain called serotonin. This altering of the brain's chemistry causes a sense of euphoria, a sense of mental clarity, the feeling of being very emotionally close to other people and hallucinations such as floating. These effects are at the center of why Ecstasy is often found at parties but they only last a couple hours. Some users try to deal with this time limitation by repeatedly taking the drug but that can lead to serious medical consequences such as heart failure and severe heat stroke.

There is a lengthy list of negative effects of using Ecstasy. These include (among others) anxiety, paranoia, depression, impaired judgment and concentration, insomnia, vertigo, nausea, tremors, increased body temperature and suppressed appetite, thirst and sleepiness. The combination of increased body temperature and reduced thirst commonly result in a user suffering from dehydration. Chronic use of Ecstasy can lead to a long-term brain chemistry change in the user. Ecstasy use is also associated with an increased chance of becoming HIV+ because it causes a user to have poor judgment and that causes him to do things he would otherwise not do.

Question: What are the risks involved in using poppers?
"Poppers" is the street name for a class of drugs called alkyl nitrates. The class includes various formulations such as amyl nitrate, butyl nitrate, isobutyl nitrate, isopropyl nitrate and pentyl nitrate. All of them are illegal in the United States for human consumption but are sold legally for commercial uses such as head cleaning or room deodorizing. They are illegal for any purpose in the United Kingdom and Canada.

"Poppers" is a liquid that is packaged in a small bottle. Most commonly its vapor is inhaled from the original bottle although sometimes a small amount of liquid is transferred into another small bottle that is filled with cotton so that the cotton absorbs the poppers and then the substance is inhaled from that bottle. The usual dose is one or two sniffs. It causes a warm head and body rush and relaxes the body's smooth muscles like the inner anal sphincter.

Users report that time seems to slow down after they use poppers. These effects are practically immediate, but they last only minutes. It also dilates blood vessels throughout the body thus causing a blood rush to the heart and brain. It is sometimes inhaled by bottoms involved in anal sex to make receiving an erect penis easier.

This drug was more widely used in the 1970s, but its popularity faded in the 80s. It has made a comeback in the gay community but is still used by only a small percentage of people. The drug rapidly loses potency once it is exposed to air or water, so it must be stored in a bottle that can be tightly sealed. It is often stored in a refrigerator then brought to room temperature before use.

Poppers are very poisonous if swallowed and, if orally ingested, may cause death. It can also burn the skin, so the user should be especially careful when using it while high or when lying down. Transferring poppers to a bottle filled with cotton reduces the chance of getting it on your skin or accidentally swallowing it. An eye dropper can be useful in that transfer since that minimizes the chance of the substance touching the skin.

Users of poppers sometimes experience headaches, sinus pain, loss of the ability to get an erection, nausea and/or vomiting after use and can experience shock, unconsciousness, heart attack or stroke. There are also reports of the drug damaging the eyes and increasing the risk of throat cancer and anal cancer. Aspiration of poppers can lead to pneumonia or death.

Poppers should not be used by anyone using drugs like Cialis or Viagra because the resulting drop in blood pressure may be fatal. It should not be used in combination with a stimulant drug such as meth, E, amphetamines or cocaine. It should also not be used by anyone using a protease inhibitor such as those used in HIV treatment or by anyone who has a preexisting condition related to the heart, brain or nerves. HIV+ individuals should note that poppers have been reported to temporarily suppress the immune system thus it might compound the immune system problem they have already.

Question: What risks are involved in methamphetamine use?

Methamphetamine is a highly addictive synthetic stimulant drug. The term "synthetic" means that it is created by someone in a laboratory. The word "stimulant" means that when used it at least temporarily increases activity in the brain. The word "addictive" means that with repeated use the user will become dependent on the drug, will need higher and higher doses over time to feel "normal" and will go through physical withdrawal if he stops using the drug.

Methamphetamine is also known by a lot of other names such as meth, chalk, crystal, glass, ice, speed, Tina and crank. It is made by cooking down (reducing) the ingredients. The primary ingredient is ephedrine or pseudoephedrine which is acquired by the drug producer through the purchase or theft of sizeable quantities of certain cold medications, diet pills or allergy medications. To that is added substances that have known impact on the brain. This can include antifreeze, iodine crystals, drain cleaner, isopropyl alcohol and other toxic substances. The typical cook down yields about one pound of drug for every five pounds of waste. The waste is so toxic that special suits must be worn by law enforcement agents when they clean up lab sites.

Meth can be smoked, injected, inhaled or taken orally depending upon the form it is in. It very rapidly changes the brain and thereby causes feelings of pleasure, increased energy and an elevation of mood. That often changes over time into feelings of anger, edginess and fear. The user commonly has the sense that his thoughts are very rapid. He feels hot and may have the sensation that bugs are crawling on him. He experiences rapid changes in mood so that he might be happy in one moment, angry or violent in the next, tired in the moment after that and very agitated in the next. The user also typically has an irregular heartbeat, elevated blood pressure and may experience psychological problems. Chronic use can yield long term mental disorders, memory loss and severe dental problems. Methamphetamine is associated with an increased willingness to take part in risky sexual practices (Mansergh and Shouse, 2005; Molitor and Truax, 1998). It also tends to accelerate the aging process and make the user look much older than he is.

Question: What are the risks involved in using marijuana?

Marijuana is the shredded flowers, stems, seeds and/or leaves of the plant cannabis sativa although users typically remove the seeds and stems before use. The primary psychoactive chemical in marijuana is delta-P-tetrahydrocannoabinol (THC). It can be smoked in a cigarette (joint), blunt or pipe, eaten in food products like brownies or drank as a tea. It varies in potency depending on the type and form used. Smoking or eating the plant itself is by far the most typical use. Hashish is a more concentrated form and is more potent. Hashish oil is several times more potent than hashish and is therefore a lot more expensive.

THC temporarily interacts with the endocannabinoid receptors in the brain. These receptors regulate the sense of pleasure, the memory, thinking processes, concentration, awareness of the senses, the perception of time and coordination. Users often report an elevation of mood, a reduction of stress, muscle relaxation, a sense of euphoria, a feeling of sedation and an increased sense of hunger. The CDC says 1 in 10 users will become psychologically addicted and the number climbs to 1 in 6 when the use begins prior to age 18.

Studies suggest that marijuana may have negative effects in some people and that this varies based upon age at first use, frequency of use and the level of THC used. Studies also suggest that younger people and older people are at elevated risk and that the ingestion of THC may worsen preexisting medical or psychiatric conditions. There have been no reports of death directly caused by using marijuana although there are reports of lethal accidents wherein marijuana use may have been a factor. Any kind of smoke affects the lungs negatively.

The negative effects of use can include an increased heart rate and an impaired heart rhythm which may lead to a heart attack. This heart attack risk is especially true for older users or users with a preexisting heart condition but is not typical for healthy users. Marijuana use impairs coordination and judgment. Therefore, persons under the influence have a higher accident rate than non-users do. Mixing marijuana use and alcohol use makes this much worse. Marijuana is linked to getting HIV only in that it impairs judgment, so a user might do things while using that he otherwise would not do.

A high dose of THC can cause temporary psychosis, but this is not common. This becomes more problematic if the user has a preexisting mental health issue. Heavy use of THC has been shown to be linked to high job turnover, dropping out of school and being involved in accidents. Chronic use can lead to a permanent decrease in the connections in the brain related to memory and concentration although that is not common.

Question: What are the risks involved in amphetamine use?

Amphetamine is a class of drugs all of which act as a stimulant on the nervous system. Of all illegal drugs, only marijuana, cocaine, Ecstasy and methamphetamine are more widely used in the United States than are amphetamines. Street names for drugs in this class are (among others) black beauties, dexies, pep pills, speed, uppers, Christmas trees and double trouble.

Amphetamines work by increasing the release of the neurochemical dopamine and then altering how the brain uses it. The user will rather quickly have a sense of euphoria, an increased sex drive and an increased sense of alertness and self-confidence. He may also feel a heightened sense of aggression and/or paranoia. Also, on the negative side, the users commonly experience hyperactivity, headache, insomnia, tremors, itchy skin, teeth grinding, diarrhea, fever and acne.

The most dangerous effect of amphetamine use however is a seriously increased heart rate which can lead to a heart attack or stroke. People with heart disease, high blood pressure, hardening of the arteries, hyperthyroidism, glaucoma and those using other medications or alcohol should strictly avoid the recreational use of amphetamines. Those with an anxiety disorder, diabetes, motor or phonic tics, or a seizure disorder such as epilepsy are also at a heightened risk if using this class of drug.

Heavy or long-term use of amphetamines substantially increases the user's risk of stroke, heart attack, seizures, coma and death. There are also documented cases of amphetamine related psychosis which may be short-term or long-term. Amphetamines are highly addictive and are associated with the body developing an increased tolerance for them which, of course, means that more and more must be used. Withdrawal symptoms will occur if the drug is stopped. This should be done under the care of a qualified professional because it sometimes involves depressive episodes, great fatigue, weight loss, hallucinations, aggression and suicide ideation.

Question: What are the risks involved in using Ketamine?

Ketamine is a "club drug" belonging to a class of drugs called dissociative anesthetics. Dissociative anesthetics act to disrupt one's sense of awareness, identity, perception and memory. The user does not experience reality as it is and therefore cannot function within it rationally or safely. Street names include: K, special k, cat valium, KitKat, vitamin k, and horse tranquilizer. The latter name comes from the fact that ketamine is primarily used in veterinary medicine.

Ketamine is addictive. It always has a very quick but unpredictable effect. This can include visual or auditory hallucinations, a sense of floating and being detached from one's body, a loss of coordination, confusion, tremors, changes in sensory perceptions and anxiety or fear. Users sometimes go into a "K Hole" in which they experience delusions but are unable to move or communicate.

Users also experience increases in blood pressure, heart rate, respiration, body temperature and pressure in the brain and eyes. It is especially dangerous for those with preexisting medical or psychiatric conditions, those who are senior citizens or who use alcohol or nervous system depressants. It can affect a user's judgement, memory and health long after its immediate effects wear off.

Question: What are the risks involved in using GHB?

GHB (Gamma-Hydroxybutyrate) is a central nervous system depressant. It is among the type of drugs that are called "club drugs" and "date rape" drugs. It may be in the form of a pill or capsule, but it is usually in the form of an odorless and colorless liquid or powder that is commonly mixed together with alcohol to hide its soapy or salty taste. Its street names include Liquid X, Liquid Ecstasy, Liquid G, Georgia Home Boy, and Grievous Bodily Harm.

It is used in clubs primarily because it causes feelings of euphoria and tranquility and an increased sex drive. Studies show it causes unconsciousness 69% of the time which, of course, is why it is used as a date rape drug. The negative effects include nausea, headaches, hallucinations, amnesia, confusion and loss of muscle control. It is addictive if used repeatedly and withdrawal symptoms are typically severe. It is particularly dangerous when used with other drugs or alcohol because the mixture can cause the aspiration of vomit, central nervous system impairment and breathing difficulties.

Question: What are the risks involved in using Rohypnol?

Rohypnol (flunitrazepam) is a central nervous system depressant which has various street names such as Roofies, Ruffles, La Rocha, Roach, and Wolfies. It is among a group of drugs called "club drugs" and "date rape" drugs. It is usually in the form of a tasteless, odorless powder or tablet which dissolves easily. As a date rape drug, it is typically mixed into the drink of an unsuspecting person. It commonly causes drowsiness, sleep and amnesia which may prevent the victim of a sexual assault from resisting or possibly even remembering what happened.

When used as a club drug it is usually in the form of a tablet that is either swallowed or crushed then snorted. It is commonly used at clubs and parties to enhance the effects of other drugs or alcohol intoxication. It is also used to decrease the negative effects of coming down from a cocaine or crack high.

The negative effects of Rohypnol include amnesia, decreased reaction time, impairment of mental functioning/judgement, confusion, and aggression. It can also cause loss of motor coordination, headache, slurred speech, and difficulty with breathing. An overdose can cause unconsciousness, slowed heart rate, suppression or arrest of respiration or death.

There is no recognized medical use for Rohypnol and the importation, manufacture, possession, and use of it is illegal in the United States. It is typically smuggled into our country from Mexico or manufactured in underground labs which, of course, means there is no oversight of what ingredients are used.

Question: What are the risks involved in using LSD?
LSD (lysergic acid diethylamide) is among a group of drugs called hallucinogens. It has a variety of street names some of which are: Acid, Blotter, Dots, Lucy, Tabs, Yellow Sunshine, and Cubes. It is made from ergot which is a grain fungus. It may be found in the form of tablets, capsules, liquid, on blotter paper which is divided into squares called "tabs", on sugar cubes or in squares of gelatin all of which are typically used orally. Liquid LSD is clear and has a bitter taste.

LSD has no medically recognized use. It is used recreationally or as a spiritual enhancement because it produces altered awareness, feelings, perceptions, sensations, and/or images that are different of a person's true, objective reality. It takes very little of it to produce these reactions.

The effects of LSD are variable depending on the amount used and the state of the person using it. It typically reduces the appetite, dilates the pupils and causes sleeplessness. It may also cause nausea, an increase of heart rate, an elevated blood sugar level, sweating, increased blood pressure, a higher body temperature, tremors and dry mouth.

A negative psychological reaction to LSD may cause extreme anxiety, panic attacks, aggression toward others, suicidal ideation and mood swings. These may occur in "flashbacks" long after the use of the drug has stopped. It has been associated with the onset of psychosis in some cases. This is especially possible among those with an earlier mental health condition. Studies show that LSD is not addictive but repeated use can result in a tolerance to the drug so that an increased dose is needed to create the effect.

Question: Does being a drug user mean I won't be helped by HIV treatment?

This is something you need to talk to a physician about but having a history of drug use is unlikely to prevent you from taking HIV medication and taking part in treatment. People with a history of drug use respond to antiretroviral medications just as well as non-drug users (Beyrer and Malinowska-Sempruch, 2010). If you have HIV you should be under the care of a HIV knowledgeable doctor and following a treatment plan. It is very important that a person not hide his/her drug use from his/her physician. This is especially true when medication is involved.

Question: Is there a link between drug abuse and mental disorders?

The National Institute on Drug Abuse (NIDA) asserts that drug abuse can cause or worsen mental disorders. Likewise, a mental disorder can lead a person into drug abuse. Drug abuse and mental illness have common risk factors which is why the link between the two is present. These risk factors include an overlapping genetic vulnerability, overlapping environmental triggers, and involvement of similar regions of the brain. The NIDA reports that person with a mood or anxiety disorder are twice as likely to also have a drug disorder and a person with a drug disorder is twice as likely to have a mood or anxiety disorder. Several studies show that gays and bisexuals are more likely than heterosexuals to be depressed (a mood disorder) or anxious. This is common for any minority that feels rejected and/or threatened by the majority.

Question: What is depression, what are its symptoms and what can I do if I have it?

Depression is a general class of mood disorder. A mood disorder is a problem related to one's underlying emotional state of being. Depression presents itself in several forms but they all have some common underlying characteristics. Some of the markers of depression are:
1. Feeling depressed (sadness, irritableness or an empty feeling)
2. Having a lack of interest in things
3. Having an unusual increase or decrease in appetite

4. Sleeping too much or too little
5. Not being able to think or concentrate
6. Having thoughts about suicide or self-harm

It is very important that you see a qualified medical or psychological professional if you have these symptoms. You need to be completely honest with the professional about what you are feeling and experiencing. Although depression sometimes reoccurs it is manageable with proper treatment.

Question: What is anxiety, how do I know if I have it and what can I do if I do?

Anxiety has many faces but generally it is the mental and emotional state of being uneasy or worried about some future event or about the result of some event. Some degree of anxiety is perfectly normal and can be very healthy in that it motivates us to create and use methods or mechanisms that will aid our well-being. The creation and maintenance of civilizations and laws, for example, are based on the need to deal with anxiety.

Anxiety becomes a mental health issue when it causes interpersonal problems, interferes with one's functioning in life or causes physical illness. Among the more common types of anxiety related mental health issues are:

1. Panic attack. The person has physical symptoms because of his fear that he is in a situation where escape is very difficult or impossible. Symptoms of a panic attack might include things like sweating, rapid pulse, chest pain, a tremor, shortness of breath, nausea, or feeling dizzy.
2. Obsessive-compulsive disorder (OCD). This condition is often diagnosed when a person obsessively (persistently) has unwanted thoughts that lead him into compulsively (uncontrollably) repeating behaviors.
3. Social phobia. This is the avoidance of social situations in which the person fears he will be among people he does not know and/or where he might be judged or embarrassed. This is not the same as shyness because while a shy person may blush, have difficulty with talking in public, feel nauseous, sweat or tremble just as person with social phobia would he will steel himself and push his way through it. The person with social phobia either will not do so or he may experience a panic attack if he does.

4. Post-traumatic stress disorder (PTSD). A person with PTSD has experienced or seen a serious situation that involved significant injury, death or the threat of significant injury or death and he is unable to work his way through it psychologically or emotionally. Instead he dreams about or remembers the situation repeatedly and continues to experience the feelings he had associated with the experience. This may cause him to become apathetic, emotionally numb/volatile, irritable, withdrawn and/or sleepless.
5. Generalized anxiety. The person persistently worries about a lot of things. He may also be on edge, easily fatigued, irritable and/or tense and may have insomnia and difficulty with concentration. The person finds that his worrying is interfering with his life and/or is at the root of physical illness.

LGBT people have some anxiety disorders at a higher rate than heterosexuals. There are no studies that show homosexuality per se is the cause of that difference. There are studies however that show homosexuals are more likely to be rejected socially by family or society, more likely to be discriminated against, more likely to be homeless, more likely to be assaulted verbally or physically and, thus, much more likely to hide who they are than heterosexuals are. The homosexual also has a very different experience during the formative years of his life than does the heterosexual. These facts point to the conclusion that anxiety is a response that is learned. In short, there is nothing in homosexuality that dictates these higher rates of anxiety. It is homophobia and heterosexism that are at the root of the problem.

If you have symptoms of unhealthy anxiety you need to see a medical professional. That professional will decide if your symptoms are generated by some sort of medical problem or if it is a mental health issue. Most cases of anxiety are successfully dealt with using therapy and/or medication. Your doctor can refer you to a qualified mental health professional if that course is chosen.

Question: How can I tell if someone is suicidal and what can I do if I think someone is?
While it is true that gays and lesbians think about and try suicide at a much higher rate than heterosexuals there is no data that supports the notion that we commit suicide at a higher level

(Movement Advancement Project, 2017; Haas and Eliason, 2011; Muerhrer, 1995). A recent study found that gay men do not have a higher rate of suicide than other men (Cochran and Mays, 2011).

Suicide ideation, suicide threats and suicide completion are not just LGBT issues. Per the National Vital Statistics Report, suicide is the third leading cause of death in the United States for those 15-24 years of age and the fourth leading cause of death for those 24-44. Women are reported to think about suicide more often than men do but men complete the act more often. We have long known that those who think about or attempt suicide often also have a problem with depression and/or drug abuse.

It is not possible to predict who is going to commit suicide, but an earlier attempt greatly increases the chance that another attempt will occur. This is especially true in the first year after an attempt. Warning signs of include:

1. Verbal threats or hints about suicide.
2. An attempt to find a way to commit suicide (like looking for pills or getting a weapon).
3. Verbalizations of hopelessness or feeling trapped in his life or situation.
4. Verbalizations about feeling deep physical or psychological pain.
5. Talk about feeling like a burden to others.
6. Increased use of drugs and/or alcohol (these are used to deaden feelings and to lower personal barriers to suicide).
7. An earlier suicide attempt (an earlier attempt makes other attempts easier).
8. Reckless behavior (many deaths which are counted as accidental are suicides).
9. A personality change involving social withdrawal, increased anger or mood swings.
10. Depression (signaled by an increase/decrease in sleep or appetite or feelings of sadness or apathy).
11. Giving away possessions or settling affairs (paying off bills, quitting a job, etc.).
12. Visiting people to say goodbye when no trip has been planned.

If you know someone who has these symptoms you should talk to the person frankly and openly about suicide. You should listen to his/her words and his feelings. You should not be judgmental, aloof or allow yourself to be sworn to secrecy. The suicidal person also needs to be evaluated by a medical professional and perhaps referred to a mental health therapist soon. In most cases this problem can be managed with the proper treatment. Try to avoid leaving them alone and call someone who is trained to deal with the problem such as the ***National Suicide Prevention Lifeline (1-800-273-8255)***.

Question: Are homosexuals less mentally healthy than heterosexuals?

No. Per the National Alliance on Mental Illness (NAMI) mental illnesses are "medical conditions that disrupt a person's thinking, feeling, mood, ability to relate to others and daily functioning". Homosexuals are diagnosed with stress related conditions such as some types of depression, some types of anxiety, suicide ideation/attempts, some types of eating disorders and substance abuse more often than heterosexuals are. These sorts of conditions are common among those who perceive themselves as not accepted by the larger society and/or discriminated against are (Kessler & Mickelson, 1999). Homosexuals and bisexuals have more of these stressors than heterosexuals do (Mays & Cochran, 2001) and this commonly begins in adolescence or before.

Those facts however are not the entire picture nor are they a basis to say homosexuals, as a group, are less psychologically healthy than heterosexuals. They are certainly not a reason to cast a negative light on the LGBT community. The fact is a large majority of Americans, gay, straight and bi, are mentally healthy (NAMI, 2007). There is no difference in the overall mental health of homosexual people and heterosexual people (Gay and Lesbian Medical Assoc., 2010; Rothblum and Factor, 2001; Gonsiorek, 1982). Most gay and bisexual men do not meet the criteria for any mental health disorder (Cochran and Mays, 2008). They cope with life reasonably well. It was shown in a study as far back as 1957 that when the psychological tests taken by heterosexual males and homosexual males were given to experts for review, the experts could not tell the two groups apart (Hooker, 1957).

One very useful study (Berg and Mimiaga, 2008) points to the kind of things gay and bisexual men use mental health services for. Primarily the issues dealt with are depression, anxiety and relationship problems. Other common topics are current and past abuse, financial/employment problems, grief because of a loss, and substance abuse. These are very human problems. Reaching out for help is very human too if you are brave enough to do it.

The National Alliance on Mental Health asserts that LGBT people account for around 4% of those who have a serious or major mental illness (NAMI, 2007). That is about what many authorities count the LGBT community as being in proportion to the society at large so we are not overrepresented in that mental health sector. There is, in fact, no significant difference between LGBT people and non-LGBT people in the rates of psychiatric hospitalization (Hellman and Sudderth, 2002). LGBT mental health issues are commonly treatable on an outpatient basis and, as noted previously, LGBTs are more likely to seek help.

The picture of mental illness existing within the homosexual community is often painted with too broad a brush. It is not uncommon to see authorities say that LGBT have a higher psychiatric morbidity (rate of incidence) or a poorer mental health outcome. That is an overgeneralization. Homosexuals are not overrepresented in all categories or kinds of mental illness. There is some evidence, in fact, that in some areas of mental health gay men are disproportionately fewer in number than would be expected given our proportional presence in society. Most of the areas related to psychotic disorders are an example of that (Hellman and Sudderth, 2002). There is also a study of monozygotic twins with discordant sexual orientations (one hetero, one homo) that found the heterosexuals had greater issues related to hostility, anger, paranoid ideation and psychoticism than did their gay brothers (Sanchez and Bocklandt, 2013).

It should be added that there are some types of mental illness such as transvestic fetishism that are wholly or primarily found in the heterosexual community. There are other forms of mental illness such as pedophilia (child molestation), medication related disorders and elimination disorders that have nothing to do with sexual orientation at all. It is also true that in those mental health areas where gays are overrepresented the degree of difference is sometimes moderate or small.

The fact that homosexuals seek out the help of mental health professionals more often than heterosexuals do is sometimes used as a negative indicator. It is used to signal a higher level of mental illness. Factually however looking for professional help is a positive coping mechanism. Long term and short-term outcomes related to mental health issues are often greatly improved by getting proper treatment. The act of seeking treatment shows the ability to recognize and accept that there is a problem and that help is needed with it. Indeed, the fact that heterosexual men do not often seek out mental health help is a negative mental health indicator.

Question: Are heterosexual men happier with their bodies than homosexual men are?

Most men, gay and straight, are happy with their body. Happiness with how they look is more common among hetero men, as a group, however. Gay men, as a group, tend to have body concerns that are comparable to hetero women (Peplau and Frederick, 2007). These concerns center on weight and attractiveness issues. Both straight women and gay men are interested in men as sex partners, so it is not unusual or unexpected that they would respond in similar fashion to the fact that men, straight and gay, are highly visual in selecting sex partners and prefer good looking partners. At the same time, it must be noted that gay men are a very diverse group so naturally the type of body they prefer and are happy with varies too. Bears and gay Leathermen, for example, tend to not worry much about weight while clubbers and gay youths do.

The higher rate of body acceptance that hetero men enjoy as a group is not entirely a plus for them because it lets them to be happy with a body that is overweight or obese. Hetero men not only are more likely to accept their body if it is overweight or obese, but they are also more likely to accept their male friends being that way. This is a major negative health factor in that being overweight or obese is associated with a variety of health concerns.

Question: Do gay men have a higher rate of eating disorders?

Eating disorders is a category of emotional dysfunction in which a person has an ongoing disturbance in his/her pattern of eating or otherwise dealing with food or non-food substances. The most common forms of this are anorexia nervosa (persistent pattern of not eating due to the fear of being fat), binge eating (pattern of eating a lot of food due to the feeling that one has no control over it) and bulimia nervosa (pattern of binge eating due to a lack of control then vomiting due to the fear of getting fat). These conditions commonly co-occur with other mental health issues and they also very commonly have medical consequences such as low blood pressure, low heart rate, muscle loss and osteoporosis. They can also lead to death.

As of 2007 the lifetime prevalence (proportion of the population having a condition in a lifetime) in the United States of anorexia nervosa is 0.9% for females and 0.3% for males. The lifetime prevalence for bulimia nervosa is 1.5% for females and 0.5% for males. The lifetime prevalence for binge eating is 3.5% for females and 2.0% for men (Hudson and Hiripi, 2007). Gay and bisexual men have eating disorders at a significantly higher rate than heterosexual men do (Feldman and Meyer, 2007). Forty-two percent of the men having an eating disorder are gay (National Eating Disorders Assn, 2014). Gays are less than 10% of the general population.

Question: Does penis size matter?
The average range of a penis is 1 to 5 inches in length when soft and 5 to 6 inches in length when erect. The average circumference is 4.8 inches (Kinsey Institute, 2010). Gay men, on average, have a slightly larger (length and circumference) penis than straight men do (Bogaert & Hershlberger, 1999). It is thought this may because of hormonal differences in the womb.

Penis size is not related to the ability to find a sex partner, frequency of sex, or condom use. It is also not related to HIV status or getting hepatitis B, hepatitis C, syphilis, crabs, lice or scabies. Having a larger than average penis is however positively correlated to getting anal or genital warts (HPV), anal or genital herpes (HSV-2), gonorrhea, chlamydia and urinary tract infections (Grov & Parsons, 2010).

Experienced gay men know that whether you prefer to be a "top" (anal or oral insertive), a "bottom" (anal or oral receptive) or a "versatile" (will take either role) has more to do with what is going on in your head than with what you have hanging between your legs but one's perception of his penis size has been shown to be statistically related to whether a gay man is a "top" or a "bottom". A man who perceives himself as having a larger than average penis is more likely to be a "top" while a man who views his penis as smaller than average is more likely to be a "bottom". Men who perceive their penis as being smaller than average also tend to score worse than other men on measures of psychosocial adjustment (Grov & Parsons, 2010). This may reflect the view that the penis is an object of power and status among men.

Question: Is there any association between prostate cancer and how often a man ejaculates?

There is no positive relationship between frequent ejaculation and getting prostate cancer. There may however be a negative association. In other words, frequent ejaculation does not increase the odds of getting prostate cancer, but it may be somewhat protective. (Leitzmann & Platz, 2004; Giles & Severi, 2003).

Question: Do penis-enlargement products or techniques work?

Most penis-enlargement products and techniques do not work, and some may damage the penis (Mayo Clinic, 2011; Nugteeren, 2010; Martin, 2005). Pills and lotions advertised for this purpose have not been empirically proven to work and may include harmful ingredients. Long-term or incorrect use of a penile pump can damage the tissues of the penis. Exercises like jelqing have not been proven to work and may cause harmful/painful scarring of the penis. Devises that are used to stretch the penis have not been shown by high quality studies to work and may damage penis tissue. Surgical techniques may result in a slight increase in penile size, but unsatisfactory results and medical complications often occur (Vardi, 2008). Trimming one's pubic hair and losing weight will make the penis look longer and have no negative health consequences.

Chapter 7
Legal Issues

Question: Is being gay illegal anywhere?
There are, per the U.S. State Department, 195 countries on Earth. Homosexuality is illegal in seventy-six of them. Another six countries either have political subdivisions (provinces, districts, states, etc.) wherein homosexual activity is illegal or it is de facto illegal because of severe repression.

Some countries ban homosexual behavior but not gay identity. Most countries governed by Muslim Sharia law fall into this category. Other countries forbid male homosexual behavior but not lesbian behavior. Some take it further by banning both gay/lesbian behavior and having a homosexual identity. Several countries have decriminalized homosexual identity, behavior and relationships but still regulate what homosexuals can/cannot do and/or allow LGBT people to be victimized and discriminated against. A minority of countries allow homosexuals to express their identities openly and legally and give us some or all the same rights held by heterosexuals.

Homosexual behavior was illegal in many parts of the United States until 2003. That changed when the United States Supreme Court handed down its decision in the case of Lawrence vs. Texas. The court said states could not criminalize the private sexual conduct of its citizens. That effectively made homosexuality legal everywhere in this country. Gays and lesbians are still legally discriminated against in most states however.

Question: Do any countries authorize the death penalty for being homosexual?
Yes. Homosexuality can be punished by death in Iran, Saudi Arabia, Yemen, Afghanistan, Qatar, Brunei, Northern Nigeria, Somalia, Sudan, and Mauritania. Uganda has been considering making homosexuality a death penalty offense too. In addition, some countries foster, tolerate or lightly punish the tradition of "honor killing" in which a family member can kill a member of their family if that member does something to bring shame or disrepute to the family. Many LGBT people have been killed on this basis.

Question: Is anyone trying to criminalize homosexuality in the United States?

There is no sign that criminalization is going to happen here, and the trend seems to be toward a further expansion of LGBT rights and acceptance. The LGBT community cannot stop being vigilant and assertive however because there are forces in America that are actively working to undo our progress. There are lots of examples of this.

In 2012 House Republicans included anti-gay language in the National Defense Authorization Bill which authorizes the budget for the military. Both the 2012 and the 2016 Republican Party platforms explicitly opposed same-sex marriage. On July 7, 2011 People for the American Way reported that the Family Research Council asked its members to pray in support of countries that criminalize homosexual behavior. The Missoula Independent reported on July 1, 2010 that the Montana Republican Party had offered a plank in their party platform that called for the criminalization of homosexuality. The New York Daily News reported on June 22, 2010 that the Texas Republican Party voted for a plank in their party platform that would criminalize oral and anal sex and ban gay marriage. On February 9, 2010, The Michigan Messenger reported that the president of the American Family Association of Michigan had called for the criminalization of homosexuality. These are just a few examples of opposition to the idea of freedom and liberty for LGBT people.

Question: Why are gays not treated equally under the U.S. Constitution?

The Equal Protection Clause is found in Section 1 of the Fourteenth Amendment to the United States Constitution. It reads: "All persons born or naturalized in the United States, and subject to the jurisdiction thereof, are citizens of the United States and of the State wherein they reside. No State shall make or enforce any law which shall abridge the privileges or immunities of citizens of the United States; nor shall any State deprive any person of life, liberty or property, without due process of law; nor deny any person within its jurisdiction of the equal protection of the laws". The courts have held that this clause does not require that all classes of people be treated equally under the law.

The U.S. Supreme Court has found that religious groups and racial minorities are "suspect classes". A suspect class is a group that needs a higher level of judicial scrutiny when discrimination is alleged. They are, in effect, protected classes. LGBT people have not been found to be a protected class.

This may have begun its way to change however with the case of GlaxoSmithKline vs. Abbott Laboratories. In January 2012, the Ninth Circuit Court of Appeals found that "heightened scrutiny" and not the lower level of "rational basis scrutiny" is the standard to use when considering discrimination based on sexual orientation. If this is upheld on appeal or the case is not taken by the US Supreme Court LGBT people may join religious groups and racial minorities as a class receiving more protection from discrimination. It will, as a minimum, be used as precedent in other cases.

Questions: Can landlords refuse to rent to or evict people based on sexual orientation or gender identity? Can sellers refuse to sell property on that basis?

There is no federal law prohibiting sellers or landlords from discriminating against LGBT people. California, Colorado, Connecticut, Hawaii, Illinois, Iowa, Maine, Maryland, Massachusetts, Minnesota, New Hampshire, New Jersey, New York, New Mexico, Oregon, Rhode Island, Vermont, Washington, Wisconsin and the District of Columbia ban discrimination in housing based on sexual orientation. Some of these states ban discrimination in housing based on gender identity too. Many local jurisdictions also ban housing discrimination based on sexual orientation and/or gender identity.

Question: Can LGBT people be denied use of public accommodations solely because of their sexual orientation?

Title II of the Civil Rights Act of 1964 and the Americans with Disabilities Act make it illegal to deny use of a public accommodation solely because of race, religion, color, national origin or disability. LGBT people are not a protected class under federal law. Some states and some local jurisdictions however have enacted laws that forbid discrimination against LGBT people in the use of public accommodations. In these states, it is illegal for a public accommodation to refuse to serve or do business with a person based on that person's race, religion, color, national origin, disability or sexual orientation. A public accommodation has been defined as any entity that serves the public. This includes stores, rental businesses, schools, recreation facilities, establishments offering services to the public and similar places.

Question: Are there restrictions on gay men relating to donating blood?

Yes, in most cases. The Food and Drug Administration (FDA) has the legal authority under Title 21 chapter 1(f) of the U.S. Code of Federal Regulations (CFR) to regulate the collection and distribution of our country's blood supply. Current guidelines place a permanent blood donation ban on people who have ever: 1) had a positive HIV test, 2) been diagnosed as having hepatitis B or C, 3) exchanged sex for money or drugs, and 4) used non-prescribed IV drugs. A one year waiting period (from the time of the most recent event) applies to: 1) a man who has had sex with another man, 2) a woman who has had sex with a man who has had sex with another man, 3) a person who has since age 11 had hepatitis not caused by a virus, 4) a person who has been detained in a corrections facility for 72 hours or more, 5) a person who has had syphilis or gonorrhea, 6) a person has had a blood transfusion, 7) a person who has had a tattoo done by an entity not regulated by a state and/or not done using sterile needles and non-reused ink, 8) a person who has undergone ear or body piercing without the use single use equipment, and 9) a person who has had through-the-skin contact (e.g. open wound or sore, mucous membrane or needles stick) with the blood of another person (Food & Drug Admin, 2015).

Question: What are the rules related to lesbian, gays and bisexuals serving in the military?

The Department of Defense (DoD) policy regarding LGBs serving in the military is based upon Public Law 111-321 (Repeal of Don't Ask, Don't Tell), the 2013 Supreme Court case of United States v. Windsor (Marriage cannot be defined as heterosexual), and the 2015 Supreme Court case of Obergefell v. Hodges (Same-sex couples have the right to marry). DoD policy is found in DoD

Directive 1020.02E (Diversity Management and Equal Opportunity in the DoD), DoD Directive 1350.2 (as amended on 6/8/2015), a 2/11/2013 memorandum from former Secretary of Defense Leon Panetta and the DoD Human Goals Charter. Some of its provisions are:
1. Unlawful discrimination because of race, color, religion, sex, sexual orientation, or national origin will not be condoned.
2. Military personnel will not be separated from the service solely based on sexual orientation nor will anybody be denied entry into the service solely on that basis.
3. Sexual orientation will be viewed as a private matter. Commanders will not collect or keep information related to the sexual orientation of military personnel except as necessary as part of a proper investigation or official action.
4. Professional evaluations will be based on merit, fitness and capability. Sexual orientation will not be a factor.
5. No service member or spouse will be denied benefits or excluded from participation in any program or activity purely because of sexual orientation.

Question: What is the policy regarding transgender persons serving in the military?

On 7/26/2017, on the eve of the full implementation of the Department of Defense's new policy on transgender persons in the military, President Donald Trump tweeted that transgender persons would not be admitted into the military because of the negative impact that would have on the costs, readiness and cohesion of the armed services. Defense Secretary Mattis then announced he was delaying the full implementation of DoD's new policy about transgender service until the White House gave further guidance. The White House provided that in a memorandum dated 8/25/2017.

Absent that change in direction, the Department of Defense (DoD) policy regarding transgender persons serving in the military would have been based upon: 1) A RAND Corporation study which found that allowing transgender persons to serve would have little impact on the military's costs, readiness and cohesion (Schaefer, 2016), 2) DoD Instruction 1300.28 (In-Service Transition for Transgender Service Members), 3) A memorandum dated 6/30/2016 from former Defense Secretary Ash Carter, and 4) Army Directive 2016-35 (Army Policy on Military Service of Transgender Soldiers). That policy allowed qualified transgender persons to serve openly, bans discrimination against them and offers policies and procedures to ease their transition.

On 10/30/2017 District Court Judge Colleen Kollar-Kotelly issued an injunction stopping the implementation of the Trump Memo. On 11/21/2017 District Court Judge Marvin Garbis also issued an injunction. The Trump Administration asked Judge Kollar-Kotelly to delay the her injunction. She responded by ordering DoD to begin enlisting transgender people on 01/01/2018. Transgender people can enlist under current rules.

Question: Have homosexuals who were discharged from the military solely for being gay been treated equally to other soldiers who served honorably prior to discharge?
Yes and No. Prior to the end of "Don't Ask, Don't Tell" homosexuals were given "other than honorable" discharges even though they served their country faithfully and honorably. Some members of the Democrat Party in the Congress worked to correct this, but Republicans blocked those efforts. Since the end of "Don't Ask, Don't Tell" gays and lesbians have been given honorable discharges but received only half of what their separation pay should have been. The American Civil Liberties Union (ACLU) filed a class action lawsuit (Collins v. United States) to change this. That effort succeeded when, on January 7, 2013, the case was settled out of court. The U.S. agreed to treat gays equally with respect to separation pay and to apply that rule to gay members separating from the service on or after November 10, 2004.

Question: What is the Matthew Sheppard & James Byrd, Jr. Hate Crimes Prevention Act?
This is an extension of the 1964 Civil Rights Act which was the previously existing federal hate crimes law. That law made it illegal to willingly injure, intimidate or interfere with anyone based on race, color, religion, or national origin who is doing a federally protected activity such as trying to go to school, apply for a job, trying to vote, perform as a juror or using a public place.

The Sheppard and Byrd Act added gender, sexual orientation, gender identity and disability to the list of those protected. It removed the constraint that the victim must be trying to do a federally protected activity. It also lets federal agents pursue cases that state authorities decline to pursue, and it compels the FBI to keep and publish hate crime statistics.

Question: What is an assault and how is that different from assault and battery?

An assault is the threat of physical harm that causes the victim to fear he is in immediate danger. No physical touch is necessary. The threat must be unlawful, and the victim cannot have willingly given permission for it to occur. The aggressor must be physically able to follow through with the threat. The intent to do harm to the victim may or may not need to exist depending upon the situation.

An assault elevates to assault and battery when the aggressor follows through with some sort of action in which he makes physical contact with the victim or uses an object to make contact. Those who aid in an assault and battery may be liable for it also. Understanding the definition of assault and of battery is important to LGBT people because we have a higher probability of being the victim of it.

Question: What is the Health Insurance Portability and Accountability Act of 1996?

Per the U.S. Department of Health and Human Services, the Health Insurance Portability and Accountability Act of 1996 (HIPPA) sets national standards that protect personal medical records and health care information. It sets up limits on what patient information may be shared and who it may be shared with. Generally, everything in a medical file, all conversations with medical personnel and all medical billing information is covered by the law. Your medical information can, without your permission, be shared to improve your treatment, to pay medical bills, to protect public health, to make required police reports such as in the case of a gunshot wound and to assure that safe and clean care is being given in a nursing home. Your information can also be given to family or friends you name as involved in your health care or the payment of your bills. Inmates in a correctional facility may have special rules that apply to them.

HIPPA includes the right of patients to examine their medical records and to ask for corrections but does not give patients access to psychotherapy notes. It also does not protect medical information that is part of employment records nor does it prohibit an employer from asking for a doctor's note or other medical information that is necessary in administering business related things like sick leave, workman's compensation, wellness programs or health insurance. Life insurers, worker compensation carriers, schools and school districts, police agencies and some state and local governmental agencies are exempt from the law.

This law is particularly relevant to gays because many of us are in the closet and may wish to be totally honest with our doctors without risking being outed. It is also relevant to persons wishing to confidentially undergo HIV or other sex related testing or procedures. Additionally, it is relevant to LGBT people who are under the care of a mental health professional.

Question: What is the Defense of Marriage Act?
The Defense of Marriage Act (DOMA) was a federal law that was initially proposed by the Republican Party. It was approved by large majorities of both political parties in the U.S. House and Senate and signed by Bill Clinton in 1996. Section 1 of the act basically only gives the name and intent of the law. Section 2 says that no state or U.S. territory that bans same-sex marriage must honor a same-sex marriage that has been approved in another state. Section 3 forbad the federal government from recognizing such marriages and thereby denied same-sex couples from having any of the rights and privileges given under federal law to opposite sex couples. On February 24, 2011, the Obama administration notified the United States 1st Circuit Court of Appeals that the federal government would no longer defend DOMA in court because it viewed DOMA as clearly unconstitutional.

On March 4, 2011 House Speaker John Boehner (Republican) announced he was leading a group of Republicans in seeking to defend DOMA in court. Several states had by then passed legislation that were comparable to DOMA. On June 26, 2013, the

United States Supreme Court, in a 5-4 decision, ruled section 3 of DOMA to be unconstitutional. Lower courts have since then used the Equal Protection Clause of the 14th Amendment to strike down state laws banning same-sex marriage. Lower courts are also ruling that states must honor same-sex marriages performed in other states. House Republicans ended their defense of DOMA in July 2013 after spending millions of tax payer dollars on their fruitless effort.

Question: What is marriage and why do some people not want gays and lesbians to have it?

Marriage is a statutorily sanctioned union of people in wedlock that gives certain rights, benefits, privileges and obligations. It is often also a religiously sanctioned institution. The case against same-sex marriage is based on tradition, religious belief and socio/political dogma.

The tradition argument simply asserts that American society has never approved of same-sex marriage, our founding fathers would certainly be opposed to it and the traditional definition of marriage demands that it be between a man and a woman. The religious argument asserts that same-sex marriage is unnatural and against the design of God and is therefore an inherent evil. The religious argument also contends that the state has no right to force religious institutions or bodies to accept marriage as anything but between a man and a woman or to compel clerics to perform marriages between same-sex couples. The socio/political argument is that traditional marriage between a man and a woman is a critical foundation of our society which should not be devalued or diluted by allowing same-sex unions. It also says that children do best when they are raised by a married man and woman because each gender gives a child a unique kind of rearing.

Question: What rights, benefits, privileges and obligations are associated with marriage?

The U.S. Government Accountability Office lists 1,138 provisions within the United States Code in which marital status a factor in defining the rights, duties and privileges held by an individual in the United States (GAO, 2004). States have also enacted laws which offer similar rights, duties and privileges. Among these are:

1. Income tax deductions, credits and exemptions
2. Property tax breaks for the spouse of a disabled person
3. Tax free transfer of property or income between spouses
4. Joint tax filing of tax returns
5. Military benefits including housing, moving with a spouse and commissary privileges
6. Family visitation rights
7. Next of kin status in medical situations or in case of the death of a spouse
8. Funeral and bereavement leave in case of the death of a spouse
9. The ability to make funeral arrangements in case of the death of a spouse
10. The right of survivorship and inheritance
11. The right to social security payments at the rate the spouse earned if it is higher
12. Custodial status in relation to children
13. Joint property status in case of a divorce
14. Child support payments in case of a divorce
15. Joint adoption or foster care
16. The ability to make medical and legal decisions in the event that a spouse is incapacitated.
17. The right not to testify in court against a spouse
18. The right to spousal benefits and health insurance coverage
19. A spouse may have the obligation to pay the debts incurred by a spouse
20. A spouse's income is normally counted when figuring out government payments
21. A spouse's income is normally counted when applying for loans or grants

Question: What is the difference between a civil union or domestic partnership and a marriage?
This partially depends upon the state you live in. The definitions of civil union and domestic partnership vary by state. The rights, benefits, privileges and obligations that go with civil union/domestic partnership in one state may or may not the same as in other states. A civil union or domestic partnership may not carry all the rights, benefits, privileges and obligations of

marriage. Civil unions and domestic partnerships are usually recognized only in the state they were created in and that is also where they must be dissolved should that happen. The federal government recognizes same-sex marriages but not civil unions. The terms "civil union" and "domestic partnership" also do not carry the same weight in our society as the term "marriage".

Question: Are homosexuals allowed to adopt children?
Every state in the union allows a single homosexual person to petition to adopt a child. Some states allow a homosexual couple to jointly adopt a child while other states do not. Similarly, some states allow a homosexual person to petition to adopt the child of his/her same-sex partner, but other states do not. Whether a petition to adopt is successful depends both upon state law and upon how the presiding judge chooses to interpret and administer that law. You can find information about LGBT adoption and foster care on the Human Rights Campaign website: http://www.hrc.org/explore/topic/adoption.

Some adoptions agencies that are affiliated with certain religious groups will not allow homosexuals to adopt children who are in their care and custody. In some cases, state or local government has tried to intervene in that but that has not always been successful. Some of these adoption agencies have simply closed their doors. They would prefer children to be homeless rather than put them in the home of a gay or a lesbian.

Question: How does being a homosexual impact someone wanting to immigrate to the United States?
Homosexuality per se is not a reason for exclusion from entry into the United States nor is it a basis to deny someone a green card. It is also not, by itself, a reason to get to stay in this country. To gain refugee status in the United States you must prove you are a member of a "particular social group" (in this case that you are gay) and that you either have been persecuted in the past for being a member of that group or you have a well-founded fear of persecution in the future. This standard was first created in 1980 in the case of In re Toboso-Alfonso and codified in 1994 when U.S. Attorney General Janet Reno signed Order 1895-94.

Until section 3 of the Defense of Marriage Act (DOMA) was declared unconstitutional in 2013 gay Americans did not have the same rights under immigration law as straight Americans did. Under those now void rules a foreign national could get a green card by marrying an opposite sex American citizen but not by marrying a same-sex American citizen. The undoing of section 3 puts that into the rubbish bin of history and gives heterosexual and homosexual Americans the same rules. A gay immigrant can now get a green card and thereby stay in this country legally by marrying an American citizen.

Question: Does federal law explicitly ban job discrimination?

Federal law bans discrimination within the competitive service of the federal civilian workforce but there is no federal law which explicitly bans employment discrimination by private employers.

Question: What is the Employment Non-Discrimination Act?

The Employment Non-Discrimination Act (ENDA) is a law that has been proposed repeatedly by congressional Democrats since the 1970s that would make employment discrimination based on sexual orientation largely illegal in the United States. The law would have added sexual orientation to the Civil Rights Act of 1964 which banned workplace discrimination-based race, color, disability, national origin and religious affiliation. All efforts to pass ENDA have been blocked by the Republican Party.

Since 2015 congressional Democrats have proposed the Equality Act in place of ENDA. The Equality Act, if adopted, would add LGBT protections to the Civil Rights Act of 1964 in the areas of employment, housing, using public accommodations, federal funding, credit and participation in serving on juries. The Republican Party has blocked the effort to pass this law too.

Question: Does Title VII of the Civil Rights Act of 1964 protect LGBT people?

The Equal Employment Opportunity Commission (EEOC) lists Title VII of the Civil Rights Act of 1964 as being among those laws which may protect LGBT people from discrimination in employment. In 2012 it issued an administrative ruling in the case of Macy v. Department of Justice that Title VII does ban employment discrimination against transgender people and it supported that finding in 2013 in the case of Jameson v. U.S. Postal Service and again in the 2015 case of Lusardi V. Dept. of the Army.

In 2015 it issued an administrative ruling in the case of Baldwin v. Foxx that Title VII does prohibit employment discrimination which is based on sexual orientation. It said this is so because Title VII explicitly bans employment discrimination based on the sex of the individual. It reasoned that discrimination based on sexual orientation necessarily entails the use of sex-based factors. In other words, the employer would make a judgment that a male who was attracted to another male or a female who was attracted to another female would not be treated the same as an employee who had only opposites sex attractions.

This EEOC view was in line with the policy of the Department of Justice under the Obama Administration but it is not in line with that of the Trump Administration. Attorney General Jeff Sessions has issued legal opinions and has argued in court that Title VII does not protect LGBT people from employment discrimination. He is actively working now to enforce that view.

The courts have ruled on both sides of the issue. Several district courts and some appellate courts have sided with the EEOC but not all. In 2000 the Second Circuit Court of Appeals in the case of Simonton v. Runyon declined, on technical grounds, to say that Title VII protection includes LGBT people. It was also found to not apply to LGBT people in the Eleventh Circuit case of Jameka Evans v. Georgia Regional Hospital (2017).

There are however several cases wherein Title VII was found to apply to LGBT people. They include: Schwenck v. Hartford (9th Circuit, 2000), Rosa v. Parks W. Bank & Trust (1st Circuit, 2000), Smith v. City of Salem (6th Circuit, 2004), Barnes v. City of Cincinnati (6th Circuit, 2005), Glenn v. Brumby (11th Circuit, 2011), Chevez v. Credit Nation Auto Sales (11th Circuit, 2016), Hively v. Ivy Tech Community College of Indiana (7th Circuit, 2017).

The U.S. Supreme Court has twice found Title VII to apply to LGBT people. In 1989 it said in the case of Price Waterhouse v. Hopkins that employment discrimination based on sex stereotypes is unlawful under Title VII and that an employer must prove by a preponderance of the evidence that it would have made the same employment decision in the absence of discrimination.

In 1998 Justice Scalia said, in a unanimous opinion in Oncale v. Sundowner Offshore Services, that sex discrimination extends to "sex-based" harassment under Title VII if it places the victim in an objectively disadvantaged situation at work regardless of that person's gender.

Question: How do I file a discrimination complaint with the Equal Employment Opportunity Commission?

According to the Equal Employment Opportunity Commission (EEOC), such a complaint is called a "charge of discrimination". It is a signed statement which charges that an employer has engaged in employment discrimination. The workplace discrimination could be based on race, color, religion, sex (including pregnancy), national origin, age (40 or older), disability, genetic information, sexual orientation or gender identity.

The EEOC must, by law, act on complaints but it can only do so after the charge has been filed. The law also requires that a charge be filed before a lawsuit can be filed. There are time limits of 180 day or 300 days (depending upon the situation) that apply to the complaint process. The time starts ticking when the act of discrimination occurs.

For an explanation of the complaint process go to the EEOC website at: https://publicportal.eeoc.gov/. This site will offer you a three-minute video tutorial in English and Spanish. You will then be directed to the correct portal to begin the process.

You can also visit a local office of the EEOC. You can find more about that at: https://www.eeoc.gov/ field/ index.cfm. Alternatively, you can telephone the EEOC at 1-800-669-4000 to discuss your case.

Question: Does the Civil Service Reform Act of 1964 protect LGBT people?

Section 2302 (10) of that law says (under federally prohibited practices) an agency shall not "discriminate for or against any employee or applicant for employment on the basis of conduct which does not adversely affect the performance of the employee or applicant or the performance of others; except that nothing in this paragraph shall prohibit an agency from taking into account in determining suitability or fitness any conviction of the employee or applicant for any crime under the laws of any State, of the District of Columbia or of the United States".

Question: Are there any presidential executive orders that protect LGBT people?

Executive Order 11478 (Nixon, 1969) prohibited discrimination in the competitive service of the federal civilian workforce based on race, color, religion, sex, national origin, handicap and age. Executive Order 13087 (Clinton, 1998) amended that order to include sexual orientation. Executive Order 13672 (Obama, 2014) amended 11478 to include sexual orientation and gender identity. Executive Order 13673 (Obama, 2014) required federal contractors to prove with documentation that they were following all federal laws and executive orders. Executive Order 13782 (Trump, 2017) rescinded Executive Order 13673 which means businesses can get a federal contract without proving they do not discriminate against LGBT people.

Question: What protections do the states offer LGBT people?

Most states do not offer any protections specifically to LGBT people. Some states ban discrimination within their state government but allow private entities to do it. Other states ban discrimination more broadly. What is offered in the states varies by location and may be added to by cities. For a description of what is offered go to: www.hrc.org/state-maps.

Question: What constitutional right to have counsel during a criminal trial is given under Gideon v. Wainwright?

All Americans, including LGBT ones, should know about the case of Gideon v. Wainwright (372 U.S. 335). It is a case decided by the U.S. Supreme Court in 1963 which compels the states to offer an attorney to those in custody for a criminal offense and are too poor to hire an attorney themselves. A person in law enforcement custody can simply ask for an attorney to get to talk to one. There is then a process through which the court will decide if the person meets the income requirements needed for an appointed attorney to be given and paid for by the government. This ruling is important to the LGBT community because we have a proportionately higher number of poor people within our ranks than the hetero community does.

Question: What rights do people in police custody have prior to interrogation under Miranda v Arizona?

This is a U.S. Supreme Court case that was decided in 1966. It requires that the following information be given to an arrested person (including LGBT ones) before the police can use the result of their questioning of a suspect in court:
1. You have the right to stay silent.
2. Anything you say may be used as evidence against you.
3. You have the right to have an attorney.
4. If you cannot afford an attorney one will be given prior to questioning.

Persons in police custody have the right to ask for an attorney prior to saying anything or at any time during the questioning. Your silence after being arrested cannot be used against you in court. However, in the case of Salinas v. Texas (2013) the US Supreme Court ruled that a prosecutor can mention, and a judge or jury can consider the defendant's refusal to answer questions prior to arrest when they are weighing guilt or innocence. A person in custody may choose to stay silent or he may choose to stop talking at any time during questioning.

The US Supreme Court ruled, in the case of Berghuis v. Thompkins (2010), that a suspect who has been given his Miranda and understands them must explicitly invoke his right to stay silent. That right is not invoked by merely staying silent or by the fact that he has not waived his rights. The court ruled that any free and deliberate comment or word spoken after the Miranda warning is given is an implicit waiver of the right to stay silent. A waiver of Miranda rights cannot be the product of coercion or intimidation and it must be made "with full awareness of both the nature of the right being abandoned and the consequences of the decision to abandon it". In short, if a suspect wants to exercise his right to stay silent he must explicitly say he does not want to answer questions and then say nothing except that he wants to speak to an attorney. The police must stop their questioning at that point.

The courts have also ruled that in most situations the Miranda warnings do not have to be given while pre-arrest questioning is taking place. The major exception is a situation in which a person reasonably believes he is in police custody and is not free to leave but has not been formally arrested. To use the accused's answers in court the Miranda warning must be given prior to questioning being done once an arrest is made or when an arrest is imminent. If you think you are in custody but the police have not explicitly said you are you have the right to ask if you can leave.

Question: What rights to personal safety do LGBT jail inmates have?

Farmer v Brennan 511 US 825 (1994) concerned a male preoperative transsexual who was incarcerated with other males. After being beaten and raped by other inmates he was transferred to a higher security facility which housed inmates that historically were more dangerous and troublesome. He was placed in general population. He sued saying the government had acted with deliberate indifference to his safety. The district court gave a summary judgement to the government holding that the petitioner (the inmate) had not shown officials had "actual knowledge" of potential dangers since he had not expressed any concerns about his safety to them.

The Supreme Court ruled that actual knowledge was not necessary because the officials had acted with "deliberate indifference" to his safety. It said prison officials must give humane conditions and must protect inmates from violence at the hands of other inmates when failure to do so could yield a "sufficiently serious" result. An inmate does not have to suffer actual harm to seek relief in the courts. He/she only must show "deliberate indifference".

Question: Can the government criminalize private same-sex sexual intimacy between consenting adults?

The U.S. Supreme Court said "No" to this question in the case of Lawrence v Texas 539 US 558 (2003). It ruled the state has "no legitimate interest which can justify its intrusion into the personal and private life of an individual" and such intrusion violates the Due Process Clause.

Question: Can a state pass a law that bans its subdivisions from enacting local measures that would protect homosexuals as a class from discrimination?
This question was taken to the courts because the people of Colorado passed an amendment to the Colorado state constitution which forbad subdivisions of the state from adopting measures that would protect homosexuals as a class from discrimination. The state courts prevented the amendment from taking effect and that was appealed to the US Supreme Court. In Romer v Evans 517 US 620 (1996) that court upheld the lower courts saying the amendment was a violation of the Equal Protection Clause of the Fourteenth Amendment and that the state had no legitimate government interest in doing harm to homosexuals as a solitary class simply because they were a politically unpopular group.

Question: Does the U.S. Constitution compel states to license marriage between same-sex couples and does it compel states to recognize same-sex marriages legally performed in other states?
The US Supreme Court said "yes" to both questions in Obergefell v Hodges (2015). It ruled that marriage is a fundamental right and that this right is protected by the Due Process Clause and the Equal Protection Clause in the same way for same-sex couples as they protect opposite-sex couples. Overturning this decision is a primary goal of the Republican party.

Question: Can a school be held liable if it acts with deliberate indifference to student on student harassment?
The Supreme Court answered this question in Davis v Monroe County Board of Education (1999). It said schools could be held liable under Title IX of the Education Amendments of 1972 when officials act with deliberate indifference to student on student harassment if it is so severe that it prevents the victim from enjoying the educational opportunities that are available. Such deliberate indifference is a form of discrimination.

Question: Can a school deny a LGBT student the right to express his/her sexual orientation or gender identity?
This question was answered in the 1969 case of Tinker v. Des Moines Independent Community School District. The case involved a small group of high school students who planned to wear black armbands to protest the war in Viet Nam. School officials disallowed this and sent those students home who wore an armband then refused to remove it. The parents sued and lost in both the district court and the appellate court. They appealed to the Supreme Court.

The court, in a 7-2 decision, said while children may not have all the rights of adults, they do have the constitutional right to free speech and expression and those rights are not shed at the schoolhouse door. Justice Fortas (the majority opinion writer) said the armbands where prohibited by the school officials because they wished to avoid discomfort but that was not a sufficient reason to ban them. He said the test of whether the students' freedom of speech and expression could be censored is whether the conduct "materially and substantially" interferes with the requirements of appropriate discipline in the operation of a school. The court found that test was not met in this case and reversed the lower court.

According to the American Civil Liberties Union (ACLU) this case means an LGBT student can express his/her sexual orientation or gender identity at school so long as it is not truly disruptive. He/she also has the right to express an opinion related to that if it is done appropriately.

If your school does not allow that you may wish to contact the ACLU. You can find summaries of your rights at www.aclu.org/files/assets/Prom_rights.pdf and at www. aclu.org/files/images/asset_upload_file94_28337.pdf. For more help go to: www.aclu.org/issues/lgbt-rights/lgbt-youth or call them at (212) 549-2673.

Question: What constitutional rights do juveniles have during a criminal proceeding in juvenile court under In re Gault?
In re Gault is a case decided by the United States Supreme Court in 1967. It requires that all juveniles who are facing charges which may result in the loss of liberty be given the following:

1. A written notice of what the charges are and what proceedings will be held.
2. Notice of the right to have an attorney.
3. A written record of what occurred at all proceedings.
4. Notice that the child has the right against self-incrimination.
5. The right to confront his accuser and that accuser must appear at the hearing.
6. The accused or his attorney must be given the opportunity to cross-examine witnesses.

This law is important to our community both because juveniles tend to not know their rights and because the LGBT community has a high percentage of homeless youths in our ranks who do not have adults to help them when they get in legal trouble.

Question: Can private organizations exclude homosexuals solely upon sexual orientation?

The United States Supreme Court ruled in Boy Scouts of America v. Dale (2000) that private organizations can exclude anyone based on the constitutionally guaranteed freedom of association when "the presence of that person affects in a significant way the group's ability to advocate public and private viewpoints". In this case the Boy Scouts had dismissed and expelled a scout leader solely because he was gay. That was declared legal by the court.

Question: What is the Administrative Procedure Act?

The Administrative Procedure Act is a federal law that was passed in 1946. It compels all federal agencies to publish their rules, regulations and procedures. They are published in the Federal Register in chronological order. It can be found at most large libraries and at the website http://www.gpoaccess.gov/fr/. Most states and cities also have a version of this law that covers agencies in that jurisdiction. That can be found at most large libraries or possibly online.

This is important to LGBT people because our community is actively discriminated against and because we are actively working to get equal rights. Many of us are therefore likely to appear before state or local agencies. Such an agency is often a near law unto itself in that it gets to decide on its own rules, regulations and procedures and has the power to enforce them. It is a good thing to know that agency's rules, regulations and procedures prior to dealing with it.

Question: What is the Affordable Care Act?
The Affordable Care Act is health insurance reform legislation that was signed into law on March 23, 2010 by President Obama. This law is extremely important to the LGBT community because of the substantial number of people within it that do not have health insurance. Many of us cannot get health insurance through our job, are unemployed or health insurance costs too much when bought by an individual without a government subsidy to help pay for it. The law not only gives access to affordable health insurance but also ends some practices done by insurance companies that have negatively impacted LGBT people. A summary of the provisions of the law can be found at http://www.hs.gov/healthcare/about-the-aca/ index.html. A recap of some of the major provisions of the law follows:
1. People cannot be denied coverage because of pre-existing conditions.
2. Insurance companies can no longer cancel coverage after you get sick by finding an error or technical mistake in application paperwork.
3. Insurance companies cannot discriminate based on sexual orientation, gender identity or HIV status.
4. There are no annual or lifetime limits.
5. Insurance companies can no longer impose an annual or lifetime limit on how much you can claim in benefits. This is especially important to people who are chronically ill due to things like cancer and AIDS.
6. Plan members now have a way to appeal insurance company decisions that is independent from the company.
7. Small businesses are given tax credits to help them offer coverage to employees.
8. People under 26 years of age can stay on their parent's insurance plan.
9. Federal funding to Medicaid has been increased so more of the poor can be covered.
10. Senior citizens are eligible for free preventive healthcare and the Medicare gap in the coverage of prescription drugs called the "donut hole" is gone.

11. Health insurance is more affordable for the poor and the middle class because of a system of tax credits and reduced cost sharing such as lower deductibles and co-pays.
12. Those who cannot get affordable health insurance through their job can get it through an Affordable Insurance Exchange.
13. Preventive healthcare like HIV screening, depression screening and tobacco screening is covered.
14. Low income people may qualify for a government subsidy that will help pay for the insurance.

The Republican Party has vehemently opposed this law and promises to repeal it. The 2016 election gave the Republicans, the power to do that and they moved forward with that repeal legislatively. That effort has failed so far but their effort continues.

Question: What is sodomy?
It is commonly believed that sodomy is the act of anal intercourse between homosexual men. This belief has become so common that some dictionaries now define "sodomy" that way. That definition is incorrect or at least imprecise.

Sodomy is, from the religious and legal history perspective, any sexual act that is not at least potentially procreative. It includes masturbation, anal sex and oral sex whether done as a homosexual act or a heterosexual one and any sex act done with an animal (Peakman, 2014; Crawford, 2010; Meer, 2003; Eder & Hall, 1999). Sodomy has, over the course of history, sometimes been legal and even socially acceptable under certain conditions while at other times it has been viewed as a social evil and even as a capital crime. In the latter case sodomy between men has been viewed as the very worst kind.

Criminalization of male with male sodomy in Western civilization began in 390 A.D. with a decree by the Roman emperor Theodosius at the insistence of Ambrose Bishop of Milan who used the new law to rid himself of political opponents. Anti-sodomy laws rose and fell periodically over the following centuries. Those laws, for the most part, have covered both male and female sodomites but the male with male variety continued to be viewed more harshly. Many political leaders such as Justinian I, Phillip IV of France, Henry the VIII and Elizabeth I of England, Adolf Hitler, and former U.S. Senator Joseph McCarthy have followed the example of St. Ambrose in using sodomy as a political tool.

Thomas Aquinas wrote *Summa Contra Gentiles* from 1259-1264 A.D. and *Summa Theologica* from 1265-1273. In these works, he expanded on the ideas of Plato and Aristotle concerning natural law. Aquinas wrote that an act of sodomy is an act against nature thus it is against the will of God. He asserted that it is the second worse (next to murder) offense a person could do because it denies life to a potential person. These writings became fundamental to the teachings of the Roman Catholic Church and some protestant denominations. They also became a justification for the persecution, prosecution and execution of sodomites including homosexual and bisexuals. Aquinas' natural law theory continues to be used by anti-LGBT forces to this day.

Be that as it may, research shows that over 80% of heterosexuals have taken part in opposite-sex oral sex, 38.9% of heterosexual men have been involved in anal sex with a woman and 33.1% of heterosexual women have done so with a man (Chandra, 2011). Studies show 70-80% of gay men have been involved in anal intercourse (Levin, 2009; Bell, 1999; Laumann & Gagnon, 1994). An equal number or more take part in fellatio. Laumann & Gagnon (1994) puts it at 89.5% while Rosenberger (2011) puts it at 75.0% for giving and 73.4% for receiving it. Private sexual acts done between consenting adults, including acts of sodomy, were formally legalized by the U.S. Supreme Court in 2003. The French government did the same thing but did so 212 years earlier.

Chapter 8
Sex Education

Question: How do I choose a condom?
There are two general kinds of condoms. One is the male condom which is applied over an erect penis and the other is the female condom which during heterosexual sex is usually inserted into the vagina. In some cases, as in homosexual sex, it is also inserted into the anal cavity. Most gay males never use the female condom, but some find them to be a desirable choice for anal sex.

Male condoms come in a variety of sizes (length and diameter), shapes, colors and flavors. Some are pre-lubricated, and some have spermicide on them. Male condoms are usually made of lamb's intestine, latex (natural rubber), polyisoprene (synthetic rubber) or polyurethane (plastic). Some condoms have talc in them to increase the ease of using them.

Latex condoms are the most popular choice because they are easily found, relatively inexpensive and are typically very durable if they are used correctly. Plastic condoms are somewhat more expensive, and they can be a little stiff during use, but they are a right choice if an oil-based lubricant such as petroleum jelly, vegetable oil, baby oil, mineral oil, petroleum-based talcum powder or massage lotion is going to be used during sex or foreplay since oil-based products destroy latex and polyisoprene. Lamb intestine is not a proper choice for gays because these condoms have microscopic pores in them that allow viruses to pass through. Condoms with spermicide on them are also not a desirable choice since the spermicide tastes awful, eases the transmission of HIV and it can irritate the lining of the anus.

Condoms may come pre-lubricated on the inside and/or on the outside. The condoms that are lubed on the outside are designed for vaginal sex and don't have enough lubrication on them to use for comfortable anal sex so added lube is usually called for. Condoms that come without lubrication on them naturally involve the user adding lube if it going to be used at all. This may be viewed as a plus since it allows the user to have some control over what lube ingredients he uses. It is not uncommon for these condoms to be used without lubrication during oral sex. Some are, in fact, recommended by the manufacturer for that purpose.

Men with certain medical problems should take care in using flavored, pre-lubed or talc condoms because they can have glycerin, artificial sweeteners or parabens (a synthetic preservative) in them. Condoms having glycerin should not be used for anal sex because glycerin has been shown to increase the odds of infection. Flavored condoms are often in this category and should be used for oral sex only. That is the reason they are flavored after all.

Men who have a history of an allergic reaction to latex may choose to use polyurethane or polyisoprene condoms to avoid any potential problem. This includes both the insertive and the receptive partners. If you have an allergy to latex is it wise to carry your own alternative ones because most of your sex partners will have latex ones.

Most gay men believe the size and shape of a condom is their personal choice. This is only true within certain limits however. A condom should be neither real tight nor real loose when fitted on the erect penis. Selecting the wrong size will significantly increase the chance of the condom breaking or slipping off during use and thereby potentially spread an infection.

When selecting a condom, it is essential that the purchaser be aware of the products end date. Using a condom beyond that date increases the odds that it will fail during use. The end date can be found both on the package the condoms came in and on the individual wrapper of each condom. If the end date has passed throw the condom away unused.

Condoms should be kept in a cool, dry place and away from direct sunlight. Wallets, cars and pants pockets are awful places to store condoms because those places tend to be very warm or hot. If you are using a condom someone else is offering pay attention to where he is getting it from. The safest choice is to always carry a condom yourself, so you can supply your own protection. This is especially true if you are the one being penetrated orally or anally since your risk of infection is higher.

Question: What is the correct way to use a condom?
There is a right way and plenty of wrong ways to use a condom. The correct way starts by reading the box the condoms come in to find out what the recommended use of the condoms inside is.

Some condoms, for example, are not recommended for anal sex and some, such as edible ones, are intended as novelty items only.

The next step is checking the end date on the condom wrapper and discarding any that are out of date. You should also look the wrapper over to ensure that it hasn't been damaged. If the wrapper is in bad shape the odds are that the condom inside it is also damaged.

The third step is to be careful when the condom wrapper is opened. Don't use teeth or any sharp object to do this since doing so may damage the condom. It is also a good practice to open condom wrappers from the corner with a sideways motion along the edge instead of in the middle since the act of tearing toward the condom puts it at risk.

A condom should only be placed on an erect penis. This allows the user to judge the fit and the proper positioning of the condom. If the person wearing the condom isn't circumcised push back the foreskin just prior to removing the condom from its wrapper. Put the rolled-up condom on the head of the erect penis then pinch the closed end of the condom to remove any air. Not doing this pinching may result in the condom failing.

Once the rolled-up condom is in place roll it down the penis while continuing to pinch the end of it. You should assure that a half inch or so of the condom is under the area you are pinching so the ejaculated sperm has a place to go. This is especially true if the condom is designed with a rounded head rather than a head with a nib that acts as a reservoir. The failure to do this process may result in the condom breaking or in ejaculate spilling out of the condom.

The condom should roll easily down the penis. It should be rolled down to the base of the penis. A regular sized condom is typically at least seven inches long, so most men should be able to do this. If the penis is longer than that a longer condom is needed.

If the condom doesn't roll down the penis easily you have probably placed it on the head of the penis upside down. Consider throwing away this condom because if you turn it over and roll it down the penis the inside part that that touched the penis head before is now the outside part of the condom. It is therefore a potential source of bacteria and virus transmission.

Once the condom is in place it is important to remove any air bubbles that may be in the condom. Not doing this may result in the condom breaking during use. The condom's fit should also be checked to assure that it is not too loose (which may cause it to slip off the penis) or too tight (which may cause the condom to break).

Some gay men believe that if using one condom gives a safer sex act then using two is better. They put on one condom then put another one over that. This is called "double bagging". Others believe using two condoms increases the chance of condom failure during sex because of the friction between the condom surfaces. There is no creditable evidence that using two condoms at once increases the chance of breakage and the admonishment against "double bagging" as based on myth (Planned Parenthood, 2011).

Properly removing a condom from the penis after ejaculation is straight forward. The penis should be pulled out before it softens to lessen the chance that the condom will slip off while it is still inside the receptive partner. That would greatly increase the odds of spillage. The insertive partner should hold the condom against the base of his penis as he pulls it out gently. It is wise for both insertive and receptive partners to shower after sex using plenty of soap and water.

Many gay men use condoms while engaged in oral sex. This reduces the chance of getting an STI and is therefore a safer sex practice. It is important for the receptive partner to hold the condom at the base of the erect penis since that will assure that the condom does not slip off while it is in his mouth or throat. That, of course, could cause choking. This is especially true if deep throating is involved.

Condoms are not reusable, so you shouldn't use a condom more than once or for multiple sex acts. You can't clean and safely use them again. Once used a condom should be wrapped in a tissue and thrown in the garbage. Never flush a condom down the toilet since they are not biodegradable and may damage a septic or sewer system.

Question: What should I do if a condom breaks or slips off during sex?
If a condom slips down the penis prior to ejaculation it can be adjusted back into place. If it slips all the way off it should be retrieved and thrown away. A new condom should replace it.

If a condom slips off or breaks the partner who becomes aware of it should inform the other partner at once. This is especially important if this happens during or after ejaculation since one or both partners may wish to get tested for STIs. If a condom breaks during oral sex the insertive partner should check to make sure the receptive partner is breathing normally and doesn't have a piece of the condom stuck in his throat.

Question: How do you choose a personal lube?
Gay men should never use a lube that has Nonoxynol-9 (N-9) in it. This applies to both lubes that are pre-applied to condoms by the manufacturer and lubes that are applied by the user. Many gays believe this ingredient reduces the chances of getting STIs including HIV, but this is not true. Studies show that N-9 increases the chances of getting HIV (Heise, 2002; Centers for Disease Control and Prevention, 2002).

Lubes come in solid, liquid, cream, gel, spray and powder forms and are water-based, silicone based, or petroleum/oil based. These categories branch out into a variety of products that include a variety of features.

Flavored lube is designed to enhance oral sex. Stimulating lubes have ingredients such as menthol that increase sensation. Numbing lubes have ingredients such as benzocaine that are intended to reduce pain during anal sex. Glycerin-free lubes are available for those who prefer to avoid the possible complications involved in introducing sugar or sugar-like substances into the body. There are also paraben-free lubes available for those who prefer to avoid artificial preservatives. Parabens are banned throughout Europe. There are also organic lubes and earth-friendly lubes. Which of these you use is, within limits, a personal choice.

Water-based lubes are the most commonly used. They are condom safe, can be used with any sex toy and are easily cleaned up. They tend to dry out over time but can be reactivated with a few drops of water. Some people find these lubes to be a bit sticky. They cannot be used in water.

Silicone lubes are condom safe but cannot be used with silicone-based sex toys. This type of lube stays slick, but some people find them to be too slick. Silicone lubes can be used in the water which makes them a desirable choice for in the pool or shower. These lubes have a smooth, silky feel and are never sticky. They can be hard to cleanup since they are not water soluble.

Petroleum/Oil based lubes are not a good choice if you are using anything made of natural rubber (latex) or synthetic rubber (polyisoprene) since it can cause both to break. It can be used on silicone, glass or metal sex toys and with polyurethane (plastic) condoms. It will stay slick, but it can be difficult to cleanup. It can also foster infection if used internally as in anal sex. These lubes are often used for masturbation.

Many gay men use saliva (spit) as a lube in anal sex. This is not a good choice because it dries out rather quickly and it can carry infections such as herpes and hepatitis B. It is also related to cancers such as Kaposki sarcoma (Butler & Osmond, 2009). These infections can enter the body through mucous membranes such as those found in the rectum.

Some gay men use lube that comes from a tub-type jar that allows the user to dip his finger into the container to take a bit of lube. This practice may be acceptable if nobody else uses the lube but if someone else touches it the lube may then carry bacteria or viruses. It is better to use containers that have a pump dispenser or compel the user to turn the container over and squeeze out some of the contents. This precaution is especially important for those who have more than one sex partner or the lube is being used for anal sex.

Question: What is fellatio and how is it done?
Fellatio (pronounced fah lay she oh) is a form of oral sex in which a person stimulates the genitals of a male partner using the lips, tongue, mouth and/or throat. It is also called a blow job, a knob job, giving head, cock sucking and sucking someone off. This is a very common form of sex within the gay male community. One study found that 89.5% of gay men take part in giving and/or receiving fellatio (Laumann and Gagnon, 1994). If done with a condom this activity is relatively safe.

There are several ways to perform fellatio. Perhaps the most common method is to begin by getting your partner's permission to blow him. Few guys will say "no" but lots of guys like their partner to ask before physical contact is made. After getting permission gently handle your partner's penis and testicles as you say something nice about his equipment or his looks. If you like the idea of cock worship this is the time to do it.

Follow that by licking the head of the penis for a few seconds then placing your lips back over your teeth just prior inserting the erect penis into your mouth. You then slide your lips and perhaps your tongue up and down the penis by bobbing your head toward and then away from the base of the penis. This repeated piston motion will cause your partner to orgasm. This method is functional and effective, but it is not the technique used by guys who are good at fellatio.

A good fellator knows there are really three parts of giving a mind-blowing head job. The first part is an understanding of male anatomy and psychology. The second part is having a repertoire of techniques and changing which of those methods is used based upon what is pleasing to the recipient at the time. The third part is communication.

The first thing to know about fellatio is that men think about sex a lot. Males are designed physically and psychologically to have sex often. Some men are capable of and willing to have sex multiple times a day and, indeed, it is not uncommon for young men to be able to ejaculate again relatively quickly after an earlier ejaculation. Some rare men can do it again at once. All of this means that if you want to be a fellator you probably won't have much trouble finding a willing subject to do it with.

The second thing to know is that male genitals are very sensitive. Men are especially protective of their testicles because if bumped, thumped or handled roughly they can cause a lot of pain. Many men therefore voice a preference to have their testicles left alone during sex. If you are going to be your best at fellatio, you will probably have to overcome your partner's hesitancy in this regard. Manipulation of the testes can give a lot of pleasure and pleasure is the name of the game for a quality fellator.

The head of the penis is also very sensitive. It has a great many nerve endings and is easily stimulated. Those nerve endings are connected directly to the brain and when properly aroused they tend to make the brain focus entirely on them. This is important because as a world-class schwanzlutsher you must stimulate your partner without making him ejaculate until you want him to. Lengthening the timespan wherein your partner is sexually aroused will make it a better experience for him and it will make his orgasm more powerful. To do that however you must know when and where to stimulate and when to ease off, so he doesn't ejaculate. This is done through communication.

The first part of communicating with your partner is paying attention to what he says and the noises he makes. These oral messages will tell you what is working and what isn't. It is important to show him that you will respond to these messages. Your response will tell him that your focus is on his pleasure and he will find that very pleasing and very sexy.

The second part of communication is paying attention to what his body is doing. His body will tense when you hit a sweet spot. If you are looking him in the face you will also be able to clearly read it when that is happening. This communication will help you know what is pleasing him, what is driving him crazy with lust and what isn't working so well.

You should mix the things that merely please him with the things that drive him crazy, so he will like what is happening but won't shoot for a while. You will know when orgasm is about to happen because his abdomen and butt muscles will tense, and his erection will enlarge just a bit. If you don't want him to orgasm you need to back off and do something that is less stimulating. You may even need to stop entirely and firmly place a finger or two on the underside of his erection at the base. That will normally prevent ejaculation unless you do it too late.

The third part of communication is being in touch with yourself. A good blow job doesn't just happen. It must be intentionally built, and the other person needs to see that you are enjoying being the carpenter. You build it by paying attention to your partner's verbal and nonverbal messages and responding to them so that you get the result you want. This means your actions should be intentional and not hurried. It means that you allow yourself to enjoy what you are doing and that you express that. That can be done with words, with noises or even just a joyful smile. Every man likes to be called "sexy" and all of us like hearing that we have a great dick.

You should also not become self-conscious if you create a lot of saliva and start to drool. That happens even to very experienced fellateurs and it aids the activity because it lubricates things. You will learn to swallow saliva as part of your technique but don't work toward keeping things dry. That isn't going to happen, and you don't want it to.

All the above is useful but it is only the bare bones of a good blow job. The meat of the process is the techniques you use and how you mix them. Many guys think that to be a good fellator you must deep throat but that isn't true. Most of the nerve endings on an erection are in the first inch or so. The mouth cavity is more than twice that in depth, so you can give and get a lot of pleasure without ever putting a dick down your throat. You can give the sensation of full encasement by holding the shaft of the penis in your fist.

The number one rule for in giving fellatio is that your partner should never feel your teeth. If you can't train yourself to never touch a penis with your teeth, then fold you lips over them. Even if you decide you don't really like the guy you're blowing, and you don't want to see him again you should follow this rule. He is after all likely critique the job you did when he talks to his friends and that may become part of your reputation as a sex partner. The only exception to this rule is if you know your partner well and he is a pain pig. That guy may like your teeth.

Position is important when doing fellatio. You are going to have to find the position that suits you best and you may find that changes from situation to situation or from moment to moment. Kneeling or crouching between the partner's legs while he is standing sometimes works best. Sometimes that position while he is seated works best. Many people prefer their partner lying on his back while they approach him from above. The important thing is to find a position that is comfortable and to feel free to change when necessary. In a long session, it will be necessary to change because your jaw, leg and other muscles will tire and possibly cramp if you don't reposition or rest them occasionally.

Many guys start a head job by opening their mouths wide and putting the erection in. This gets the job done but it is not sexy and it's not the best you can do. A better way is to tongue and kiss your partner's penis and testicles for a bit and let him know you love doing it by the words and sounds you make. Open your mouth just wide enough to accept the erection then slide it in so that it rubs against the lips. This allows your partner to feel some friction. That friction will stimulate the nerve endings in his penis.

Many fellators think giving a blow job involves only oral activity. It is called "oral sex" after all. This is not true however if you want to give your partner the best experience he can have. You should also keep your hands busy and in contact with your partner's body. This might involve lightly holding his testicles, rubbing his genital area, caressing his chest or abdomen, lightly pinching or playing with his nipples or even fingering his anus. The important thing is to use your hands to give him a varying experience with pleasure.

There are a variety of techniques that can be used in fellatio. Most of them are enhanced if you lightly cup his testicles in your hand as you start them. One technique is to place the top of your tongue flat on the penis head as you hold the erection in your hand. Use your tongue to wash up and down the penis on all sides. When you are ready wash just the head of the penis then slide it up your tongue and into your mouth. Move your head in a circle as you purse your lips so that the penis is moving around in your mouth. Let it glide over the various surfaces found in there so that it receives light friction. Stroke the penis with your tongue as you do the circle. Please don't forget that a circle can go in two directions so mix it up.

Another technique is to imagine that the erect penis is a lollipop. Starting at the base of the ball sac lick upwards a few times then put the head in your mouth to savor it. Move the penis around in your mouth like a lollipop then take it out and start all over again.

A third technique is to flutter the tongue on the underside of the penis head for a bit then back off. If you do the flutter for very long your partner is going to orgasm because that part of the penis is the most sensitive. Wash the shaft of the erection with your tongue or lightly kiss and nibble it. This is much less stimulating, but the motion is still erotic. As you flutter take the head into your mouth make a light vacuum by holding your breath and sucking inward. Again, if you do this too long your partner will probably ejaculate before you want him to.

There are other techniques also, but space disallows including them here. The one that must be included however is deep throating because that seems to be the gold standard for many men who enjoy fellatio. Many men love the physical and psychological feelings they get as their erection moves in another person's throat. Lots of guys (and gals) love the feeling they get by taking an erection down their throat all the way to its base. This is not a technique all fellators have mastered however because Mother Nature tends to act against it.

The primary reason many people cannot deep throat is that they can't stop their gag reflex. Nature gives that reflex to prevent us from inhaling or swallowing foreign objects that might cause choking. To deep throat that natural reflex must be overcome. That is easier for some people than for other people. Some people seem to have no gag reflex and can deep throat the first time they try it (they are called naturals) while some are never able to do it.

Most people are not able to control their gag reflex during their early attempts. Most must learn to do it and they do that through practice. Practice means repeatedly trying to move an object passed the point of the gag reflex. This allows the body and the brain to get used to deep penetration into the throat. That, in turn, allows you to relax the throat so that it can accept an erection.

Practice is potentially dangerous, so it should only be done using an object with a broad base which cannot be accidentally swallowed or become an airway obstruction. A simulated penis (dildo) that has simulated testicles permanently attached might be such an object. No dildo that has ever been shared or used anally should ever be placed in the mouth. It must be clean.

Practice not only allows you to work on quieting the gag reflex, but it also allows you to work on technique. Your practice should be directed toward having an erection in your mouth without your teeth touching it. It should also not touch the back of your oral cavity because that will trigger the gag reflex. Once you get the penis passed that point you must learn to take it down the throat. That will mean learning to relax your throat muscles. Once you have done that you need to get used to the feeling and learn to breathe.

Having an erection in your throat will prevent you from breathing. If you leave it there very long you will pass out due to oxygen deprivation. The technique used to prevent this is to find a rhythm wherein the erection moves in and out of the throat. You breathe through your nose as it leaves the throat and hold your breath as it enters. It is important for you to keep control over that rhythm because only you know what you are feeling and when you need air.

The use of a condom during oral sex is wise since it greatly reduces the chances of transmitting disease but doing so during deep throating is a serious decision. If a condom is used when taking an erection deep into the throat it is important for you to grasp it at the base of the penis. Your goal in that is to assure that the condom will not slip off while it is down your throat. If that happens you may, at least temporarily, have a condom blocking your airway. That of course creates a medical emergency.

Some men find that they can't get their partner's penis into their mouth because the penis is too big to fit. This obviously will prevent the fellator from doing some of the techniques described above but it does not mean great oral sex is not achievable. The fellator will simply have to use his hands, tongue and lips on his partner's perineum, balls, penis shaft and penis head. He also needs to remember that great sex is not just physical. It is also psychological. The fellator needs to make his partner believe that he (the partner) is the sexiest, most desirable thing in the world. That is done by giving verbal and nonverbal messages.

The final thing offered here about fellatio concerns what happens during and right after your partner orgasms. You must decide where the ejaculate is going and what you are going to do. Is the condom going to stay on and collect the semen or is it coming off, so the ejaculate can go elsewhere? Are you going to accept it in your mouth or on your body? Are you going to swallow it? Your partner probably would like you to swallow it, but you are the one that should decide that because the risks involved in that are all yours.

Your pleasure is also something you may want to consider during and after fellating your partner. The rule among gay men is that during a sexual encounter both men get to orgasm if they want to. You therefore need to decide what you want and how you want that to happen. Some fellators simply masturbate. Other men want their partner to exchange roles with them. If the latter is true in your case your partner needs to know it before the encounter begins. He can't give you what you want if he doesn't know what it is.

Question: What is irrumatio and how is it done?
Irrumatio is also known as irrumation. It is a form of oral sex in which a man stimulates his erect penis using the lips, tongue, mouth and throat of another person. It differs from fellatio both in who the active party is and how it is done. It also differs in the fact that irrumatio is commonly done forcibly as a means of showing domination or superiority. That, of course, doesn't necessarily mean that it is nonconsensual or that mutual satisfaction is not achieved.

In fellatio, the active party is the person giving the blow job while in irrumatio the active party is owner of the erection. Irrumatio is done simply by taking a firm hold on someone's head, inserting one's erection into his mouth then moving one's hips forwards and backwards repetitively in a piston motion. Because of this irrumatio is commonly known as "skull fucking", "face fucking" or "throat fucking". Irrumatio often includes rubbing or tapping one's erection on the face of the receiving person before or after inserting into his mouth.

The active person performing irrumation controls the encounter. He decides how fast, at what depth and with what force he will use the other person's mouth and throat. It is common therefore for the recipient to gag and drool. Sometimes his nose will run. The recipient may also experience some concern about breathing if the erection is in his throat for long or irregular periods of time. Condoms are commonly not used during irrumatio and that, of course, increases the risk of transmitting an STI.

The recipient of irrumation does not have to be totally passive or helpless unless he is physically restrained in some way as in BDSM. He can force the other person take shorter strokes by grasping the erection with his fist. He can also stop the process entirely by turning way as the other person strokes outwardly or by pushing him away and verbally telling him to stop or change what he is doing. This doesn't usually occur however because it is common for the encounter and all that goes with it to be consensual and mutual. If it is not consensual it is classed as a sexual assault and battery.

Question: What is anilingus and how is it done?

Anilingus is also called rimming or a rim job. It is a form of oral sex wherein the buttocks and anus of one person is stimulated by the lips and tongue of another person. Due to the many nerve endings in and around the anus and the nature of the activity this can be highly pleasurable. Rimming is often used to prepare the person being rimmed for anal penetration by an object such as a dildo, one or more fingers or an erect penis.

Rimming, at its most basic, involves a person kissing, licking, sucking or tonguing the ass cheeks, crack and/or anal sphincter(s) of the other person. It may include doing so on just the surface of the body or pushing the tongue into the rectum to some degree. The tongue can be used slowly while moving flatly on the surface or in a quick flittering motion. The technique may also include humming as the lips move around the anal area and especially around the outer anal sphincter. The vibrations created by that humming can be very stimulating. It is often found that making noises and sharing other verbal messages enhances the encounter.

Rimming is not a safer sex practice and it is even less so if the parties do not use an effective barrier of some kind. In that case both parties (esp. the person doing the rimming) are at risk of catching an STI such as hepatitis, herpes or gonorrhea or of getting a parasite. It is possible to get HIV through anilingus but that is rare. The human papillomavirus (HPV) can also be transmitted through rimming and that virus, of course, is associated with throat cancer (D'Souza & Kreimer, 2007). Those choosing to assume the risks involved in taking part in anilingus are therefore wise to use a barrier.

At a minimum, the person being rimmed should wash his anal area well with soap and water before the encounter. If douching is done it should occur well before anilingus occurs to ensure that the fluid has either been completely expelled or absorbed. If the recipient wants to shave his anal area prior to the encounter he will probably make the activity more hygienic but will increase his risk of getting an STI because the act of shaving will cause skin abrasions.

The most common barrier used for rimming is probably plastic wrap. The user should remember however that some plastic wrap is microwavable without venting because it is more porous than other wraps. Something that is less porous is a better choice because of the possible presence microorganisms. The Centers on Disease Control and Prevention caution that there is one study showing that plastic wrap may be an effective barrier in the transmission of herpes but none showing it is an effective barrier against other STIs or HIV.

Other barriers that are used for rimming are dental dams, condoms and rubber gloves. Dental dams are large, thin layers of latex or silicon that are used in various oral procedures by dentists. They can be difficult to find in stores, but they can be bought online from outlets such as Amazon.com. Some manufactures have created a line of dental dams specifically designed for anilingus. They tend to be more expensive than other options, but they are well suited for their designed purpose.

If a less expensive choice is wanted a barrier can be created out of commonly found items. A condom, for example, can be made into a useful barrier by unrolling it then cutting off the closed end. You follow that by cutting it length ways down the side and laying it out flat. Make sure the end date has not passed and that the condom is not damaged. Some people prefer to use a non-lubricated condom in its dry form while others prefer to start with a dry condom then add a bit of lube between the anus and the latex. Many people enjoy using a flavored condom when they perform anilingus in this way. Few people, on the other hand, like the taste of spermicide thus prefer to use condoms without it when doing any form of oral sex.

There are two ways to use a latex or polyisoprene glove as a barrier. In one method, you cut all the fingers off the glove while leaving the thumb on the glove. You then cut the glove length ways on the side opposite from the thumb. This method works well if the rimmer intends to insert his tongue into the anus. He will find the thumb of the glove useful for that.

The other method involves cutting off the middle three fingers of the glove while leaving the pinky finger and the thumb intact. Once this is done, cut down the center of the palm and lay the condom out flat. You will then have a barrier with a handle on each side. The handles will help control the position of the dam while you use it.

There are several positions that can be used during anilingus. Which of these is used is a matter of personal choice and creativity. The position sometimes seen in porno films is not really a good technique however. In that method, the person being rimmed is flat on his stomach on a bed while his partner (also on the bed) bends over him. This method causes the person rimming to tire rather quickly and that leads to muscle fatigue or cramping. It is better for the rimmer's mouth to be nearly at the same level as the recipient's anal area.

A commonly used method is for the recipient to kneel with his buttock high and his head low. His partner can then approach him from the rear and perform without having to bend over very much. It also allows the rimmer to change positions readily if his legs begin to tire as he kneels or crouches.

Another common position is for the recipient to lie on his back and then draw his legs back, so his knees touch or nearly touch his shoulders. This, of course, exposes the buttock. The disadvantages of this position are that it is difficult to keep unless something is used to hold the legs back and it can cause the rimmer to tire quickly. The latter problem can be overcome if the recipient positions himself at the edge of a bed while the rimmer kneels or crouches on the floor.

Question: What is anal intercourse and how is it done?
Anal intercourse, as the name suggests, is a form of anal sex in which an erect penis penetrates the anus of another person. It is also called "sodomy" and "butt fucking". The term "sodomy" carries with it a high degree of negative interpretation in some cultures. It is viewed as immoral or unnatural because of religious tradition or cultural norms. When viewed objectively however there is nothing immoral or unnatural about it.

Many men, both straight and gay, find anal intercourse to be highly pleasurable. Bottoms (persons being penetrated) like it because anal intercourse is perhaps the most intimate thing gay men can do, the sensations resulting from it can last for days and the movement of the penis inside them strokes against their prostate gland and rectum walls. This offers a very pleasing sensation in most men.

Tops (persons penetrating an anus) like it not only because of the high degree of intimacy but also because the rectum and anus is tight enough to offer a high degree of friction on an erection. That commonly yields a remarkable orgasm. It is no surprise then that research shows that 75-80% of gay men are involved in anal intercourse (Bell, 1999; Laumann & Gagnon, 1994).

Many gay men believe that being the bottom during anal intercourse is very painful. This is true in many cases. The pain a bottom may feel when he is anally penetrated is very real, but it often exists because those involved don't know how to do it. Anal intercourse doesn't have to be painful and, in fact, it usually shouldn't be. Pain, after all, is nature's way of telling us to stop doing what we are doing because there is something physically wrong happening to us. If pain is involved in anal sex it is being done wrong and it should stop.

The primary reason anal intercourse is painful is that the people doing it don't understand anatomy or don't care about it. They should however because that understanding is the ticket to better sex for both the top and the bottom. Understanding the anatomy of the anus and rectum and using that knowledge is a means to abolish pain and to a happy anal sex experience for both parties.

The opening of the anus has two sphincters. Both are normally closed very tightly to prevent fluids and feces from leaking. The visible pucker seen on the surface of the ass is the outer sphincter but there is also another one inside that. A person can consciously relax the outer sphincter. The inner one however works independently of a person's will so a person cannot consciously get it to relax. It must relax on its own. Both sphincters are made of tissues that are easily damaged so forcing them open is a bad choice.

Just inside the inner sphincter is the anal canal. It is about one and a half inches long and connects to the rectum which is about five inches long. It is a very soft and delicate tube which expands naturally as feces enters it. Above that is the lower end of the intestines which is called the sigmoid colon. This is where feces accumulate until the body sends it into the rectum to await elimination from the body. Except for traces of feces left after a bowel movement there is usually little or no fecal matter in the rectum.

The anus, rectum and intestines are designed to expel waste and gas and to be very absorbent. Given this purpose, involuntary farting by the bottom may be unavoidable during anal sex. As noted previously, there is normally little or no fecal matter in the rectum unless a bowel movement is imminent, but it may exist there at any time. What is in the lower intestine may be drawn down into the rectum as the intercourse proceeds.

The parties involved in anal sex should accept that feces or gas may be involved in their activity by clinging to the penis/condom when it is removed from the ass or because the bottom accidentally defecates or farts when the penis is removed. There is no way to end the chance that these things will occur, but the chances can be greatly reduced if the bottom cleans out his ass. Some bottoms do that with a lubed finger while others choose to douche.

Experienced tops know that if his bottom accidentally expels gas or feces during sex it is his job as the top (and a fellow human being) to comfort and reassure the bottom because doing this will be very embarrassing. It will certainly alter the mood in the room for both parties. If the top responds to the situation with maturity and caring, he will be earning the trust and respect of the bottom and the bottom will be more likely to agree to anal sex in the future. The bottom will know that the top cared more about him than he did about the stink or mess. If the top does not follow this course the bottom will always remember the top as part of an unpleasant situation.

Anal intercourse should always be consensual. This not only removes it from the realm of sexual assault, but it also is a step toward better sex because it allows the parties to relax and enjoy the experience. Relaxation is a key if the bottom is going to be penetrated without pain.

Bleeding may occur during or after anal intercourse. This is usually a sign that entry was too rapid and forceful and that not enough lube was used. It is commonly also a sign that you have a ruptured hemorrhoid or anal fissure. The treatment for that may or may not involve seeing a medical professional but usually does not. Blood can also signal something more serious like a perforation (hole) in the colon. This is a medical emergency. Further information can be found at: http://www. mayoclinic .org/symptoms/ rectalbleeding/sym-20050740.

It is necessary for the parties involved to be concerned about hygiene and the spread of disease. Anal intercourse is not a safer sex practice and it is especially hazardous if a condom is not used (this is called "barebacking") or not properly used. This is because the rectum and lower intestine will readily absorb any bacteria or virus introduced into them by the top and the top may be exposed to any bacteria, virus or parasite that was within the bottom. The bottom however is at more risk than the top during anal intercourse.

These risks can often be partially managed by following simple procedures. The parties should assure that they have washed well with soap and water prior to the encounter. The bottom may also wish to douche out his rectum and lower intestine. Douching should be done correctly, far enough in advance so that all fluid is either eliminated or absorbed and with the knowledge that douching may irritate the lining of the rectum and thereby increase the bottom's chances of getting an STI or HIV. The top should wear an intact, correctly fitting condom because an ass is much tighter than a vagina. It is much more likely to cause an ill-fitting condom to break or slip off. These procedures will reduce the risks involved in having anal intercourse in most cases.

The reason many people find anal intercourse to be painful is that they don't take their time. They are in a hurry to experience the many pleasures involved in anal sex, so the bottom is not prepared correctly. The result is that he either experiences pain when the penis penetrates him and directly after or he can't manage to take the penis at all.

If the bottom can't comfortably take the erection he shouldn't be scorned or coerced. This outcome can usually be prevented however. A top who is willing to delay his pleasure as he works with the bottom toward a non-painful experience will be valued by the bottom.

It is essential that both the top and the bottom be completely relaxed and open to the experience that is to come. Men who are new to topping may be nervous about what will happen, and even experienced tops may be concerned about causing the bottom to experience pain. The bottom is going to be aware of any anxiety felt by the top. Even if he is the more experienced of the two that anxiety will affect his ability to relax and fully enjoy the tryst. In this case the bottom will need to help the top become more calm and comfortable.

A bottom can often help the top relax by relieving him of the feeling that he must perform even if he doesn't want to and by engaging in some intimate foreplay or other form of sex with him. The bottom can direct the top's hand toward his (the bottom's) ass as part of that and tell him how good that ass play feels. He can ask the top, in a nondirective way, to do specific things that are focused toward the anal area such as fingering, rimming or massage. When something feels good the bottom should let the top know it with words or noises. That positive feedback will give the top confidence and will encourage him to go further.

Relaxing the bottom's ass can start by massaging his butt cheeks. A thin, condom friendly (not oil or petroleum based) lube can be used during this massage both because it will make the massage more sensuous and because using it now will make your use of lube on his hole later a nearly seamless part of the scene. It should be understood however that if a barrier is not used this lube will get on the top's face and probably in his mouth if he rims. The massage should slowly move toward and into the bottom's ass crack. Once there the top can move the massage toward his partner's ass pucker (outer sphincter).

There are two movements that are commonly used in massaging the outer sphincter. One is a light, circular motion using the fingers and thumbs on and around the pucker. In the other method, you place your hands on his ass cheeks, so a thumb is on each side of his hole. You then move the thumbs in an upwards direction while your hand stays in contact and lightly massages his ass. If you are going to rim him now is probably the time to transition to it. If not, you can add some lube to his hole and try to put your index finger into his ass but no further than the first finger joint. Wearing gloves makes this safer for both parties but, at a minimum, the top's fingernails should be cut and filed so there are no sharp or long edges.

The finger should be inserted several times but should never be forced in. Force will cause the sphincter to resist entry and it may increase the bottom's anxiety level which, of course, will tense him up. Sometimes the ass pucker will not accept anything more than the front pad of the finger, but you should let it do what it is going to do. It will accept your finger if you give it a bit of time. You can add lube as necessary, but the goal is to get the first bit of your finger inside without causing any pain. The bottom can help with this by consciously trying to relax his outer sphincter.

Once you can get the first part of your finger into your partner's ass add more lube and try to push it a bit further in. Once again, you don't want to force it. It will slide in easily if you give it a bit of time. Work the finger in and out of the ass as you push it deeper. Once you have it all the way in, let it rest there for a few seconds then try to slowly move it in and out and in a circular motion that gently stretches the sphincters. Neither party should do anything else that might sexually stimulate the bottom since that will tense his body and cause the sphincters to close.

Once the bottom is comfortably taking one of your fingers you can repeat the process using two fingers. Once he is taking two fingers easily you can move on to three fingers. When three fingers go inside comfortably the bottom can probably take most erect penises without experiencing much pain if lots of lube is used. He should be in control of the insertion however. If he feels any pain the top should stop the process and work on it some more.

The bottom can help taking the erection by pretending to take a bowel movement and breathing deeply as the penis slowly enters him. The top should push his penis into the bottom as the bottom exhales. The top can help the encounter be pain free by taking short strokes until the bottom says he is ready for longer ones and by using circular motions instead of piston motions. The top should stop thrusting when the bottom wants that.

Some inexperienced bottoms prefer to take their first erections by sitting on the lap of the top. This gives them a lot of control, but the top must be careful because if the bottom sits but misses getting the penis into his anal hole the penis can be damaged. This is usually avoided by the bottom finding his hole with a finger then sliding the erection along the finger into his anus or by having the top slowly guide the erection in for him.

There are several positions which may be used in anal sex. Which of them is chosen is usually a matter of personal preference. The exception to this arrives when a man is bottoming for someone new. In this case it is wise to only use positions which allow him to face the top since that allows him to better ward off an attack or other unwanted action if things go wrong.

A man who wants to learn to bottom comfortably can take it upon himself to practice using his fingers or a dildo. He can also help his sphincters learn to accept intercourse by learning to take a lubed butt plug slowly into his anal cavity. Novices should start with a small one and go slow however. Over the course of time and with experience many bottoms learn to accept penetration without much preparation. Lube should always be used however because anal tissue can tear or be otherwise damaged. The lube reduces the surface resistance that causes that.

Some people who take part in anal intercourse believe that a bottom can be helped to take an erection if he uses a muscle relaxant such as "poppers" (alkyl nitrate) or he uses a local anesthetic such as lidocaine. Poppers are sometimes used in anal sex because they are said to not only relax the anal sphincters but also to increase the intensity of an orgasm. Local aesthetics are also used because they because the numb the ass to pain.

Poppers are illegal under federal law for human consumption and present a serious health risk if taken with certain other medications such as Viagra, Cialis or Levitra. They can also cause a dramatic drop in blood pressure and burn human tissue. Anesthetics present a health risk because they may prevent the bottom from knowing he is being injured (Dean, 2011).

Question: Why do some tops slap their sex partner on the butt during sex?

It varies from top to top. Some like to feel dominant. Some like rough sex. Some believe it makes the bottom clench his ass muscles, so the top has a tighter fit. Some believe it will cause the bottom to produce endorphins which will reduce whatever pain that may be involved in anal sex and it will thereby make the sex better for both partners.

There are no studies on whether slapping someone's butt improves sex but pain does cause the release of endorphins and endorphins are known to reduce pain, to increase the level of sex hormones in the body and to cause some degree of euphoria in some people. Endorphin production however varies from person to person so the level of benefit (if any) won't be universal. If a bottom doesn't like being slapped, it should not be done.

Question: What is anal douching and how is it done?

Anal douching is the act of cleaning out the rectum and intestine using a stream of fluid. It is also called an enema. The website for the US Department of Health and Human Services (AIDS.com) asserts that douching before sex increases the risk of getting HIV because it can irritate the lining of the rectum. The website suggests, as an alternative, that the bottom gently clean out the rectum with a soapy finger and water.

Many gay men assume the risks involved in douching. It is in fact a widespread practice within our community. This is rather obviously why so many retailers in gay communities sell items that are designed for anal douching. These include mechanisms that attach to a faucet or shower, douching bulbs that resemble a turkey baster, enema bags, and small enema bottles. All douching equipment needs a thorough cleaning after use.

Most drug stores sell prepared enema fluid in small enema bottles. The bottles may have a membrane that allows fluid to travel only outwards. Most gay men dump out the fluid that comes in them (it irritates the anal lining) and replace it with water. These bottles are so small that you may have to refill them with water several times if you want to be cleaned out well.

The mechanisms that attach to faucets and showers use water pressure to keep backwash out. Care should be used with any mechanism that attaches to a faucet or shower because the water coming out of it may be hot enough to burn you internally and the water pressure may be high enough that it will damage your inner tissues.

When douching prior to anal play use plain water. Other fluids may cause irritation inside the rectum and intestine. Check the temperature to make sure the fluid is cool or lukewarm. If a douching tool is connected to a water source such as a shower it is wise to assure that any machine or other person having access to your water supply doesn't create a change in the temperature of the water going into your body. In some homes, for example, turning on the cold water in the kitchen makes the water hotter in the bathroom and turning on the hot water will do the opposite. Getting burned internally is not only painful but it also increases the risk of getting an STI. Cold fluid will shrink your Willy and kill your libido for a while.

Douching should be done well before any kind of anal sex because you will want to assure that the fluid is either completely evacuated or absorbed prior to the encounter. It is wise not to eat between the time you douche and the time of your tryst. You should also not douche often because it will dehydrate your body, wash out mucous, bacteria and fluids that your body needs, and it may make your body dependent upon having enemas to evacuate wastes. If you are concerned that you might have feces in your rectum as you move closer to anal sex you can check with a lubed finger. Any feces found can then be removed with that lubed finger.

You will want to use plenty of lube when you are inserting the head of the douche. The douching tool is not a sex toy so don't treat it like a dildo. Its purpose it to fill your innards with enough water that you can get cleaned out. If you are going to douche in the shower or tub you should remove plate that covers the drain and then accept that this drain was not designed to deal with large clumps of feces, so you may have to clean up that separately.

Some people choose to repeat the douching process until the water comes out clean while others limit the cleaning to just the lower intestine and rectum. The former choice usually assures that fecal matter will not be part of your anal sex experience, but it also presents the possibility that water than has been trapped inside the intestine will flow out during sex. This will not happen using the latter way but that also increases the odds of fecal matter becoming part of your anal sex experience since it can be drawn down into the rectum during sex. Many men choose not to douche at all and just accept that fecal matter may be part of what happens.

Some people use fluids other than plain water for anal douching. Urine, warm coffee and alcoholic beverages are examples of these. None of these are a safe idea however. Urine can spread disease. There are documented cases of people dying after getting a coffee enema. Alcohol will move through the intestines much faster and in much higher concentration than it does through the stomach. This presents the very real possibility of damaging a bottom's internal organs. It can also be lethal.

Question: What is felching and how is it done?
Felching is a form of anal sex in which the semen of one person is sucked out of the anus of another person. It is done either directly with the lips and mouth or with a straw. It therefore involves semen being introduced into the rectum of the bottom and semen that is potentially contaminated with feces and microorganisms being sucked into the mouth. This puts both the top and the bottom at risk of getting an infection. This is a high-risk activity.

Question: What is "scat play?
Scat is a fetish involving being sexually aroused by, fantasizing about, or deriving sexual pleasure from feces. Any behavior involving one or more of those things is called "scat play". It may be looking at feces, smelling feces, watching someone defecate or having actual contact with feces. This may include smearing feces on your own or someone else's body, having it spread on you, one person defecating on another person or eating it.

Scat is categorized as a paraphilia which means it is viewed by our society as abnormal. It is practiced by a very small minority of heterosexual and homosexual people and is rare even in the kink community. Scat is a very high-risk behavior. The potential for those involved in scat to get hepatitis is very high.

Question: What is frottage?
Frottage is the act of gaining sexual gratification by rubbing one's genitals against the body of another person. It is classed as a paraphilia (a sexual abnormality) called frotteuristic disorder and a violation of law when done without the consent of the target person. It is typically done in a crowded place to conceal the offender's intent.

When done with the consent of the other person it can be, and often is, an act of sexual intimacy that gives both parties great satisfaction. It is a very common practice among gay males and is used both as foreplay and as part of the main event. In this case one person's penis is rubbed against the thighs, chest, armpits or genitals of his partner and is commonly accompanied by romantic holding, kissing and solo or mutual masturbation. It is colloquially called dry-humping, frot, or the Princeton rub.

Question: What is a "ménage è trois"?
Americans usually call a ménage è trois a threesome or a three way. It is simply three people having sex together. It can be any mixture of males and females but in gay male sex it is obviously three men. This arrangement should be consensual by all of those involved.

Whether a threesome is positive experience for all of those involved absolutely depends upon the expectations and activity of those involved. They can be highly pleasurable or disappointing. There are many pitfalls and they sometimes do not end satisfactorily for some or all of those who took part simply because one or more of the participants does not have his wants fulfilled.

There are guidelines for threesomes that can help make the threesome good for everyone. They certainly don't assure that everyone will leave the encounter happy, but they make the odds better. They are:

1. The threesome is consensual. Everyone knows who will be involved and agrees to it.
2. There are agreed upon rules and limits. No person's limits will be violated.
3. Everyone receives and gives, and nobody expects to be the center of attention.
4. Everyone stays involved in the encounter and nobody becomes a mere observer unless they want to.
5. Everyone understands that ejaculation may mean the end of the encounter.
6. All of those involved understand that the encounter is about sex and not about making a relationship.
7. Nobody expects the host to invite him to stay overnight. If the host doesn't give an invitation the others leave gracefully.
8. Everybody is truthful about their HIV and STI status.
9. Everyone practices "safer sex" unless everyone willingly agrees to do otherwise.

Question: What is public sex?
It is exactly what it sounds like ... sex in a public place. That place could be almost anywhere, but the most usual places are at a park, in a car, at the movies, in front of an unshaded window and a public toilet. This activity is illegal in all or nearly all legal jurisdictions, so it carries a risk of arrest and conviction for a public indecency or morals violation. The thrill of experiencing that risk is often why people do it.

Question: What is a "tearoom" and what happens there?
A tearoom is a public toilet where sex between men occurs. The toilet is usually one that is little used by the public but has been found by gay men as a good place to look for sex. Typically, one man will stand at a urinal as if he was about to urinate. Another man will take a place at the urinal next to him as if he is going to

urinate too. One man says something to the other man, so he can get a sense of his demeanor. If he thinks it may be safe he then looks at the other guys penis. If the other guy does likewise he can ask if that man is interested in having sex. If there is an agreement about that the sex usually occurs in a stall or they go somewhere else.

A variation of this involves the use of a "glory hole". A glory hole is a hole that has been created in the partition between stalls. A man wanting to have sex will look through the hole at the man using the adjacent stall. If he finds that man sexually appealing he can express that interest by moving his foot to the far edge of the stall that is nearest to the other man's stall. If the other man moves his foot so it is near to that foot and taps with is toes both parties know the other one is interested in sex. That can occur when one man puts his penis through the hole, moves to the other stall or they go somewhere else. Having sex or looking for it in a public toilet is illegal in all or nearly all legal jurisdictions so it carries the risk of arrest and conviction on a public indecency or morals charge.

Question: What is a JO club and what happens there?
The "JO" in the name JO club stands for "jackoff". In other words, a JO club is a masturbation club. It is typically a small group of men who meet in a private place to socialize. Part of that is either publicly masturbating themselves or each other. It typically includes total nudity but does not include any form of sexual penetration. There is usually a fee involved which is used to cover the cost of refreshments, lube and paper towels.

Question: What is a sex party and what happens there?
A sex party is just what it sounds like. In the gay male world, it is a group of guys that have gotten together to have sex in an atmosphere that is like a party. Sometimes the men involved get together before the sex happens to share chit chat, a meal or a movie. It is common for the host to ask guests for a small amount of money to cover the lube, condoms and whatever else is provided. Sometimes sex parties are arranged by personal invitation and sometimes they are open to men who answer an advertisement and then are screened by the host of the party. If

you are invited always ask if it is a bareback party because safer sex practices will not be used there.

Sex parties have a start time and sometimes have a set time after which nobody else will be admitted. Normally the host will be attentive to who comes in the front door and will meet and greet until the entry cutoff time arrives. After that it is likely that the front door will be locked, and nobody will answer it. The host will be busy with other things. Some hosts hire male prostitutes or performers to entertain his guests but that is not common.

Those attending a sex party will either get naked soon after they arrive, or they will have a preliminary period to interact with other guests before clothes are shed. At some point clothes and personal belongings will be put into bags and stored in a corner or otherwise set aside. Those things are probably safe at that point, but it is wise not to bring anything to a sex party that you can't afford to lose.

The environment at a sex party will probably include music. There may be a gay male porno movie playing somewhere and one of the rooms may hold a sling waiting for someone to occupy it. There will be sheets covering furniture and possibly some areas of the floor. Condoms and cleanup towels will be available around the main room and probably in the other rooms of the building as well. Use a new condom after each sexual encounter.

There will also probably be containers of lube available. If this comes in a tub type container that allows everyone to touch the lube it may become contaminated with microorganisms. Lubes that squirt or pump onto the hand are more sanitary.

The host may or may not allow drugs or alcohol. If he does you can probably bring your own if you are willing to share. If he doesn't allow it and you bring it anyway you may be asked to leave or to at least not bring it into the party. Sex parties allowing drugs and alcohol are different from those that don't simply because of what substance use does to the human brain and body.

The people at sex parties will vary in age. Some of them may be older and out of shape too. What they lack in physical appearance however they often make up for in enthusiasm and skill. The host will work to assure that people are interacting, and everyone is busy having fun. He is likely to ask anyone that seems to be killing the fun to leave. That does not mean that each person should be involved in sex all the time. It just means that whether they are having sex or not they are having fun and sharing the good time.

People will tend peel away from the group in pairs or trios. They go to various locations throughout the house or building but usually respect the host's wishes if some rooms are considered off limits. They also respect the host's wish to protect his floors and furnishings by leaving anything covering them in place. The sounds of men having sex will be heard over the music and the smell of sex will grow.

Men may come together to mingle, to have group sex or to watch some sort of sex scene. They may also take part in taking turns with using anyone who has gotten into or has been placed into the sling or who otherwise makes himself available for group use. Sex and other interaction will continue until the host asks people to leave.

Question: Is it alright to talk dirty during sex?
Whether a person likes dirty talk during a sexual encounter is a personal preference but including it should be agreed upon by both parties in a situation before it is done. Dirty talk is a turn-on for some men but a real mood killer for others. It is fine to ask the other person how he feels about it and it is also fine to say you like it or don't like it.

It is rude however to just blurt it out. Hearing yourself being called a whore or a pussy boy or hearing someone say they are going to rape your slut ass can be rather jarring if you are unprepared for it and you don't know it is just part of the scene. It can be downright offensive if you have made it known that you don't like that kind of talk. On the other hand, for some men dirty talk is the difference between good sex and sex that racks the body, moves the soul and pushes the mind to places good boys never experience.

Question: How do you clean sex toys?
The methods you can use to clean sex toys depend upon what the toy is made of and whether it is battery activated or electrical. If the toy is electrical, vibrates or uses batteries you should avoid using fluids directly on it. It is important not to get water or another fluid in the battery compartment or the motor of a toy since that will not only cause the toy to not work but may also

cause injury. This type of toy can be cleaned by putting a small amount of cleaning agent on a clean cloth and then using that to clean the toy. The cleaning agent can then be removed using a clean damp cloth. The toy should be dried before storing it.

Toys made of porous materials can be difficult to clean well so you should always cover them with a non-lubricated condom when you are using them. When you clean one of these toys you can use an anti-bacterial soap and warm (not hot) water. You can then let it air dry.

Cleaning toys made of nonporous material such as glass, medical silicone, rigid plastic, steel or acrylic is much easier. You can wash them in the dishwasher on the top shelf. Rigid plastic and glass toys can be cleaned using alcohol or an anti-bacterial soap. These cleaning agents should be thoroughly rinsed off.

You can also clean nonporous materials using a mixture of one-part bleach and nine parts of water. The formula should be sprayed or wiped onto the toy because some of these materials will respond poorly to being immersed or soaked in this mixture. The bleach solution should be cleaned off thoroughly with a damp cloth and the toy should be allowed to air dry.

Unless a glass toy is already structurally compromised cleaning one on the top shelf of the dishwasher is usually safe and easy. Never expose glass dildos or any glass toy to extreme temperatures. Doing so may cause them to crack, break or chip. You don't want a glass toy breaking or chipping while it is in your ass, down your throat or wrapped around your penis.

Leather toys are not really water friendly but can be cleaned using a damp, soapy cloth or with a commercial leather cleaner. Dry it off and use a premium quality leather conditioner after cleaning it. Make sure the metal parts to these toys (grommets, buckles, snaps, etc.) are dry.

Question: How do you remove pubic hair/buttock hair?
This depends upon the look you want to achieve by doing it, how coarse the hair is, how densely growing it is, the skin type, how modest you are and how much time and money you want to spend. It also depends upon how much pain and suffering you are willing to risk because that risk is always present. If something is done wrong or goes wrong the result can be bumps or pimples, ingrown hairs, blisters, cellulitis (bacterial infection of the

scrotum and penis), chemical burns, boils/carbuncles, rashes, cuts/lacerations, infections including folliculitis (inflammation of the hair root), razor burn and/or an irrepressible itch from hell.

If you are a furry guy or you want to minimize your risks, you might settle for trimming the hair down to a presentable length. So long as you don't make the hair too short most of the problems noted above will probably not arise. You will have to be careful with your scissors or clippers of course since a nicked penis, scrotum or anus will certainly bleed, seriously hurt and may result in an infection. You will have to do this trimming regularly if you want to keep the look because human hair grows about half an inch every month until you die. Nobody cares about it then of course.

Shaving is the most commonly used method of removing pubic and butt hair. Start the process by gently pulling up on the hair and clipping it off to make it less than ¼ inch long. Use small safety tipped manual scissors or electric clippers that has a guard. Take a hot shower or bath to soften the hair. Use an unscented foam or cream that is made for shaving pubic hair rather than one that is designed for shaving the face. Never shave without this and always test it on another body part to assure that you are not allergic to it.

When you select your razor know that the more blades it has the closer the shave will be and the more likely you will be to have ingrown hairs. Stretch the skin tight and make it as flat as possible. Shave in the direction that the hair is growing and go slowly and carefully. Check the shaved area for missed hairs and stubble. Use a moisturizer that is made for the intimate areas but do not use aftershave unless you enjoy pain. If all goes well, then all that is left is to clean up and wait to see if you've done it wrong. That will be clear rather soon.

Over the counter depilatories/hair removers are also sometimes used. Products that are specifically designed for use in the pubic and butt areas are best because the skin in those areas is more sensitive and delicate. Test it on another body part to assure that you are not allergic to it. Do not put a depilatory directly on or in the anal hole unless you enjoy pain. Follow the directions on the package exactly as written.

Waxing is a method of hair removal that involves a thin layer of wax being spread over the hair that is to be removed. A thin cloth strip is then placed in the wax. Once the wax hardens the cloth is rapidly yanked away without even a hint of mercy. The hair, of course, has no choice but to go with the wax and cloth. This method is very painful but it is effective in the short term. It is best to do this procedure at a salon or spa that does it regularly and has routinely passed government inspection. You will have to leave your modesty at home. Those who are diabetic or use Retin-A, Renova, Differin or Isotretin should talk to a doctor before waxing their intimate areas.

Laser hair removal uses a light beam to destroy hair follicles. It may take multiple sessions to achieve a satisfactory result and each session can be expensive. The sessions vary in length depending upon what you want and your skin/hair type. There is some pain involved and, in time, some hair regrowth in the treated area is common. The procedure should only be done by a technician or doctor who is trained and certified to do it. It is up to you to check on his/her credentials. You should consult with the treatment provider before you do the procedure and follow his/her instructions exactly.

Electrolysis uses energy to destroy hair. A very fine electrified needle penetrates the hair follicle, the hair is zapped then removed with tweezers. Obviously, since this is a hair by hair process, it will take some time so it is expensive. It does involve pain or at least discomfort but he results are permanent. You may have trouble finding a provider who will do the pubic and butt area so call around. If you find one that is willing, have a consultation with him/her and check their credentials. Also check the equipment. The only method of electrolysis that gives permanent results uses a needle so if a provider is using electric tweezers or photoepilators, you may want to walk away.

You may wish to consider why you have pubic and ass hair before you remove it since it is, in fact, very functional. It reduces friction when skin contacts skin or objects and thereby reduces chaffing, irritation and rashes. It acts as a barrier against STIs although this function is more effective in females than males. It signals sexual maturity to those who have something in mind they might do with a sexually mature person. It carries pheromones which may attract a mate. It keeps the genitals warmer although, once again, this works better for females than males. It helps keep dirt out if the urethra (pee hole). If you remove it after it has done of all that you risk being thought of as ungrateful.

Question: What is a cock ring and how are they used?

A cock ring is exactly what its name suggests it is: a strap or ring that is placed around a penis. Most men who use a cock ring do so to keep their erection from softening. The ring is placed at the base of the penis so that when the penis becomes erect the ring becomes tight enough to prevent blood from flowing out of the erection. Blood entering the penis is, of course, what causes an erection and keeping it there keeps it hard. A ring used in this manner should be worn only 20-30 minutes at the most. Wearing it longer can cause damage to the penis.

Men also use a cock ring for a variety of other reasons. Some wear one as a form of body jewelry or as a fashion statement. Some like the way their body feels when they wear the ring. Some men say the orgasm they have while wearing a ring is deeper. Some men like to wear a cock ring because knowing they have it on makes them feel very sexual. Others like to do it because they know that most guys don't wear one. They like the feeling of being different and they like the response their sex partners usually give when they first see the ring.

Selecting a cock ring is obviously an intimately personal choice. Before you buy a ring however you need to ask yourself if you are willing to trim back your pubic hair. You don't have to do that trim to wear a ring but if you don't you need to accept that long pubic hair will interfere with putting the ring on and taking it off. You also need to accept that at some point long pubic hair is going to get painfully pulled on as you deal with your ring.

Cock rings can be made of a variety of materials and come in several configurations. The most commonly used material is some type of jelly, rubber or silicone that stretches to allow an easier placement and removal of the ring. Another ordinary form of cock ring is a leather strap that has snaps placed at intervals which allow the ring to adjust to many sizes and to be easily removed. Vendors also offer cock rings made of neoprene, wood and a variety of metals. The metals ones can be found in assorted colors and in chromed format.

Buying a cock ring that doesn't stretch or come with snaps is a serious choice. If you buy one that is too small and are unlucky enough to get it on you are at risk of having genital pain soon because you may not be able to get it off. Your penis at that point will not be a happy camper. Like all unhappy campers, it will make sure that it is the most significant thing in your life until it is happy again. That will undoubtedly demand an embarrassing visit with a doctor. Hopefully the doctor will say no lasting damage was done to your Willy. On the other hand, damaged penises have the reputation of often not healing well.

When buying a cock ring you first should decide what its purpose is. If that purpose is to keep your erection, then you need a ring that will be tight enough to prevent blood from flowing out of your erect penis, but you also need one that will be removable once your erection has sprouted. None of the other reasons men use a cock ring demands that it be this tight. All you really need is a ring you can feel and one that doesn't fall off as you move around during your day. As noted above the rings that restrict blood flow can be worn for a maximum of 20-30 minutes. Typically, men who wear a ring for any reason other than keeping their erection want to wear it much longer than that, so they will need a ring that allows blood to flow freely.

If you want a nonadjustable cock ring, you should measure yourself, so you get a good fit and you can get it off when you want to. The smallest size of ring a man can wear is traditionally found by measuring the erect penis at the rear of the scrotal sac. Once that circumference is found the diameter is obtained by dividing it by pi (3.14). Again, this size is not the one you want if you want anything other than keeping your erection. This size will be harder to get off than a larger size would be.

Putting on a nonadjustable cock ring is straight forward. Pull the scrotal sac through the ring. Work one testicle through the ring and then do the same with the other one. Once that is done work the flaccid penis through the ring. Removing the ring is done by simply reversing the process. Taking a ring off while still erect is difficult at best. Not being able to remove a nonadjustable ring is a risk that comes with using one.

Question: What is a harness and how are they used?
A harness is an arrangement of connected straps and buckles that are designed to fit the human torso and/or waist. They are most commonly made of leather but may be made of other materials

such as chain, neoprene, or PVC. They may or may not be classed as fetish wear depending upon the motivation of the wearer. They are sometimes worn as a fashion statement and can be aesthetically striking. They are also often used in a more functional and utilitarian way. This is especially so in the Leather subculture and in the D/s, S&M or B&D worlds. In this case a purchaser should opt for a harness that what will standup to hard use if it is to be worn by a bottom.

Harnesses come in a variety of configurations but basically there are three types: the torso or body harness, the dildo harness and the anal (butt plug) harness. The most commonly used of these is the torso harness. It will be present and worn by many men at any Leather subculture venue. This type of harness exists in a variety of styles but generally can be classed as chest only, full torso and those with a collar and/or cock ring included. It is imperative that this type of harness be worn correctly and that it fits well. Buying this kind of harness from a leather shop that specializes in this kind of product is a plus.

There is no exception to the rule that a person who wears a torso harness is making an intentional statement. Sometimes it is a fashion statement. Often it is a sexual statement. Torso harnesses are, after all, routinely used by a top to hold his bottom in place as he penetrates him anally. Once the top firmly grasps the bottom's harness that bottom isn't going anywhere. It is however incorrect to assume that a man wearing a chest or torso harness is a bottom.

A dildo harness is what it sounds like it is. It is a harness that fits around the waist and between the legs that allows a dildo to be attached to it. It is sometimes used by lesbians to simulate penis to vagina sex, sometimes used a top who wants to penetrate his partner with a larger phallus than he has naturally and sometimes used in D/s scenes to keep a sub in his proper place and mind set when the sub penetrates the top.

An anal (butt plug) harness is configured so that a strap fits around the waist and another goes between the legs. That strap is slightly wider as it passes over the anus. This strap holds a butt plug securely in place within the ass. It is not possible to wear this harness and plug without feeling to some degree submissive, humiliated and/or sexually stimulated. This is heightened by the fact that this type of harness can be locked into place.

Question: How is a good kiss done?
Whether a kiss is good depends upon the situation and the people involved. A kiss that is right for one situation, person or relationship may be all wrong for another one. Some men don't like being kissed at all under any situation, but most do.

Kisses can be boiled down into two types: romantic and non-romantic. A non-romantic kiss might be a peck on a cheek or even a quick, light kiss on the lips as a greeting or a sign of friendship or affection. It might be a kiss on the hand as a sign of respect. What is proper is based on cultural norms and the norms of those directly involved. Most of us learn how and when to do this kind of kiss as we grow into adulthood and, most often, we are confident in our knowledge and ability in this area.

The romantic kiss is, for many of us, another matter entirely. It can be quite complicated and learning how to do it can cause some anxiety. We may worry that we are bad kisser or that the other person will respond badly or apathetically to our kiss and thereby to that intimate expression of our feelings. There are some general guidelines that may help. They are:

1. Don't have bad breath when you lean in for a kiss. If you aren't sure about it use a mint or a breath freshener.
2. Don't lick or wet your lips or produce a lot of saliva prior to kissing because that will contribute to your kiss being sloppy and wet.
3. Don't pucker or stick out your lips if you intend the kiss to be romantic or erotic.
4. Don't make a smacking noise when you kiss.
5. Don't leave your kissing technique to chance. Practice it on the back of your hand.
6. Don't ignore how other people kiss. You can learn from both the good and the bad examples.
7. Don't bite or play with any piercings the other person has. They might be sensitive so be gentle with them.
8. Don't be a boring kisser. Vary the rhythm, the pressure of the kiss and the technique.
9. Use your hands to caress your lover's body and head.
10. Use your voice to say something sensual occasionally.

11. Use the alternate lip kiss. You kiss his upper lip while he kisses your lower lip then you switch. He doesn't have to know how to do it. Your lip position will decide his.
12. Use the lip sucking kiss. When kissing him gently suck on his lower lip for a moment. This is not a "first date kiss". If you want a lasting relationship with the other guy you should wait until you know him well before you do this. The exception to that rule is when you have done or are doing the act of sex. In that case, you obviously know the guy well enough to do this.
13. Use the open kiss. Put your wide-open mouth on his. Use this only after you know your man for a while or you have had sex with him because it can freak out a new guy.
14. Use the nibble kiss. Gently nibble (don't bite) on his lip for a moment. You can nibble his ear too.
15. Use the peripheral kiss. Kiss his shoulders, neck, eyes and behind the ear. This may include briefly licking his ear.
16. Use the vacuum kiss. When open kissing gently suck air out of his mouth. Again, any kind of open kiss should be saved until you know the other guy for a while or you have had sex with him.
17. Use the French kiss. A French kiss involves use of the tongue. You can touch the tip of his tongue with yours, flutter the end of the tongue, gently suck on your partner's tongue, circle his tongue with yours or gently push each other's tongue around. If you use this kiss before you know a man well, you are at elevated risk of scaring him off.
18. If you want to kiss but you aren't sure the other person wants to kiss move closer, smile, touch him, look him in the eyes then look at his lips. He will then probably give you some sign if he wants a kiss. If he moves away don't move too because he isn't interested. If he doesn't move away, you can move closer then stroke his arm or take his hand. If he doesn't pull or turn away at that point, lean in and look him in the eyes. If he doesn't turn away, you can probably gently kiss him. If you are still not sure if he wants a kiss, ask him if it is alright.
19. Don't kiss after a coffee date.

Question: How is a "quickie" sexual encounter done?
A "quickie" is a fast, intense expression of carnal lust and physical sex. It is completely about satisfying sexual needs. It is commonly

anonymous and there are no strings attached. Taking part in one only requires that you find someone who is willing to have sex with you and a place to do it. Some gay bars have backrooms that are unofficially used for this. Alleys and toilet stalls are also occasionally used although that can be dangerous. Sometimes contact information is exchanged but it is common for that information to be thrown away.

Question: How is a "one-night stand" done?
A "one-night stand" involves one person inviting another person to spend the night or evening with him. There is a clear message in that invitation that sex is going to be a major thing on the agenda. If you accept or offer such an invitation it is wise to let someone know where you are going to be and who you are going to be with. At a minimum you should leave a note about that at your home which could be found later if needed. You should also have your own means of transportation.

A one-night stand is not a date since it is not meant to be a phase in a potential or existing romantic relationship. The invitee isn't going to the host's place for drinks, dinner and conversation but offering a guest something to drink is mannerly. It should be simple things like coffee, beer or an easily-made mixed drink like run and coke. This minimizes the distraction from what both parties are there for.

Polite conversation is fine, but it shouldn't be deep or related to personal information. Saying one or two things you like about the other guy is an effective way to start but it should be true rather than rehearsed lines. Never mention another guy. Keep the focus on the two people in the room.

Someone needs to start things off so if nothing but conversation is happening the host can move things along by taking off his shirt or unbuttoning it. That will let the other guy know he has a green light. If he responds the host can then heat things up by rubbing the other guy's chest though his shirt and leaning in for a kiss. If the other guy doesn't object to kissing, then nature will take its course from there.

Requests and feedback should stay fairly "vanilla" and shouldn't sound like you are correcting him. Leave any kind of kink for a time after you get to know him better. This especially goes for bondage. If he pressures you to do that as part of a one-night stand you should leave since signals a potentially dangerous situation.

After the sex is over cues and clues are critical. It is okay for the guest to say something like, "That was great, but I have to go" and then just leave. It is also fine for him to stay and talk for a bit but if the host doesn't ask him to stay within a brief time he should leave. If he is asked to stay but he doesn't want to he should thank the host and make some excuse for not staying. The host will probably know it is an excuse but should let the guest leave gracefully.

If the host asks the guest to stay for the night, it probably means he wants to have sex in the morning. If the guest isn't willing to do that he should leave. Sometimes a guest will accept the invitation and then slip out quietly before the host wakes up. A host might find that offensive but all it really means is that the guest changed his mind.

A guest should not expect the host to offer him breakfast. It is fine for a guest to ask to use the shower but if breakfast isn't offered soon after both parties are awake, the guest should take the hint and leave. If the host wants to offer breakfast simple foods like cereal or pastry and coffee are fine but something like pancakes and eggs will impress.

It is okay to give the other guy contact information and it should be accepted even if there is no intention of ever using it. Any attempts at contact should be done within day or two and that should be limited to a simple message like, "I really enjoyed what we did. When can we do it again?" If the other guy doesn't respond within a couple of days to your attempts to contact him he probably isn't going to. That is the time to remember that one-night stands are usually about sex and little more.

Question: How does a "fuck buddy" relationship work?
A fuck buddy is a guy that a person has sex with occasionally over time. The key to this relationship is to like having sex with him and possibly even seeing him as a friend but not seeing him as anything more than that. When love creeps into a fuck buddy relationship it transforms it into something else. There is no stepping back from "I love you".

A fuck buddy relationship is primarily about sex. He is a guy you call when you want to have sex, but you cannot or do not want to find someone else. He is doing the same thing with you. It is important therefore that you are just as available to him as he is for you. It is also important for him to know that you like him and that he is good in bed.

Question: How is a coffee date done?
A coffee date is a brief get together at a coffee shop or a similar venue. It is commonly done as a first meeting which is aimed at deciding whether another person is someone you want to get to know better or have sex with. Coffee dates are usually arranged online or after two people meet socially somewhere.

There are general guidelines to follow: 1) Pick a place that is mutually acceptable and that you are familiar with. 2) Have your own, separate means of transportation. 3) Dress to look nice but don't dress up. 4) Arrive on time or offer an explanation if you can't help being late. 5) Listen as much as you talk, stay away from giving negative messages and don't talk about other guys. 6) Talk about what you like to do on your free time and not about your job. 7) Use nonverbal messages to express interest and to be interesting. Ways of doing that include widening your eyes when you first see him, looking at him and slightly smiling or licking you lips occasionally, centering your attention on him, being polite to the coffee shop staff and the others around you, and letting your sense of humor and your interests show.

You can also communicate nonverbally with your hands and arms. Keeping your arms relaxed at your side, on your lap or slightly behind you is a gesture of openness and welcoming. Arms that are crossed in front of you signal that you are closed off and not welcoming. If you talk while gesturing, try to keep your palms open. Touching a coffee date very briefly on the shoulder, knee, hand or forearm is usually taken as an attempt to connect but don't touch him anywhere else. Never touch him on the inner thigh, chest, crotch or butt.

Coffee dates are short dates. If you are still talking after an hour or so you are probably ready to take the relationship to the step of a real date. You can ask to see him again or invite him to go somewhere with you. If he accepts, all is well. If he declines you can tell him that you enjoyed the coffee date and ask for another one. You can also exchange contact information but don't try to kiss him. Instead, as you walk away, turn to look at him then smile.

Sometimes coffee dates don't go well because the people are a bad fit. If that happens it is important to treat the other guy well and to not rudely just drop him. Another date isn't going to happen, but he is going to talk to his friends about you. One or two of them might be guys that would be a good fit for you, but they won't be interested if he tells them you are a jerk. You should also consider what might happen if he or his friends can help or hurt you at some point in the future.

Question: How can I make a first date a pleasant experience for both of us?
The foundation of a good first date is staying within or close to the comfort zone of both parties. The way to do that is to learn some basic things about each other and to talk about where you are going and what you are going to do before it happens. Coffee dates, having lunch together, chats on the phone, texting and email exchanges are primary in that. Pay attention to what he says, look for themes and ask questions. Figure out what, if anything, you have in common. A first date is not the time to open new doors unless you agree to do it before it happens.

First dates are not typically about sex. They are about getting to know someone and finding out if there is a connection between you. Where you go and what you do should foster that. You don't want a place like a noisy bar that will hamper conversation or a place like a theater where you must stay quiet and inactive. Select a place where you can talk and interact as you share the experience.

The primary rule in going on a date (be it the first or the ninety first) is accepting that he is the one you are with. It is not acceptable to leave him to go off with someone else even for a little while. The general rules of a coffee date also apply on a first date. Showing your date that you like being with him is essential.

If you ask someone out it is customary that you pay the bill unless you have agreed in advance to share the expense or your date offers to pay. If you are the one who has been asked out it is okay to offer to pay. If your date declines don't argue about it. If you want to take someone out but you can't afford the tab be honest with him about it. Most people understand the constraints of a budget and your honesty puts the possibility of going "Dutch" on the table.

A first date should end as a natural extension of how it started. If you met somewhere at the beginning of the date you can part and go your separate ways after leaving the last place you go to as a couple. If the date started at his place or your place that is where it should end. It is not acceptable to invite yourself into another man's home at the end of a first date. It is also not customary to kiss after a first date. If you want another date you should say so after saying that you very much enjoyed the one you just had. As you part, look at him and smile.

It is important to follow up a date by calling or texting the next day. Make the call or text short and simple. Don't tell him that you are already falling in love with him even if you are because that may freak him out. The words, "I love you" should be saved until you know each other much better. That will take some time.

If the other guy doesn't respond to you after two or three calls or texts he probably isn't going to so let it go and move on. Just because you had an enjoyable time and want the relationship to continue doesn't mean the other guy feels the same way. If you keep trying to make contact, you will not only increase your own level of stress but will also quickly become a pest. Just accept that you had fun and make it a positive experience.

Question: How is the classic pick up done?
A pick up is the act of connecting with a random guy you don't know to have sex. Going out and about with the purpose of doing that is called "cruising". It can be done almost anywhere but some places are safer than others. Most large cities have parks, paths, stores, bars or other cruising areas where gay men tend to go because they have a reputation for being fruitful, safer places. Never cruise when you are drunk, high or otherwise not in control of yourself since doing it safely and successfully without getting arrested demands good judgement.

The foundation of the classic pick up is the "look, pass then look back" technique. This involves seeing a guy you are interested in, looking him in the eyes for a few seconds as you walk toward him, passing by him then looking back at him. If you look back and he is looking back too you have the first signal that he may be interested.

If you are a self-confident, assertive person you can then say something to him or even try to start a conversation. If you prefer to take less risk, simply stop walking, look at the other guy while you smile then wait for several seconds for him to make his move on you. If he is doing the same thing, you need to be bolder and say something to him. Anything that will break the ice, such as a comment about the weather, will do if that is all you can think of. Your goal is to start communication that can lead to going somewhere with him or agreeing to have sex.

Question: How do I pick up someone in a bar?
The easiest way is to get some other guy to pick you up. You do that by putting yourself in places other gay men go, looking good while you're there, positioning yourself so you can be seen and by correctly responding to signals. If you prefer men with certain traits go to places that would interest someone like that. Sports enthusiasts tend to like sports bars for example.

Once you are there make it clear that you are not with anyone by moving around the room, interacting with a variety of people and by not staying with anyone long. You also want to appear as though you are having a good time but not drunk or high and that you are not a bore.

If you want to be picked up, you need to look attractive and use good grooming and hygiene habits. If you wear cologne use only a light touch and understand that some people are allergic to it. Keep the jewelry you wear to a minimum. Behave confidently but not aggressively. Hands and arms are used to communicate so do not put your hands in your pockets or cross your arms in front of you. Don't chew gum or ice. If you want to look masculine don't use the stirring straw that came with your drink for anything but stirring.

Looking attractive demands that you pick clothing that fits properly and that you wear it only when it is clean and unrumpled. You want to look comfortable but not like a slob. Your shirt should be tucked in unless it is a t-shirt or a polo shirt. If you wear any other kind of shirt untucked, it will look sloppy and people will wonder whether you are trying to hide a gut. Don't wear sports related clothing that does not reflect who you really are. If you are asked about the team you are wearing you want to be able to say, "Yes, I am a fan" and then be willing to talk about it. Do not wear a cap backwards. Pick the colors you wear carefully because they can wash you out or overpower you. They can also overpower and scare off guys who are watching you.

If you see someone in a gay friendly place who interests you, look at him for a bit then look away. Keep doing that until he looks at you. Keep eye contact for a few seconds then look down and smile. Follow that by looking at him again then moving a little closer to him. If he looks at you again you can simply acknowledge his look with a nod. If he is interested, he will probably move over to you and say something. Your response should be natural, unrehearsed and upbeat. If the place is noisy use that as an excuse to lean in, touch him on the arm or shoulder then say something nice in his ear. If he offers you a drink, take it.

Taking the drink does not end the process of being picked up. Now that you have him, you need to keep him. You do that by showing you are interested in him and interesting to be with and by understanding that cruising is about sex. If you do not, within a few minutes, give some sign that sex may be in the cards, you risk being labelled a "cock tease" and having the guy move along to someone else.

Nearly any method of delivering that message will do. It is often done with a short, friendly verbal exchange which at least hints about an interest in sex. It can also be done by just glancing at his crotch or licking your lips with the tip of your tongue. Pickups should be done with the understanding that there are lots of gay men who will use other gays badly if they can.

Bars that cater primarily to a straight crowd can be places for gay men to find a good time and good company, but they typically are not good places to hook up with other guys. Nearly all the men there will be straight, and some will be insecure about their masculinity. It may be best, if you are out and proud, to become a regular at a bar and to get to know the other regulars before you use it for a pick-up place. The others will come to know that you respect their boundaries, you are not a threat and you can be good company, but you may respond to opportunity knocking.

If a straight bar is a poor place for an out and proud gay man to find a hookup it is more so for a closeted one. It is also a risky environment for someone who is trying to hide his sexual orientation while, at the same time, trying to get picked up by a guy. The safest way to do this is to let the other guy take most of the risks. Your job here is to covertly get the attention of the gay or bi guys in the room and to then trust the fact that gay men are more likely to detect other gay men than straight men are.

Doing this will require that you try to conform to some of the stereotypes that are commonly viewed as gay. You will want to use only very subtle ones that the straight guys in the room are unlikely to notice or understand. At the same time, you cannot use ones that are so subtle that they will be missed by those you are fishing for. It will do no good, for example, to order wine or a vodka-based drink because most gays do not know that, per capita, gay men drink a whole lot more of those things than straight men do.

Gay men are pigeon-holed as being more concerned about their appearance than straight men are so be that when you go to the bar. Gay men are naturally attracted to other men so look and act attractive. Do not use cologne or scented products. Keep the jewelry you wear to a minimum but do wear a plain ring on your right hand since that signals you do wear rings but not on your left-hand ring finger. Politely rebuff any women that attempt to make a connection. The rules for what to wear apply even in a straight bar so your clothes must be clean, pressed and fit well and of a color and style that is proper for the venue you will be in. Do not pay rapt attention to whatever sport may be on the television set.

Most of the beer consumed in America is, by a wide margin, downed by hetero men and they overwhelmingly prefer domestic beers such as Budweiser, or light beers. As an attractive, dapper man you will be noticed by other gays when you enter the bar, but you can up that a notch by ordering a foreign beer and pouring it into the glass correctly. Most bars carry Heineken, Corona, and Guinness but something like Moosehead, Negra Modelo or Beck's Stout will be noticed if you place the bottle next to your glass after you pour. That simple act will further separate you from the other men in the room in the eyes of other gay men if they are there and make you someone they watch.

Your goal is to attract another gay man and draw him over, so you can talk to him. The only reason he is going to talk to you is that he has identified you as a possible, albeit very temporary, sex partner which is, of course, also why you want to talk to him. He will be willing to move to a more private place to talk or for sex, but he is not going to spend a lot of time waiting for you to deal with your insecurities. He will move along if he comes to think you are not going to give him what he wants. If you are not willing to do that, do not start the process.

Some straight men like sex with gay men but most will avoid contact with anything that might be taken to show they might be gay or bisexual. A few may respond to any perceived gayness around them with visible discomfort or even with verbal aggression. A few of those will be willing to show you that they can use the word "faggot" as a noun and an adjective in the same sentence as they simultaneously attach their fist to your face. This is more likely to occur if you are not a regular at the place or after you leave the bar. They commonly choose a place that has no witnesses and where nobody is likely to intervene.

If you want to pick someone up, you need to be assertive. Gay men most often do this in places that are known to be good pickup spots, but it can work elsewhere too. Wherever it is you must take the risk of going to the guy you are interested in and starting a conversation even though you don't know him. It is common to start that by talking to him for a bit then offering to buy him a drink. If the drink is accepted follow it up briefly with a little more chit chat which should include a comment about something you like about him. Make it in the form of a question so he can't just say "thanks" then go silent but don't get too personal. If he is physically fit something like, "I wish I could be as fit as you seem to be. What do you have to do to stay looking this good"?

Remember however that picking a guy up has two steps. Before you make a move, you need to know if he is alone because it is both rude and potentially hazardous to try to pick up someone else's date. The only way to do that is to watch him for a little while to see who he is interacting with. Whether he is alone or not will soon become clear.

Question: How can I find a partner using the internet?
The first step in doing this is deciding what you are looking for before you go online. Some websites specialize in certain kinds of relationships or client profiles. Some sites like Grindr, Manhunt.com and Gay.com are usually for men who are looking

for a hookup while other sites like Tinder, Match.com and GKiss.com are for people who want a longer relationship or at least a date. The website EliteSingles.com caters to professional people most of whom have college degrees while the website Caffmocommunity.com carters to Bears and older men. Other popular sites include: OneGoodLove.com, MyPartner.com, Adam4Adam, CompatiblePartners.net and GayCupid.com. It is wise to investigate a website before you use it to make sure that it is reputable.

It is critical when using the internet to meet people that you have the best internet security program you can afford and that you keep it updated. Dating websites are sometimes targeted by malicious hackers and identity thieves. The major dating websites try to keep their sites secure but if hackers can enter the Pentagon's computers they can enter those of a business.

You should try to avoid giving a website information that is linked to a bank account and never use a debit card to pay membership fees. Use a credit card that is a standalone account and has a good record for helping clients with disputes about charges or use a service like PayPal.

When you meet someone interesting on a site it is wise to chat online until you know more about them. That can progress to phone calls and then perhaps to a coffee date. Always tell someone who you are chatting with or meeting and always meet in a public place that you are familiar with. Don't invite a stranger to your home. It is wise to remember that there are lots of liars and predators on the internet so be cautious.

Question: What happens in a bathhouse?
While all bathhouses have shower facilities and most have a whirlpool, a sauna and/or a steam room, no gay bathhouse exists so someone can have a sweat, a steam or a bath. They are entirely about male with male interactions, lust and sex. They exist solely because the male sex drive is very strong and having sex is fun. Bathhouses offer a place where consenting adults can usually relieve sexual tension and have fun in the process in a relatively harmless way.

Douching or fingering out your ass is probably something you should do before you go to a bathhouse. Some gay men don't care about contending with fecal matter as they sodomize another guy, but most do. You will probably want to avoid the fuss, mess and embarrassment that can bring. Don't assume you are not going to be anally penetrated since such things happen occasionally and unexpectedly even to total tops.

It is not advisable to brush your teeth or floss during the hour or two before going to a bathhouse. Doing so may cause scrapes or other openings in the mouth that microorganisms can enter the body through. Shaving the face or body just prior to going is also a mistake for the same reason. You have no way of knowing what kind of bacteria or virus you may meet in a bathhouse and your skin is your first line of defense. Don't screw it up.

The first step in entering a bathhouse is showing a government issued ID with your birthdate on it. No minors allowed inside. If you are visibly drunk or high or a known prostitute you will probably also be rejected. Possession of drugs or weapons is banned. You then pay a fee, show a membership card or both.

In exchange, you will get a key to a locker or a room, a towel, a condom and maybe some lube. The key may have an elastic band attached to it, so it can be worn on the wrist or ankle. The fee you pay for entry will vary based on what you want, and prices are usually available on the bathhouse's website. A locker is the least expensive choice and commonly costs around $15. The price of a room varies based upon its size, amenities and location. The range is commonly $25 to $40. Always keep your key with you.

Don't take anything of value to a bathhouse. You are probably going to be either completely nude or wearing just a towel while you are there, so you won't need it anyway. What you have will be in a locker or in you room but neither of those is very secure. You will need a reliable, inexpensive watch that is waterproof since lockers and rooms are sometimes rented on a time specific basis. An illuminated dial on the watch is best because bathhouse lighting is dim.

Once inside, most men stow their things away, wrap their towel around themselves then walk around the place. This allows them to see what and who is there, what is going on and it allows other men to see them. If someone asks for your name just give a first name and it doesn't have to be your real one. Don't give any personal information since you have no way to know if that is safe.

If you have a room, leave the door open when you are inside alone. Guys will pass by or stop and look in. If you see someone you like, invite him in. What happens then is between two consenting adults but both people are free to say "no" to any sex act. If you want privacy while having sex, close the door because people will watch if it is open. Your open door makes that acceptable. Never knock on a closed door and don't go into a room unless you are invited in.

Bathhouses commonly have an area called a maze. It is a series of rooms or areas offering various sexually oriented amenities. Among these may be a porn lounge, a room with a sling, a computer room, a weight room, open areas with beds and some rooms with glory holes. Many bathhouses also have a room where men can just go to talk.

Steam rooms or dry saunas are commonly found in a bathhouse. Inside these are usually some tiered seating. Laying on them is fine if the room is uncrowded although it may be taken as an offer or signal. The men using this room will usually wear a towel around their waist, but some may be nude. It is common for men to sit after they lay their towel across the seating, so they do not touch the germs that may be on the bench.

Most people using a steam room or sauna do so to relax. You can talk softy in them, but it is often quiet. Some of the men in these rooms will be looking for signals of sexual interest. If you want sex look at another guy, briefly lock eyes with him then smile or start a conversation to break down barriers. Most guys, but not all, go somewhere else to have anal sex.

Using safer sex techniques is very important at a bathhouse since there is no way to tell who has an STI. You can ask people about their STI/HIV status but that offers no guarantees since people can lie. It is your job to protect yourself so use your own condoms. Using PrEP is probably a wise idea too.

Some bathhouses are reasonably clean while other are not. Even ones that are cleaned regularly are too big to clean well so use flip flops instead of going barefoot. It is also best to shower as soon as you get home and to wash your clothes in hot water right away.

Question: Does wearing keys or an earring on the right or left side mean anything?
In the 1980s wearing keys or an earring on the left side meant you were gay and wearing them on the right side meant you were

straight. Now it means nothing more than you prefer wearing those things there. The exception to this is that in certain subsets of the gay community, such as BDSM or Leather, tops may wear their keys on the left and bottoms wear them on the right.

Question: What is "flagging" and how does it work?
Flagging is a means within certain subsets of the gay community to advertise what specific sexual activities a person likes to take part in to attract a willing partner. It is done by placing a colored handkerchief in your right or left rear pocket thus it is called a "handkerchief code". Specific colors stand for certain activities. A handkerchief in the right pocket means you are a bottom who wants that activity while a handkerchief on the left means you are a top who wants that activity. There are as many colors and combinations of colors as kinds of sexual activities. That of course means there are a lot of them. The meaning of some colors may vary from region to region. Some of the codes are:

Beige = Rimming
Black = S/M
Black/white checked = Safe Sex
Charcoal = Latex Fetish
Fuchsia = Spanking
Gold = Three way or more
Gray = Bondage
Hunter Green (left) = Daddy
Hunter Green (right) = boy
Kelly Green = Prostitution
Light Blue = Fellatio
Mosquito Netting = Outdoor Sex
Mustard Yellow = Large Penis
Navy Blue = Anal Sex
Orange = Open to Anything
Red = Fisting
Robin's Egg Blue = 69
White = Masturbation
Yellow = Water Sports
Zip Lock Bag = Drugs

Citations

Abel, Gene and Becker, Judith et al – Multiple paraphilic diagnoses among sex offenders – Journal of the American Academy of Psychiatry and Law (vol. 16 issue 2, 1988).

Adams, Henry and Wright, Lester et al – Is homophobia associated with homosexual arousal? - Journal of Abnormal Psychology (vol. 105 issue 3, 1996).

Ahmed, Ali and Hammarstedt, Mats – Sexual orientation and earnings: A register data-base approach to identify homosexuals – Journal of Population Econ. (vol. 23 issue 3, June 2010).

Albelda, Randy and Badgett, M.V. Lee et al – Poverty in the lesbian, gay, and bisexual community – The Williams Institute (March 2009).

Allen, Laura and Gorski, Roger – Sexual orientation and the size of the anterior commissure in the human brain – Proceedings of the National Academy of Sciences, USA (vol. 89 issue 15, 1992).

Alford, John and Funk, Carolyn et al – Are political orientations genetically transmitted? – American Political Science Review (vol. 99 issue 2, 2005).

Ambady, Nalini and Hallahan, Mark et al – Accuracy of judgments of sexual orientation from thin slices of behavior – Journal of Personality and Social Psychology (vol. 77 issue 3, 1999).

American Association for Clinical Chemistry – Lab Tests Online – Urinary Tract Infection – This can be retrieved at: http://www. labtestsonline.org/understanding/conditions/uri/.

American Association of Suicidology – Elderly Suicide Fact Sheet (2012) – This can be retrieved at: http://www.suicidology.org/Portals/14/docs/Resources/FactSheets/Elderly/2012.pdf

American Civil Liberties Union – Collins v United States: Class Action for Military Separation Pay (May10, 2011) – This can be retrieved at: http://www.aclu.org/ lgbt-rights/collins- v. united-states-class-action-military-separation-pay.

American Lung Association – Smoking Out a Deadly Threat

– 2010.

American Medical Association – American Medical Association Complete Medical Encyclopedia (New York, NY: Random House, 2003).

American Psychiatric Association – APA Statement on DSM-5 Error (Oct. 31, 2013). This can be retrieved at http://www.dsm5.org/Documents/13-67-DSM-Correction-103113.pdf.

American Psychiatric Association – Diagnostic and Statistical Manual of Mental Disorders, Fourth Edition – Revised Text (Arlington, VA: American Psychiatric Association, 2000).

American Psychiatric Association – Diagnostic and Statistical Manual of Mental Disorders /Fifth Edition (DSM5) (Washington, DC & London, England: American Psychiatric Publishing, 2013).

American Psychological Association – Answers to Your Questions: For a better understanding of sexual orientation & homosexuality (2008). This can be retrieved at: http://www.apa.org/topics/lgbt/orientation.pdf.

American Psychological Association – Being gay is just as healthy as being straight (2003).

American Psychological Association – Resolution on appropriate affirmative responses to sexual orientation distress and change efforts – (Aug. 5, 2009).

American Psychological Association – Sexual orientation and homosexuality – This can be retrieved athttp://www.apa.org/helpcenter/sexual-orientation.aspx.

American Psychological Association – Statement on Homosexuality – July 1994.

American Red Cross – Eligibility for donating blood –This can be retrieved at: http://www.redcrossblood.org

American Sociological Association – Amicus Curiae Brief to The United States Supreme Court – Hollingsworth v. Perry (2013).

Amerson-Zavala, Sameria – Preparing for repeal of DADT brings training for soldiers – Army News Service (June 28, 2011).

Amodio, David and Jost, John et al – Neurocognitive

correlates of liberalism and conservatism – Nature Neuroscience (vol. 10 issue 10, 2007).

Annenberg Political Fact Check – What is a Civil Union? – FactCheck.org (Aug. 9, 2007).

Aosved, Allison and Long, Patricia – Co-occurrence of rape myth acceptance, sexism, racism, homophobia, ageism, classism, and religious intolerance – Sex Roles (vol. 55 issues 7-8, 2006).

Badgett, M.V. Lee and Mallory, Christy – Patterns of relationship recognition for same-sex couples: Divorce and terminations -The Williams Institute (December 2014).

Bailey, J.M. and Dunne, M.P. et al – Genetic and environmental influences on sexual orientation and its correlates in an Australian twin sample – Journal of Personality and Social Psychology (vol. 78 issue 3, 2000).

Bailey, J.M. and Gaulin, S. et al – Effects of gender and sexual orientation on evolutionary relevant aspects of human mating psychology – Journal of Personality and Social Psychology (vol. 66 issue 6, 1994).

Baker, Judith and Fishbein, Harold – The development of prejudice towards gays and lesbians by adolescents – Journal of Homosexuality (vol. 36 issue 1, 1998).

Baker, Warren – The Complete Word Study Old Testament (Chattanooga, TN: AMG Publishers, 1994).

Bakker, A. and van Kestern, P.J.M. – The prevalence of transsexuals in the Netherlands – Acta Psychiatrica Scandinavica (vol. 87 issue 4, 2007).

Bakker, Floor and Sandfort, Theo et al – Do homosexual persons use health care services more frequently than heterosexual persons: Findings from a Dutch population survey – Social Science and Medicine (vol. 63 issue 8, 2006).

Balthazart, Jacques – Minireview: Hormones and human sexual orientation – Endocrinology (vol. 152 issue 8, 2011)

Banks, Amy and Gartrell, Nanette – Hormones and sexual orientation: A questionable link – Journal of Homosexuality (vol. 28 issue3/4, 1995).

Bao, Ai-Minn and Swabb, Dick – Sexual differentiation of

the human brain: Relation to gender identity, sexual orientation and neuropsychiatric disorders – Frontiers of Neuroendocrinology (vol. 32 issue 2, 2011).

Bara Group, Ltd – Bara Group 2009 survey: Spiritual profile of homosexual adults provides surprising insights (June 22, 2009). It can be retrieved at: http://www.barna.org/barna-update/article/13-culture/ 282-spiritual-profile-of- homosexual-adults-provides-surprising-insights.

Baral, Stefan and Poteat, Tonia et al – Worldwide burden of HIV in transgender women: A systematic review and meta-analysis – The Lancet Infectious Diseases (vol. 13 issue 3).

Baumeister, Roy and Catanese, Kathleen et al – Is there a gender difference in strength of sex drive? Theoretical views, conceptual distinctions, and a review of relevant evidence – Personality and Social Science Review (vol. 5 issue 3, 2001).

Bell, Robin – Homosexual Men and Women – British Medical Journal (vol. 318 issue 7181, 1999).

Bentz, Eva-Katrin and Hefler, Lukas et al – A polymorphism of the CYP17 gene related to sex steroid metabolism is associated with female-to-male but not male-to-female transsexualism – Fertility and Sterility (vol. 90 issue 1, 2008).

Berg, Michael and Mimiaga, Matthew et al – Mental health concerns of gay and bisexual men seeking mental health services – Journal of Homosexuality (vol. 54 issue 3, 2008).

Berg, Nathan and Lien, Donald – Measuring the effect of sexual orientation on income: Evidence of discrimination? – Contemporary Economic Policy – (vol. 20 issue 4, 2002).

Berglund, H., Lindstrom, P. and Savic. I. – Brain response to putative pheromones in lesbian women – Proceedings of the national Academy of Sciences (vol. 103 issue 21, 2006).

Berk, Laura – Human Development Through the Lifespan – (New York: Allyn & Bacon, 2010).

Berkowitz, Dana and Liska Belgrave, Linda – She works

hard for the money: Drag queens and the management of their contradictory status of celebrity and marginality – Journal of Contemporary Ethnography (vol. 39 issue 2, 2010).

Beyrer, Chris and Baral, Stefan et al – Global epidemiology of HIV in men who have sex with men – The Lancet (vol. 380 Issue 9839, 2012).

Beyrer, Chris and Malinowki-Sempruch, Kasia et al – 12 Myths about HIV/AIDS and people who use drugs – The Lancet (vol. 376 issue 9737, 2010).

Binson, Diane and Dolcini, Margaret et al – Multiple sexual partners among young adults in high-risk cities – Family Planning Perspectives (Nov. 1993).

Binson, Diane and Michaels, Stuart et al – Prevalence and societal distribution of men who have sex with men: United States and its urban centers – Journal of Sex Research (vol. 32 Issue 3, 1995).

Black, Dan and Gates, Gary et al – Demographics of the gay and lesbian population in the United States: Evidence from available systematic data sources – Demography (May 2000).

Blumstein, Philip and Schwartz, Pepper – American Couples: Money, Work and Sex (New York: William Morrow & Co., 1983).

Bockting, Walter and Benner, Autumn et al – Gay and bisexual identity development among female-to-male transsexuals in North America: Emergence of transgender sexuality – Archive of Sexual Behavior (vol. 38 issue 5, 2009).

Boehmer, Ulrike and Bowen, Deborah et al – Overweight and obesity in minority women: Evidence from population-based data – American Journal of Public Health (vol. 97 issue 6, 2007).

Boehmer, Ulrike and Miao, Xiaopeng et al – Cancer survivorship and sexual orientation – Cancer (vol. 117 issue 16, 2011).

Boehmer, Ulrike and Miao, Xiaopeng et al – Sexual minority population density and incidence of lung, colorectal and female breast cancer in California – BMJ Open (vol. 4 issue 3, 2014).

Bogaert, Anthony and Friesen, Chris et al – Age of puberty and sexual orientation in a national probability sample – Archives of Sexual Behavior (vol. 31 issue 1, 2002).

Bogaert, Anthony and Hershlberger, Scott – The relation between sexual orientation and penile size – Archives of Sexual Behavior (vol. 28 issue 3, 1999).

Bolingbroke, Henry St. John – Letters on the Study and Use of History (1735).

Brand, Chad and Draper, Charles et al (eds.) – Holman Illustrated Bible Dictionary (Nashville, TN: Holman Bible Publishers, 2003).

Brennan, David and Ross, Lori et al – Men's sexual orientation and health in Canada – Canadian Journal of Public Health (vol. 101 issue 3, 2010).

Brown, Raymond – Introduction to the New Testament (New York, NY: Doubleday,1997).

Brusch, John – Urinary Tract Infection in Males – Medscape Reference (Feb. 21, 2012) – This can be retrieved at http://emedicine.medscape.com /article/231547-overview.

Bureau of Justice Statistics – Hate Crime Victimization, 2003-2011 – This can be retrieved at: http://www.bjs. gov/index.cfm?ty=pbdetail&iid=4614.

Burkhalter, Jack and Hay, Jennifer et al – Perceived risk for cancer in an urban minority – Journal of Behavioral Medicine (vol. 34 issue 3, 2011).

Buss, David 0and Schmitt, David – Sexual strategies theory: An evolutionary perspective on human mating – Psychology Review (vol. 100 issue 2, 1993).

Butler, Lisa and Osmond, Dennis et al – Use of saliva as a lubricant in anal sexual practices among homosexual men – Journal of Acquired Immune Deficiency Syndromes (vol. 50 issue 2, 2009).

Camperio-Ciani, Andrea and Corna, Francesca et al – Evidence of maternally inherited factors favouring male homosexuality and promoting female fecundity – Proc. Biol. Sci. (vol. 271 issue 1554, 2004).

Camperio-Ciani, Andrea and Fontanesi, Lilybeth et al – Factors associated with higher fecundity in female maternal relatives of homosexual men – J. Sexual

Medicine (vol. 9 issue 11, 2012).

Cantor, JM and Kabani, N. et al – Cerebral white matter deficiencies in pedophilic men – Journal of Psychiatric Research (vol. 42 issue 3, 2008).

Carden, Michael – Sodomy: A History of Christian Biblical Myth (London & New York: Routledge, 2004).

Carpenter, Christopher – Sexual orientation, work, and income in Canada – Canadian Journal of Economics (vol. 41 issue 4, 2008).

Carpiano, Richard and Kelly, Brian et al – Community and drug use among gay men: The role of neighborhoods and networks – Journal of Health and Social Behavior (vol. 52 issue 1, 2011).

Cass, V.C. – Homosexuality identity formation: A theoretical model – Journal of Homosexuality (vol. 4 issue 3, 1979).

Centers for Disease Control and Prevention – Almost half of Americans use at least one prescription drug Annual Report on Nation's Health shows – Press Release: Dec. 2, 2004. Centers for Disease Control and Prevention – Basic Information about HIV and AIDS – This can be retrieved at: http://ww.cdc.gov/hiv/topics/basic/print/index.htm.

Centers for Disease Control and Prevention – Basic Information about HPV and Associated Cancers – This can be retrieved at: http://www.cdc.gov/cancer/hpv/basic info/

Centers for Disease Control and Prevention – Calculating HIV and Syphilis Rates for Risk Groups: Estimating the National Population Size of Men Who Have Sex with Men – Retrieve at: http://www.cdc.gov/hiv/topic/msm/resources/msm.htm.

Centers for Disease Control and Prevention – Estimated Per-Act Probability of Acquiring HIV from an Infected Source, by Exposure Act (2014) – Retrieve at: www.cdc.gov/hiv/.../risk.html.

Centers for Disease Control and Prevention – Fact Sheet: HIV and AIDS among Gay and Bisexual Men (June 2010).

Centers for Disease Control and Prevention – For Your

Health: Recommendations for a Healthier You – This can be retrieved at: http://www.cdc.gov/msmhealth/for-your-health.htm.

Centers for Disease Control and Prevention – Genital Herpes: CDC Fact Sheet – This can be retrieved at: http://www.cdc.gov/std/herpes/STDFact-Herpes.htm.

Centers for Disease Control and Prevention – Gonorrhea: CDC Fact Sheet – This can be retrieved at: http://www.cdc.gov/std/gonorrhea/STDFact-gonorrhea.htm.

Centers for Disease Control and Prevention – Hepatitis A Information for the Public – This can be retrieved at http://www.cdc.gov/hepatitis/A/index.htm.

Centers for Disease Control and Prevention – Hepatitis B Information for Health Professionals – This can be retrieved at: http://www.cdc.gov/hepatitis/HBV/index.htm

Centers for Disease Control and Prevention – Hepatitis C FAQ for Health Professionals – This can be retrieved at: http://www.cdc.gov/hepatitis/HCV/HCVfaq.htm.

Centers for Disease Control and Prevention – HIV Surveillance Report: Cases of HIV infection and AIDS in the United States and Dependent Areas, 2005 (vol. 17) – This can be retrieved at: http://www.cdc.gov/hiv/pdf/statistics-2005-HIV-surveillance-report-vol-17.pdf.

Centers for Disease Control and Prevention – HIV Transmission – This can be retrieved at: http://www.cdc.gov/hiv/resources/qa/transmission.htm.

Centers for Disease Control and Prevention – HPV and Men: Fact Sheet – This can be retrieved at: http://www.cdc.gov/std/hpv/STDFact-HPV-and-men.htm.

Centers for Disease Control and Prevention – Morbidity and Mortality Weekly Report: Likely Female-to-Female Sexual Transmission of HIV, Texas 2012 – This can be retrieved at: http://www.cdc.gov/mmwr/preview/mmwrth/mm6310a1.htm.

Centers for Disease Control and Prevention – National Survey of Family Growth - This can be retrieved at http://www.cdc.gov/nchs/nsfg/key_statistics/s.htm.

Centers for Disease Control and Prevention: New CDC Studies Shed Light on Factors Underlying High HIV

Rates Among Gay and Bisexual Men – Press Release July 8, 2002 – This can be retrieved at: http://www.cdc.gov/media /pressrel/r020710.htm.

Centers for Disease Control and Prevention – Oral Sex and HIV Risk – This can be retrieved at: http://www.cdc.gov/hiv/resources/factsheet/pdf/oralsex.pdf.

Centers for Disease Control and Prevention – Parasites: Lice –This can be retrieved at: http://www.cdc.gov/parasites/lice.

Centers for Disease Control and Prevention – Parasites: Scabies – This can be retrieved at: http://www.cdc.gov/parasites/scabies.

Centers for Disease Control and Prevention – Questions and Answers for the General Public: Revised Recommendations for HIV Testing of Adults, Adolescents, and Pregnant Women in Health Care Settings – This can be retrieved at: http://www.cdc.gov/hiv/topics/testing/resources/qa/print/qa/general-public.htm.

Centers for Disease Control and Prevention – Sexual identity, sex of sexual contacts, and health-related behaviors among students in grades 9-12 – United States and selected sites, 2015 – MMWR Surveillance Summaries (vol. 65 issue 9, Aug. 12, 2016).

Centers for Disease Control and Prevention – Sexually Transmitted Diseases – This can be retrieved at: http://www.cdc .gov/msmhealth/STD.htm.

Centers for Disease Control and Prevention – Substance Abuse – This can be retrieved at: http://www.cdc.gov/msmhealth/substance-abuse.htm.

Centers for Disease Control and Prevention – Syphilis: CDC Fact Sheet – This can be retrieved at: http://www.cdc.gov/std/syphilis/STDFact-Syphilis.htm.

Centers for Disease Control and Prevention – Trichomoniasis: CDC Fact Sheet – This can be retrieved at: http://www.cdc. gov/std/trichomonas/stdfact-trichomoniasis.htm.

Centers for Disease Control and Prevention – Viral Hepatitis –This can be retrieved at: http://www.cdc.gov/hepititus.

Cerny, Jerome and Janssen, Erick – Patterns of sexual arousal in homosexual, bisexual, and heterosexual men – Archives of Sexual Behavior (vol. 40 issue 4, 2011).

Chaladze, Giorgi – Heterosexual male carriers could explain persistence of homosexuality in men: Individual-based modeling simulations of a x-linked inheritance model - Archives of Sexual Behavior (vol. 45 issue 7, 2016).

Chandra, Anjani and Mosher, William et al – Sexual Behavior, Sexual Attraction, and Sexual Identity in the United States: Data from the 2006-2008 National Survey of Family Growth – National Health Statics Reports (Number 36 March 3, 2011).

Chase, Anthony – Violent reaction: What do teen killers have in common – In These Times (vol. 25 issue 16, 2001).

Clark, Russell and Hatfield, Elaine – Gender differences in receptivity of sexual offers – Journal of Psychology and Human Sexuality (vol. 2 issue 1, 1989).

Clines, D.J.A. – Pentateuch - In: The Oxford Companion to the Bible – (New York, NY: Oxford University Press, 1993).

Cochran, Susan – Emerging issues in research on lesbians' and gay men's mental health: Does sexual orientation really matter – American Psychologist (vol. 56 issue 1, 2001).

Cochran, Susan and Ackerman, Deborah et al – Prevalence of non-medical drug use and dependence among homosexually active men and women in the US population – Addiction (vol. 99 issue 8, 2004).

Cochran, Susan and Keenan, Colleen et al – Estimates of alcohol use and clinical treatment needs among homosexually active men and women in the U.S. population – J. of Clinical Psychology (vol. 68 issue 6, 2000).

Cochran, Susan and Mays, Vickie – Prevalence of Primary Morbidity and Suicide Symptoms among Gay and Bisexual Men – In: R.J. Wolitski, Ron Stall et al (Eds.) Unequal Opportunity (New York, NY: Oxford University Press, 2008).

Cochran, Susan and Mays, Vickie – Sexual orientation and mortality among US men aged 17 to 59 years: Results from the National Health and Nutrition Examination Survey III – American Journal of Public Health (vol. 10 issue 6, 2011).

Cochran, Susan and Sullivan, J. Greer et al – Prevalence of mental disorders, psychological distress, and mental health services use among lesbian, gay, and bisexual adults in the United States – Journal of Consulting and Clinical Psychology (vol. 71 issue 1, 2003).

Coffman, Katherine and Coffman, Lucus et al – The Size of the LGBT Population and the Magnitude of Anti-Gay Sentiment are Substantially Underestimated – National Bureau of Economic Research (NBER working paper No. 19508 Oct. 2013).

Cohen, C.E. and Giles, A. et al – Sexual trauma associated with fisting and recreational drugs – BMJ (British Medical Journal) (vol. 80 issue 6, 2004).

Cohen, L.J. and Galynker, I.I. – Clinical features of pedophilia and implications for treatment – Journal of Psychiatric Practice (vol. 8 issue5, 2002).

Cohen, L.J. and Nickiforov, K. – Heterosexual male perpetrators of childhood sexual abuse: A preliminary neuropsychiatric model – Psychiatric Quarterly (vol. 73 issue 4, 2002).

Columbia University – Go Ask Alice! Anal protrusions after anal sex – This can be retrieved at: http://goaskalice.columbia.edu/anal-protrusion-after-anal-sex.

Conley, T.D. and Ziegler, A. et al – A critical examination of popular assumptions about benefits and outcomes of monogamous relationships – Personality and Social Psychology (vol. 17 issue 2, 2013).

Connell, Raewyn W – Masculinities (2nd ed.) (Berkeley, CA: Univ. of California Press, 2005).

Connolly, Pamela – Psychological functioning of bondage/domination/sado-masochism (BDSM) practitioners – Journal of Psychology & Human Sexuality (vol. 18 issue 1, 2006).

Conron, Kerith and Mimiaga, Matthew et al – A population-based study of sexual orientation identity and gender differences in health – American Journal of Public Health (vol. 100 issue 10, 2010).

Consumer Healthcare Products Association – Consumer Survey on Self-Medication – This can be retrieved at: http://www.chpa-info.org.

Contraception Technology Update (January 2011) – Ask the Experts: What's the evidence for using two condoms?

Copeland, William and Wolke, Dieter et al – Psychiatric outcomes of bullying and being bullied by peers in childhood and adolescence – JAMA Psychiatry (vol. 7 issue 4, 2013).

Corliss, Heather and Rosario, Margaret et al – Sexual orientation and drug use in a longitudinal cohort study of U.S. adolescents – Addictive Behavior (vol. 35 issue 5, 2010).

Cornwell, Benjamin and Laumann, Edward et al – The social connectedness of older adults: A national profile – American Sociological Review (vol. 73 issue 2, 2008).

Crawford, Katherine – The Sexual Culture of the French Renaissance – (New York: Cambridge University Press, 2010).

Critchlow, J.F. and Houlihan, M.J. et al – Primary sphincter repair in anorectal trauma – Diseases of the Colon & Rectum (vol. 28 issue 12, 1985).

Cruz, Michael – "Why Doesn't He Just Leave?": Gay male domestic violence and the reasons victims stay – Journal of Men's Studies (vol. 11 issue 3, 2003).

Dean, John – Anal Sex – netdoctor (May 05, 2009) – This can be retrieved at http://www.netdoctor.co.uk/sexandrelationships/analsex.htm.

Dancey, Christine – Sexual orientation in women: An investigation of hormonal and personality variables – Biological Psychology (vol. 30 issue 3, 1990).

DeAngeles, Tori – New data on lesbian, gay and bisexual mental health – American Psychological Association (vol. 33 issue 2, 2002).

De Bakker, J.K. and Bruin, S.C. – Successful laparoscopic repair of a large traumatic sigmoid perforation – Journal of Surgical Care Reports (vol. 2012 issue 2, 2012).

De Graaf, Hanneke and Sandfort, Theo – Gender

differences in affective responses to sexual rejection – Archives of Sexual Behavior (vol. 33 issue 4, 2004).

DeNavas-Walt, Carmen and Proctor, Bernadette et al – Income, poverty, and health insurance coverage in the United States: 2009 – U.S. Census Bureau, Current Population Reports.

De, Preeti and Farley, Amanda et al – Systematic review and meta-analysis: Influence of smoking cessation on incidence of pneumonia in HIV – BMC Medicine (vol. 11 issue 15, 2013).

Dever, William – What Remains of the House That Albright Built – In: George Wright, Frank Cross et al – The Bible Archeologist – American School of Oriental Research (vol. 56 issue 1, 1993).

Devinsky, Orrin and Lai, George – Spiritual and Religious Epilepsy – Epilepsy & Behavior (vol.12 issue 2, 2008).

Diamond, Lisa – Emerging perspectives on distinctions between romantic love and sexual desire – Current Directions in Psychological Science (vol. 13 issue 3, 2004).

Diamond, Lisa – Female bisexuality from adolescence to adulthood: Results From a 10-year longitudinal study – Developmental Psychology (vol. 44 issue 1, 2008).

Dickson, Nigel and van Roode, Thea et al – Stability and change in same-sex attraction, experience, and identity by sex and age in a New Zealand birth cohort – Archives of Sexual Behavior (vol. 42 issue 5, 2013).

Dixit, Jay – Five Shocking Facts about Men and Sex - Psychology Today (June 28, 2010).

Dreyer, P.H. – Sexuality during Adolescence. In: B.B. Wolman (Ed.), Handbook of Developmental Psychology (Englewood Cliffs, NJ: Prentice-Hall, 1982).

Drummond, Kelly and Bradley, Susan et al – A follow-up Study of the girls with gender identity disorder – Developmental Psychology (vol. 44 issue 1, 2008).

D'Souza, Gypsyamber and Kreimer, Aimee et al – Case-control study of human papillomavirus and oropharyngeal cancer – New England Journal of Medicine (vol. 356 issue 19, 2007).

Durso, L.E. and Gates, G.J. – Serving Our Youth: Findings

from a National Survey of Service Providers Working with Lesbian, Gay, Bisexual, and Transgender Youth Who Are Homeless or at Risk of Becoming Homeless – Los Angeles: The Williams Institute with the True Colors Fund and the Palette Fund (2012).

Eder Franz and Hall, Lesley et al (editors) – Sexual Cultures in Europe Natural Histories – (Manchester & New York: Manchester University Press, 1999).

Egan, V. and Kavanaugh, B. et al – Sexual offenders against children: The influence of personality and obsessionality on cognitive distortions – Sex Abuse (vol. 17 issue 3, 2005).

El-Rouayheb, Khaled – Before Homosexuality in the Arab-Islamic World 1500-1800 (Chicago: University of Chicago Press, 2005).

England, Paula and Brown, Eliza – An unequal distribution of partners: Gays versus straights – Contexts (July 1, 2016) – This can be retrieved at: https://contexts.org/blog/ an-unequal-distribution- of-partners/. Contexts is a publication of the American Sociological Association.

Factor, R.J. and Rothblum, E.D. – A study of transgender adults and their non-transgender siblings on demographic characteristics, social support, and experiences of violence – Journal of LGBT Health Research (vol. 3 issue 3, 2007).

Federal Bureau of Investigation – Hate Crime Statistics 2011- This can be retrieved at: http://www.fbi.gov/about-us/cjis/ucr/hate-crime/2011.

Feldman, Matthew and Meyer, Ilan – Childhood abuse and eating disorders in gay and bisexual men – International Journal of Eating Disorders (vol. 40 issue 5, 2007).

Feldman, Matthew and Meyer, Ilan – Eating disorders in diverse lesbian, gay, and bisexual populations – International Journal of Eating Disorders (vol. 40 issue 3, 2007).

Ferguson, Kristin and Bender, Kimberly et al – Social control correlates of arrest behavior among homeless youth in five cities – Violence and Victims; New York (vol. 26 issue 5, 2011),

Finkelstein, Israel and Silberman, Neil, - The Bible Unearthed – (New York: Touchstone, 2001).

Finley, Barbara and Scheltema, Karen – The relation of gender and sexual orientation to measures of masculinity, femininity, and androgyny: A further analysis – Journal of Homosexuality (vol. 21 issue 3, 1991).

Fisher, Helen – Anatomy of Love – (New York: W.W. Norton Co. 1992).

Fisher, Terry – Gender differences and similarities in sexuality – The Society for the Scientific Study of Sexuality, 2012 – This can be retrieved at http://www.sexscience.org/PDFs/Gender%20Differences 20andSimilarity%20Final.pdf.

Flora, Carlin – The Puzzle of the Pretty Boy – Psychology Today (vol. 43 issue 6, 2010).

Flores, Stephen and Mansergh, Gordon et al – Gay identity-related factors and sexual risk among men who have sex with men in San Francisco – AIDS Education and Prevention (Apr. 2009).

Food and Drug Administration (FDA) – Revised recommendations for reducing the risk of human immunodeficiency virus transmission by blood and blood products: Questions and Answers (2015) – This can be retrieved at http://www.fda.gov/BiologicsBloodVaccines/BloodBloodProducts/QuestionsaboutBlood/ucm108186.htm.

France, David – The Science of Gaydar – New York Magazine (June 17, 2007).

Franklin, Karen – Antigay behavior among young adults: Prevalence, patterns, and motivations in a noncriminal population – Journal of Interpersonal Violence (vol. 15 issue 4, 2000).

Fredricksen-Goldsen, Karen et al – The unfolding of LGBT lives: Key events associated with health and well-being in later life – The Gerontologist (vol. 57 issue S1, 2017)

Freeman, Jonathan and Johnson, Kerri et al – Sexual orientation perception involves gendered facial cues – Personality and Social Psychology Bulletin (vol. 36 issue 10, 2010).

Freund, Kurt and Heasman, Gerald et al – Pedophilia and heterosexuality vs. homosexuality – Journal of Sex and

Marital Therapy (vol. 10 issue 3, 1984).

Freund, Kurt and Watson, Robin et al – Heterosexuality, homosexuality and erotic age preference – Journal of Sex Research (vol. 26 issue 1, 1989).

Freiss, Steve – Behind Closed Doors: While America wakes up to straight domestic violence, most of those abused in same-sex relationships still can't find a safe bed for the night – The Advocate (Dec. 9, 1997).

Friedman, Richard – Who Wrote the Bible (New York: HarperOne, 1997).

Frisch, Morten and Smith, Else et al – Cancer in a population-based cohort of men and women in registered homosexual partnerships – American Journal of Epidemiology (vol. 157 issue 11, 2003).

Frost, David and Meyer, Ilan – Internalized homophobia and relationship quality among lesbians, gay men, and bisexuals – Journal of Counseling Psychology (vol. 56 issue 1, 2009).

Galperin, Andrew and Haselton, Martie et al – Sexual regret: Evidence for evolved sex differences – Archives of Sexual Behavior (vol. 42 issue 17, 2012).

Garcia-Falgueras, Alicia and Swabb, Dick – Sexual differentiation of the human brain in relation to gender identity and sexual orientation – Journal of Functional Neurology (Jan. 2009).

Garcia-Falgueras, Alicia and Swabb, Dick – Sexual hormones and the brain: An essential alliance for sexual identity and sexual orientation – Journal of Pediatric Neuroendocrinology (vol. 17, 2010).

Garofalo, Robert and Wolf, R. Cameron et al – The Association between health risk behaviors and sexual orientation among a school-based sample of adolescents – Pediatrics (vol. 101 issue 5, 1998).

Gartrell, Nanette and Bos, Henny – US National Longitudinal Lesbian Family Study: Psychological adjustment of 17-year old adolescents – Pediatrics (volume 126 issue 1, 2010).

Gates, Gary – How many people are lesbian, gay and transgender? – The Williams Institute (April 2011).

Gates, Gary – New Census Data Show Annual Increases in

Same-Sex Couples Outpacing Population Growth – The Williams Institute (Oct. 4, 2010).

Gates, Gary and Macomber, Jennifer et al – Adoption and Foster Care by Gay and Lesbian Parents in the United States – The Williams Institute/The Urban Institute (March 2007).

Gaudio, Rudolf – Sounding gay: Pitch properties in the speech of gay and straight men – American Speech (vol. 69 issue 1, 1994).

Gaul, Shaina – Golden showers from a health perspective – Women's Health on Line/EmpowHER – This can be Retrieved at: http://www.empower.com/ conditions/sexually-transmitted-diseases.

Gayle, Helene Asst. Secretary for Legislation - Dept. of Health and Human Services – Statement for the Record on HIV Prevention (Feb. 14, 2000).

Gay and Lesbian Medical Association & LGBT Health Experts – Healthy People 2010: Companion Document for Lesbian, Gay, Bisexual, and Transgender (LGBT) Health (San Francisco, CA: Gay and Lesbian Medical Assn. 2010).

Gay, Lesbian and Straight Education Network – The 2003 National School Climate Survey: The School Related Experiences of Our Nation's Lesbian, Gay, Bisexual and Transgender Youth.

Geddes, Linda – Gene variant more prevalent in transsexuals – New Scientist (vol.199 issue 2667, 2008).

Gifford, Robert and Katzourakis, Aris et al – A transitional endogenous lentivirus from the genome of a basal primate and implications for lentivirus evolution – Proceedings of the National Academy of Sciences, USA (vol. 105 issue 51, 2008).

Gilbert, Paul and Brewer, Noel et al – HPV vaccine acceptability in heterosexual, gay and bisexual men – American Journal of Men's Health (vol. 5 issue 4, 2011).

Giles, GG and Severi, G. et al – Sexual factors and prostate cancer – British Journal of Urology International (vol. 92 issue 3, 2003).

Glick, Sara and Morris, Martina et al – A comparison of sexual behavior patterns among men who have sex with men and heterosexual men and women – Journal of Acquired Deficiency Syndrome (vol. 60 issue 1, 2012).

Gomez-Gil, Ester and Esteva, Isabel et al – Familiality of gender identity disorder in non-twin siblings – Archives of Sexual Behavior (vol. 39 issue 2, 2010).

Gonsiorek, John – Results of psychological testing on homosexual populations – American Behavior Scientist (vol. 4 issue 4, 1982).

Government Accountability Office (GOA) – Defense of Marriage Act: An Update to Prior Report – Document No. GAO-04-353R Jan. 23, 2004.

Govier, Ernest and Diamond, Milton et al – Dichotic listening, handedness, brain organization, and transsexuality – International Journal of Transgenderism (vol. 12 issue 3, 2010).

Grant, Jamie – Outing Age 2010 – National Gay and Lesbian Task Force Policy Institute.

Graves, Robert and Patai, Raphael – Hebrew Myths: The Book of Genesis – (New York: Anchor Books, 1964).

Greenberg, Gary – 101 Myths of the Bible (Naperville, IL: Sourcebooks, Inc., 2000).

Grigoriou, Tina – Friendship Between Gay Men and Heterosexual Women: An Interpretive Phenomenological Analysis (London: South Bank University Press, 2004)

Grossman, Igor – Reasoning about social conflicts improves into old age – PNAS (vol. 107 issue 16, 2010).

Grov, Christian and Parsons, Jeffrey et al – The association between penis size and sexual health among men who have sex with men – Archives of Sexual Behavior (vol. 39 issue 3, 2010).

Guèguen, N. – Effects of solicitor sex and attractiveness on receptivity to sexual offers: A field study – Archives of Sexual Behavior (vol. 40 issue 5, 2011).

Guillamon, Antonio and Carme, Junque et al – A review of the status of brain structure research in transsexualism – Archives of Sexual Behavior (vol. 45 issue 7, 2016).

Haas, Ann and Eliason, Mickey et al – Suicide and suicide risk in lesbian, gay, bisexual, and transgender populations: Review and recommendations – Journal of

Homosexuality (vol. 58 issue 1, 2011).

Halkitis, Perry and Palamar, Joseph et al – Poly-club-drug use among gay & bisexual men: A longitudinal analysis – Drug and Alcohol Dependence (vol. 89 issue 2-3, 2007).

Hall, J.A.Y. and Kimura, Doreen – Dermatoglyphic asymmetry and sexual orientation in men – Behavioral Neuroscience (vol. 108 issue 6, 1994).

Hall, J.A.Y. and Kimura, Doreen – Sexual orientation and performance on sexually dimorphic motor tasks – Archive of Sexual Behavior (vol. 24 issue 4, 1995).

Hall, Ryan and Hall, Richard – A profile of pedophilia: Definition, characteristics of offenders, recidivism, treatment outcomes, and forensic issues – Mayo Clinic Proceedings (vol. 82 issue 4, 2007).

Hamer, Dean and Hu, S. et al – A linkage between markers on the X chromosome Xq28 in males but not in females – Archives of Sexual Behavior (vol. 26 issue 5119, 1993).

Hatzenbuehler, Mark and Bellatorre, Anna et al – Anti-gay prejudice and all-cause mortality among heterosexuals in the United States – American Journal of Public Health (vol. 104 issue 2, 2013).

Healthcommunities.com – High Risk Sexual Behavior – This can be retrieved at: http://www.healthcommunities.com/std/fetish.shtml.

Heard, Richard – Introduction to the New Testament (New York, NY: Harper & Brothers, 1950).

Heise, Lori – HIV Transmission: Scientists and health groups call for removal of N-9 from condoms, lubricants – AIDS Weekly (Oct. 21, 2002).

Helleberg, Marie and Afzal, Shoaib et al – HIV/AIDS: Mortality attributes to smoking among HIV-1-infected individuals: A nationwide, population-based cohort study – Clinical Infectious Diseases (vol. 56 no. 5, 2013).

Hellman, Ronald and Sudderth, Lori et al – Major mental illnesses in a sexual minority psychiatric sample – Journal of the Gay and Lesbian Medical Association (vol. 6 issue 3-4, 2002).

Helminiak, Daniel – What the Bible Really Says About Homosexuality (Tajique, NM: Alamo Square Press, 2000).

Hennen, Peter – Faeries, Bears, and Leathermen: Men in Community Queering the Masculine (Chicago: University of Chicago Press, 2008).

Henningsson, Susanne and Westberg, Lars et al – Sex steroid genes and male-to-female transsexualism – Psychoneuroendocrinology (vol. 30 issue 7, 2005).

Herbenick, Debra and Reece, Michael et al – Sexual behavior in the United States: Results from a national probability sample of men and women ages 14-94 – Journal of Sexual Medicine (vol. 7 Supplement 5, 2010).

Herek, Gregory and Kimmel, Douglas et al – Avoiding heterosexual bias in psychological research – American Psychologist (vol. 46 issue 9, 1991).

Herek, Gregory – Beyond "Homophobia": Thinking about sexual prejudice and stigma in the twenty-first century – Journal of the NSRC (vol. 1 issue 2, 2004).

Herek, Gregory – Black heterosexuals' attitudes toward lesbians and gay men in the United States – Journal of Sex Research (vol. 32 issue 2, 1995).

Herek, Gregory and Norton, Aaron – Demographic, psychological, and social characteristics of self-identified lesbian, gay, and bisexual adults in a US probability sample – Sexual Research and Social Policy (vol. 7 issue 3, 2010).

Herek, Gregory – Hate crimes and stigma-related experiences among sexual minority adults in the United States: Prevalence estimates from a national probability sample – Journal of Interpersonal Violence (vol. 24 issue 1, 2009).

Herek, Gregory – Heterosexuals' attitudes toward bisexual Men and women in the United States – Journal of Sex Research (vol. 39 issue 4, 2002).

Herek, Gregory – The psychology of sexual prejudice – Current Directions in Psychological Science (vol. 9 issue 1, 2000).

Herek, Gregory and Garnets, Linda – Sexual orientation and mental health – Annual Review of Clinical Psychology (vol. 3, 2007).

Heslin, Kevin and Gore, John et al – Sexual orientation and testing for prostate and colorectal cancers among men in California – Medical Care (vol. 46 issue 12, 2008).

Hess, Eckerd and Seltzer, A.L. et al – Pupil response of the hetero and homosexual males to pictures of men and women: A pilot study – Journal of Abnormal Psychology (vol. 70 issue 3, 1965).

Heywood, Todd – Family group says it wants homosexuality criminalized – Michigan Messenger (Feb. 9, 2010).

Hite, Shere – The Hite Report on Male Sexuality – (New York: Ballantine Books, 1981).

Hodson, Gordon and Busseri, Michael – Bright minds and dark attitudes – Psychological Science (vol. 23 issue 2, 2012).

Hoff, Colleen and Beougher, Sean et al – Relationship characteristics and motivations behind agreements among gay male couples: Differences by agreement type and couple serostatus – AIDS Care (vol. 22 issue 7, 2010).

Holmes, William and Slap, Gail et al – Sexual abuse of boys: Definition, prevalence, correlates, sequelae, and management – JAMA (vol. 280 issue 21, 1998).

Hooker, Evelyn – The adjustment of the male overt homosexual – Journal of Projective Techniques (vol. 21 issue 1, 1957).

Hopkins, Steven – "Let the Drag Race Begin": The rewards of becoming a queen – Journal of Homosexuality (vol. 46 issue 3/4, 2004).

Horton, Mary Ann – The Prevalence of SRS Among US Residents – Out & Equal Workplace Summit (Sept. 2008). This can be retrieved at: http://www.tgender.net/tlaw/thbcost.html#prevalence.

Houston, Erik and McKirnan, David – Intimate partner abuse among gay and bisexual men: Risk correlates and health consequences – Journal of Urban Health (vol. 84 issue 5, 2007).

Hudson, James and Hiripi, Eva et al – The prevalence and correlates of eating disorders in the national comorbidity survey population – Biological Psychiatry (vol. 61 issue 3, 2007).

Huff, C.C. and Beougher, S.C. et al – Relationship

characteristics and motivation behind agreements among gay male couples: Differences by agreement type and couple serostatus – AIDS Care (vol. 22 issue 7, 2010).

Human Rights Campaign – Adoption Laws: State by State – This can be retrieved at: http://www/hrc.org/issues/parenting/adoptions.2375.htm

Human Rights Campaign Foundation – Corporate Equality Index: A Report Card on Lesbian, Gay, Bisexual and Transgender Equality in Corporate American – This can be retrieved at: http://www.hrc.org/cei.

Human Rights Campaign – HRC Youth Survey Report: Growing Up LGBT in America (June 2012) – This can be retrieved at: www.hrc.org/files/assets/resources/growing-up-lgbt-in-america-report.pdf.

Hu, S-h and Wang, Q-D – Haemodynamic brain response to visual sexual stimuli is different between homosexual and heterosexual men – Journal of International Medical Research (vol. 39 issue 1, 2011).

Hu, S-h and Wei, N. et al – Patterns of brain activation during visually evoked sexual arousal differs between homosexual and heterosexual men – American Journal of Neurology (vol. 29 issue 10, 2008).

Iemmola, Francesca and Camperio-Ciani, Andrea – New evidence of genetic factors influencing sexual orientation in men: Female fecundity increase in the maternal line – Archives of Sexual Behavior (vol. 38 issue 3, 2009).

Inter-University Consortium for Political and Social Research (ICPSR) – United States General Election Poll Series (Voter News Service Poll, Nov. 2008).

Janus, Samuel and Janus, Cynthia – The Janus Report on Sexual Behavior – (New York: John Wiley & Sons, 1993).

Jefferson, Thomas – Letter to William Short, April 13, 1820.

Jenny, Carole and Roesler, Thomas et al – Are children at risk for sexual abuse by homosexuals? – Pediatrics (vol. 94 issue 1, 1994).

Johnson, Kerri and Gill, Simone et al – Swagger, sway and sexuality: Judging sexual orientation by body motion and morphology – Journal of Personality and Social

Psychology (Sept. 2007).

Just, Felix – A Brief Overview of each Book and Letter of the New Testament (updated: 2012) – This can be retrieved at: http://www.catholic-resources.org/Bible/NT Overviews_htm#2Peter.

Kanai, Ryota and Feilden, Tom et al – Political orientations are correlated with brain structure in young adults – Current Biology (vol. 21 issue 8, 2011).

Kanazawa, Satoshi – Intelligence and Homosexuality – Journal of Biological Science (vol. 44 issue 5, 2012).

Keiller, Scott – Abstract reasoning as a predictor of attitudes toward gay men – Journal of Homosexuality - (vol. 57 issue 7, 2010).

Kellogg, S.K. – The Book of Leviticus - In: W. Robert Nicoll (ed.) - The Expositor's Bible (New York, NY: Funk & Wagnall, 1900).

Kessler, RC and Mickelson KD et al – The prevalence, distribution, and mental health correlates of perceived discrimination in the United States – Journal of Health and Social Behavior (vol. 40 issue 3, 1999).

Kimmel, Michael – Masculinity as Homophobia: Fear, Shame, and Silence in the Construction of Gender Identity – In: Research on Men and Masculinity Series: Theorizing Masculinities (Brod, H. and Kaufman, M. (eds.) – Thousand Oaks, CA: Sage Publishing, 1994).

Kinsey, Alfred and Pomeroy, Wardell et al – Sexual Behavior in the Human Female (Philadelphia: Saunders Publishing, 1953).

Kinsey, Alfred and Pomeroy, Wardell et al – Sexual Behavior in the Human Male – (Bloomington, IN: Indiana University Press, 1948).

Kinsey Institute – Frequently Asked Sexuality Questions to The Kinsey Institute (2010). This can be retrieved at http:// www.iub.edu/~kinsey/resources/FAQ.html.

Kirkpatrick, R.C. – The evolution of human sexual behavior – Current Anthropology (vol. 41 issue 3, 2000).

Klar, A.J. – Excess of counterclockwise scalp hair-whorl rotation in homosexual men – Journal of Genetics (vol. 83 issue 3, 2004).

Klein, Kevin – Sexual orientation, drug use preference

during sex, and HIV risk practices and preferences among men who specifically seek unprotected sex partners on the internet – International Journal of Environmental Research and Public Health (vol. 5 issue 5, 2009).

Klusmann, Dietrich – Reported by the BBC August 14, 2006 – This can be retrieved at: http://news.BBC.co.uk/2/hi/health/4790313.stm.

Kohlberg, Lawrence – A cognitive-developmental analysis of children's sex role concepts and attitudes - In: Maccoby, Eleanor (ed.) – The development of sex differences (Stanford, CA: Stanford University Press, 1966).

Kraanen, Fleur and Emmelkamp, Paul – Substance misuse and substance use disorders in sex offenders: A review – Clinical Psychology Review (vol. 31 issue 3, 2011).

Kruijver, F.P. and Zhou, J.N. – Male to Female transsexuals have female neuron numbers in a limbic nucleus – Journal of Clinical Endocrinology and Metabolism (vol. 85 issue 5, 2000).

Kurdek, Lawrence – Are gay and lesbian cohabiting couples really different from heterosexual couples? – Journal of Marriage and Family (vol. 66 issue 4, 2004).

Kurdek, Lawrence – Differences between partners from heterosexual, gay, and lesbian cohabiting couples – Journal of Marriage and Family (vol. 68 issue 2, 2006).

Kurdek, Lawrence – Relationship outcomes and their predictors: Longitudinal evidence from heterosexual married, gay cohabiting and lesbian cohabiting couples – Journal of Marriage and the Family (vol. 6 issue 3, 1998).

Lalumiére, M.L. and Blanchard, R. et al – Sexual orientation and handedness in men and women: A meta-analysis – Psychological Bulletin (vol. 126 issue 4, 2000).

Lasco, M.S. and Jordan, T.J. et al -A lack of dimorphism of sex or sexual orientation in the human anterior commissure – Brain Research (vol. 936 issue 1-2, 2002).

Laumann, Edward and Gagnon, John et al – The Social Organization of Sexuality (Chicago: University of

Chicago Press, 1994).

Lee, I-Ching and Crawford, Mary – Lesbians and bisexual women in the eyes of science - Feminism & Psychology (vol. 17 issue 1, Feb 2007).

Leitzmann, Michael and Platz, Elizabeth et al – Ejaculation frequency and subsequent risk of prostate cancer – Journal of the American Medical Association (vol. 291 issue 13, 2004).

Lemelle, Anthony and Battle, Juan – Black masculinity matters in attitudes toward gay males – Journal of Homosexuality (vol. 47 issue 1, 2004).

LeVay, Simon – A difference in hypothalamic structure between heterosexual and homosexual men – Science (vol. 253 issue 5023, 1991).

LeVay, Simon and Hamer, Dean – Evidence for a biological influence in male homosexuality – Scientific American (May 1994).

LeVay, Simon – Gay, Straight and the Reason Why (New York, NY: Oxford University Press, 2011)

LeVay, Simon – Queer Science (Cambridge, MA: MIT Press, 1996).

Levin, Elizabeth and Koopman, James et al – Characteristics of men who have sex with men and women who have sex with women and men: Results from the 2003 Seattle Sex Survey – Sexually Transmitted Diseases (vol. 36 issue 9, 2009).

Linville, S.E. – Acoustic correlates of perceived versus actual sexual orientation in men's speech – Folia Phoniatrica et logopaedica (vol. 50 issue 1, 1998).

Lippa, Richard – Handedness, sexual orientation, and gender personality traits in men and women – Archives of Sexual Behavior (vol. 32 issue 2, 2003).

Lippa, Richard – Sexual orientation and personality – Annual Review of Sex Research (vol. 16, 2005).

Lippa, Richard – Sex differences and sexual orientation differences in personality: Findings from the BBC survey – Archives of Sexual Behavior (vol. 37 issue 1, 2008).

Lombardi, Emilia and Wilchins, Rikki Anne et al – Gender violence: Transgender experiences with violence and discrimination – Journal of Homosexuality (vol. 41

issue 1, 2001).

Luders, Eileen and Sànchez, Francisco – Regional gray matter variation in male-to female transsexuals – Neuroimage (vol. 46 issue 4, 2009).

Maccoby, Hyram – The Mythmaker: Paul and the Invention of Christianity (New York: HarperCollins, 1987).

Maes, M. and De Vos, N. et al – Pedophilia is accompanied by increased plasma concentrations of catecholamines, in particular epinephrine – Psychiatry Research (vol. 103, issue 1, 2001).

Maes, M. and van West, D. et al – Lower baseline plasma cortisol and prolactin together with increased body temperature and higher mCPP-induced cortisol responses in men with pedophilia – Neuropsychopharmacology (vol. 24 issue 1, 2001).

Mansergh, Gordon and Shouse, Roy et al – Methamphetamine and sildenafil (Viagra) use are linked to unprotected receptive and insertive anal sex, respectively, in men who have sex with men – Sexually Transmitted Infections (vol. 82 issue 2, 2006).

Marshal, Michael and Friedman, Mark et al – Individual trajectories of substance use in lesbian, gay and bisexual youth and heterosexual youth – Addiction (vol. 104 issue 6, 2009).

Martin, Frank and Bolton, John – Penis Enlargement – British Medical Journal (vol. 330 issue 7486, 2005) – This can be retrieved at: http://www.ncbi.nlm.nih.gov/pmc/ articles PMC548174.

Martins, Yolanda and Preti, George et al – Preference for human body odors is influenced by gender and sexual orientation – Psychological Science (vol. 16 issue 9, 2005).

Massachusetts Department of Elementary and Secondary Education and the Massachusetts Department of Public Health – Health and Risk Behaviors of Massachusetts Youth (2006).

Maslow, Abraham – Motivation and Personality (New York: Harper and Row, 1954).

Mayo Clinic – Diseases and Conditions: Hemorrhoids

/causes – This can be retrieved at: http://www.mayoclinic.org /diseasesconditions/hemorrhoids/basics/causes/con-2002952.

Mayo Clinic – Penis-enlargement products: Do they work? – May 21, 2011. This can be retrieved at: http://www.mayoclinic.com/health/penis/MC00026.

Mayo Clinic – Women's Health – Sept. 26, 2009. This can be retrieved at: http://www.mayoclinic.com /health/health-issues-for-lesbians/MY00739.

Mayrer, Jessica – GOP aims to criminalize homosexuality – Missoula Independent (July 1, 2010).

Mays, Vickie and Cochran, Susan – Mental health correlations of perceived discrimination among lesbian, gay, and bisexual adults in the United States – American Journal of Public Health (vol. 91 issue 11, 2001).

McFadden, Dennis and Pasanen, Edward – Comparison of the auditory systems of heterosexuals and homosexuals: Click-evoked otoacoustic emissions – Proceedings of the National Academy of Sciences (vol. 95 issue 5, 1998).

McFadden, Dennis and Schubel, E. – Relative lengths of fingers and toes in human males and females – Hormones and Behavior (vol. 42 issue 4, 2002).

Metz, Michael and Rosser, Simon et al – Differences in conflict-resolution styles among heterosexual, gay, and lesbian couples – Journal of Sex Research (vol. 31 issue 4,1994).

Meyer, IIan – Prejudice, social stress, and mental health in lesbian, gay, and bisexual populations: Conceptual issues and research evidence – Psychological Bulletin (vol. 129 issue 5, 2003).

Meyer-Bahlburg, Heino – Psychoendocrine research on sexual orientation: Current status and future options - In: De Vries, G.J and De Bruin (eds.) – Progress in Brain Research volume 61 (Amsterdam: Elsevier Science Press, 1984).

Middleton, Laura and Barnes, Deborah et al – Physical activity over the life course and its association with cognitive performance and impairment in old age – Journal of the American Geriatrics Society (vol. 58 issue 7, 2010).

Midgley, Ruth (editor) – Sex: A User's Manual – (New York: Perigree Books, 1981).

Miller, J. Maxwell and Hayes, John – A History of Ancient Israel and Judah (London: Westminster John Knox Press, 1986).

Molitar, Fred and Truax, Steven et al – Association of methamphetamine use during sex with risky sexual behaviors and HIV infection among non-injecting drug users -Western Journal of Medicine (vol. 168 issue 2, 1998).

Moore, Megan and Kelle, Brad – Biblical History and Israel's Past – (Grand Rapids, MI: Wm. B. Eerdmans Publishing Co., 2011).

Moore, Peter – A third of young Americans say they aren't 100% heterosexual – LGBT Omnibus, Life, Omnibus Research (August 20, 2015).

Moore, Susan and Rosenthal, Doreen – Sexuality in Adolescence – (London & New York: Routledge, Taylor & Francis Group, 2007).

Morin, Stephen and Garfinkle, Ellen – Male Homophobia – Journal of Social Issues (vol. 34 issue 1, 1978).

Morrow, Daniel and Leirer, Von et al – When expertise reduces differences in performance – Psychology and Aging (vol. 9 issue 1, 1994).

Movement Advancement Project and the American Foundation for Suicide Prevention – Suicide and LGBT Populations (2017) – This can be retrieved at: http:www.afps.org/wp-content/uploads/2016/01/talking-about-suicide-and- lgbt populations,2nd edition.pdf.

Muehrer, Peter – Suicide and sexual orientation: A critical summary of recent research and directions for future research – Suicide and Life-Threatening Behavior (vol. 25 issue Supp. S1, 1995).

Mulder, M.J. – Sodom and Gomorrah – In: D.N. Freedman (ed)– The Anchor Bible Dictionary volume 6 (New York: Doubleday, 1992).

Murdock, D.M. – Did Moses Exist? The Myth of the Israelite Lawgiver – (Seattle, WA: Stellar House Publishing, 2014).

Murray, John – Psychological profile of pedophiles and

child molesters – The Journal of Psychology (Vol. 135 issue 2, 2000)

Muscarella, Frank and Elias, Vanessa et al – Brain differentiation and preferred partner characteristics in heterosexual and homosexual men and women – Neuroendocrinology Letters (vol. 25 issue 4, 2004).

Mustanski, Brian and DuPree, M.G. – A genome-wide scan of male sexual orientation – American Journal of Human Genetics (March 2005).

Nagoshi, Julie and Adams, Katherine et al – Gender differences in correlates of homophobia and transphobia – Sex Roles (vol. 59 issues 7-8, 2008).

Nam Aidsmap – Fingering and Fisting (April 7, 2009) – This can be retrieved at: http://www.aidsmap.com/print/Fingering-and-fisting/page1323538/

Nash, G. - The subversive male: Homosexual and bestial images on European Mesolithic rock art – In L. Bevin (Ed), Indecent Exposure: Sexuality, Society and the Archeological Record (Glasgow, UK: Cruithne Press, 2001).

National Alliance on Mental Health – What is Mental Illness: Mental Illness Facts – This can be retrieved at: http://www.nami.org/PrinterTemplate.cfm ?section= about_mental_health.

National Association of Mental Illness (NAMI), - Mental Health Issues Among Gay, Lesbian and Transgender (GLBT) People – June 2007. That can be retrieved at: http://www.nami.org/TextTemplate.cfm?Section= Fact_Sheet1...cfm...

National Center for HIV/AIDS – HIV among gay, bisexual and other men who have sex with men – Centers for Disease Control and Prevention (Sept. 2010).

National Center for HIV/AIDS – Fact Sheet: HIV and AIDS In the United States – Centers for Disease Control and Prevention (July 2010).

National Eating Disorders Association – Eating Disorders in LGBT Populations (2014) – This can be retrieved at: https://www. nationaleatingdisorders.org/eating-disorders-lgbt populations.

National Human Genome Research Institute – Genetic

Variation (4/25/2008) – This can be retrieved at: https://www.genome.gov/pages/education/modules/geneticvariation.pdf.

National Institute of Mental Health – Depression: Treat it. Defeat it. (June 1999). This can be retrieved at: http://www.nimh.nih.gov/depression/genpop/gen_fact.htm.

National Institute of Mental Health – Older Adults: Depression and Suicide Fact Sheet (1999).

National Institute on Aging – New Research Illuminates Memory Loss and Early Dementia (2009) – This can be retrieved at: http://www.nia.nih.gov/Alzheimers/ResearchInformation/Newsletter/Spring 2009.

National Institute on Drug Abuse – Addiction and Health – This can be retrieved at: http://www.nida.nih.gov/scienceofaddiction/health.html.

National Institute on Drug Abuse – Comorbid Drug and Mental Illness – This can be retrieved at: http://www.nida.nih.gov/tib/comorbid.html.

National Institute on Drug Abuse – Drug Abuse and Addiction – This can be retrieved at: http://www.nida.nih.gov/scienceofaddiction/addiction.html.

National Institute on Drug Abuse – Medical Consequences of Drug Abuse – This can be retrieved at: http://www.nida.nih.gov/consequences/.

National Kidney and Urologic Diseases Information Clearing House (NKUDIC) – What I need to know about urinary tract infections – This can be retrieved at: http://www.kidney.niddk.nih.gov/kudiseases/pubs/uti_ez/.

Navin, Helen – Medical and surgical risks in handballing: Implications of an inadequate socialization process – Journal of Homosexuality (vol. 6 issue 3, 1981).

Neal, Rome – Is Coffee Beneficial or Bad for Americans – CBS News (Sept. 7, 2003).

Newport, Frank – Americans Continue to Shift Left on Key Moral Issues – Gallup Inc. (May 28, 2015). Retrieve at: http://www.gallup.com/poll/183413/americans-continue-to-shift-left-on-key-moral-issues.aspx.

Nicholas, Cheryl – Gaydar: Eye-gaze as identity recognition among gay men and lesbians – Sexuality & Culture (vol.

8 issue 1, 2004).

Northrup, Chrisanna, Schwartz, Pepper and Witte, James – The Normal Bar – (New York: Harmony Books, 2012).

Nugteren, Helena and Balkema, G.T. et al – Penile enlargement: From medication to surgery – Journal of Sex and Marital Therapy (vol. 36 issue 2, 2010).

Nunes, Ashley and Kramer, Arthur – Experience-based mitigation of age-related performance declines: Evidence from air traffic control – Journal of Experimental Psychology: Applied (vol. 15 issue 1, 2009).

NYU Medical Center – Anal Cancer – This can be retrieved at: http://www.med.nyu.edu/crs/info/anorectal10.html.

Office of National Drug Control Policy – Drug Use Trends 2002 – This may be retrieved at: http://www.whitehousedrugpolicy.gov.

O'hEineachain, Roibeard – Urine eye drops a dangerous practice – EuroTimes (vol. 13 issue 3, 2008).

Olfson, M. and Pincus, H.A. et al – Outpatient mental healthcare in nonhospital settings: Distribution of patients across provider groups – American Journal of Psychiatry (vol. 153 issue 10, 1996).

Oliver, M.B. and Hyde, J.S. – Gender differences in sexuality: A meta-analysis – Psychological Bulletin (vol. 114 issue 1, 1993).

Olyslager, Femke and Conway, Lynn – On the calculation of The prevalence of transsexualism – Presented at the World Professional Association for Transsexual Health (WPATH) 20th International Symposium in Chicago, Illinois (Sept. 2007).

Ott, Miles and Corliss, Heather et al – Stability and change in self-reported sexual orientation identity in young people: Application of mobility metrics - Archives of Sexual Behavior (vol. 40 issue 3, 2011).

Oxley, Douglas and Smith, Kevin et al – Political attitudes vary with physiological traits – Science (vol. 321 issue 5896, 2008).

Parrot, Dominic – Aggression toward gay men as gender role enforcement: Effects of male role norms, sexual prejudice, and masculine gender role stress – Journal of Personality (vol. 77 issue 4, 2009).

Parsons, Jeffrey and Halkitis, Perry et al – Club drug use among young adults frequenting dance clubs and other social venues in New York City – J. of Child and Adolescent Substance Abuse (vol. 15 issue 3, 2006).

Parsons, J.T. and Starks T.J. et al – Non-monogamy and sexual relationship quality among same-sex couples – Journal of Family Psychology (vol. 26 issue 5, 2012).

Payne, Jessica – What can body odor tell us about sexual attraction and sexual orientation? – The Observer (April 14, 2010) – This can be retrieved at: http://ndsmcobserver. com/ 010/04/what-can-body-odor-tells- us-about-sexual-attraction-an...

Peakman, Julie – A Cultural History of Sexuality in the Enlightenment – (London: Bloomsbury Publishing, 2014).

Peplau, Letitia and Frederick, David et al – Body image satisfaction in heterosexual, gay, and lesbian adults – Archives of Sexual Behavior (vol. 38 issue 5, 2007).

Peplau, Letitia - Human Sexuality: How do men and Women differ? – Current Directions in Psychological Science (vol. 12 issue 2, 2003).

Pew Research Center – A Survey of LGBT Americans (June 13, 2013) – This can be retrieved at: http://www.pewsocialtrends.org/2013/13/a-survey-of-lgb.

Pew Research Center – Changing Attitudes on Same-Sex Marriage (May 12, 2016) – This can be retrieved at: http://www.pewforum.org/2016/05/12/changing-attitudes-on-gay-marriage.

Pew Research Center – U.S. Muslims Concerned About Their Place in Society, but Continue to Believe in the American Dream – July 26, 2017.

Phillips, Gregory and Ybarra, Michael et al – Low rates of human immunodeficiency virus testing among adolescent gay, bisexual, and queer men – Journal of Adolescent Health (vol. 57 issue 4, 2015).

Piaget, J. – The Psychology of the Child (New York: Basic Books, 1972).

Pierrehumbert, Janet and Munson, Benjamin et al – The influence of sexual orientation on vowel production (L) – Journal of the Acoustical Society of America (vol. 116

issue 4, 2004).

Pitts, Marian – Bisexuality and Health Psychology: Strange Bedfellows? – Health Psychology Update (vol. 14 issue 2, 2005).

Planned Parenthood – Safer Sex ("Safe Sex") – This can be retrieved at: http://www.plannedparenthood.org/health-topics/stds-hiv-safer sex/safer-sex-4263.htm.

Planned Parenthood – Fact Sheet: The Truth About Condoms (July 2011) – This can be viewed at: http://www.planned parenthood. org/files/PPFA/truth_about_condoms.pdf

Porter, Robert (Editor in chief) – Bacterial Urinary Tract Infections – Merck Manual for Health Care Professionals (2007) – This can be retrieved at: http://www.merckmanuals.com/professional/index.html.

Poteat, V. Paul and Anderson, Carolyn – Developmental change in sexual prejudice from early to late adolescence: The effects of gender, race, and ideology on different patterns of change – Developmental Psychology (vol. 48 issue 5, 2012).

Purcell, David and Johnson, Christopher et al – Estimating the population size of men who have sex with men in the United States to obtain HIV and syphilis rates – The Open AIDS Journal (vol. 6 issue Supp. 1, 2012). This can be retrieved at: http://www. benthanscience.com/open/toaidj/articles/V006/S10065TOAIDJ/98TOAIDJ.pdf.

Rahman, Qazi and Wilson, Glenn – Born Gay? The psychobiology of human sexual Orientation – Personal and Individual Differences (vol. 34 issue 8, 2003).

Rahman, Qazi and Abrahams, Sharon et al – Sexual orientation related to differences in verbal fluency – Journal of Neuropsychology – (vol. 17 issue 2, 2003).

Rahman, Qazi and Bhanot, S. et al – Gender nonconformity, intelligence, and sexual orientation – Archives of Sexual Behavior (vol. 41 issue 3, 2012).

Rahman, Qazi and Kumari, Veena et al – Sexual orientation related differences in pre-pulse inhibitions of the human startle response – Behavioral Neuroscience (vol. 117 issue 5, 2003).

Rahman, Qazi and Wilson, Glenn – Sexual orientation and

the 2nd to 4th finger length ratio: Evidence for organizing effects of sex hormones or developmental instability – Psychoneuroendocrinology (vol. 28 issue 3, 2003).

Rahman, Qazi and Wilson, Glenn – Sexual orientation related to differences in spatial memory – Journal of the International Neuropsychological Society (vol. 9 issue 3, Feb. 2003).

Rametti, Giuseppina and Carrillo, Beatriz et al – The microstructure of white matter in male to female transsexuals before cross-sex treatment. A DTI study – Journal of Psychiatric Research (vol. 45 issue 7, 2011).

Rametti, Giuseppina and Carrillo, Beatriz et al – White matter microstructure in female to male transsexuals before cross-sex hormonal treatment. A diffusion tensor imaging study – Journal of Psychiatric Research (vol. 45 issue 2, 2011).

Raymond, Nancy and Coleman, Eli et al – Psychiatric comorbidity in pedophilic sex offenders – American Journal of Psychiatry (vol. 156 issue 5, 1999).

Regan, Pamela and Medina, Roberta et al – Partner preferences among homosexual men and women: What is desirable in a sex partner is not necessarily desirable in a romantic partner – Social Behavior and Personality (vol. 29 issue 7, 2001).

Regan, Pamela – The role of sexual desire and sexual activity in dating relationships – Social Behavior and Personality (vol. 28 issue 1, 2000).

Reinisch, June - The Kinsey Institute New Report of Sex – (New York: St. Martin's Press 1990).

Remafedi, Gary and French, Simone et al – The relationship between suicide risk and sexual orientation: Results of a population-based study – American Journal of Public Health (vol. 88 issue1, Jan. 1998).

Resnikoff, Serge and Pascollini, Donatella et al – Global data on visual impairment in the year 2002 – Bulletin of the World Health Organization (vol. 82 issue 11, 2004).

Richards, Julie and Hawley, R. Scott – The Human Genome: A User's Guide 3rd edition (New York, NY: Academic Press, 2011).

Richters, J. and De Visser, R.O. – Demographic and psychosocial features of participants in bondage and discipline, "sadomasochism", dominance and submission (BDSM): Data from a national survey – J. of Sexual Medicine (vol. 5 issue 7, 2008).

Rieger, Gerulf and Chivers, Meredith et al – Sexual arousal patterns of bisexual men – Psychological Science (vol. 16 issue 8, 2005).

Rieger, Gerulf and Savin-Williams, Ritch – The eyes have it: Sex and sexual orientation differences in pupil dilation patterns – PLOS ONE (vol. 7 issue 8, 2012).

Robertson, B.A. – Translations and interpretations of same-sex behavior in Leviticus 18:22 – This can be retrieved at: http://www.religioustolerance.org/hom_bibh5.htm.

Robertson, M.J. and Toro, P.A. – Homeless Youth: Research, Intervention & Policy – United States Department of Health and Human Services (1998).

Rodger, Alison and Lodwick, Rebecca et al – Mortality in well controlled HIV in the continuous antiretroviral therapy arms of the SMART and ESPRIT trials compared to the general population – AIDS (vol. 27 issue 6, 2013).

Roese, Neal and Pennington, Ginger et al – Sex differences in regret: All for love or some for lust? – Personal and Social Psychology Bulletin (vol. 32 issue 6, 2006).

Rogers, Carl – A theory of therapy, personality and interpersonal relationships as developed in the client-centered framework – In: S. Koch (Ed.) Psychology: A Study of a Science. Volume 3: Formulations of the Person and the Social Context (New York, NY: McGraw Hill, 1959).

Romero, Adam and Baumle, Amanda et al – Census Snapshot – Williams Institute (Dec. 2007).

Rosario, Margaret and Scrimshaw, Eric et al – The coming out process of young lesbian women: Are there Butch/Femme differences in sexual identity development? – Archives of Sexual Behavior (vol. 38 issue 1, 2007).

Rosenberg, Eli and Sullivan, Patrick et al – Number of casual male sexual partners and associated factors among men who have sex with men: Results from the National HIV Behavioral Surveillance system – BMC Public Health (vol. 11 issue 189, 2011).

Rosenberger, Joshua and Reece, Michael et al – Sexual behaviors and situational characteristics of most recent male-partnered sexual event among gay and bisexually identified men in the United States – Journal of Sexual Medicine (vol. 8, 2011).

Rosenberger, Joshua and Schick, Vanessa et al – Sex toy use by gay and bisexual men in the United States – Archives of Sexual Behavior (vol. 41 issue 2, 2012).

Rosenthal, A.M. and Sylva, David et al – Sexual arousal patterns of bisexual men revisited – Biological Psychology (vol. 41 issue 1, 2012).

Rosenthal, A.M. and Sylva, David et al – The male bisexuality debate revisited: Some bisexual men have bisexual arousal patterns – Archives of Sexual Behavior (vol. 41 issue 1, 2012).

Rothblum, Esther and Factor, Rhonda – Lesbians and their sisters as a control group: Demographic and mental health factors – Psychological Science (vol. 12 issue 1, 2002).

Royal College of Psychiatrists – Submission to the Church of England's Listening Exercise on Human Sexuality (Oct. 31, 2007).

Rule, Nicholas and Ambady, Nalini et al – Brief exposures: Male sexual orientation is accurately perceived at 50 ms – Journal of Experimental Social Psychology (vol. 44 issue 4, 2008).

Russell, Stephen and Joyner, Kara – Adolescent sexual orientation and suicide risk: Evidence from a national study – American Journal of Public Health (vol. 91 issue 8, 2001).

Rust, Paula – Bisexuality: The state of the union – Annual Review of Sexual Research (vol. 13, 2002).

Ryan, Caitlin and Futterman, Donna – Lesbian and Gay Youth: Care & Counseling – (New York: Columbia University Press, 1998).

Ryan, Caitlin and Huebner, David et al – Family rejection as a predictor of negative outcomes in White and Latino lesbian, gay and bisexual young adults – Pediatrics (vol. 123) 2009.

Saad, Lydia – Majority in U.S. Drink Alcohol, Averaging Four Drinks a Week – Gallup Poll (August 17, 2012).

Saewyc, Elizabeth – Research on adolescent sexual orientation: Development, health disparities, stigma, and resilience – Journal of Research on Adolescence (vol. 21 issue 1, 2001)

Safron, A. and Barach, B. et al – Neural correlates of sexual arousal in homosexual and heterosexual men – Behavior Neuroscience (vol. 121 issue 2, 2007).

SageUSA and Movement Advancement Project (MAP) – Understanding Issues Facing LGBT Older Adults (2017) – This can be retrieved at: www.sageusa.org/resources/publications.cfm?ID=304

Sánchez, FJ and Bockladt, S. et al – The relationship between help-seeking attitudes and masculine norms among monozygotic male twins discordant for sexual orientation – Health Psychology (vol. 32 issue 1, 2013).

Sanders, Alan and Beecham, Gary et al – Genome-wide association study of male sexual orientation – Scientific Reports (vol. 7 number 16950, 2017)

Sandfort, Theo and de Graaf, Ron et al – Same-sex sexual behavior and psychiatric disorders – Archives of General Psychiatry (vol. 58, 2001).

Sandovski, R – Prevalence and recognition of stress in elderly patients – American Academy of Family Physicians (vol. 57 issue 5, 1998).

Sartorius, Alexander and Ruf, Matthias et al – Abnormal amygdala activation profile in pedophilia – European Archives of Psychiatry and Clinical Neuroscience (vol. 258 issue 5, 2008).

Satcher, David – The Surgeon General's Call to Action to Promote Sexual Health and Responsible Sexual Behavior – A Letter from the Surgeon General (US), Dept. of Health and Human Services (June 28, 2001).

Savic, Ivanka and Berglund, Hans et al – Brain response to putative pheromones in lesbian women – Proceedings of the National Acad. of Sciences (vol. 103 issue 21, 2006).

Savic, I., Garcia-Falgueras, A. and Swaab. D.F. – Sexual

differences of the human brain in relation to gender identity and sexual orientation – Progress in Brain Research (vol. 186, Dec. 3, 2010).

Savic, Ivanka and Lindstrom, Per – PET and MRI show differences in cerebral asymmetry and functional connectivity between homosexual and heterosexual subjects – Proceedings of the National Academy of Sciences (July 2008).

Savin-Williams, Ritch and Joyner, Kara et al – Prevalence and stability of self-reported orientation identity during young adulthood – Archives of Sexual Behavior (vol. 4 issue 2, 2012).

Savin-Williams, Ritch and Ream, Geoffrey – Prevalence and stability of sexual orientation components during adolescence and young adulthood – Archives of Sexual Behavior (vol. 36 issue 3, 2007).

Schaefer, Angus Gereban et al – Assessing the implications of allowing transgender persons to serve openly (Rand Corporation, 2016).

Scheibe, Suzanne – The Golden Years of Emotion – Observer (Assn For Psychological Science) (vol. 25 issue 9, 2012).

Schiavi, Raul and White, Daniel – Androgens and male sexual function: A review of human studies – Sex and Marital Therapy (vol. 2 issue 3, 1976).

Schiffer, Boris and Krueger, Tilmann et al – Brain response to visual sexual stimuli in homosexual pedophiles – Journal of Psychiatry and Neuroscience (vol. 33 issue 1, 2008).

Schiller, Jeannine and Lucus, Jacqueline et al – Summary Health Statistics for U.S. Adults: National Health Interview Survey 2011 – National Center for Health Statistics – Vital Health Statistics (vol. 10 issue 256, 2012).

Sell, Randall – Defining and measuring sexual orientation: A review – Archives of Sexual Behavior (vol. 26 issue 6, 1997).

Sessions-Stepp, Laura – A Lesson in Cruelty – Washington Post (June 19, 2001).

Settle, JE and Dawes, CT et al – Friendships moderate an

association between dopamine gene variant and political ideology – Journal of Politics (vol. 72 issue 4, 2010).

Shahid, Aliyah – Texas GOP platform: Criminalize gay marriage and ban sodomy, outlaw strip clubs and pornography – New York Daily News (June 22, 2010).

Shankar, Prinja and Jeet, Gursimer et al – Validity of self-reported morbidity – Indian Journal of Medical Research (vol. 136 issue 5, 2012).

Shaw, Philip and Kabani, Noor et al – Neurodevelopmental trajectories of the human cortex – Journal of Neuroscience (vol. 28 issue 13) Apr. 2, 2008. Note: For an explanation of the article in common language refer to the National Institute of Mental Health's (NIMH) Science Update June 5, 2008 entitled The Maturing Brain Parallels its Evolution.

Shook, Natalie and Fazio, Russell – Political ideology, exploration of novel stimuli, and attitude formation – Journal of Experimental Psychology (vol. 45 issue 4, 2009).

Singh, Devendra and Vidaurri, Melody et al – Lesbian erotic role identification: Behavioral, morphological and hormonal correlates – Journal of Personality and Social Psychology (vol. 76 issue 6, 1999).

Silva, David and Rieger, Gerulf, et al – Concealment of sexual orientation – Archives of Sexual Behavior – (Feb. 2010).

Skinner, William – The prevalence and demographic predictors of illicit and licit drug use among lesbians and gay men – American Journal of Public Health (Aug. 1994).

Sousa, João Dinis and Müller, Viktor et al – High GUD incidence in the early 20th century created a particularly permissive window for the origin and initial spread of epidemic HIV strains – PLOS One (vol. 5 issue 4, 2010).

Stall, Ronald and Greenwood, Gregory et al – Cigarette smoking among gay and bisexual men – American Journal of Public Health (Dec. 1999).

Stall, Ronald and Paul, Jay et al – Alcohol use, drug use and alcohol-related problems among men who have sex with men: The Urban Men's Health Study – Addictions (vol.

96 issue 11, 2001).

Stall, Ronald and Wiley, James – A comparison of alcohol and drug patterns of homosexual and heterosexual men: The San Francisco Health Study – Drug and Alcohol Dependence (vol. 22 issue 1-2, 1988).

Stark, Margret M. (ed.) – Clinical Forensics: A Physician's Guide / 3rd edition (Springer-Verlag: New York, 2011).

Steensma, Thomas and Biemond, Roeline et al – Desisting and persisting gender dysphoria after childhood: A qualitative follow-up study – Clinical Child Psychology and Psychiatry (vol. 16 issue 4, 2011).

Steensma, Thomas and Kreukels, Baudewijntje et al – Gender identity development in adolescence – Journal of Hormones and Behavior (vol. 64 issue 2, 2013).

Strong, James – Strong's Exhaustive Concordance of the Bible (Peabody, Mass: Hendrickson Publishers, 2007).

Stop AIDS Project – Giving Head: Risky or Not? – This can be retrieved at: http://www.stopaids.org/resources/how-risky-it/giving-head-risky-or-not.

Stipek, Deborah and Gralinski, J. Heidi et al – Self-concept development in the Toddler Years – Developmental Psychology (vol. 26 issue 6, 1990).

Substance Abuse and Mental Health Services Administration/Office of Applied Studies – National Household Survey on Drug Abuse 1994.

Substance Abuse &Mental Health Services Administration – Results from the 2008 National Survey on Drug Abuse and Health: National Findings (Office of Applied Studies 2009, NSDUH Series H-36, HHS Publication No. SMA 09-4434) Rockville, MD.

Swaab, D.F. and Garcia-Falgueras, A. – Sexual differentiation of the human brain in relation of gender identity – This can be retrieved at: http://wwwshb-info.org/sexbrain.html.

Swaab, D.F. and Gooren, L.J. et al – Brain research, gender and sexual orientation – Journal of Homosexuality (vol. 28 issue 3-4, 1995).

Swaab, D.F. and Hofman, M.A. – An enlarged suprachiasmatic nucleus in homosexual men – Brain Research (vol. 537 issue 1-2, 1990).

Symons, D. – The Evolution of Human Sexuality (New York: Oxford Univ. Press, 1979).

Tashman, Brian – FRC: Pray for the Criminalization of Homosexuality – People For the American Way/RightWingWatch.org (July 7, 2011).

Theodore, Peter and Basow, Susan – Heterosexual masculinity and homophobia: A reaction to the self? – Journal of Homosexuality (vol. 40 issue 2, 2000).

Thompson, Sanna and Sayfer, Andrew et al – Differences and predictors of family reunification among subgroups of runaway youth using shelter resources – Social Work Research (vol. 25 issue 3) 2001.

Tilghman, Andrew – Pentagon outlines new training on gays – Army Times (Jan. 28, 2011).

Tohme, R.A. and Holmberg, S.D. – Is sexual contact a major mode of hepatitis C transmission? – Hepatology (vol. 52 issue 4, 2010).

Trocki, Karen and Drabble, Laurie et al – Use of heavier drinking contexts among heterosexuals, homosexuals and bisexuals: Results from a household probability survey – Journal of Studies on Alcohol and Drugs (vol. 66 issue 1, 2005).

Truman, Jennifer and Planty, Michael – National Crime Victim Survey – United States Department of Justice/Bureau of Justice Statistics – October 2012.

Tulloch, Trisha and Kaufman, Miriam – Adolescent Sexuality – Pediatrics in Review (vol. 34 issue, 2013).

Turner, Bruce – Management of retained foreign bodies and rectal sexual trauma – Nursing Times.net (vol. 100 issue 38, 2004).

Turner, JM and Rider, AT et al – Behavioral predictors of subsequent hepatitis C diagnosis in a UK sample of HIV positive men who have sex with men – Sexually Transmitted Infections (vol. 82 issue 4, 2006).

Tuttle, Gordon and Pillard, Richard – Sexual orientation and cognitive abilities – Archives of Sexual Behavior (vol. 20 issue 3, 1991).

UNAIDS – UNAIDS: Report on the global Aids epidemic, 2010 – This can be retrieved at: http://www.unaids.org/globalreport/global_report.htm.

United States Department of Health and Human Services – Health Information Privacy: Summary of the HIPPA Privacy Rule – This can be retrieved at: http://www.hhs.gov/ocr/ privacy/hippa/understand/summary/index.html.

Unites States Department of Health and Human Services – Safe Sex – This can be retrieved at: http://www.nlm.nih.gov/medlineplus/ency/article/001949.htm.

United States Department of Health and Human Services: Strategic Plan on Homelessness (March 2007).

United States Dept. of Health and Human Services, Substance Abuse & Mental Health Services Administration - National Life Survey – This can be retrieved at: http://www.oas.samhsa.gov.

United States Food and Drug Administration – Have you given blood lately – This can be retrieved at: http://www. fda.gov/ForConsumers/ConsumerUpdates/ucm048368.html.

Urinary Care Foundation (American Urinary Assoc.) – Urinary Tract Infections in Adults – This can be retrieved at: http://www.urologyhealth.org/urology/index.cfm?article=47&display=1.

Utah Department of Health – Hand Washing Information (2005) – This can be retrieved at: http://www. health.utah.gov/epi/fact sheet/handwash.htm.

Van Horn, Linda and Fukagawa, Naomi et al – Report of the Dietary Guidelines Committee on the Dietary Guidelines for Americans, 2010 – United States Department of Agriculture and the United States Department of Health and Human Services (May 2010).

Valentova, Jaroslava and Havlìček, Jan – Perceived sexual orientation based on vocal and facial stimuli is linked to self-rated sexual orientation in Czech men – PLOS ONE (vol. 8 issue 12, 2013).

Valentova, Jaroslava and Rieger, Gerulf – Judgments of sexual orientation and masculinity-femininity based on thin slices of behavior: A cross-cultural comparison – Archives of Sexual Behavior (vol. 40 issue 6, 2011).

Van der Meek, Theo – Sodomy and the Pursuit of a Third Sex in the Early Modern Period – In: Third Sex Third

Gender: Beyond Sexual Dimorphism in Culture and History – Gilbert Herdt (ed.) - Period – (New York: Zone Books, 2003).

Vardi, Yoram and Har-Shai, Yaron et al – A critical analysis of penile enhancement procedures for patients with normal penis size: Surgical techniques, success and complications – European Urology (vol. 54 issue 5, 2008).

Waite, Teresa – Sexual Behavior Levels Compared in Studies in Britain and France – New York Times (Dec. 8, 1992).

Wallien, M.S.C. and Cohen-Kettenis, P.T. et al – Psychosexual outcome of gender-dysphoric children – Journal of the American Academy of Child and Adolescent Psychiatry (vol. 47 issue12, 2008).

Warin, Jo – The attainment of self-consistency through gender in young children – Sex Roles (vol. 42 issue 3-4, 2000).

Webster's New World College Dictionary - Agnes, Michael (ed.) (Cleveland, Ohio: Wiley, 2006).

Weinstein, Netta and Ryan, William et al – Parental autonomy support and discrepancies between implicit and explicit sexual identities: Dynamics of self-acceptance and defense – Journal of Personal and Social Psychology (vol. 102 issue 4, 2012).

Wellings, Kaye and Collumbien, Martine et al – Sexual and reproductive health 2: Sexual behavior in context: A global perspective – The Lancet (vol. 368 issue 9548, 2006).

Wenham, Gordon – The Old Testament attitude to homosexuality – Expository Times (vol. 102 issue 12, 1991).

Wheeler, Charles – Interview with Henry Ford – Chicago Tribune (May 25, 1916).

The Williams Institute – Same-sex Couples and the Gay, Lesbian, Bisexual Population: New Estimates from the American Community Survey – Oct. 2006.

Wilson, Barrie – How Jesus Became Christian (New York: St. Martin's Press, 2008).

Wismeijer, A.A. and van Assen, M.A. – Psychological

characteristics of BDSM practitioners – J. of Sexual Medicine (vol. 10 issue 8, 2013).

Wolfe, Alan and Toh, Evelyn et al – Evidence of uncultivated bacteria in the adult female bladder – Journal of Clinical Microbiology (vol. 50 issue 4, 2012).

Women's Institute at GMHC – HIV Risk for Lesbians, Bisexuals & Other Women Who Have Sex with Women – (June 2009).

Wong, Carolyn and Weiss, George et al – Harassment, discrimination, violence, and illicit drug use among young men who have sex with men – AIDS Education and Prevention (vol. 22 issue 4, 2010).

Woolery, Lisa – Gaydar: A Social-Cognitive Analysis – Journal of Homosexuality – (Vol. 53 issue 3, 2007).

Woolf, Linda – Gay and lesbian aging – Siecus Report (vol. 30 issue 2, Dec. 2001/Jan.2002).

World Health Organization (WHO), 2009 – Condoms for HIV prevention – This can be retrieved at: http://who.int/hiv/topics/condoms/en/.

World Health Organization (WHO), 2012 – Press release: World Health Organization Releases Groundbreaking Report Condemning "Conversion" Therapies – This can be found at: http://www.dayagainsthomophobia.org/Media-Release-World-Health,1557.

Worobey, Michael and Gemmel, Marlea et al – Direct evidence of extensive diversity of HIV-1 in Kinshasa by 1960 – Nature (vol. 455 issue 7213, 2008).

Wright, Les – The Bear Book (New York: Routledge, 2013).

Yang, Yang – Social inequalities in happiness in the United States, 1972 to 2004: An age-period-cohort analysis (vol. 73 issue 2, 2008).

Yumiko, Aratani and Cooper, Janice – The effects of runaway-homelessness episodes on high school dropouts – Youth and Society (vol. 47 issue 2, 2015).

Zhou, Jiang-Ning and Hofman, Michel et al – A sex difference in the human brain and its relation to transsexuality – Nature (vol. 378 issue 6552, 1995).

Zucker, Kenneth and Bradley, Susan et al – Gender Identity Disorder and Psychosexual Problems in Children and Adolescents (New York: Guilford Press, 1995).

www.ingramcontent.com/pod-product-compliance
Lightning Source LLC
Chambersburg PA
CBHW052010070526
44584CB00016B/1687